Contents

PART III Systems and Software

10   Data Base Systems 280

PART IV   Designing and Implementing Information Systems

11   Programming Concepts 306

12 System Analysis and Design 330

13 Management Support Systems 356

PART V   Computers and Society

Preface

Understanding Computers is an introductory book about computers and their use. It is an easy reading book which primarily addresses personal computing with occasional looks into the world of mainframes. Understanding computer concepts is the base upon which applications software is presented, leading to the practical use of the PC through the use of software tutorials provided as a supplement to the book. We think students will find the book interesting and relevant to their use of computers both in school and in the business world. Instructors will find that the text supports them with coverage of the many topics needed for an introductory course as well as with the accompanying supplement package.

THE CONTENT

Understanding Computers covers the topics needed for the introductory computer course that is microcomputer oriented. Included are the topics of the uses of computers, hardware devices, data storage concepts, data communications, operating systems, programming concepts, systems analysis and design, and management information systems. Four full chapters are devoted to application software including word processing, desktop publishing, spreadsheets, integrated packages, presentation graphics, and data base management. A final chapter addresses the current issues of computer phobia, software piracy, licensing, computer crime, viruses, security, privacy, and computer careers.

CHAPTER ORGANIZATION

Understanding Computers is organized into five sections that each focus on a central theme. This structure works well for most instructors but offers the flexibility needed for those who wish to follow a different route. The chapter content is summarized as follows.

PART I—COMPUTERS AND INFORMATION SYSTEMS

This section introduces the reader to the world of computers. Topics include why computers are needed, what is a computer, different types of computers, and a general introduction to the types of software used on today's computer systems. This section gives the student an exposure to the concepts and terms that will be developed in greater depth throughout the course.

Complex topics are introduced early in the book and then covered in depth in later chapters. For example, the subjects of computer hardware, input/output, spreadsheets, word processing, data base, integrated software, and communications are each introduced briefly in Chapter 1. Later chapters develop each topic more fully.

PART II—HARDWARE SYSTEMS

The four chapters in this section cover the major topics relating to computer hardware. This ranges from a discussion on bits and bytes to laptops, from RAM and ROM to data communications. Included are topics such as microprocessors, PS/2, data entry, display screens, printers, plotters, disk storage devices and file organization, networks, communication systems, and micro-mainframe links. Most of the material relates to PC hardware and covers the hardware in widespread use as well as newer developments such as the 80286 and 80386 based computers, VGA and Multi-sync screens, and CD ROMs.

PART III—SYSTEMS AND SOFTWARE

This section contains five chapters on software and related topics. The section begins with a discussion on operating systems, primarily PC-DOS. The use of DOS and some basic commands are discussed. Next an overview of application software is presented with a discussion on the use of menus, templates, help screens, and how software is installed. The last three chapters cover the major software applications: word processing, spreadsheets and data base management. Other related material is provided on desktop publishing, three dimensional spreadsheets, integrated software, resident software, presentation graphics, CAD/CAM, and project management.

PART IV—DESIGNING AND IMPLEMENTING INFORMATION SYSTEMS

This section proceeds from the micro to the macro view of systems. It begins with programming concepts and establishes why programs are necessary. Program development tools such as structured methodology are discussed as are the major procedural languages. Fourth generation languages are also examined and why they are so important today. Next we cover systems analysis and design covering the life cycle from the feasibility study, through analysis, design, programming, implementation, and maintenance.

PART V—COMPUTERS AND SOCIETY

The text is ended with a discussion of social issues that have been introduced as a result of the computer impact. These issues include computer phobia, software piracy, software licensing, computer crime, viruses, privacy, security, and ethics. The last section of Part V discusses various computer careers that are of interest to the student who wants to pursue a computer based career.

APPENDICES

Some topics are considered optional by instructors of an introductory computer course. These have been collected into the appendices and can be used as required or left out of the mainstream of the course at the professor's discretion. Included in Appendix A are computer history, computer generations, the history of languages and software and the first PCs. Appendix B covers number systems as they relate to the computer.

FEATURES

Writing Style

The writing style is conversational in tone and attempts to be light and interesting to retain the attention of the student and to encourage further involvement in the subject matter.

Use of Photographs and Figures

The book is highly visual in the sense that there are figures, photographs, and/or graphic art on most pages to support the textual material. These are accompanied by descriptive captions that provide further support to the related topic in the text.

Inserts

Most chapters have inserts on special topics such as "Why the Need for Large Memory Capacity," "E-Mail—The Alternate to a Postage Stamp," and so on. Inserts are also used when a particularly difficult concept is presented in order to give an alternate perspective on the topic.

Photo Essays

Photo essay inserts are also included in most chapters. These essays add spice to the chapter by presenting a visual tour of a specific topic such as WordPerfect 5.0, desktop publishing, expert systems, and Microsoft Excel, that is related to the chapter content. One of these essays is used in Chapter 1 to show a variety of fields where computers are being used. Another is used to show the benefits of desktop publishing in Chapter 8.

LEARNING AIDS IN THE BOOK

Each chapter begins with chapter objectives which are called "A View of the Chapter Ahead." Objectives are stated in a manner to promote "understanding" as suggested by the book title.

Each chapter ends with a series of review questions. Answers will be provided in the instructor's manual. There are three types of questions used: 1) Fill-in Questions, 2) Matching Questions, and 3) Discussion Questions.

Chapters contain boldfaced keywords with a summary of terms at the end of the chapter. A chapter summary highlights and reviews major topics at the end of each chapter which is useful for test preparation. An extensive glossary and complete index are included at the end of the book.

SUPPLEMENTS PACKAGE

A collection of booklets are available for both students and instructors of the course. These supplements are as follows.

1. Software Tutorial—*Learning DOS, WordPerfect 4.2, Lotus 1-2-3 (2.01)/TWIN, and dBASE III Plus*—This tutorial gives introductory coverage of DOS and the three major software packages in use today. The tutorial contains instruction on the use of the software, and keystroke exercises and other challenging exercises are included. Student versions of the software are available with this tutorial.

2. Software Tutorial—*Learning DOS, WordPerfect 5.0, Lotus 1-2-3 (2.2), and dBASE III Plus*—This tutorial gives the same coverage as the one above but uses the most recent release of the three major software packages.

3. A separate *BASIC programming manual* is available for courses that teach this language. The BASIC used is IBM PC BASIC but mostly uses the generic commands that are found on most BASIC interpreters. As a result of this treatment the instructor can use this manual for most versions of BASIC.

4. *Study Guide*—This guide written by Anne Kelly and Franca Giacommelli is available to assist the student in preparing for tests and exams. Included is an overview of the chapter, summary, sample test questions, and learning aids, such as crossword puzzles.

5. *Instructor's Manual*—Prepared by the author of the text, this manual supports the book with chapter descriptions, learning objectives, vocabulary, teaching tips, and answers to review questions.

6. *Test Bank*—A set of test questions is included in the instructor's manual for each chapter of the text. Each section includes fill-in, matching, and multiple choice questions with answers provided.

7. *Hypergraphics*—A software package that provides automated presentation graphics for instructor support. Using a PC and projector screens graphics are presented to support the course lectures. Review and test questions with automatic marking are also provided. See your Prentice Hall representative for further details.

OTHER SUPPLEMENTS

Prentice Hall also provides a number of supplements to support instructors of introductory computer courses. Included are transparency masters and test generation software. Ask your Prentice Hall representative for details.

ACKNOWLEDGMENTS

A book of this scope represents the efforts of many people representing a diversity of skills and backgrounds. Each has made a unique contribution which is much appreciated by the author. First are the reviewers. These professors took time out from their full schedules to read the manuscript and comment on their reaction to its content. Although it wasn't possible to include every change suggested much of this feedback made a valuable contribution to the final revision. Thank you goes to

- R. A. Barrett, Indiana University/Purdue University
- Joyce L. Capen, Central Michigan University
- George P. Grill, University of North Carolina
- David Harvey, Ryerson Polytechnical Institute
- Seth A. Hock, Columbus State Community College
- Peter L. Irwin, Richland College
- Herman Kempe, Lampton College of Applied Arts and Technology
- Randall L. Lechlitner, Collin County Community College
- Paul E. Lecoq, Spokane Falls College
- Anthony P. Malone, Raymond Walters College
- Charles Miri, Delaware Tech
- Thomas W. Osgood, Indiana University East
- Ernest Philipp, Northern Virginia Community College
- Guy W. Pollock, Mountain View College
- Frank Relotta, DeVRY Technical Institute
- David J. Rooser, Essex County College
- Daniel Rota, Robert Morris College
- Edward Solinsky, Purdue School of Engineering and Technology
- Julia Tinsley, Indiana University at Kokomo
- Anthony L. Tiona, Broward Community College
- John P. Traynor, Northern Illinois University
- Dennis L. Varin, Southern Oregon State College
- Barbara Walters, Ashland Community College

When this book was originally conceived it was with the direction and prompting of Marcia Horton, Editor Computer Science, and Jim Fegen, Executive Editor Computer Science and Engineering who both gave of their constant support and encouragement. More recently editorial support was provided by Dennis Hogan, Editor-in-Chief Business and Economics, and Gary June, Editor Business Computing, whose insights and energy helped bring this book to production. When Gary was promoted to Marketing Manager, Ted Werthman took over the editorial responsibilities and continued to bring the results of everyone's labor to fruition. Barbara Grasso, production editor, nurtured the book from manuscript to the final text. Caroline Ruddle, Marketing, Jenny Kletzin, Supplements, Laura Weinberg, Market Research, Lee Cohen, Design, Dottie Baldi, Photo Research, and Lori Morris-Nantz, Photo Editor, are all professionals at Prentice Hall whose contribution is much appreciated.

The World
of Computers

A VIEW OF THE CHAPTER AHEAD

After Reading This Chapter You Will Understand:

- The need for computers and information systems in business and industry.

- When it is useful to use a computer and when purchasing a computer might not be the best solution to a business problem.

- The concept of a computer system and the basic components it contains.

- The concept of productivity software and will identify the main types of software in this category.

Y ou may be taking this course about computers for one of several reasons. Possibly you are a business student who will soon be using the computer in other courses in your business program and eventually in your job after graduation. Or maybe you are looking for a career in computers and the course you are taking is an introduction to the subject. Many students from other disciplines ranging from engineering to health sciences also take an introductory computer course as part of their program.

Whatever the reason for taking this course, it is important to recognize that computers are becoming an integral part of life in our society. It seems that no matter what career you follow, whether you are self-employed, work for a small to medium-sized company, or get a job with one of the largest corporations, the computer will likely be one of the tools you will use in your job. For that reason, most schools offer introductory computer courses to prepare their graduates for the future.

This book is a general treatment of the subject of computers, especially personal computers. Using it will not make you a computer expert, but you will gain a broad understanding of computer concepts and become familiar with the use of several computer programs that are widely used in business. Doing hands-on activities with the computer will help to build confidence in your ability to use a computer and to apply it to real-life problems.

In this chapter we will look at why computers are used and how they came into being. The origin of the computer is a fascinating subject (see Appendix A), and it is exciting to see how quickly it has become an important tool used to expand our abilities. Some writers have called the computer "the mind tool," and so it is, because of its ability to store facts, recall them quickly, and do many types of processes with them. But in the process of learning about the computer, you will need to apply your mind to the learning process. That means you will need to read and absorb new concepts, make notes, and do some old-fashioned studying.

Computer training is an essential component of most business programs as well as many technology and educational programs in today's colleges. Employees in small to large companies are also being trained to use the personal computer, a skill that can contribute to their employability and eventual promotion.

Courtesy of Texas Instruments.

WHY DO WE NEED COMPUTERS?

What is it that an accountant, a novelist, a restaurateur, a business executive, an electronics engineer, a salesperson, and an investment counselor have in common? They all use a computer to supply, store, and process information to do their job or run their company more effectively.

The accountant uses a personal computer to help analyze clients' taxes, keep track of the payroll, and prepare year-end reports. A novelist, of course, uses a computer to write books, and the restaurateur uses the computer to record sales of meals, keep track of the waiters' gratuities, and tabulate the amount owed to the credit card companies. The business executive uses the computer to monitor the performance of the company and its various functions. The computer can help the executive to identify business trends, make better informed business decisions, and plan new directions for the company.

Courtesy of IBM.

Courtesy of Ted Thai/Sygma.

Courtesy of IBM.

Courtesy of Sperry Corp.

Courtesy of Hewlett-Packard.

Courtesy of IBM.

People from all walks of life use computers. Whether a person's occupation is as an accountant or a novelist, a restaurateur or an executive, an electronics engineer or an investment counselor, the computer can be a valuable tool.

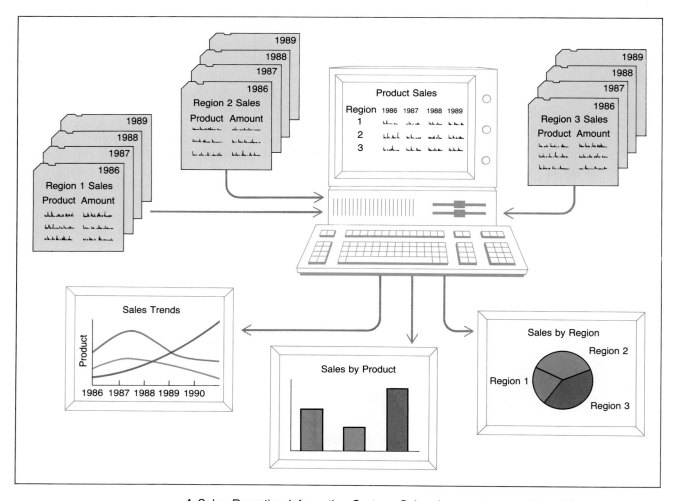

A Sales Reporting Information System. Sales documents are gathered from each region of the company and entered into the computer for processing. Numerous interpretations of the data are possible, including both numeric and graphic displays of the results. Some of these displays depict total product sales by region for each of the previous four years, a line graph showing sales trends, a pie chart showing percentage distribution of sales by region, and a bar graph comparing sales for each product.

The electronics engineer uses a computer to save time over manual methods in designing circuits and to try out different circuit designs without having to wire many components together for initial testing. The salesperson uses a personal computer to keep track of sales, customers' likes and dislikes, and customers' past spending habits so that more time can be devoted to promoting the products that will satisfy customer needs. The computer can even recommend optimum intervals for meeting with a customer, ensuring that both the salesperson and the customer's time is used profitably.

Investment counselors use computers to analyze their clients' investment goals and suggest investment strategies, track the clients' investments, and calculate the potential effect of choices made in the investment program.

While the personal computer is an important part of any job function, there are two other important ingredients required for a successful operation: personnel and quality of information. Although the computer may have specific

When the IBM personal computer was introduced in 1981 the name PC became synonymous with the IBM PC. Since the release of that historic computer, millions of personal computers have been purchased by corporations, small companies, educational institutes, and individuals.

Over the intervening years the name PC has become a generic one. Today most desktop computers are called PCs, whether produced by IBM, Compaq, Tandy, or any one of many other corporations that build competing computers. Even the more advanced models, such as ATs or PS/2s, are frequently called personal computers.

In this book the terms PC and personal computer are intended to refer to the complete range of personal computers whether they are the IBM PC, PC/XT, PC/AT, or PS/2 or computers from any number of competitors. Where a computer has a feature that is unique to that model, a more direct reference will be made to that computer.

programs that relate to accounting, restaurants, or investment, it cannot begin to replace the professionals who bring their expertise to the jobs described. Knowledgeable people are needed to use the computer effectively, and without them the computer might just as well be used to play games or as a boat anchor.

Stock Investing by Computer. Using data communications lines and a personal computer, a financial analyst can access current stock market prices. Stock analysis programs can be used to graph the price trends of a specific stock over a period of time. Some analysts use these programs to help predict the future performance of the stock. The PC simplifies the recording of investment data for quick and easy access as investment decisions are required. Reports for both the analyst and the client may be produced directly from the personal computer.

Photo courtesy of New York Stock Exchange.

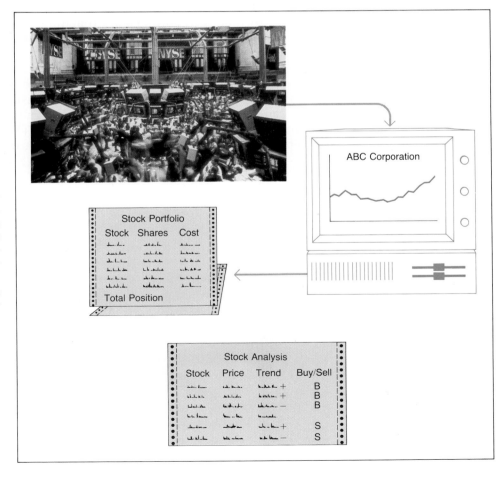

Then there is the matter of relevant information. The kind of information used can vary greatly, and how it is used can also vary. For the accountant, information will exist primarily as numbers that represent debits and credits in the accounts of clients. By contrast, the novelist uses ideas and words as information. The engineer might also use ideas but also uses the rules of electronics as information that determine how these ideas might be used.

All these new directions in our society show an increased need for information, and the computer is often the central tool for providing this information. This trend has resulted in a new type of employee called the knowledge worker. A **knowledge worker** is a person whose job depends largely on the use of knowledge or information. Clearly people in many different career paths are knowledge workers because they use information as a primary ingredient of their job. Now let's consider what a computer is.

WHAT IS A COMPUTER?

There are a lot of concepts that are needed for a full understanding of the computer, and in the next few chapters we will be expanding on the basics given here. But first, let's use the analogy of a television set to draw some parallels. A television set uses an antenna or cable to capture a signal from the TV station and feed it into the electronic circuits. The electronics are then used to process the signal and convert it into a picture and sound.

In reality there are many signals, from different channels, that are captured by the antenna, and the TV set must separate these into a signal for the channel that you select. Not only that, but the signal received is extremely weak and must be amplified for it to produce a good picture and quality sound. Part of the processing also involves identifying the various colors in the picture and displaying them on the screen to give you a pleasing color picture.

In computer language we can think of the antenna as the input that reads or captures the signal. The electronics of the TV set is the processor that processes the signal and creates the information or output that you require.

The computer receives its input from several sources, including the keyboard, mouse, and floppy disk. After processing the data, output is created on the display screen, printer, or disk.

Courtesy of IBM.

And the picture and sound are outputs that are created as a result of the processing. Each of these terms—input, process, and output—have similar counterparts in the computer.

- **Input** refers to a device, like the keyboard, that provides data for the computer to process or act upon.
- **Process** refers to the computer's processor and related electronics that act on the data to provide a variety of useful information such as reports.
- **Output** is the result of processing and can be displayed on the screen, similar to the television, or printed on paper for a permanent copy of the results.

Interestingly, television sets are moving closer to the computer in the way that they operate. Digital selection of channels, on-screen channel and time display, and integration with video cassette records (VCRs) and computers are all a result of computer technology. However similar the two may be, there are still many features and concepts that are unique to the computer.

DATA AND INFORMATION

When we discuss computers, the terms data and information are often used. (See Figure 1–1.) **Data** refers to the raw material or facts that are gathered and used for input to the computer. **Data entry** is the process of entering data into the computer, often by typing. Items such as name, description, year, age, program number, grade received, phone number, course number, and so on are all examples of data. Data is something like the signal that is received by a television antenna. By itself it is not very useful. Just as the television can only give a useful image after the signal is amplified and processed, so can data be useful only after it has been collected and processed.

FIGURE 1–1

Data is the raw material that represents the facts, while information is a collection of the data into a meaningful pattern.

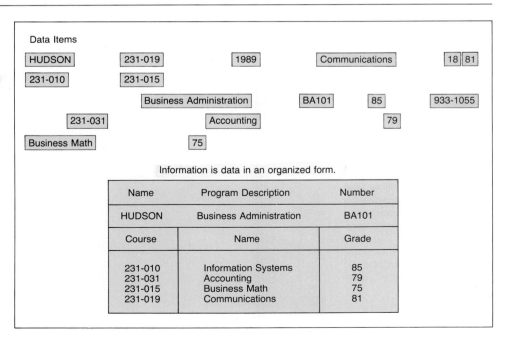

Information is data that has been processed and organized into a useful pattern. This is comparable to the TV picture that results only after the processing of the television signal. Similarly, the data items just described can be organized into a student record to provide meaningful information. The system that collects and organizes the data into a useful form is called an **information system.** Well-designed information systems contribute to worker productivity and increase excellence in the workplace.

In this book we will be mainly concerned with the use of computers and information in business, but occasionally we will look at other areas that are important to understanding the use of computers.

INFORMATION SYSTEMS

Computers and Information Systems

With management's need for timely and accurate information, the computer has become an instrumental part of a **management information system (MIS).** These systems use computers to collect data, process it, summarize it, and use it to generate a variety of reports that provide all levels of management with the information they need. A sales reporting system may not only provide lists of customers who have made purchases or whose payment is outstanding, but may also identify trends in sales so that management may guide the company's efforts more intelligently.

When information from a computer is used for decision making, we call this a **decision support system (DSS).** The term "decision support" suggests that management relies on the computer for more than just the day-to-day operation of the company. Indeed, the computer is used for making decisions that have long-term implications in the welfare of the company and its employees.

Information systems have not always depended upon the computer; some still don't. Manual systems of collecting information and analyzing it were

Introducing personal computers into a company results in decentralization of the computing resource. Although most large companies still depend on the central mainframe computer for many large or complex tasks, the PC has moved computer power to the individual user in many departments throughout the organization. The PC has also made computing affordable for the smaller company that could not previously afford the expensive mainframe computer.

Courtesy of Unisys.

the most common method used until the advent of the computer. These systems were called **business systems,** and although some of them used electromechanical devices such as the accounting machine or the calculator, others were completely manual. Now the computer is changing all of that, resulting in a group of specialists whose work revolves around the use of the computer.

Information Systems Departments

Manufacturers, banks, franchise operations, retail stores, insurance companies, government, and school systems all depend on information and the use of computers for their operation. Until the 1980s these organizations used centralized computer systems with a staff of computer professionals to design, implement, and maintain the system. The **information systems (IS)** or **data processing**

Different kinds of systems.

Photos courtesy of (top to bottom): NASA; IBM; G. Contorakes/The Stock Market; ISSCO Graphics.

System	ORBITS OF THE PLANETS	An organization of elements or things into a workable order or scheme.	Solar system, telephone system.
Information System (IS)		A system that provides information for the function of an operation.	A cash register may provide information for the operation of a company.
Management Information System (MIS)		A system that collects information for management's use in making the daily decisions about the operation of the company.	Sales reports, inventory, profit, and accounts provide this information.
Decision Support System (DSS)	ACCUMULATIVE PRODUCT INSTALLATIONS ACCELERATE WITH NEW PRODUCTS	A system that helps management to make decisions regarding the future or long term direction of the company and its products or services.	DSS may start with the same information as an MIS but goes beyond it to consider market and social trends.

Centralized mainframe computers are supported by a staff of information system professionals who in turn support the many users located throughout the company. The information systems or data processing department consists of people trained in computer programming, systems analysis, computer operations, and data entry. These professions develop and implement computer applications, run the computers, and enter data.

Photos courtesy of: (top left) Micro Data Base Systems; (top right) Holiday Inn.

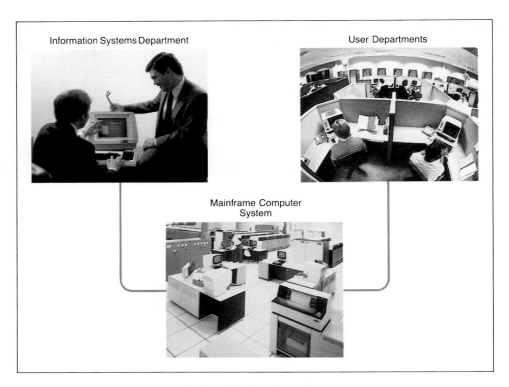

Information Systems Department

User Departments

Mainframe Computer System

(DP) department was self-contained and provided the company with much of its information requirements.

These departments were staffed with computer operators, programmers, systems analysts, and data entry operators who had the responsibility for running the computer, entering the data, and designing, implementing, and maintaining the information system. The **users** were the accounting, payroll, personnel, and order departments who depended on the central mainframe computer system and the IS department for their support. These users concentrated on the role of accounting or payroll, and so on, while the information systems department provided the technical expertise.

By the late 1970s, the personal computer came on the scene, and within a few years its price, capacity, and speed made it possible for each user department to have its own computer or, if necessary, to have a computer for each person. As we move into the 1990s a computer on every desk is no longer a dream but a reality in many organizations. Concurrently, the mainframe computer has also developed higher speeds and greater capacity for less money and is still a major force in computing. As we will see, the mainframe computer often works directly with the personal computer, sometimes supplying it with information and at other times collecting information that is available to it from the personal computer.

While most large organizations have a centralized information systems department, much of the computing is now done on the desktop of individual workers in the company. The personal computer also brings computing power to the smallest company where there is no information systems department, but individuals in various job functions who depend on the computer to do their tasks.

FACTORS TO CONSIDER FOR COMPUTER USE

Often computers seem to be a pat solution to many problems. If operating expenses are higher than management would like, if personnel are too costly, and if efficiency of the operation is low and not responsive enough, a frequent response is to get a computer. But often this is not the right answer or may only be part of a complete solution. The following are some considerations for using or not using a computer.

- **A job is routine and repetitive.** Computers tend to be able to handle repetitive tasks more effectively than tasks that involve decision making and tasks that take training and skill to manage effectively. Accounting, payroll, expense accounts, and budgets are usually well-defined repetitive tasks that are easily implemented on the computer. More advanced software is placing many applications within reach of the computer. Even tasks that are often considered to be creative and not previously suitable for computer implementation, such as engineering or architectural design, are now finding the computer to be a useful tool.

- **Software already exists to do the task required.** Software is generally quite expensive to develop and may require years of work before it is completed. Thus the value saved may be more than offset by the cost of developing the software. However, there are many software packages available for a wide variety of applications in business and industry. This software may be purchased at a fraction of the cost it would take to develop and therefore may be a cost effective way to implement a solution on the computer.

- **Using a computer would be more expensive or unwieldy than doing the job manually.** Although the computer can manage payroll applications, it would not make much sense for a company that had only a few employees. A manual system would probably work just as well and at considerably less cost.

- **A service company will do the job at a fraction of the cost.** Just as it may not be worthwhile to use a computer to do payroll for only two or three employees, service companies exist that also do jobs such as payroll, and because they are doing these tasks for many different companies, they can do them for less cost than an individual firm could with its own computer.

WHAT IS A COMPUTER SYSTEM?

What image comes to mind when you hear the term "computer system"? Do you think of a home computer that is attached to a television set or monitor and includes a joystick and a keyboard? Or do you think of an IBM personal computer or compatible with a floppy disk drive, display screen, keyboard, and printer? Maybe you have seen a large mainframe business computer with many different devices such as processors, operator consoles, disk storage devices, and printers. A computer system such as this would occupy a large room.

All these descriptions may apply when the term computer system is used. A **computer system,** then, is an electronic device that consists of several components that together provide the capability of executing a stored program for input, output, arithmetic, and logical operations. The physical computer and its devices are the hardware, while the stored program that supplies its instructions is called the software.

Certainly there is considerable difference among computers. A low-cost home computer is usually used for fun and enjoyment, whereas a large mainframe computer is serious business and may be used for significant applications such as recording and tracking reservations for a major airline. In the latter case, speed and efficiency are important as is the accuracy of processing data. Of course there are many sizes of computers with a wide range of capability between the two extemes.

Sizes of Computers

Computers come in all sizes. At the low end there is the **microcomputer,** which is becoming better known recently as the **personal computer** or **desktop computer.**

Next is the **minicomputer,** which is somewhat larger and more expensive than the micro, with correspondingly greater speed and storage capacity. Some minis are desktop, but most are larger and must occupy their own floor space. Usually a mini is a multiuser system whereas a micro is a single-user system. However, some upscale micros now boast a capability that is comparable to the minicomputer.

At the next level of speed and capacity we have the **mainframe computer.** It again is physically larger and may often require a specially designed room with extra air conditioning and a subfloor to run cables between the input and output devices and the processor. Full-time specially trained operators are usually required to operate these computers as are a staff of programmers to develop the application software.

The fourth level of computer is the **supercomputer.** This computer is designed for large-scale, complex, scientific applications such as weather forecasting, seismic activity research, and aerospace. These computers are very expensive, often costing in the millions of dollars to purchase.

While it is convenient to think of computers in these clearly defined categories, the reality is somewhat different. There are microcomputers that have comparable power to minis. And there are minis that could be classed as mainframes. The reverse is also true. So these terms are used to give a relative difference between major groupings of computers.

General-Purpose Computers

Computers used in business for accounting, payroll, word processing, reservations, and so on are called **general-purpose computers.** Most computers that we are likely to see or use on a day-by-day basis fall into this category. The home computer, small business computer, and even the mainframe are all capable of doing many different jobs and are therefore general purpose.

Special-Purpose Computers

Other computers that do only one specific function are called **special-purpose computers.** These are often hidden in places where we are unlikely to see them because they are simply a part of the device they help to operate. A commonly used special-purpose computer is that used on the fuel injection system of today's cars. Other specially designed computers are also used in digital watches, refrigerators, microwave ovens, and video cassette recorders to name a few applications.

Courtesy of Apple Computer Inc.

Courtesy of IBM.

Courtesy of Tandy Co.

Several types of microcomputers.

A microcomputer or personal computer is used in homes, offices, scientific labs, and even student dorms. The PC is priced to be affordable by a wide range of users, both individual and corporate. PCs are user friendly and have no unusual power or environmental requirements. Some computers, such as the IBM PS/2, can be connected with mini- and mainframe computers.

Courtesy of Harris Corp.

Courtesy of Honeywell.

Minicomputers used by business.

The minicomputer is refrigerator sized and usually sits on the floor. Minis can serve several users each located at separate terminals in the office. A mini is a natural step up for a company that has used a personal computer but due to the growth of the business has increased storage and processing needs requiring more computer power.

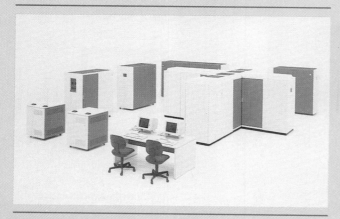

Courtesy of IBM.

Courtesy of IBM.

Centralized mainframe computer systems.

A computer center with a mainframe computer system. Medium- to large-sized businesses use the mainframe because its large storage and processing capacity simplifies the sharing of information within the company. A single mainframe computer can service hundreds of people at one time, while a personal computer can service only one person. However, companies with mainframes are using PCs for many computing needs throughout the company because the PC is inexpensive and easy to use.

Courtesy of Cray Research.

A Cray supercomputer.

A supercomputer such as this Cray system is used for very specialized computing needs, for example, weather forecasting. Compared to mainframe computers, only a small number of systems such as this exist, and scientists and researchers often need to book computer time on them months in advance.

This computer is used to control the fuel injection system on a Chrysler Corporation car. A special-purpose computer like this is designed for one purpose and cannot readily be reprogrammed to do other duties such as accounting, for which it is ill suited.

Courtesy of Chrysler Corp.

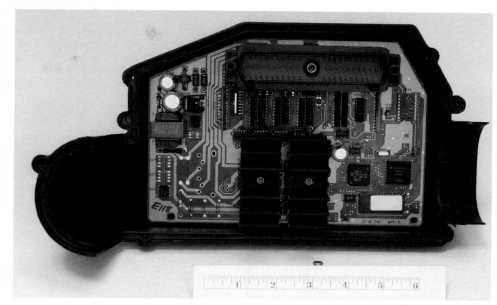

COMPONENTS OF THE COMPUTER

To understand the computer concept fully, it is important to recognize that a computer consists of several components (see Figure 1–2). In a large-scale computer system, these components may number in the hundreds, but usually we think of the computer in terms of only a few parts. These components may be broadly defined into three categories: processor, input, and output.

The Processor

The **processor,** often called the **central processing unit** or **CPU** and sometimes called the system unit, is the brains of the computer system. All activity in the system originates here under the control of a program that is stored in the processor. The processor is made of one or more silicon chips. A processor typically has three major components regardless of whether it is a personal or mainframe computer.

1. **Primary storage section.** The primary storage section or **memory** is used for several purposes. It provides storage space for data that is arriving from an input device, such as a keyboard, or going to an output device, such as the display screen. Primary storage is also used to store the program while it is executing. Finally, primary storage acts as a temporary scratch pad for the computer to use while doing calculations and other operations required by the program.
2. **Arithmetic and logic unit.** The arithmetic and logic unit or **ALU** for short, is where all the calculations take place in the computer. Calculations such as addition, subtraction, multiplication, and division are done here under control of the program. For example, a payroll program might read the number of hours and the rate of pay for an employee and give an instruction to multiply these numbers to give the gross pay earned for the week. It is the function of the arithmetic portion of the ALU to do this type of operation.

FIGURE 1–2 **Personal computer components.** The central processor of the computer consists of a processor, memory, and arithmetic and logic unit. Input devices include the keyboard, light pen, mouse, and document reader, while output devices include the display screen, printer, and plotter. A modem operates as both input and output. Devices such as disk and tape provide for secondary storage and provide both input and output.

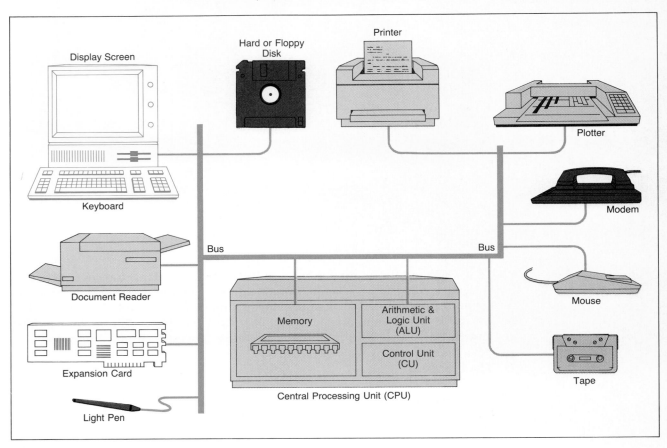

The logic side of the ALU does comparisons or logical operations. These operations compare values for greater than, less than, or equal to some other value. For example, in payroll the program may instruct the logic unit to compare the gross salary to $100 for the purpose of deducting income tax. If the salary is less than $100, then it determines that no tax deduction is necessary. But if the gross is equal to or greater than $100, then a tax deduction is necessary.

The logic unit may also compare alphabetic data. Thus the name Henderson is less than the name Jones because Henderson begins with an H, which alphabetically precedes J in Jones. Similarly, the name Smythe is greater than the name Smith because the letter y in Smythe is alphabetically greater than the letter i in Smith.

3. **Control unit.** The control unit is somewhat analagous to the conductor of a symphony. It directs the activity of the processor and determines which component should play its part and when. It is the control unit that decides when the ALU is to do an arithmetic or logical operation or data is to be transferred from an input device to memory. The control unit decodes each instruction received from

the program and acts on the instruction. By translating each instruction, it determines the action to be taken and then communicates the necessary instructions to the other components of the processor.

Other Components in a Computer

Computers also contain several components along with the processor to create a fully functioning unit. There are usually three of these features as described here.

1. The **bus** is an electronic circuit that sends data and messages between the other components of the system.
2. **Ports** are provided to attach input and output devices, such as the screen, keyboard, and printer, to the computer. Usually a port is a plug or socket located on the outside of the computer's chassis.
3. Most personal computers for business use also have **expansion slots** built internally in the computer. These allow the addition of extra features such as a mouse, memory expansion, and color graphics.

INPUT AND OUTPUT DEVICES

Imagine a stereo system without a record player, cassette player, or compact disk (CD) unit. Then suppose that it had no speakers or headphones. A stereo like this would not be of much use, and certainly there would be little pleasure derived from owning one. The devices named for the stereo system are the equivalent of the input and output devices on a computer system. Without input and output capability, the computer would be no more useful than the sound system without sound.

Input

Input devices supply data for the computer to act upon. Some devices are meant for human interaction with the computer and are usually relatively slow in speed. Others are for use by the computer and usually operate at a much higher speed. On a personal computer, the keyboard is the most common input device for human use. Other human use devices are a mouse, digitizer, and light pen. Devices that provide input for use by the computer are the floppy disk drive, hard disk, and modem. Some less frequently used input devices on the PC are tape, compact disk (CD) read-only memory (ROM), and a voice reader.

Output

Output devices are like the speakers or headphones on a stereo system. They either let us see the results of the computer's operation or are used to store these results for later use. As for input there are slower-speed output devices for human use, while the outputs that the computer may use to store data are generally much faster in operation.

On the personal computer, the display screen is the most common output device, while the printer is second in use. Displayed output, called **soft copy**, is temporary (although there is no practical limit to how long data may be

Input devices

Keyboard

Courtesy of IBM.

Modem

Courtesy of Hayes Microcomputer.

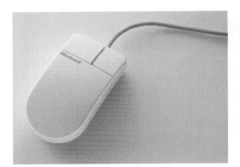

Mouse

Courtesy of Microsoft.

Disk Drive

Courtesy of Toshiba.

Output devices

Display Screen

Courtesy of IBM.

Plotter

Courtesy of Hewlett Packard.

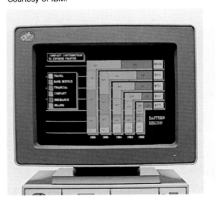

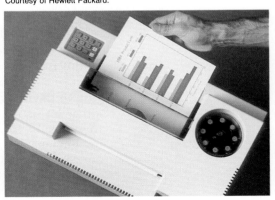

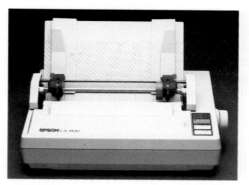

Printer

Courtesy of Epson America, Inc.

Hard Disk

Courtesy of Seagate.

displayed), while printed results, **hard copy,** are more or less permanent. Other output devices that the PC may use are the floppy or hard disk. These devices are both known as **secondary storage devices** because they store data for later use by the computer.

A personal computer may also use a plotter to create quality graphics, magnetic tape storage, a modem, and voice output.

SOFTWARE

All computers require a program to function. The program supplies the instructions for the computer to follow. Just as we may follow instructions in a recipe to prepare a soufflé, the computer follows instructions in the form of a program to complete a given task.

Computer software is supplied on one or more floppy disks, which may be loaded directly into the computer. Documentation for the software is provided in manuals that are supplied with the software package. Other materials such as a keyboard template and a command summary card may also be provided by the software manufacturer.

Courtesy of WordPerfect.

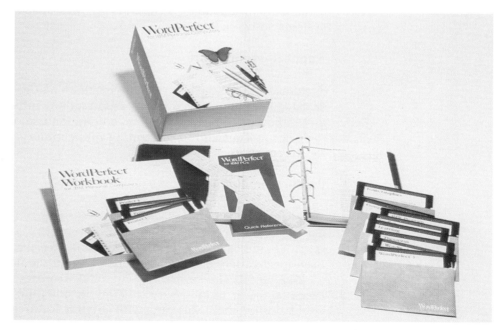

Programs are called software because they are not a physical object as is the hardware. Instead, software consists of commands or instructions that are placed into memory from a floppy or hard disk or some other device. The program is located in memory only during the time that the computer requires it. Because the program in memory is a copy of what was read from disk, the program may be used by the computer over and over again.

Early computer users were technically trained programmers who knew a great deal about the inner workings of the computer. Business users simply supplied the data and received the results without a need to know how the computer accomplished its task. But today many businesspeople use a computer directly in their jobs. If they are to use a computer effectively without the need for a lot of technical knowledge, then programs known as systems software and applications software will be essential.

Systems Software

These are general-purpose programs that enable the computer and other software to function more effectively and apply to all computer users. The most important program classified as **systems software** is the operating system that originated with mainframe computers. On today's personal computers, this program is commonly called **DOS,** which is an acronym for **disk operating system.** The word "disk" means that this program is located on disk and that it is used to assist in any activities that use the disk. DOS is used to read and write data to and from the disk, to load programs, to look at the disk contents, and to perform many other operations. Later, in Chapter 6, we will discuss DOS in more depth.

Other systems software programs are also available to enhance the use of the computer and make it function more effectively. These programs may provide features such as the ability to print graphs, the ability to reserve part of memory to act like a disk (called RAM disk), or the ability to connect (via a modem) to a remote computer. We will discuss many of these forms of systems software later in the book.

Applications Software

Systems software, such as DOS, is general in nature while applications software tends to have more specific uses. **Applications software** is designed to perform a specific function. For example, a common use of the personal computer is to do accounting, and so accounting applications packages are widely available for that purpose.

Productivity Software

Some software is not so clearly defined for a specific use such as an accounting package. This software includes word processing, spreadsheets, data base, and graphics and is called **productivity software.** Productivity software can be used for a variety of purposes depending on the needs of the user.

Figure 1–3 shows that the computer requires both systems software and applications or productivity software to function. While program developers could design their software with all the features provided by the systems software, this would be like reinventing the wheel. Instead, most programs

FIGURE 1–3

At the first layer in the hierarchy, we have the computer hardware. Next is the systems software, such as DOS, which attends to basic operations like accessing data from disk. The last level is the applications or productivity software. This is the software that interacts with the user of the system.

Hierarchy of Computer Functions

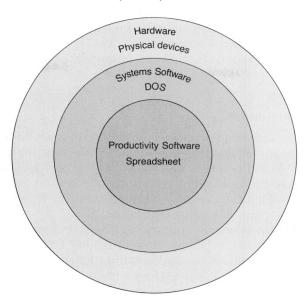

Hardware
Physical devices

Systems Software
DOS

Productivity Software
Spreadsheet

Types of productivity software

Word Processing
Courtesy of WordPerfect.

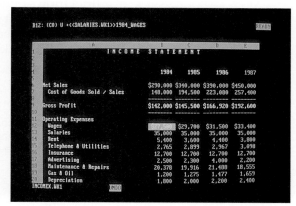

Spreadsheet
Courtesy of Lotus Development Corp.

Data Base
Courtesy of Ashton Tate.

Graphics
Courtesy of Harvard Graphics.

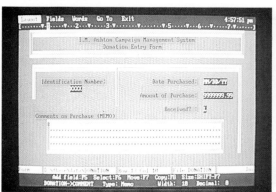

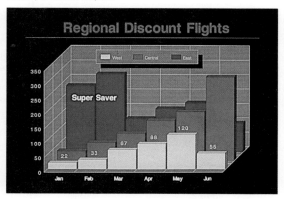

call on DOS to provide the capabilities of the system software. They will, for example, use the DOS functions for reading from disk, writing to disk, displaying information on the screen, and so on. This approach greatly simplifies program development and also makes it easier for the user of the software to understand the commonly used features.

Spreadsheets

Spreadsheets are among the most widely used software on personal computers. A **spreadsheet** is a program that permits the entry of data and formulas in rows and columns on the screen. As new values are entered, all formulas are automatically recalculated, and the results are shown immediately on the screen. Thus the user may ask questions, called "what if" questions, by entering new data and observing the results.

In the information processing time frame, spreadsheets are a recent development. In 1978, a college student named Dan Bricklin was sitting in class at Harvard Business School watching his professor create a model budget on the blackboard. As the professor changed a value in one column of the model, it was necessary to recalculate related numbers in the other columns. This is typical of an operation done when creating a budget, where values are adjusted—some increased, and others decreased—to try and stay within the financial limits assigned.

Bricklin was puzzling over the need for constant recalculations and suddenly realized that a computer could do all the recalculations if the data could be represented in rows and columns. He discussed this concept with a friend, Robert Frankston, who was an experienced computer programmer. To-

---

FIGURE 1–4 A spreadsheet program is used for many different applications within the company. Here, a spreadsheet is used by management to help predict financial requirements for budgets over a five-year period.

```
B13: (,2) @SUM(B7..B11)                                          READY
```

	A	B	C	D	E	F	G
1				Budget Spreadsheet			
2							
3	Budget	Budget	Projected	===>			
4	Category						
5		1988	1989	1990	1991	1992	1993
6							
7	Supplies	150.75	162.81	175.83	189.90	205.09	221.50
8	Travel	1,200.00	1,296.00	1,399.68	1,511.65	1,632.59	1,763.19
9	Phone	300.00	324.00	349.92	377.91	408.15	440.80
10	Mail	425.00	459.00	495.72	535.38	578.21	624.46
11	Manuals	290.00	313.20	338.26	365.32	394.54	426.11
12							
13	Totals	2,365.75	2,555.01	2,759.41	2,980.16	3,218.58	3,476.06
14							
15							
16							
17							
18							
19							
20							

gether they realized that even if they could create such a program it would need to be marketed, so they took the project to Dan Fylstra, a fledgling software publisher. Between them, the program VisiCalc was developed, which became an instant hit in the marketplace.

Today there are spreadsheet applications for budget planning (Figure 1–4), financial forecasting, depreciation, loan amortization, and virtually any application that uses rows and columns of data. Lotus 1–2–3, a competing spreadsheet package, has outdistanced VisiCalc to become by far the best selling program followed by other competitors such as SuperCalc[4] and Multiplan, and recently Microsoft Excel. Current spreadsheets offer important features such as windows, graphing, and data base capabilities. Later in the book, in Chapter 9, we will examine spreadsheets in more detail.

Word processing

Anyone who has become reasonably competent at using a word processing program on a personal computer would not be easily persuaded to return to the typewriter. Gone is the need for retyping a page if too many errors have been made. There is no need to use correction fluid or special correcting ribbons. Neither is a copier needed if two or three extra copies of the document are required.

A **word processing program** (Figure 1–5) aids in the typing of text ranging from short memos to manuscript-length documents. Word processors first became available on specialized computers that were devoted entirely to word processing. These machines were called **dedicated word processors** because that was the only task they could do. When personal computers arrived, they were truly general-purpose computers because word processing was only one of many duties they were capable of performing.

Word processor features vary a lot, and so does the price, from as low as $19.95 to hundreds of dollars. Most word processors provide for automatic

FIGURE 1–5
A word processing program improves the productivity of tasks that are typing intensive. Good word processors enable easy correcting or updating of documents and creating form letters from a file of names and addresses. Advanced systems also have automatic spelling checkers and a thesaurus.

Courtesy of Apple Computer, Inc.

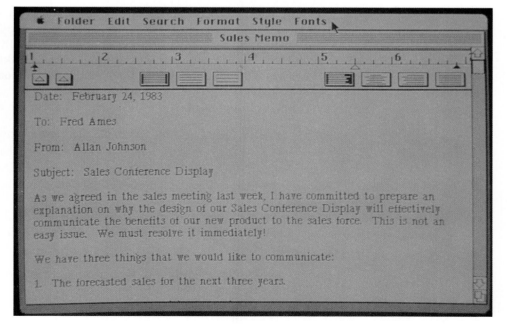

word wrap at the end of a line; correcting typing errors; underlining; centering; and changing the location of words, sentences, or paragraphs in the text. Others create automatic headers and footers and provide for searching and replacing of text in the document. Full-feature word processors also provide a merge capability for creating form letters; they may have a spelling checker, a thesaurus, and even line drawing ability.

Of course, a word processor must interface with a printer, and a good one will permit a variety of printers to be used with it. Another feature that is important to many users is known as **WYSIWYG** meaning, "What you see is what you get." This expression means that the document on the screen appears as it will be printed, so that the user will know what to expect when the command to print is given.

But using the best word processing software does not of itself produce a better writer. Rather, the program is just a tool to help in the processing of words. Some widely used word processing programs for personal computers are WordStar, WordPerfect, Microsoft Word, and Multimate. Later in the book in Chapter 8, we will look at word processors in much greater depth.

Data base management systems (DBMS)

Imagine a filing cabinet with hundreds of pages of information about each of a company's customers and the orders they have placed. There is a second file that contains the current inventory of items in stock. Now, a customer calls to find out the status of the order and is required to wait several minutes while the file is manually searched for the order and then the separate inventory file checked to determine if the shipment of parts has been received.

If the company has used a data base program, instead of the manual system, then the customer data, orders, and inventory could all be recorded on a hard disk on a personal computer. By entering the appropriate commands to the data base program, the computer can provide the information the customer requires within a few seconds.

A **data base** program, such as the one just described, permits the storing of data in a systematic way on a disk file so that it may be easily retrieved and updated as required. Data base programs can easily do things that are often too time consuming in a manual system. Suppose we want to know all the customers who have ordered a specific part. In a manual system, every customer's record would need to be examined, taking many hours of labor. However, a simple **query** (Figure 1–6) on a data base program could find the answer in as little time as a few minutes.

Some of the features of a data base program are as follows.

1. The ability to add new records to the file as new activity occurs.
2. The ability to revise existing records as data about that record changes.
3. The ability to delete records that are no longer required.
4. A query capability that permits asking questions about the contents of the data base.
5. The ability to organize or sort large amounts of data into a more usable form.
6. The ability to generate reports from the data base with appropriate totals or summarizing of data.

Some commonly used data base programs for personal computers are dBASE IV, R:base System V, PFS File, and Q&A.

FIGURE 1–6
Data stored in a data base management system may be accessed in a variety of ways. Here a query operation is used to find out which customers have ordered RGB screens for their computers.

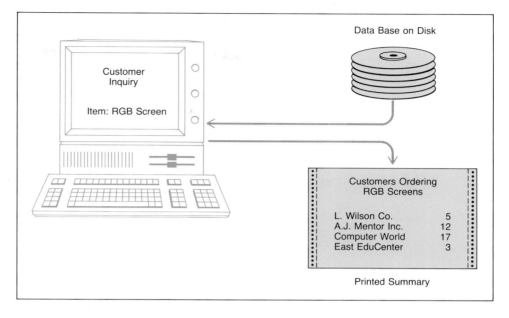

Graphics

To rephrase an ancient saying, a graph is worth a thousand words. A **graph** portrays numerical data pictorially. Using graphs to communicate the relationships between numbers can be much more effective than trying to explain the same data (Figure 1–7). Graphs can also help in the analysis of the numbers when a simple mathematical formula just won't do.

Although many spreadsheet programs produce graphs, they do not have the specialized abilities of the graphics software packages. Sometimes data is

FIGURE 1–7
Graphics displays are used to enhance the presentation of numerical data.

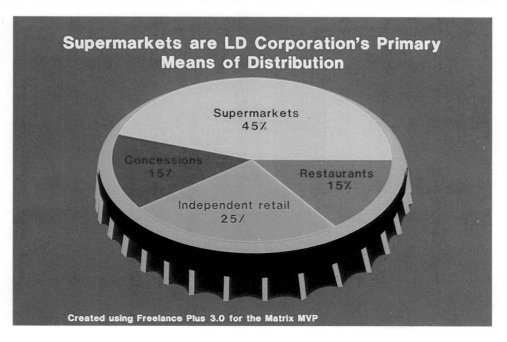

organized in a spreadsheet such as Lotus 1–2–3, and a rough graph is produced by 1–2–3 to give a feel for the presentation. Then the data is sent to one of the specialized graphics programs that can produce dazzling graphs with high-quality output.

Some graphics programs are essentially charting programs that produce a variety of bar or pie charts with various type styles on a dot matrix printer, laser printer, or plotter. Others can create an animated presentation that is projected like a slide projector for use in business meetings or sales presentations.

Specialized graphics packages can be used to create flowcharts, organization charts, or other analytical graphics. Many graphics programs work with specialized output devices such as a film recorder or camera that create high-quality 35mm slides of the graph. Because these devices are often more expensive than the computer, a service bureau that specializes in creating quality graphs is often used.

Some widely used graphic programs are Lotus Freelance Plus, Harvard Presentation Graphics, and Chart-Master.

Integrated software

When a computer user has become skilled in the use of the major software programs, including spreadsheets, word processing, and data base management, the next major need usually is the ability to transfer data between each of these programs. Often a manager who is creating a report will require some data that exists on the data base as well as some statistics and graphs provided by the spreadsheet. Pulling these together into a single report can be the task of the word processor.

Achieving these tasks with most software is either impossible or quite complex, so the manager will create each part of the report with the appropriate

FIGURE 1–8
Lotus Symphony is an integrated software package that provides the user with word processing, spreadsheet, data base, graphics, and communications capability.

Courtesy of Lotus.

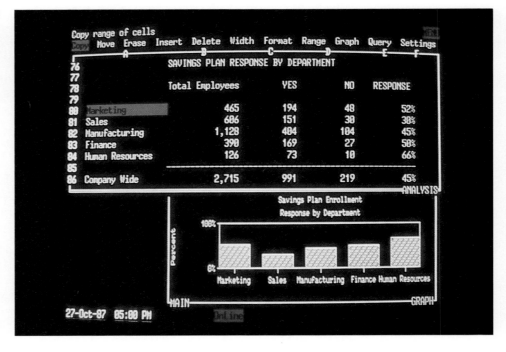

software, using two or three different packages in the process. Often the results are combined by cutting and pasting on paper and finally reproducing on a copier.

Integrated software provides all the foregoing capabilities and more in a single software solution. **Integrated software** (Figure 1–8) often supplies five functions in the one package: word processing, spreadsheet, data base, graphics, and communications. Some integrated programs now available are Enable, Framework, Lotus Symphony, and Microsoft Works. While integrated software has been slow getting started, and some of the initial results have been less than satisfying, they are now becoming a realistic alternative to having several different software packages.

COMMUNICATIONS

Many personal computers operate as **stand-alone** machines, which means that they function independently of other computers. But, for systems like this, it is difficult or inefficient to share information between them. To solve this problem, many computers are being connected together (Figure 1–9) so that they may share common data and even access the same files on a common disk.

Computers in close proximity to each other, such as several PCs in an office space, can be connected by electrical wires using what is called a **local area network.** More remote systems, such as computers located in different cities or even different countries, use established telephone systems or telecommunications networks to communicate. When computers are connected either locally or at a distance, additional hardware and software are required to make communication possible.

There are many reasons for communicating with a remote computer. One is to let the computer have access to electronic mail or electronic bulletin boards for the exchange of information of common interest. Another is to let the personal computer access a mainframe system that contains public data

FIGURE 1–9   A modem is used to connect a computer to a communication line so that it may communicate with a remote computer that is similarly equipped.

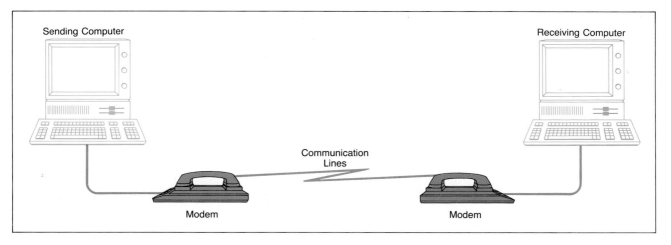

Sending Computer

Receiving Computer

Communication
Lines

Modem

Modem

bases such as stock market information, news, or travel information. Personal computers with communication capability may also act as a remote terminal for a mainframe computer to collect data that is forwarded to the mainframe system.

Many software packages recognize the need that computer users have for linking with other computers and now provide built-in features for data communications. This capability reduces the need to have separate communications software. Built-in communication capability is a common component of integrated software.

COMPUTERS AND YOUR WORLD

In the discussion and photographs of this chapter you have been given a general idea of what computers are all about. We have looked at what computers are and why they are useful. We have seen that for computers to be used in business, both hardware and software is necessary. Hardware is the processor and several input and output devices, including a keyboard, screen, printer, disk drive, and other devices. Software is both systems software and application or productivity software. Software can be specialized, as when accounting software is used, or generalized, as is the case with spreadsheets, word processing, data base, graphics, and integrated systems. As you read the following chapters you will gain a fuller understanding of the computer and how it is being used in your world.

CHAPTER SUMMARY

1. Many businesspeople use a personal computer to supply, store, and process information so that they may do their job or run their company more effectively.

2. Although the computer may have specific programs that relate to accounting, restaurants, or investment, it cannot begin to replace the professionals who bring their expertise to the jobs described. Information is required for either the professional or the computer to work effectively.

3. Data represents the raw facts, while information is data that has been collected and presented in a meaningful way.

4. An information system is a system that collects and organizes data into a form that has meaning for a specific business function. An information system is necessary for the businessperson, manager, or professional to do their job effectively, and most often this system requires the use of a computer.

5. Large companies have information systems or data processing departments that are self-contained and provide the company with all its information requirements. These departments consist of computer operators, programmers, systems analysts, and data entry operators who have the responsibility for the computer and information systems.

6. Mainframe computer systems are intended for centralized use and require computer professionals for their implementation and operation.

7. A personal computer can be used by one person. These computers are easy for anyone to use in all areas of business and personal applications, from spreadsheets to financial planning, accounting, and computer graphics, and with a minimum of training.

8. The computer is an electronic device that is only as good and as accurate as the people that use it. Although it may be extremely fast, it depends on the user's instruction for effective operation. A computer system consists of several compo-

nents that together provide the capability of executing a stored program for input, output, arithmetic, and logical operations.

9. It is not always appropriate to use a computer to solve a business problem. Use a computer when a job is easily defined and repetitive or if software already exists to do the job. Sometimes a manual system will work just as well. A service company can often provide computer support for less money than the cost of buying a system.

10. Computers come in all sizes. At the low end there is the microcomputer, also known as the personal computer or desktop computer. Next is the minicomputer, which varies from desktop size to refrigerator size. Then there is the mainframe computer, which requires special facilities such as air conditioning and a subfloor. Last is the supercomputer, which is used for complex, large-scale, scientific operations.

11. General-purpose computers are used for accounting, payroll, and reservations systems; special-purpose computers are used for only one function such as an automotive fuel injection system.

12. Computer components fall into three categories: processor, input, and output. The processor consists of primary storage or memory, the arithmetic and logic unit, and the control unit. A computer also has a bus for sending data between components in the system, ports to attach input/output devices, and expansion slots to add new features.

13. Input devices supply data for the computer to act on. Humans use devices that include a keyboard, mouse, digitizer, and light pen, while devices used by the computer are the floppy disk drive, hard disk, and modem.

14. Output devices let us see the results of the computer's operation or store the results for later use. Devices for human use are the display screen, printer, and plotter, while computer use output devices can be the floppy disk drive, hard disk, or modem.

15. Software is a program that supplies the instructions for the computer to follow. Programs are called software because they are not a physical object such as the hardware.

16. Systems software makes the computer and its applications programs function more effectively. The most widely used systems software is the disk operating system.

17. Applications software is designed to do a specific function such as accounting. Other software is not so easily defined because its purpose is more general, such as data base or spreadsheet software.

18. A spreadsheet is a program that permits the entry of data and formulas in rows and columns on the screen. As new values are entered, all formulas are automatically recalculated, and the results are shown immediately on the screen.

19. A word processing program aids in the typing of text, ranging from short memos to manuscript-length documents. The program aids in underlining, formatting, boldface, reorganizing, and error correction and may provide other advanced features such as headers and footers, spelling checks, and form letters.

20. A data base program permits the storing of data in a systematic way on a disk file so that it may be easily retrieved and updated as required.

21. A graph portrays numerical data pictorially. Using graphs to communicate the relationships between numbers can be much more effective than trying to explain verbally the same data.

22. Computers in a local setting may communicate with one another using a local area network, while other computers located at a distance may use telephone lines or communication facilities to transfer data. Personal computers may also access public data bases for information about the stock market, news, or travel. Usually communication software and a modem are required for this activity.

23. Integrated software provides the capability of several different types of software packages. Usually this includes spreadsheets, word processing, and data base and often includes graphics and communications as well.

Applications software
Arithmetic and logic unit
Bus
Business system
Central processing unit (CPU)
Computer system
Control unit
Data
Data base management systems (DBMS)
Data entry
Decision support system (DSS)
Desktop computer
Disk operating system (DOS)
Expansion slots

General-purpose computers
Graph
Graphics
Information systems department
Information system (IS)
Information
Input device
Integrated software
Knowledge worker
Local area network
Mainframe computer
Management information system (MIS)
Memory
Microcomputer

Minicomputer
Output device
Personal computer (PC)
Ports
Primary storage section
Processor
Query
Secondary storage devices
Software
Special-purpose computers
Spreadsheet
Summarizing
Supercomputer
Systems software
User
Word processing

REVIEW QUESTIONS

Fill-in Questions

1. Data is first input to the computer. The computer will then _____ the data and create output from the result of this step.
2. The term _____ refers to the raw material or facts.
3. When these facts are collected and organized in a meaningful pattern, they are called _____.
4. A(n) _____ is someone who is not a computer professional but makes use of the computer in his or her daily work.
5. An error in the _____ is more likely to be a source of a problem than a hardware error.
6. The _____ computer is a computer used by one person.
7. The _____ is where the computer does its calculations and performs decision making.
8. A(n) _____ is also known as a personal or desktop computer.
9. Devices such as the screen, printer, and plotter are called _____ devices.
10. _____ software includes programs such as accounting and spreadsheets.
11. A(n) _____ contributes to the productivity of people who work with words, whether they are writing memos or manuscripts.
12. A data base user will use a(n) _____ to determine all customers who have ordered a specific part.
13. _____ software provides multiple capabilities that would ordinarily require several different programs.

Matching Questions

Match each term with the description given.

a. spreadsheet   d. personal computer
b. MIS   e. software
c. mainframe   f. hardware

_____ 1. Another name for a microcomputer that is widely used today.
_____ 2. A computer used by most major corporations and large organizations.
_____ 3. This is a type of software that records data and formulas in rows and columns.
_____ 4. This is another name for the program that supplies the computer with its instructions.
_____ 5. A system that provides management with the information needed to run the company.
_____ 6. The physical components of the computer.

Discussion Questions

1. Why is it that information systems are so important to a broad variety of businesses today?
2. Besides the computer, what other ingredient is important for the professional to work effectively? How is this ingredient used?
3. Describe what is meant by an information system and how it fits into an organization.
4. Why is it that large organizations usually have an information systems department while smaller companies seldom do, although both may use computers?
5. What are the differences between a computer professional and a user?
6. What were the factors that made the personal computer so popular?
7. Describe situations where a computer is useful and some where a computer may not be the best choice for solving a business problem.
8. What is the definition of a computer system? What are the various components of a computer system?
9. Explain the three components of the processor and the additional components that will be found in a personal computer.
10. What is the purpose of input and output devices? Name some of these devices.
11. What is software? Explain the purpose of both sysems and application software and some commonly used software packages.
12. Describe the purpose and function of each of the following software. What are some of the most popular software programs in each category?
    a. A spreadsheet.
    b. Word processing.
    c. A data base program.
    d. Graphics.
13. Discuss the need for communications capabilities in computers explaining how computers communicate with one another in different settings.
14. Explain what is meant by the term integrated software. What do these software packages often include? Name some of the well-known integrated packages.

Computer Hardware

A VIEW OF THE CHAPTER AHEAD

After Reading This Chapter You Will Understand:

- The major components of the processor, including the CPU, memory, and buses, and the terminology used to compare them.

- Letters, digits, and other characters that are represented in ASCII code.

- The characteristics of integrated circuit technology that made personal computers possible.

- The importance of computer interfaces.

- The impact of compatibles on the market and the features they offer to create a niche in the market.

- Some of the differences between the PC and the mainframe processor and why the mainframe is still widely used in business.

When the decision has been made to purchase a computer, the first question often asked is: "what computer should I buy?" This question may seem to be easily answered when personal computers are the objective, but even with the desktop computer, there are many factors to be considered. Making the right decision about the type of processor, the memory size, processing speed, display and communication capabilities, available secondary storage, and printer compatibility are all determined in relation to the processor or components that are directly attached to it.

Even when the choice of computer has been made by management consensus or some other process, the knowledge of the processor components is important. By understanding the function of the various components of the processor, you will be better equipped to determine what activities can be realistically done on the computer. This knowledge will let you know if graphs can be displayed or printed, whether the memory is sufficient to handle a specific piece of software effectively, or whether data from another computer made by a different manufacturer will be able to be processed on yours.

PROCESSOR CHARACTERISTICS

Bits, Bytes, and Words

When computer designers began using electronic components back in the early 1940s, they soon realized that using decimal numbers to represent data did not work very well. This was because electronic components were essentially switches: they could be in one of two states—on or off. As Figure 2–1 shows,

FIGURE 2–1
A binary number is formed from a combination of zeros and ones. Common devices such as a light bulb or a wall switch can be used to represent binary values. If the light bulb is on, then it represents the value 1, but if it is off, it represents binary zero. Such a method of coding is used with magnetic spots to record data on the surface of a disk.

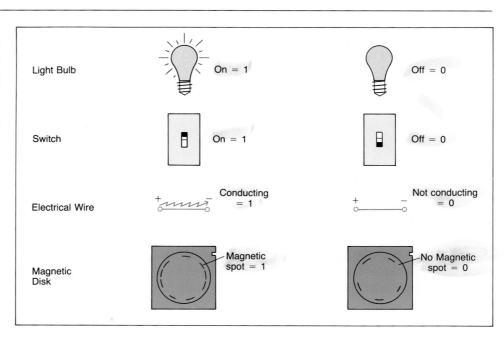

an on or off state can represent only two values—zero or one—which are the fundamental properties of the binary number system.

Bits

The decision to base computer design on the binary number system turned out to be a wise choice because many of the advances in electronics and micro technology have been developed from the binary number principle. It is from the binary number that we get the term "bit." The word bit is derived from **bi**nary digi**t**. A **bit** is the smallest element or value that is represented in the computer, and, as we have seen, it represents the value zero or one.

Bits are used in many areas in the computer. Data in memory is represented at its most basic level by bits. Data flows from the processor to other input or output devices as a stream of bits, and it is stored on secondary storage devices such as magnetic disk in the form of magnetic bits. So you can see that the use of a bit is fundamental to most operations in the computer.

HOW MANY BITS IS YOUR COMPUTER?

A computer is often described as having a 16-bit or a 32-bit processor, which describes the size of the word used within the computer. The bits measurement refers to the number of bits that the computer can process in one operation. For arithmetic, a 16-bit compuuter may require several steps to complete the operation on a large number, while a 32-bit computer may be able to do the same operation in one step, thus completing the calculation much more rapidly.

8-Bit Computers

A computer that processes only 8 bits at a time is typical of a home computer like the Commodore 64 and Apple IIC. Generally, an 8-bit system is useful for games, nondemanding word processing and spreadsheet tasks, and some educational applications.

16-Bit Computers

This class represents by far the largest number of personal computers in use today. The IBM personal computer is the best known example of a 16-bit computer; of course the many compatibles offered by companies such as Compaq, Leading Edge, Texas Instruments, and Zenith are included in this group. Some minicomputers are also 16-bit computers. Sixteen-bit computers are good at a variety of tasks, including spreadsheets, word processing, data base management, and many other business and even scientific applications.

32-Bit Computers

In the mid-1980s a new class of personal computer emerged. Although 32 bits and more were not unusual on minicomputers and mainframes, they were previously too expensive for PCs. The Apple Macintosh was the first of the 32-bit personal computers and was soon followed by others. IBM brought out a new version of the PC called the PC/AT (for "advanced technology") followed by the Personal System/2. Thirty-two-bit systems have greater memory

Courtesy of Commodore.

An 8-bit computer.

Courtesy of IBM.

A 16-bit computer.

Courtesy of Compaq.

A 32-bit computer.

capacity and higher speeds than do 16-bit computers and are used where very large spreadsheet applications, networking, and multitasking are necessary.

Bytes

Although bits are useful when discussing electronic components, most humans find them difficult to work with, and so another representation is necessary. A **byte** is the term used to describe a group of 8 bits and is the basic unit of data in the computer. A byte can be used to represent a character, such as an upper- or lowercase letter, a number, a punctuation symbol, or even a graphic symbol. Because there are 8 bits in a byte and a bit can be one of two values, a byte can represent 2^8 or 256 different values, which is more than enough for most applications.

The byte is used as a measure of the computer's memory size and of disk storage capacity. Because memory is usually in the thousands of bytes, the letter "K" is used to represent kilo, which comes from the Greek language meaning thousand. K in computer talk, however, refers to 1,024 bytes. Larger sizes are also represented by letters as shown in the accompanying table.

Term	Number of Bytes	Prefix	Meaning	Greek	Original Meaning
Kilobyte	1,024	kilo	thousand	khilioi	thousand
Megabyte	1,048,576	mega	million	megas	great
Gigabyte	1,073,741,824	giga	billion	gigas	giant
Terabyte	1,099,511,627,776	tera	trillion	teras	monster

Source: *PC Magazine*, November 25, 1986, p. 150.

TABLE 2–1
Using Powers of 2 to Show the Number of Bytes that Represent Different Storage Sizes in the Computer

Powers of 2	No. of Bytes	Shorthand	Typical Memory and Disk Sizes	
0	1			
1	2			
2	4			
3	8			
4	16			
5	32			
6	64			
7	128			
8	256			
9	512			
10	1,024	1K (kilobyte)		
11	2,048	2K		
12	4,096	4K		
13	8,192	8K		
14	16,384	16K		
15	32,768	33K	32K	8-bit computer
16	65,536	66K	64K	
17	131,072	131K	128K	16-bit computer
18	262,144	262K	256K	
19	524,288	524K	512K	
20	1,048,576	1M (megabyte)	1M	32-bit computer
21	2,097,152	2M		
22	4,194,304	4M		
23	8,388,608	8M		
24	16,777,216	17M	20M	PC fixed disk
25	33,554,432	34M	30M	
26	67,108,864	67M		
27	134,217,728	134M	100M	Mainframe disk
28	268,435,456	268M		
29	536,870,912	537M		
30	1,073,741,824	1G (gigabyte)		

Table 2–1 shows how size in bytes is measured by both primary storage (memory) and secondary storage (disk).

A typical office computer has 640K of memory and a fixed disk drive with a 20M capacity. Memory of this size is the maximum for most PCs but can be expanded with add-on boards for special applications such as spreadsheets when 640K is not enough. Computers like the IBM PS/2 can have several million bytes of main memory. By contrast, disk drives of much higher capacity are available, and if one is not enough, then two or more may be used on the computer. Although major expansion is possible for both memory and disk, many office systems get along quite nicely with 640K and 20M of hard disk.

Courtesy of IBM.

Words

A **word** is a logical unit of information consisting of a number of bits. In an 8-bit microprocessor, a word is 8 bits in length, which is the same as a byte. You might have guessed that a 16-bit processor's word is 16 bits long and therefore consists of two bytes. It is this measurement that determines the size of the data that can be processed or transferred at one time and thus affects the speed of the computer.

Components

We have already seen in Chapter 1 that the computer's processor consists of several components that operate together to make up a functional computer. The main components found with the computer's processor are shown in Figure 2–2. These components are

1. The **central processing unit (CPU)** or **microprocessing unit (MPU),** as it is sometimes called, follows the directions in the program to determine the actions to be taken by the computer. Most processors in today's personal computers reside on a single integrated chip. A 16-bit processor can do operations on data that is 16 bits or 2 bytes in length. Larger numbers, or operations on more than 2 bytes, will require two or more operations for each calculation.

2. The **memory** is the device that stores the program and the data being processed. Memory consists of a number of integrated chips. A maximum memory size of 640K is typically available on a 16-bit computer such as the IBM PC, while a 32-bit system like the Apple Macintosh, IBM PC/AT, or PS/2 can potentially have millions of bytes of memory.

3. A **data bus** is the path through which data or instructions flow between the components of the computer. The IBM PC has a 16-bit microprocessor and an 8-bit data

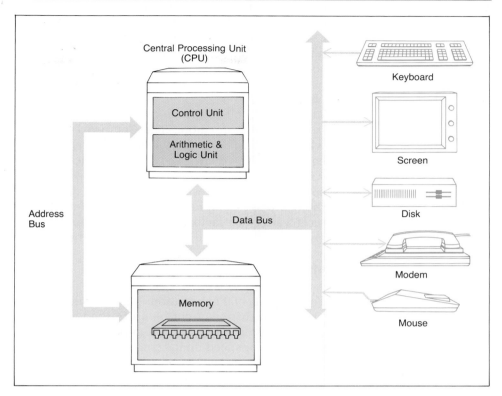

FIGURE 2–2
The primary components of the computer's processor.

bus. The PS/2 has a 16-bit data bus, called a Micro Channel, which allows for much faster data transfer than the PC.[1] The **address** bus carries memory addresses to all devices that are connected to the data bus. The bit size of the address bus determines the size of memory that may be addressed. Early 8-bit computers had a 16-bit address bus and could address 2^{16} (65,536) bytes of memory. The IBM PC has a 20-bit address bus thus allowing a theoretical maximum of 1 million bytes of memory while the AT and PS/2 use a 24-bit address bus that can address 16 megabytes.

The characteristics of these components of the computer determine to a large extent the capabilities of the system. The specifications of the processor determine the type of software that can be used on the computer and the speed at which the programs will run. Because hardware manufacturers have selected only a few different types of processors, the selection is relatively easy to make.

Speed

We have seen that the more bits a processor or bus can handle, the faster the computer will operate. Another factor that affects the speed of the computer is the clock. Each personal computer contains an electronic clock in its circuitry that acts as a timer to ensure that all the activity going on in the computer is coordinated. If a new activity begins before a previous one is finished, the

---

[1] Some models of the IBM PS/2 do not use the Micro Channel. Models such as the 25 or 30 operate similarly to the 16-bit PC.

computer will simply fail to operate accurately, and so the clock controls the timing of all events.

The speed of the clock is measured in **megahertz (MHz),** which is a term referring to the number of cycles per second at which it operates. This is something like a stop watch that measures time in thousandths of a second, except that time in a microcomputer is measured in megahertz or millionths of a second.

A typical clock speed on a 16-bit PC is 4.77 MHz while a 32-bit computer is 6 or 8 MHz or more. The Compaq Deskpro 386/20 operates at 16 MHz, while the IBM PS/2 Model 80–111 operates at 20 MHz. Some systems are equipped with a dual-speed capability such as 4.77 or 7.16 MHz, so that software will run faster and yet provide compatibility with earlier systems. To change speed simply requires the user to flick a switch. Ultimately, the speed at which the computer completes a given task depends not only on clock speed, but on a variety of factors that include the type of processor, disk speed, the type of software used, and the way the bus is designed.

Multiple Processors

For some special applications such as scientific or engineering work, the main processing chip may not be up to the tasks required of it. In such situations a second processor, called a **coprocessor,** may be installed in the computer to enhance or speed up the computer's operation. In the IBM PC and computers similar to it, an 8087 coprocessor chip may be used when applications, such as spreadsheets, require a lot of mathematical operations for faster operation.

Reliability

Naturally the company that installs personal computers would prefer that they are 100 percent reliable. But, just like a car, reliability is a factor of many components, and ultimately one of them is likely to fail. Electronic components, such as integrated circuits and memory chips, tend to be extremely reliable while electromechanical devices, such as printers or keyboards, are more susceptible to failure.

FIGURE 2–3
Improvement in mean time between hardware failure in computer systems.

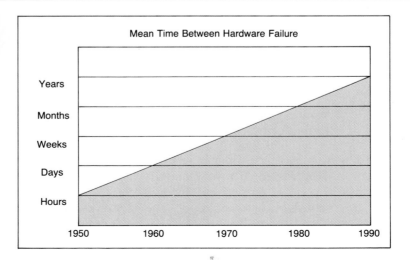

Early computers that used vacuum tubes broke down frequently, but as transistors and integrated circuits replaced the tube, computers became vastly more reliable. Figure 2–3 shows the improvement in the mean failure time as computer technology advanced.

COMPUTER CODES

Although numbers in a computer are described by a number system such as binary, the actual binary digits can be used to represent all kinds of data, including letters and numbers. (See Appendix B for more detail.) In addition to binary, all computers use some kind of internal code to represent characters, that is, digits, letters, and special symbols. The most widely used code for personal computers is the **American Standard Code for Information Inter-**

TABLE 2–2
A Table of ASCII
Character Set Values

Decimal Value	Character	Decimal Value	Character	Decimal Value	Character
32	space	65	A	97	a
33	!	66	B	98	b
34	"	67	C	99	c
35	#	68	D	100	d
36	$	69	E	101	e
37	%	70	F	102	f
38	&	71	G	103	g
39	'	72	H	104	h
40	(	73	I	105	i
41	)	74	J	106	j
42	*	75	K	107	k
43	+	76	L	108	l
44	,	77	M	109	m
45	-	78	N	110	n
46	''	79	O	111	o
47	/	80	P	112	p
48	0	81	Q	113	q
49	1	82	R	114	r
50	2	83	S	115	s
51	3	84	T	116	t
52	4	85	U	117	u
53	5	86	V	118	v
54	6	87	W	119	w
55	7	88	X	120	x
56	8	89	Y	121	y
57	9	90	Z	122	z
58	:	91	[	123	{
59	;	92	\	124	|
60	<	93	]	125	}
61	=	94	^	126	~
62	>	95	__	127	
63	?	96	`	128	?
64	@				

change (ASCII). This is an 8-bit code meaning that characters are represented with eight bits of binary digits. In most ASCII definitions, seven of these bits are used for the character, and the eighth bit is used for error checking. Using this system provides a capability for up to 128 different characters, digits, or letters in the code.

In the computer's processor and on some storage devices, such as magnetic disk, each character is represented as a binary value. For example, the number 1 is stored in ASCII as 0110001, which is equivalent to the decimal value 49. The uppercase letter A is stored as 1000001, which is decimal 65. Most operations, such as programming or other software development, use the decimal equivalent or even the character itself as it is typed at the keyboard. Table 2–2 shows a selected number of the ASCII values for a typical character set.

Some mainframe computers also use the ASCII code, but a more widely used code on IBM and other mainframes is **EBCDIC,** which is an acronym for **Extended Binary Coded Decimal Interchange Code.** This code bears some similarity to ASCII in that it also has 8 bits per character, but the coding system used is quite different.

ICs AND MICROPROCESSORS

The **microprocessor** is the chip that contains the processor, arithmetic and logic unit, and control unit. **Integrated circuits** (ICs) are silicon chips that contain a number of transistors on one chip. The transistor is a solid-state device that was invented by John Barder, William Shockley, and Walter Bratten at Bell Telephone Laboratories in 1948. (See Appendix A for more on history.) The transistor revolutionized the electronics and computer industries because of its compact size, speed of operation, and durability.

Since this time, further developments in microelectronics have enabled designers to pack more transistors into a single integrated circuit. Packing more circuits into a single IC has had several effects on computer technology, a major one being to make the personal computer a reality. Here are some of the other significant effects.

1. **Size.** The computer is much smaller in size when ICs of greater density are used.
2. **Cost.** Using ICs in computer design results in less expensive computers compared to previous technologies.
3. **Speed.** Because of the smaller size, electrons in the circuit need to travel shorter distances resulting in higher operating speeds.
4. **Power.** Electrical power consumption is less with IC components. These components also generate less heat than previous technologies, thus requiring no special cooling.

Since IC technology appeared, there has been a continual reduction in size and corresponding increase in the number of transistors packed into the IC. Several levels of design have appeared with this improving technology. Chip densities are expressed in terms of integration of scale. Low-density chips are **SSI** (small-scale integration) and **MSI** (medium-scale integration), followed by **LSI** (large-scale integration) and **VLSI** (very-large-scale integration). There is even an emergence of a higher density called **SLSI** (superlarge-scale integration). Table 2–3 shows the relative density of these chips in terms of the number of transistors they contain.

TABLE 2–3
Density of Different Levels
of Integration

IC	Number of Transistors
SSI	2 to 30
MSI	10 to 500
LSI	100 to 20,000
VLSI	10,000 to 100,000
SLSI	over 100,000

Table 2–4 shows several widely used processors in the industry today. The computers listed that use these chips are typical of the class of chip, although many other makes of personal computers may also use the same chip or an equivalent version.

TABLE 2–4
A Comparison of Popular
Microprocessors

Microprocessor	No. of Bits	Data Bus (bits)	Address Bus (bits)	Computer
MOS Technology 6502	8	8	16	Apple II Commodore 64
Intel 8088	16	8	20	IBM PC and PC/XT
Motorola 68000	32	16	24	Apple Macintosh
Intel 80286	32	16	24	IBM PC/AT and PS/2
Intel 80386	32	32	32	Compaq Deskpro 386 and some IBM PS/2s

The integrated circuit is at the heart of all computer design and construction. A chip such as this Intel 80386 is about a square inch in size and yet contains over 100,000 circuits that the computer uses in its operation.

Courtesy of Intel.

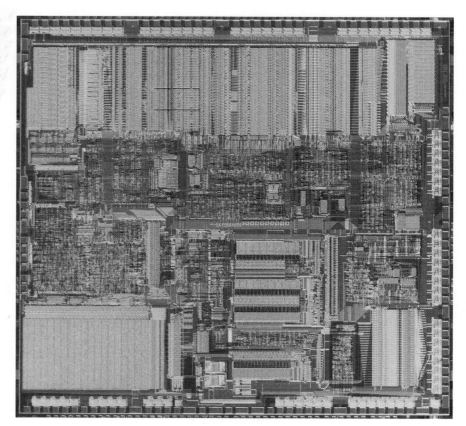

What is 50 times faster than an IBM PC and more powerful than an 80386 processor chip? It is the 80486 Intel microprocessor released in early 1989. Computers based on this 32-bit processor will offer mainframe-like performance in a desktop computer.

The 80486 is an advance on the 386 technology which already has become a widely accepted standard in the computing industry. One weakness of the 80386 was the need for extra components to speed up mathematical and graphic functions. These components are fully integrated into the design of the 80486 processor.

Intel's new chip contains 1,180,285 transistors and offers full compatibility with the 386. The new technology supports complex scientific calculations and financial modeling. It helps to manage local area networks, electronic messages and imaging such as those used in fax systems, and supports advanced graphics functions such as color separation for desktop publishing.

To take advantage of the new power and performance of the 80486 Microsoft introduced a 32-bit version of the OS/2 operating system. Some researchers believe that the 486 may also be used in smaller minicomputer systems and workstations because of its capabilities and 25 MHz clock speed, soon to be increased to 33 MHz. Prime Computer is working with Intel to develop, by 1992, a 120 Mips (million instructions per second) version of the 486 to provide mainframe power in a desktop computer.

Memory

Memory, also called primary storage, is an essential component of the computer. Memory is primarily used to store programs, which are the instructions performed by the processor, and data, which are used for the arithmetic and logical operations. Memory capacity, as we have seen, is measured in K or thousands of bytes of storage. Memory in today's computers is made from silicon chips in a similar manner to the manufacture of processor chips. There are two main kinds of memory chips in a personal computer: RAM and ROM.

RAM

The term **RAM** means **random access memory** and is the memory where a program, such as a word processing program or a spreadsheet program, is stored when it is presently active in the computer. When an expression like 640K is used to describe the size of memory, it refers to the storage capacity of random access memory.

Most RAM is **volatile,** which requires the continuous application of power to retain data and programs. The practical impact of volatile RAM is that it retains the program or data only so long as the power is applied. If the computer's power is turned off, everything in RAM is lost unless it has first been stored or saved on a disk or other secondary storage device. **Nonvolatile** RAM, which is also called CMOS RAM, can retain the contents by the use of rechargeable batteries that are part of the RAM circuit.

RAM provides large memory capacity that is relatively easy and inexpensive to expand by adding more chips to the board. Because the contents of RAM are easily changed (unlike ROM), it is simple and fast to change from a word

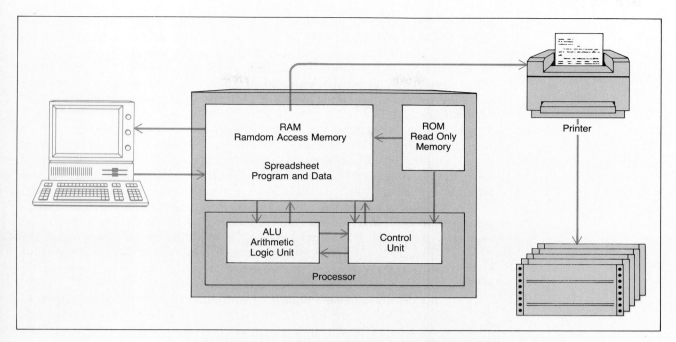

The relationship of input and output to RAM, ROM, and the processor.

processing application to a spreadsheet and then to a data base with only a few simple commands at the keyboard.

ROM

Read-only memory (ROM) is similar to RAM except that ROM chips store information permanently in the computer. The contents of ROM can be read by the processor but not written, thus the name "read only." A benefit of this property is that the contents are not lost when the power to the computer is interrupted.

Important system software is stored in ROM. One of these is a program called the **BIOS (Basic Input Output System),** which assists in the process of starting up the computer and doing such basic input/output operations as reading the keyboard or writing on the screen. Some computers even store the BASIC interpreter or a spreadsheet program in ROM. Programs in ROM are permanent and are not normally changed during the lifetime of the computer.

WHY THE NEED FOR SUCH LARGE MEMORY CAPACITY?

When the IBM PC was first announced in 1981, it had a maximum memory capacity of 640K. Other microcomputers at that time had 32K or 48K maximums, so an upper limit of 640K seemed well beyond the needs of personal computer users. Indeed, most initial purchasers of the IBM PC only installed up to 128K of memory, which was more than adequate for the software available at the time.

As new **user-friendly** software was developed that was easier to use and had many new features, more memory was required. In a few years software and user requirements (particularly spreadsheet users) pushed the computer to the limits of the 640K RAM maximum. To get around this problem, some third-party manufacturers created special expansion boards that would let some software use more than 640K. But not all software could take advantage of the added memory, and the computer's addressing scheme had to be manipulated using a technique called **bank switching** to use memory beyond its normal addressing capability.

Other uses for expanded memory appeared with the introduction of new software products. One of these products was integrated software, such as Lotus Symphony, which combined the features of word processing, spreadsheet, data base, graphics, and communications. Taking advantage of all this power required a computer with increased memory capacity.

Software also became available to use part of memory as a **RAM disk,** a **print spooler,** and even for **multitasking.** RAM disk sets aside a part of memory that acts like a disk. Files that are used frequently can be stored here, and when needed by the program, the file can be read from memory many times faster than it could from real disk, thus increasing the performance of the system.

Print spooling places a document to be printed in memory instead of directly on the printer. Then, as printing occurs, other work may be done simultaneously on the computer as the document is printed. By spooling the document into memory, the computer is not devoted to the single task of printing and can be used for a spreadsheet, data base, or other application while the document is printing.

Concurrent multitasking is the next level up from spooling. It allows two or more operations to be done concurrently on the computer by permitting several different programs to be stored in memory at the same time. You might be doing editing on a word processor at the same time that a data base program is updating a file. In a sense this is similar to an integrated package, the difference being that with multitasking, completely separate programs may be used. With a fast processor some time is allocated to each program, giving the impression that both are running simultaneously. Clearly using these programs together requires more memory capacity than using them separately.

To address the changing needs of the personal computer user, the PC/AT

Some of the uses of RAM on a personal computer.

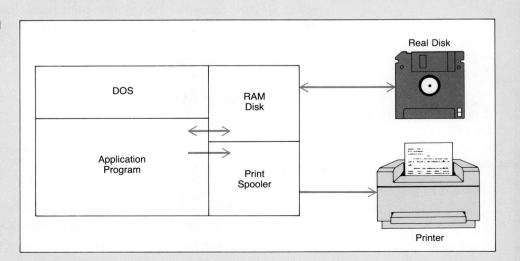

and PS/2 computers, and others like them, address up to 16 megabytes of memory, which is comparable to the addressing capability of many mainframe computers. Initial users of the AT installed 1 or 2M, but like the early PC users, this has quickly changed as new software was developed to take advantage of the larger memory capacity.

Other Memory Devices

Virtually all personal computers used in business contain both RAM and ROM memory. Some computers may also use **PROM (programmable read-only memory)** or **EPROM (erasable programmable read-only memory).** PROM is memory that can be programmed by using a special device called a PROM programmer. Once a program has been written into PROM, it becomes permanent, like the program in ROM. The advantage is that the user or computer owner can record his or her own program in the PROM.

An EPROM is like a PROM, except that the program recorded in it can be erased and then replaced by a new program. Erasure uses either an ultraviolet light or an electrical process. The advantage of EPROM is that the program is permanent like ROM but can be changed at a later time as needs change.

Both PROM and EPROM are used for special-purpose applications and are not frequently seen in the average business use of a personal computer.

Addressing Memory

Memory chips form an array of locations where data and programs may be stored. As the computer is following the instructions in the program, it needs to know where to get the data to carry out the required operation. Programs also need to branch within themselves to carry out decision making or looping. All this activity requires that the exact location or address of program instructions or data be known.

Each byte of computer memory has a unique address as shown in Table 2–5. To access an item of data, the program needs to know the address of that data and to supply it to the control unit, which in turn makes the data available to the program. Memory addressing begins at zero and increases to the value of the maximum address. A 16K computer would have 16,384 bytes of memory, and so its addressing would be from 0 to 16,383.

TABLE 2–5
Addressing 16K of memory. Each byte of memory has a unique address that is used by programs to access data at that location. Addresses begin with 0 and increase by 1 until the end of memory is reached. Addressing can be done using decimal or hexadecimal values.

Addresses Decimal Hexadecimal	0 0	1 1	2 2	3 3	4 4	5 5
Decimal Hexadecimal	16,378 3FFA	16,379 3FFB	16,380 3FFC	16,381 3FFD	16,382 3FFE	16,383 3FFF

The IBM PC/RT uses a RISC processor to increase its speed of operation four times over a standard PC.

Courtesy of IBM.

RISC MICROPROCESSORS

Computer engineers are always looking for ways to make the microprocessor operate faster and execute more program instructions. This search isn't just to lay claim to the faster computer but has practical results in the type of software that can be developed. Software for multiprocessing applications, software that creates complex high-density graphs, or simply programs that do many calculations effectively can have a need for a faster processor.

One solution to this problem is the **reduced instruction set computer (RISC,** pronounced risk). RISC is really a processor chip that uses fewer instructions in its programming language than other chips. By reducing the number of instructions, the chip can be made to operate more efficiently and therefore faster. However, some engineers claim this is not an effective solution to the speed problem because RISC offers the programmer less flexibility.

One computer using a RISC microprocessor is the IBM PC/RT. This computer operates at a speed of 2 million instructions per second, which is expressed as 2 MIPS. By contrast, the standard IBM PC operates at only 0.5 MIPS or only 25 percent of the speed of the RT. Such an improvement in speed can make a significant difference for engineering applications where the RT is frequently used.

EXPANSION SLOTS

Microprocessors need a way to communicate with input or output devices that are attached to the computer. To achieve this communication link, data are sent and received over a bus or channel that forms the pathway to the device. Because each device is different, a special board, called an expansion board, is needed to provide for the link between the bus and the device. Sometimes a separate connection is provided for devices that are always used, such as the keyboard. Using this approach, expansion cards can be used for other, less frequently used, devices.

The circuit board in many computers has a number of expansion slots into which **expansion boards** may be installed to provide for attaching different I/O devices. The number of slots varies from one computer to another. The IBM PC has five, the original Apple II computer had eight, and the more recent IBM PC/AT also has eight. The IBM PS/2 has three or more depending on the model. Fewer slots are needed because many previously add-on features are now built-in. A board placed in one of these slots may provide the capability for the computer to be attached to a given device. One board may provide a **port** or **interface** for attaching a color monitor while another may be used to connect a printer.

Boards that are built for use in these expansion slots are often provided by third-party manufacturers and not the original computer supplier. The approach is encouraged because of the **open architecture** of the design of computers like the IBM PC and compatibles that are specifically designed to permit the use of a variety of expanion boards. Some computers, such as the original Apple Macintosh, are **closed architecture** and do not have expansion slots. However, Apple is moving away from this design to provide users more choices in the way its computer is used.

A wide variety of expansion boards provide the following capabilities:

- An **RS-232C serial port** used to connect a serial printer, modem, or mouse. A serial device is one that receives data one bit at a time.
- A **parallel port** used for attaching a printer. Parallel devices receive data one byte at a time.
- Provision for memory (RAM) expansion.
- A **game port** for attaching a joystick.
- A **color/graphics adapter** for a high-quality RGB color monitor.
- A **hard card** that provides a fixed disk drive on a single expansion card.
- An accelerator board, such as PC Turbo, that speeds up the operation of the computer so it can do more work in less time.

Expansion slots are provided in most computers for expansion boards that equip the computer with a variety of functions. A board such as this one from AST Research provides for expanded memory, a clock, both parallel and serial ports, and a graphics display port.

Courtesy of AST Research.

Because there are so many possible needs for expansion boards and a limited number of slots, **multifunction** boards are a useful alternative to the many single-function boards. A multifunction board occupies one slot and yet provides six or more functions on the one board. A typical multifunction board, such as AST Research's Six-Pack Plus, contains these functions:

1. Expanded memory
2. A parallel port
3. Two serial ports
4. Color graphics port
5. Battery-backed clock/calendar

THE DIFFERENCE BETWEEN PARALLEL AND SERIAL INTERFACES

Different devices require either a serial or parallel port to be attached to the computer. Some devices, such as a printer, can be used as either a serial or a parallel device; the choice depends on the kind of interface available.

A serial interface is one where the data bits that form each character are sent to a device, such as a modem, one at a time. If a character is formed of eight bits, which is the case for ASCII code, then it will take eight units of time to send a character to the device. Serial interfaces operate considerably more slowly than do parallel interfaces, which makes them practical for slow-speed devices such as the modem or mouse.

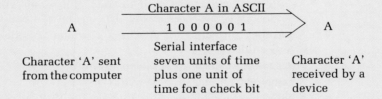

	Character A in ASCII	
A	1 0 0 0 0 0 1	A
Character 'A' sent from the computer	Serial interface seven units of time plus one unit of time for a check bit	Character 'A' received by a device

A parallel port (a common one is a Centronics interface named after the company that made it popular) sends all bits for a single character simultaneously along a line. This technique requires a wire or communications path for each bit in the character plus several control paths to identify when data is starting and stopping. A parallel interface is significantly faster than a serial interface although it is more costly. Interfaces to disk drives and many printers are parallel to optimize the transmission of data.

Character A in ASCII

	1
	0
	0
A	0	A
	0
	0
	1

| Character sent from the computer | Parallel interface 1 unit of time | Character A received by device |

PC compatibles have become popular because of their competitive pricing, generally good reliability, and compatibility with their main rival: the IBM PC. Buying a compatible requires a good understanding of your computer needs because memory size, disk drives, screens, keyboards, and software may all have special options to meet your needs at a higher price than the bottom line advertised. Some compatibles come completely equipped while others have an option list like a Chevrolet.

Courtesy of Digital Media Communications Group; Astra Chicago; Compaq; and Tandy.

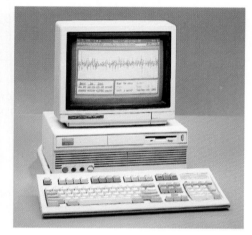

COMPATIBLES

The original IBM PC that was introduced in 1981 became the standard against which all other personal computers were measured. Within a short time of the PC's introduction other manufacturers introduced their own versions of the PC. These computers were known as **compatibles** or **clones** because they came close to duplicating the features of the IBM PC and could run all the same software. Early clones were not always 100 percent compatible; some software would run correctly while other programs ran into difficulty or would not run at all. So the quest for a true compatible continued.

Some of these compatibles were more successful than others because they offered closer compatibility to the PC at a lower price. Many purchasers learned to bring their own software to the store to make sure it would run on the clone before buying it. Other manufacturers offered clones at lower prices, faster speeds, or with free software to attract a corner of the market. One of the more successful of these companies was Compaq (see Figure 2–4) which offered a portable computer in 1982 and a desktop clone in 1984.

As newer lines such as the PC/XT and PC/AT were introduced, the compatible manufacturers followed suit. Compaq introduced an AT compatible, the Deskpro 286, in 1985, less than a year after the AT was shipped. The 286 ran at 8 MHz but a new version was announced in 1987 that had a dual

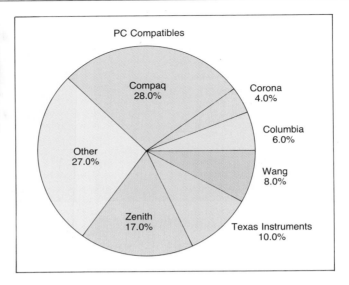

FIGURE 2–4

Although the IBM PC/XT/AT represent about 40 percent of the personal computer market, much of the remainder is represented by PC-compatible manufacturers. This chart shows how the remainder of the market is distributed.

speed of 8 or 12 MHz. In 1986 Compaq became an industry leader by introducing the Deskpro 386 using the 80386 processor chip.

FOOTPRINTS AND LAPTOPS

Personal computers are expected to be small enough to fit on a desktop and yet leave room for notes or papers that are needed by the user. However, with the demand for greater power and capacity, the physical size of the personal computer has had a tendency to increase.

But, in 1987 a new wave of PCs hit the market that were identified by a smaller footprint. The term **footprint** referred to the amount of desk space required for the computer. These computers were a third smaller than others of the same power and capacity. Most of the size reduction came not from using smaller chips as might be expected, but through careful reorganization of the location of components within the computer. As VLSI technology begins to be used in the personal computer even smaller sizes can be expected.

Another trend in downsizing personal computers is in the use of **portable computers** or **laptops** as the smaller ones are often called. These compact computers offer all the features of their big brothers with comparable memory capacity, speed, and disk storage. Some even offer a built-in fixed disk while others use the smaller $3\frac{1}{2}$-inch floppy disk. Portables have an average footprint of 11 inches by 12 inches and can vary a few inches in either dimension depending on the make. They weigh from under 10 pounds to about 20 pounds maximum.

Screens on the portable are usually a thin, fold-down screen that uses a liquid crystal display (LCD) similar to the display used on most digital watches. The screen can hold as much data as a regular desktop display. Some portables also have a built-in power supply (usually a rechargeable battery) so the computer can be used on an airplane, in the car, or out on the patio without the need to connect it to a power source.

A laptop, such as this To-shiba T1200, is truly portable. Operating from a built-in re-chargeable battery, it pro-vides the computer user with up to 7 hours of operation without a recharge. This computer comes with a stan-dard 1MB of memory and two $3\frac{1}{2}$-inch disk drives, each with a capacity of 720K bytes. The screen is a supertwist LCD display that requires only the light available in a normal room for a clear display.

Courtesy of Toshiba.

These features make the portable very useful for sales representatives, executives, reporters, and others who can work more effectively with a computer while they travel. Because these systems can use the same programs and files as the computer in the office, work done away from the office can be easily transferred from one computer to the other for complete flexibility.

IBM's PERSONAL SYSTEM/2

In the spring of 1987 IBM took steps to maintain its market share of the PC industry by announcing the new line of computers called the Personal System/2 (PS/2). Unlike the original PC, which was a single machine that eventually expanded to several models, the PS/2 is a family of computers with a wide range of capabilities and an assortment of peripheral devices.

Following in the well-established tradition of IBM mainframe computers, the PS/2 family consisted of four models: an 8086-based Model 30 with 640K of memory; Models 50 and 60, which are based on the 80286 with 1M of standard memory; and the 32-bit 80386-based Model 80, which comes with

Personal System/2 Model 30.

Courtesy of IBM.

Personal System/2 Model 50.

Courtesy of IBM.

Personal System/2 Model 80.

Courtesy of IBM.

a standard 2M of RAM. All models feature faster speed than the IBM PC/XT (even the Model 30 compares favorably with AT compatibles), higher-resolution graphics up to 1,024 by 768 pixels, and except for the Model 30, greater memory capacity.

All computers come with the smaller-sized 3½-inch diskettes that have twice the storage capacity of the larger 5¼-inch drives used on the PC. Hard disks are available for these computers with capacities from 20M bytes for the Model 30 up to two 115M byte drives for the Model 80.

To access devices effectively, a new bus architecture called the Micro Channel Architecture (MCA) was designed for the top-line models. MCA uses a 16-bit data bus on the Models 50 and 60 and a 32-bit bus on the Model 80. One feature of the MCA is that floppy disk controllers do not require an expansion slot because it is built into the system board. A communications port is also built in so that it doesn't require an extra slot.

Hardware for the MCA and other components of the PS/2 make heavy use of custom chips and surface mounting to make the computer unlike previous systems in construction. One reason for this form of construction is improved reliability. Another is to make it more difficult for clone makers to come up with compatibles that can beat IBM at its pricing scheme. Successful clones lost IBM many sales with its PC line of computers. However, competitors will no doubt find a few tricks of their own to remain in the competitive business of making computers.

Following the PS/2 release was the announcement of a new Operating System/2 (OS/2). This system supports both telecommunications and multitasking for effective office systems management: for word processing, electronic mail, spreadsheets, and data base management.

The Model 30 is compatible with previous PC, XT, and PC portables and so are the higher-level models. But the PS/2 Models 50, 60, and 80 provide the speed, power, and capability that invariably will lead to new software and new ways of information handling in the business environment. While IBM is not the first to use many of the features such as 3½-inch disks, 80286 and 80386 processors, and higher graphics resolution, its integration of them in the new generation of personal computers has drawn considerable attention from users of personal computer systems everywhere.

THE NeXT COMPUTER

Occasionally a revolution in the way we think about and do computing comes to the industry. The Apple was one of these revolutions which made the microcomputer a household word. The Macintosh legitimized the use of graphics and icons on personal computers. Possibly the third revolution will be the NeXT computer announced by Steven Jobs in 1988. Jobs, you might remember, developed the original Apple computer with his friend Steve Wozniak.

The NeXT computer is a one-cubic-foot desktop computer that offers the power of a mainframe at only a fraction of the price. In developing the computer, Jobs asked a team of 24 college professors for their wish list of computer features.

NeXT is as fast or faster than the speediest 386 computer. Operating at 32 MHz it approaches the speed of some mainframes. This speed is achieved

The NeXT Computer.

Courtesy of NeXT, Inc.

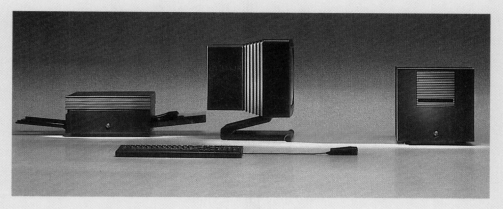

The NeXT Computer.

Courtesy of NeXT, Inc.

by using Motorola's 68030 microprocessor and two VLSI (very large scale integration) chips for high speed input and output.

Random access memory is sixteen megabytes and a new erasable optical disk provides 250 megabytes of external storage. The disk is removable, thus providing unlimited capacity. NeXT includes a built-in modem and fax and the open architecture used (typical of IBM computers) simplifies the addition of new features.

PostScript is the standard printer interface (commonly used by laser printers) and is also used for the black and white screen display that has one million pixels for high resolution graphics. The monitor also contains a speaker and a jack for Walkman-style headphones.

The operating system is called MACH. Created by Carnegie-Mellon University, it is compatible with the UNIX operating system but is reportedly much easier to use. MACH has multi-tasking capabilities, like UNIX, providing the computer with the ability to do several things at the same time.

For users who want to do more than simply process bits and bytes, NeXT provides CD-quality stereo sound. Voice is generated with digitized speech circuitry and recognized by the use of digital speech processing. Other computers require special attachments to provide these features.

Compactness is one of the features of the NeXT computer, a trend that extends to the printer. The laser printer is sixty percent of the size of most laser printers but it provides double the resolution at 400 dots per inch.

NeXT comes with a variety of software including WriteNow, a word processor; Mathematica, a symbol processor for math; Allegro CL Common Lisp, for artificial intelligence applications; and Digital Librarian, for high speed data base searching.

The optical disk also contains some widely used reference works. Among these are *Webster's Ninth New Collegiate Dictionary*, *Webster's Collegiate Thesaurus*, the *Oxford Dictionary of Quotations*, and the complete works of William Shakespeare.

NeXT software has been licensed to IBM so applications can be run on either type of computer. Although some reviewers might suggest that NeXT is not another revolution but just another step in the evolution of the computer, it has nevertheless generated a lot of excitement among computer users everywhere.

MAINFRAME PROCESSORS

We have so far discussed the concepts of the processor as it relates to the personal computer. What about the mainframe? Although the PC market has sold millions of computers, the mainframe is still in use by most large companies and continues to be an important source of computing power. A mainframe computer is a centralized source of processing that may be accessed simultaneously by many different users unlike the PC that is used by one person. So the mainframe must be quite different from the micro. In some ways it is different, but in many ways it is quite similar to a microcomputer, and with the increased speed and capacity of personal computers, the differences are becoming less obvious.

Mainframe processors have **primary storage** (memory), an arithmetic/logic unit, and a control unit. These components are made from silicon chips with generally greater speed and capacity than a microcomputer's chips. To the user of a mainframe the differences may be rather subtle, but to the programmer, there can be major differences between the two types of computers.

Speed

Because mainframes are designed to handle the processing of many users (perhaps hundreds) at the same time, the computer must function many times faster than a PC. Processors in the mainframe run at a high rate of speed often expressed in millions of instructions per second **(MIPS)**. Table 2–6 shows the units used to measure computer speed and how these relate to different generations of computers.

TABLE 2–6

The units of measure for computer speed. If you are good at arithmetic, you might multiply two 8-digit numbers together in 1 minute. In the same amount of time a computer that requires 25 milliseconds to do the operation would be able to multiply 2,400 pairs of numbers in a minute. A faster computer operating at 25 microseconds per operation could do 2.4 million multiplication operations while you do one.

Unit	Fraction of a Second	Computers
Millisecond (ms)	One-thousandth (1/1,000)	First generation
Microsecond (μs)	One-millionth (1/1,000,000)	Second generation
Nanosecond (ns)	One-billionth (1/1,000,000,000)	Third generation to present time
Picosecond (ps)	One-trillionth (1/1,000,000,000,000)	

THE LIMITS OF PI   For hundreds of years mathematicians have been interested in the number pi. You remember pi? It's the odd number expressed by the Greek symbol π used to denote the ratio of the diameter to the circumference of a circle. You might remember it best in the formula where the area is equal to π times the radius squared.

Thousands of years ago the ancient Hebrews thought of this ratio as being close to the value of 3 and a little later $3\frac{1}{7}$ or $\frac{22}{7}$, which we sometimes use even today. If you're measuring the size of a pizza, that's probably close enough. But for other measurements, such as that used in astronomy, greater accuracy is essential. At first, mathematicians occupied their time just trying to find out if there was any end to the sequence of digits in pi. You might remember the first few digits as 3.14159, but it goes on and on beyond these digits.

William Shanks, a nineteenth-century English mathematician, spent the better part of 15 years of his life calculating the value of pi. He was looking for a pattern in the sequence of numbers and calculated pi to 707 decimal places. Unfortunately for Shanks, about a century later in 1949, someone discovered an error in the 528th decimal place, thus making the remainder of his calculations incorrect. Poor Shanks had spent many fruitless years on these last decimal places, and they needed to be recalculated.

Recently a Cray 2 supercomputer at NASA devoted 28 hours to the calculation of pi. Again there was an attempt to find some pattern in the sequence of digits. The Cray crunched out 29,360,128 digits of pi but again no pattern was discovered. In 1987 a Japanese team of mathematicians planned to upstage NASA and go for 100 million or more decimal places. By now all bets are off as to whether pi has a pattern.

Memory Size

Mainframe computers have generally greater memory capacity than personal computers. Until the PC/AT and other 80286-based systems, personal computers were generally restricted to 640K or less for the maximum memory size. Mainframes, however, have had memory sizes exceeding a million bytes for many years. But since the PC/AT, maximum memory for PCs and mainframe computers is not much different; memory is a comparison of computer size that is quickly losing significance.

Software

Because mainframe computers are much faster than PCs and memory size has exceeded a million bytes for some time, mainframe software has been designed to take advantage of these factors. Operating systems on mainframes have been multiuser oriented for many years and have essentially solved the problems that a multitask environment creates. Personal computers are just beginning to get into this area of computing technology.

Special Needs

Cost is a significant factor with mainframe computers costing in the hundreds of thousands to millions of dollars. With this much at stake, many organizations rent or lease their computers. A mainframe often requires special accommodation in the form of a custom-designed computer room. Usually this room requires

A mainframe processor and its related components are usually installed in a specially designed computer room with unique power, air conditioning, and security controls. Large mainframes supply computing power to hundreds of users in a diversity of locations with a variety of needs.

These computer users communicate with the mainframe processor from their terminals. A terminal, which looks much like a personal computer, does not contain its own processor but relies on the mainframe computer for its processing needs. Using a mainframe simplifies the communication of commonly used data between many hundreds of users in a single corporation. With the centralized mainframe, a large storage capacity disk may store data for accounting, payroll, inventory, and sales in one central location. Each authorized user may then access and if necessary update this data, so that all users have current information to do their jobs.

Courtesy of Honeywell.

extra air conditioning and a special electrical power source. In many installations, sophisticated fire detection equipment and extinguishers are used. Mainframe systems are an essential component to the successful operation of most major corporations, and as a result, special security provisions are needed to protect the system from unauthorized intruders.

Fault-Tolerant Computers

Some large mainframes or supercomputers are being designed with fault tolerance, a technique used since the late 1960s by NASA on its spacecraft. These **fault-tolerant machines** are designed with multiple circuits and processors, so that if one fails, another can take over. The system must be designed with self-checking features so that errors or breakdowns can be detected before any harm is done to the processing. Fault-tolerant machines is one way computer manufacturers are responding to the market's demand for reliability. So far this type of design is limited to the larger mainframe systems and is not yet available in the personal computer.

THE PC'S EFFECT ON MAINFRAME COMPUTERS

Over the years application programs for many different needs have been developed for mainframes that reduce the need for new or original development. However, PCs are being used for many applications, which is leading to some very creative software development, which in turn is impacting the mainframe environment. An example of this trend was the development of the spreadsheet concept with VisiCalc on a personal computer. This software had such a large impact that it spawned other mainframe software developments that may not have occurred, at least not as soon, without the PC.

Until the PC, most mainframe software was developed by professional programmers. Users who needed a computer application had to wait until a program was developed, which sometimes required several years. Personal computer software made user-developed applications possible with the use of spreadsheet and data base programs. As a result many applications moved off the mainframe to the PC because the job could be done quickly and according to the users' needs.

Mainframe software has not always been considered user friendly either. Often it required technical knowledge and intensive training to be used. But since the advent of the personal computer with its user-friendly software, mainframe users have begun to demand the same treatment, resulting in much improved software. Many of the techniques used in PC software have appeared in mainframe software, leading to greater productivity and increased user satisfaction.

CHAPTER SUMMARY

1. The word bit is derived from binary digit and is the smallest element or value that is represented in the computer.

2. Personal computers can be described as 8-bit, 16-bit, or 32-bit computers. Sixteen-bit computers such as the IBM PC represent by far the largest number of personal computers in use today.

3. A byte is the term used to describe a group of 8 bits and is the basic unit of data in the computer. A byte can be used to represent a character such as an upper- or lowercase letter, a number, a punctuation symbol, or even a graphic symbol.

4. The central processing unit or microprocessing unit controls the actions taken by the computer. Most processors in today's personal computers reside on a single integrated chip. A 16-bit processor can do operations on data that is 16 bits or 2 bytes in length.

5. A maximum memory size of 640K bytes is typically available on a 16-bit computer. The memory, which consists of a number of integrated chips, stores the program and the data being processed.

6. A data bus is the path that data or instructions flow between the components of the computer. The IBM PC has a 16-bit microprocessor and an 8-bit data bus. The address bus carries memory addresses to all devices that are connected to the data bus.

7. Computer speed depends on the speed of the clock, which is measured in megahertz; a term referring to the number of cycles per second that it operates.

8. Binary numbers consist of the digits 0 and 1, decimal consists of digits 0 to 9, and hexadecimal the digits 0 to 15, where 10 to 15 are represented by the letters A to F.

9. The most widely used code for personal computers is the American Standard Code for Information Interchange (ASCII). This is an 8-bit code meaning that values are represented with 7 bits plus a check bit providing a capability for up to 128 different characters, digits, or letters in the code.

10. The term RAM means random access memory and is the memory where a program such as a word processing program or a spreadsheet program is stored when it is presently active in the computer. When the expression 640K is used to describe the size of memory it refers to the storage capacity of random access memory.

11. Read-only memory is a memory chip similar to RAM except that the ROM chip stores information permanently in the computer. ROM usually contains a program called the BIOS that assists in the process of starting up the computer and doing basic input/output operations.

12. Each byte of computer memory has a unique address. Memory addressing begins at zero and increases to the value of the maximum address.

13. Computers with open architecture contain a number of expansion slots into which expansion boards may be installed to provide additional features. One board may provide a port or interface for attaching a color monitor while another may be used to connect a printer.

14. Different input/output devices require either a serial or parallel port to be attached to the computer.

IMPORTANT TERMS AND CONCEPTS

American Standard Code for Information Interchange (ASCII)
Binary
BIOS (Basic Input Output System)
Bit
Bus
Byte
Central processing unit (CPU)

Color/graphics adapter
Compatible
Expansion slots
Integrated circuit (IC)
Interface
Kilobyte
Megabyte
Megahertz (MHz)
Memory
Microprocessor
Microsecond

Millions of instructions per second (MIPS)
Millisecond
Multifunction boards
Open architecture
Port
Random access memory (RAM)
Read-only memory (ROM)
User friendly

REVIEW QUESTIONS

Fill-in Questions

1. A(n) _____ is the smallest element or value that is represented in the computer.

2. The term _____ comes from the Greek, meaning thousand, and is used as a measure of storage capacity in the computer.

3. The _____ code is used in most personal computers to represent characters as binary values.

4. _____ is the area of the computer where the program and data are stored during program execution by the processor.

5. _____are installed in the computer to provide for the attachment of I/O devices such as a printer or modem.

6. A(n) _____ interface is more likely to be used for a printer while a _____interface would be used for a modem.

7. Computers that offer mostly the same features and performance of the IBM PC are called _____.

8. A(n) _____ computer is lightweight (under 20 pounds), offers the same features as the PC, and often is battery powered for portable operation.

Matching Questions

Match each term with the description given below.

a. 640K   d. MHz
b. 32-bit   e. byte
c. IC   f. multifunction board

_____e_____ 1. This measurement represents storage consisting of 8 bits that can represent a single character.

_____MHz_____ 2. A term that is used to define the speed at which the processor operates.

_____640k_____ 3. A typical office computer has this size of RAM installed.

_____IC_____ 4. This is the technology used to create microprocessors and memory chips.

_____b_____ 5. The IBM PC/AT and PS/2 computers are examples of computers using this size of processor.

_____f_____ 6. Using one of these adds features such as a clock, serial port, and color graphics to a PC.

Discussion Questions

1. Explain why it is necessary to use binary to represent values in a computer. What is meant by a bit?

2. Discuss what is meant by an 8-, 16-, or 32-bit computer. What are the advantages of using a computer that has a greater number of bits?

3. What is the difference between a bit and a byte? How is the term byte used in describing the characteristics of a computer?

4. Describe the purpose and characteristics of the data and address bus.

5. Explain the purpose of a clock in controlling the speed of the computer.

6. What number system, other than decimal, is commonly used to represent values in the computer?

7. Explain the purpose and characteristics of the ASCII coding system used in most personal computers.

8. Discuss the impact of using smaller or more compact ICs in computer design.

9. What terms are used to represent the storage capacity of memory? What is meant by RAM and ROM?

10. Discuss the need for and benefits received from using large memory capacity in today's computers.

11. Explain the purpose of expansion slots in the PC. How may they be used?

12. What is a port? What is the difference between a serial and a parallel interface?

13. What is meant by clone in computer lingo? Why would someone choose to purchase a compatible over the original PC.

14. Discuss some of the characteristics of a mainframe processor highlighting especially the area where it is different from the personal computer.

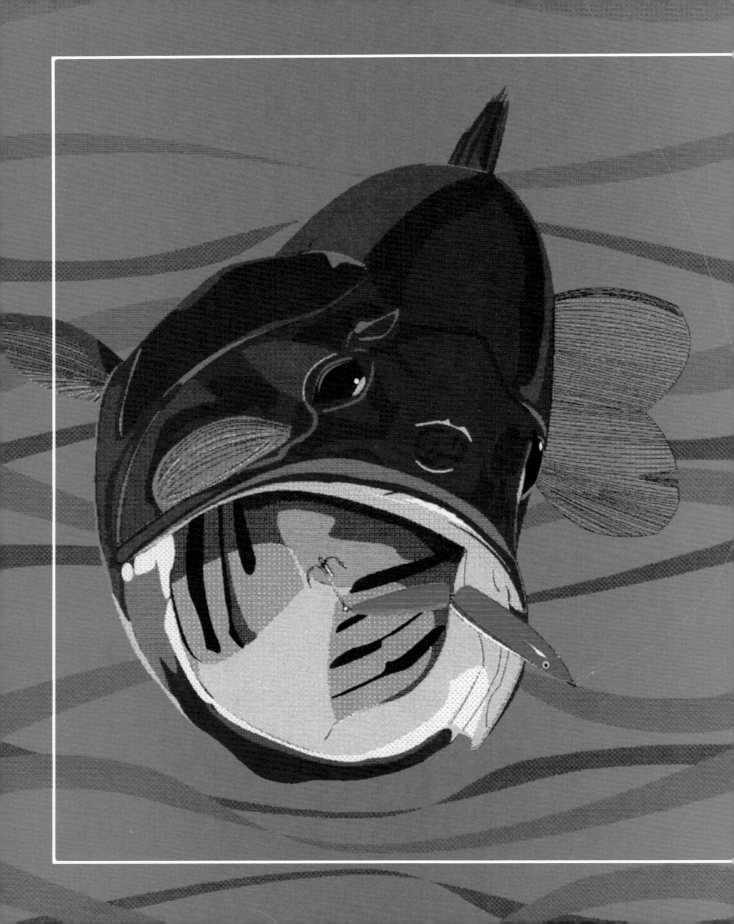

Input and Output

A VIEW OF THE CHAPTER AHEAD

After Reading This Chapter You Will Understand:

- The concepts of data entry and the differences between batch and online.

- The role of the keyboard and display screen when interacting with the computer.

- The characteristics of a monochrome or color display screen.

- The three printer types and the advantages and disadvantages of each.

B
y now you should understand that the computer consists of many components, including the processor, RAM, and ROM, and various interfaces and boards. But to use all these components requires some external devices so that we may communicate our needs to the computer and receive results from it. Input devices such as the keyboard, document reader, or mouse provide a means for supplying data or commands to the computer or, more correctly, to the program.

After the computer has acted upon our instructions or processed our data, we will want to see some results. After all, that is the main reason for entering the data. The results may tell us something about the inventory or the status of a customer's account, which we then act upon to help our business operate more effectively. Output can be displayed on the screen, printed on paper by a printer, or drawn in graphics form on a plotter.

DATA ENTRY CONCEPTS

Data entry refers to the entering of data into the computer for storage and processing. Initial data entry is most commonly done on a keyboard, but other devices may be used. As data is keyed it also appears on the screen as confirmation of what was typed. This display offers the chance to change the data entered in the event it was not entered correctly.

Fields and Records

Figure 3–1 shows a data entry screen for entering customer invoice data. Descriptions on the screen indicate the type of data that is to be entered and the order in which it is entered. These spaces where the data will be entered are called **fields.** A field refers to an item of data such as an invoice number, client, or description. All the data on the screen in this example forms a **record.** A record consists of all information that relates to a single transaction, such as the customer invoice data in this example.

As the computer user types the data into a field, the data will first appear on the screen. When the field has been filled or the enter key on the keyboard is pressed, the flashing cursor on the screen will move to the next field and wait for entry of its data. This process continues until all the necessary data has been supplied.

Trends in Data Entry

Today's computers use two basic approaches to data entry: batch and online. **Batch** refers to a data entry method where the data is collected over a period of time and entered into the computer as a group of records, while **online** data entry is a method where data is entered into the computer when it is received.

Batch Entry

Consider this example using the batch data entry approach. A company may have a department that receives orders for its customers during the day. As the orders come in, by mail, in person, or by phone, an order entry document

FIGURE 3–1
A data entry screen.

Photo courtesy of Software Solutions.

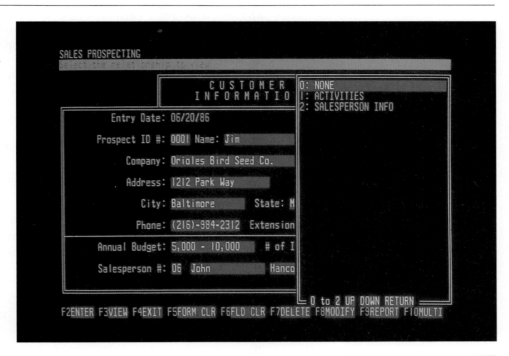

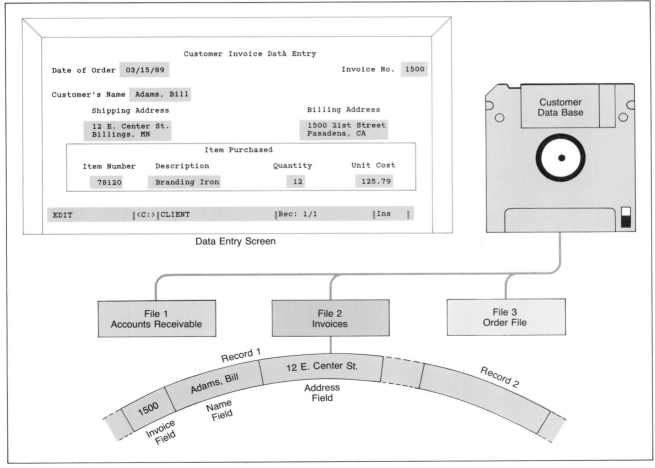

Data Entry Screen

is filled out by the order personnel. These order entry documents are accumulated in a batch during the day and then at night are keyed into the computer for processing. By contrast, with online data entry, each order would be entered into the computer as it is received.

However, there are certain advantages to be gained by using batch data entry.

1. Each person taking orders does not require a computer at his or her disposal, and therefore the cost of hardware is reduced.
2. The data entry person can be trained for that specific function and thus enters the data more efficiently than the order personnel.
3. The computer processes batches of data more efficiently than individual items entered throughout the day.

Because of these difficulties with batch data entry, there has been a move away from batch entry in personal computing systems. Although some applications still use this form, many others are now using online data entry.

FIGURE 3–2

Batch data entry accumulates data over a time period, such as a day, and then enters the data into the computer as a complete batch of records.

Photo courtesy of Peter Menzel/Stock Boston.

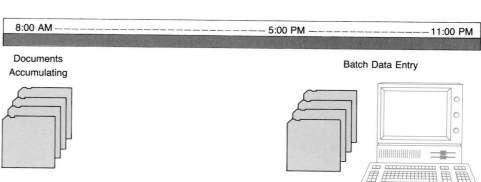

8:00 AM ————————————————————— 5:00 PM ——————————11:00 PM

Documents
Accumulating

Batch Data Entry

Eight approaches to data entry

Courtesy of Amp, Inc.

Courtesy of NCR Corporation.

Courtesy of Jervis R. Webb Company.

Courtesy of Honeywell, Inc.

Courtesy of Federal Express.

Courtesy of Diebold, Inc.

Eight approaches to data entry
(continued)

Courtesy of Intermec Corporation.

Courtesy of Eastman Kodak Company.

But there are also disadvantages to batch data entry:

1. All error checking at the source must be done manually because no computer is used to receive or validate the orders.
2. Computer records cannot be checked for availability of inventory or the customer history for a credit rating or outstanding orders.
3. The company cannot give immediate confirmation that the order has been processed.

Online Entry

Online data entry uses the computer to enter the data as it is received. Let's consider an online customer order entry system. As a customer order is received, the items ordered are immediately entered on the keyboard. The program gives direct feedback on the screen to show that there is sufficient stock available to fill the order. If there is not enough of the item in stock, the computer can immediately place a back-order and notify the customer.

Information about items that are received in stock is also entered online and thus updates the inventory file. This keeps an up to date and current record of the inventory.

Here are some of the advantages of online data entry.

1. As data is entered online, the computer can check immediately for errors and completeness. This permits the order entry personnel to get the correct information from the customer immediately.
2. Files are updated as soon as data is received.
3. Confirmation of the order status can be given to the customer immediately.
4. Although online may be less efficient for the computer, it is generally more efficient for the business operation. Because business costs are often high while computer

costs today are relatively low, realizing greater efficiency in the business operation is a worthwhile achievement.

Data Entry Error Checking

People are the main source of data entry and therefore the main source of computer errors. Figure 3–3 shows the main sources of error in a computer system, and it is clear that data entry is the main culprit. This is where we get the term **GIGO** (garbage-in, garbage-out), suggesting that what we get out of the computer is only as good as the data that was entered.

Types of error checking

The more complex the data that is used, the greater the number and type of errors that can be created. Well-designed systems will attempt to intercept most errors by using a variety of techniques. Some of the methods used for error detection are as follows:

1. *Field missing test.* Fields such as employee number and name must always be entered on a payroll system.
2. *Limit test.* Values will be permitted a maximum value beyond which an error message is displayed. For example, an employee may not earn more than $15.00 per hour.
3. *Contents test.* A data field must contain numeric values, for example, an account number that must always be numeric or a product code that is always alphabetic.
4. *Range test.* Data must fall within a given range of values. For example, numeric month values must always be between 01 and 12 inclusive.
5. *Transposition error.* A field that should contain the number 43415 but has 43145 contains a transposition of the digits 4 and 1. This is usually the result of a keying error during data entry and can be detected by requiring double-entry verification. With this method data is entered twice on the theory that the same keying error will not be made both times.

These are only a few of the types of errors that might be made in data entry. Many types of errors are specific to the application and may also vary considerably from one type of software to another. Although we are stressing data entry errors in this section, keep in mind that the actual number of errors made is usually small relative to the amount of data entered. But with good error checking, even those errors will be caught and corrected before they become part of a permanent record.

FIGURE 3–3

Sources of error in the computer.

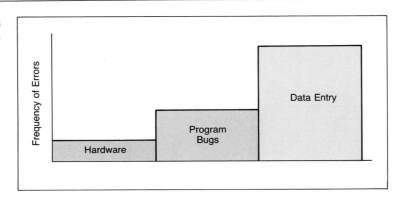

INTERACTING WITH THE COMPUTER

Almost all users of a personal computer use a keyboard and screen for their primary form of interaction with the computer. Some early computers used a **terminal** that was made of a display screen and keyboard built into the one container. Users of mainframe computers frequently employ a terminal of this type to communicate with the computer. On some of the first microcomputers, such as the Commodore PET, the screen and keyboard were built into the same case as the other components, but today most PCs have a separate screen and keyboard. Using separate components makes substitution easier so that devices appropriate to the user's needs can be attached to the computer. Having a separate screen and keyboard also permits a more flexible placement of them on the desk for ease and comfort of use.

KEYBOARDS

Computer keyboards are the most widely used device for entering data as well as commands and instructions to the software you are using. Most of the work you do on the computer will require the use of the keyboard. This doesn't mean you will need to be a skilled typist, but knowing where the keys are located will make your work much easier.

Keyboards vary from one computer to another, but the similarities are usually greater than the differences. The discussion here relates to the IBM PC keyboard shown in Figure 3–4. If you are using some other computer, you will likely find that it has all the same keys and maybe a few more. In a few cases the position or size of a key will be different.

Understanding the Keys

In this section we will look at some of the more commonly used keys on the keyboard. In Chapter 7 a more detailed description of the keys will be given for use in application software.

Some of the basic keys you will use all the time are the alphabetic and numeric keys. **Alphabetic** keys are located in the central portion of the keyboard and are organized like a typewriter. **Numeric** keys are located in the row above the alphabetic keys so they may easily be used by a typist. Uppercase alphabetics are typed by pressing and holding the Shift key down while the

---

FIGURE 3–4   Keyboards used on the IBM PC and PS/2 computers.

Courtesy of IBM.

letter is typed. The characters above the numeric keys may also be typed by holding the Shift key. Other important keys are as follows:

■ **Cursor control keys** (Figure 3–5) are used to move the cursor on the screen to the location of data that needs to be entered or changed. The **cursor** (Figure 3–6) is the flashing underscore symbol seen on the screen. Cursor traits can be different for each type of computer in use.

FIGURE 3–5
Cursor keys on the numeric key pad.

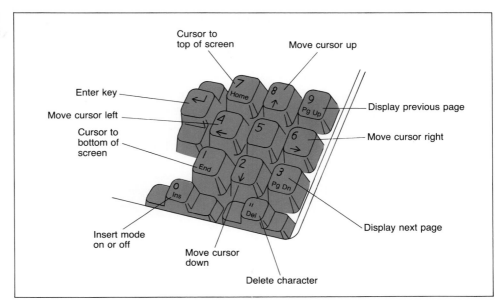

FIGURE 3–6
The cursor is a blinking symbol on the screen that shows where the next character typed will be displayed on this word processing document.

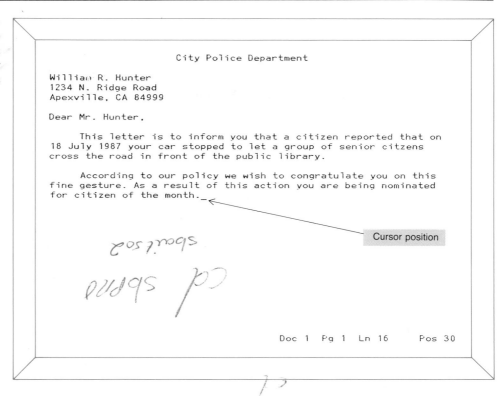

- The **Return** or **Enter** key is used to end an entry made from the keyboard. For example, in a word processor the return key is pressed at the end of a paragraph.
- The **Backspace** key is used to delete characters to the left of the cursor.
- The Delete **(Del)** key deletes the character at the cursor position.
- **Ins** is the Insert key that turns insert mode on and off.
- **Function keys** (Figure 3–7) are the keys labeled F1 to F10. Function keys may be assigned different uses depending on the needs of the software. For example, in Lotus 1-2-3 the F1 key is used to access Help information. Because function keys are assigned different uses in each program, many software companies provide an overlay template (Figure 3–8) that defines the use of function keys for their specific software package.

FIGURE 3–7
Function keys and other keys for program control.

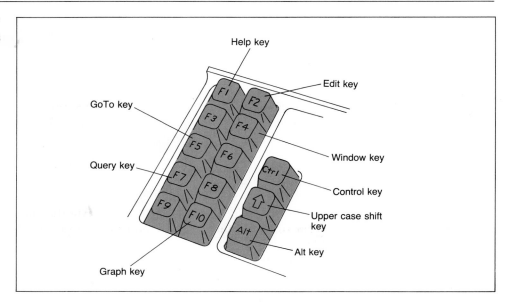

FIGURE 3–8
A function key template for use with Lotus 1-2-3.

Courtesy of Christie Tito.

- **Ctrl** and **Alt** are special keys that work together with another key. For example, the entry Ctrl T means to press and hold the Control key and then press the T key. In WordStar, this command would be used to delete a word in a document.
- The **Esc** (Escape) key is used to cancel an operation in case a command was entered incorrectly or you had a change of mind about the operation.

Choosing a Keyboard

Ordinarily you get whatever keyboard is supplied with the computer and, unlike the screen, you normally do not purchase the keyboard as a separate item. However, keyboards do vary considerably from one computer to another and, for users who must do a lot of data entry on the keyboard, choosing the right computer will ensure that the keyboard is also right. Third-party keyboards are also available for separate purchase, providing various features such as separate numeric and cursor keypads that might not be included on a standard keyboard.

The placement of the alphabetic and numeric keys will be the same on all keyboards, but other keys such as function keys, control keys, and cursor keys may vary in their location. One complaint many users had about the original IBM PC keyboard was the location and small size of the Shift and Return keys. Users familiar with the typewriter had some difficulty adjusting, but the millions in use suggest that somehow the adjustment was made. New IBM products, such as the AT and PS/2, have corrected this problem.

Another consideration in keyboard design is the feel of the keys as they are pressed. While this may seem to be a subjective matter, there are some factors that affect feel. One is the surface design of the key. A slightly curved surface works better than a flat one. Another factor is tactile feedback. This term refers to the pressure and click noticed when a key is pressed. Some keyboards have an indefinite feel, and the user is never quite sure when the key has been completely pressed. The IBM keyboard is considered to be a standard in this area because its tactile feedback is preferred by many users.

Using a quality keyboard can improve typing performance and result in less user fatigue. A few companies, such as Key Tronic Corporation, are now providing aftermarket keyboards so even if the right computer has the wrong keyboard for your needs, an improved keyboard is readily available.

DISPLAY SCREENS

Display screens are the output device where computer users usually view the results of computer processing. The display screen or monitor, as it is sometimes called, shows the results of an inquiry, presents the values for a budget, displays an account's current status, or identifies options in a program.

When a program is used, its options are displayed on the screen in the form of a menu. An option is selected by a keyboard entry, and the results of that option are displayed on the screen. Entered data is displayed on the screen and, when information from a disk file is requested, it is also displayed. It's not surprising, then, that the screen is one of the most important components of a computer system.

A **display screen** is a TV-like device that displays text or graphics depending on the needs of the program. Early computer users had a choice of monochrome for text display or color for graphics and lower-resolution text. The early Apple computers were of this type. Today's personal computers can also use monochrome, but increasingly more users are showing a preference for color monitors.

Monochrome Displays

Monochrome (Figure 3–9) refers to the type of screen that displays in one color with a contrasting background. A color in wide use on monochrome screens is green with a black background. Text characters display in green while the surrounding area is black. White on black is also used but is thought to be harder on the eyes. European systems used amber (a shade of yellow), which is considered to be easier on the eyes than most colors. Amber is becoming more widely used in North America, and several manufacturers such as Amdex and Panasonic offer amber monitors.

Monochrome displays are less expensive than color and are superior for text display such as that needed in word processing and data base applications and where graphics are not frequently needed. Although many monochrome monitors can display graphics, color usually gives superior results when graphics are needed; however, dollar for dollar, monochrome is unrivaled in clarity and sharpness of character definition. Some monochrome displays are essentially character displays, meaning they were designed to display the character set provided in the computer based on the ASCII code definition. This is how the original IBM monochrome display was designed, but by using a special adapter, such as a Hercules card, it is able to display graphics.

FIGURE 3–9
The IBM Personal System/2
monochrome display.

Courtesy of IBM.

Color Displays

A **color display** can certainly be very pleasing to the eye, and experts tell us that color communicates more information to the user, especially when graphics are involved. A basic color screen can display either 4 or 16 colors on an IBM or IBM-compatible PC. The number of colors depends on the resolution of the display, with the lower resolution having the greater color capability. In general there are two types of color monitors: composite and RGB.

A color monitor on a personal computer is pleasing to the eye as it uses colors to highlight important values in a graph. Color helps to distinguish between the values represented, so that a manager can more readily identify trends that are important to making business decisions.

Courtesy of Dell Computers.

The graphics system on the IBM Personal System/2 permits up to 256 different colors to be displayed at one time with a resolution of 320 × 200, or 16 colors using 640 × 480 pixels, thus producing startling images not previously possible on a personal computer.

Courtesy of IBM.

FIGURE 3–10
Comparison of color graphic adapters for the IBM PC and PS/2 computers.

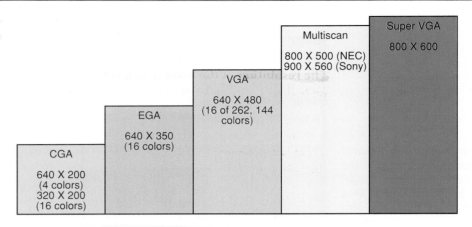

A **composite** monitor operates on the same principle as a television set in which the screen receives a composite signal on one channel containing the display information. Because these displays are similar to the TV set, they are priced comparably but lack the clarity needed to display complex graphics information. Most composite displays are limited to 40 columns of text and are primarily suited to home computers.

RBG (red, green, blue) monitors receive three different signals, one in each of the three color spectrums. These monitors yield higher definition and better clarity of the image than a composite monitor. RBG monitors may also offer a greater selection of colors, but the actual number that can be displayed depends on the software and the color adaptor board used in the computer. Choosing an adaptor board is as important as choosing the right screen as one depends on the other. Four levels (see Figure 3–10) of boards are available based on the IBM PC standard[1] and a new one for the PS/2. These are:

1. **CGA** (color/graphics adaptor). This is the basic color display board that is used on IBM PCs and compatibles with a resolution of 320 × 200 (see the discussion on resolution) and a maximum of 16 colors. CGA is widely used by basic business software such as word processing, data base, and spreadsheets.

2. **EGA** (enhanced graphics adaptor). This adaptor board, announced in 1984, offers a higher resolution of 640 × 350 with 16 colors for graphics users.

3. **PGC** (professional graphics controller). This is a step up from the EGA and offers a higher resolution of 640 × 480 and up to 256 colors. Its primary use is for computer-aided design, where high resolution is important. Because of its high cost, PGC has not been nearly as popular as the EGA.

4. **Multiscan.** This is a color graphics board that provides compatibility between the foregoing three standards, and some manufacturers provide even greater resolution (900 × 560) than the PGC standard.

    In addition to these four levels, the IBM Personal System/2 introduced a new level of graphics capability. The top-line models 50, 60, and 80 contain the video graphics array video adaptor.

5. **VGA** (video graphics adaptor). The VGA board emulates the resolution of the EGA adaptor and adds a 640 × 480 density with a 16-color mode out of 262,144

---

[1] "Behind the Screens: EGA and Multiscan Monitors," *PC Magazine*, March 31, 1987, pp. 107–145.

colors. A mode with 320 × 200 density allows 256 of the 262,144 colors to be displayed. Recently, a new display mode called Super VGA was released with a resolution of 800 × 600 pixels.

SCREEN RESOLUTION

The **resolution** of the display determines the clarity of the character displayed for text and the precision of the image for graphics. A screen with high resolution will be easier to read and less tiring on the eyes. Originally, monochrome screens offered the highest resolution, but now color is available with comparable or better images.

What determines the resolution of the screen is the screen capability and the graphic or display board used. Specifically, resolution depends on the number of dots or points of light on the display. These dots, as shown in the diagram, are called **pixels.** When more pixels are used to form a character, a clearer, sharper image is created. A standard resolution of 640 × 200 pixels provides for 128,000 points on the screen, while a higher-resolution screen of 640 × 350 provides 224,000 or almost twice the resolution.

Interpreting graphic adaptor charts, such as Figure 3–10, requires an understanding of some of the terminology used for screen specifications. These terms are used to describe screen features and are a factor in both the cost of the screen and in its usability. In the next section we will examine some of these screen features.

Resolution of standard PC screen with the color graphic adapter (CGA).

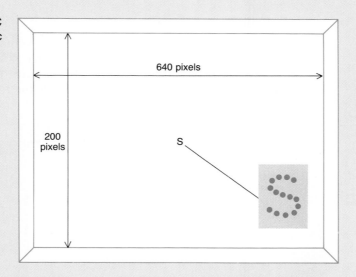

Comparison of screen resolution in pixels as defined for business PCs. The higher the resolution the sharper the image. In some applications, notably engineering, a resolution of 1,024 × 1,024 would be considered moderate.

Resolution	Pixels	Line × Column
Low	64,000	320 × 200
Medium	128,000	640 × 200
High	224,000	640 × 350
Very high	307,200	640 × 480
Super high	540,000	900 × 560

Display Features

Some features are common to all screens. Among these are the use of a cursor to show where entries are to be made. Another is the scrolling of the screen contents when more data is to be displayed at the bottom of the screen. When the screen is full and another line needs to be displayed, all lines scroll up by one line and the top line disappears off the screen.

A similar process is moving the page up or down with the Page Up or Page Down key on the keyboard. A page refers to the amount of data the screen can display, not the amount on a printed page. If the screen is currently showing the first page of a document, usually lines 1 to 23, pressing page down would cause lines 24 to 46 to appear. Page movement is a function of the software, and some programs, notably DOS, do not provide this capability even though the screen could handle it.

Figure 3–11 illustrates boldfacing, underlining, italics, and reverse video, attributes that are useful in word processing and other text-oriented programs.

Boldface characters on the screen are brighter than are the surrounding characters. On a printed page, boldface is printed darker than other characters. Underlining is used for headings or other words that need to draw the reader's attention. **Italics** are ordinarily available on high-resolution displays and are only used by some software. **Reverse video** is useful to highlight program messages or blocks of text that are to be deleted or copied by the program.

Text display

When text is displayed on the screen, the screen characteristics are described in terms of rows (or lines) and columns. A typical screen (Figure 3–12) will have 25 rows and 80 columns. For applications such as a word processor, fewer than 25 rows may be available for text because the program

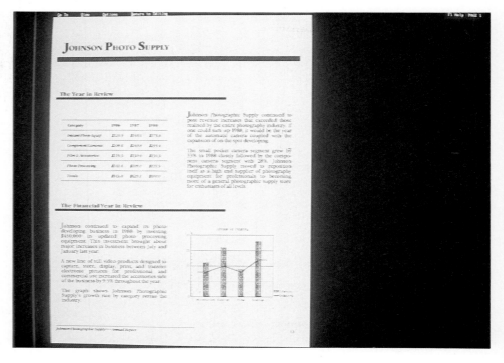

FIGURE 3–11
Use of screen features in a
word processing program.

Courtesy of MicroPro International
Corporation.

FIGURE 3–12
Allocation of rows and columns on a display screen.

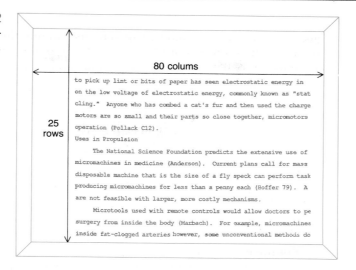

80 colums

25 rows

to pick up lint or bits of paper has seen electrostatic energy in on the low voltage of electrostatic energy, commonly known as "stat cling." Anyone who has combed a cat's fur and then used the charge motors are so small and their parts so close together, micromotors operation (Pollack C12).
Uses in Propulsion
    The National Science Foundation predicts the extensive use of micromachines in medicine (Anderson). Current plans call for mass disposable machine that is the size of a fly speck can perform task producing micromachines for less than a penny each (Hoffer 79). A are not feasible with larger, more costly mechanisms.
    Microtools used with remote controls would allow doctors to pe surgery from inside the body (Marbach). For example, micromachines inside fat-clogged arteries however, some unconventional methods do

The Apple Macintosh II has a screen resolution of 640 × 480 pixels for impressive color graphics capabilities. The Mac is promoted as a user-friendly system because its use of graphics and icons simplifies operations for the first-time computer user. Early Macintosh systems were limited by the paucity of software available, but more major software companies such as Lotus Corporation have been adapting their software for use on the Macintosh.

Courtesy of Apple Computer, Inc.

uses some of these lines for on-screen information. For example, WordPerfect uses 1 line for status information, and the remaining 24 lines may be used for text.

The Macintosh

Screens discussed in this section have been for IBM PC or IBM-compatible computers where an open architecture is used allowing for different adaptor boards and screens. On the other hand, the Apple Macintosh is basically a closed-architecture computer. It was designed to display graphics and has a standard resolution of 175,104 pixels. Because of the closed-architecture design, it was difficult for third-party manufactures to produce screens that could provide higher resolution.

However, in 1986 several companies produced large display screens for the Macintosh that can display a higher resolution. One of these companies, E-Machines, has developed a screen that can display a resolution of 1,024 × 808 (827,392 pixels) on the Macintosh. This screen requires added software to achieve this level of resolution. Other companies have achieved similar results with hardware changes. In the case of Radius, the computer must be sent to the firm's factory where the Macintosh's microprocessor is replaced and another small circuit board is installed.[2] Early in 1987, Apple announced the Macintosh II, an open-architecture computer. This new machine has a 640 × 480 pixel display with full color capabilities.

Bit mapping

Most computers display text characters based on predefined pixel formats that are part of the contents of the computer's ROM. Software packages such as dBASE III Plus use this form of text display. **Bit mapping** is an alternate technique where each pixel on the screen is controlled by the program to determine the exact format of every character. Programs, such as Microsoft Word (Figure 3–13), that depend to a large extent on graphics for displaying windows and special text fonts use bit-mapped graphics. Graphics display screens use a form of bit mapping to create on-screen characters while only some character displays use this approach.

Bit mapping has both advantages and disadvantages. The main disadvantage is that it requires more memory to set up the screen contents compared to a regular character display. Programs using bit mapping also tend to run more slowly than other programs.

FIGURE 3–13
A screen display of Microsoft Word using bit mapping.

Courtesy of Samna Corporation and Alexander Communications.

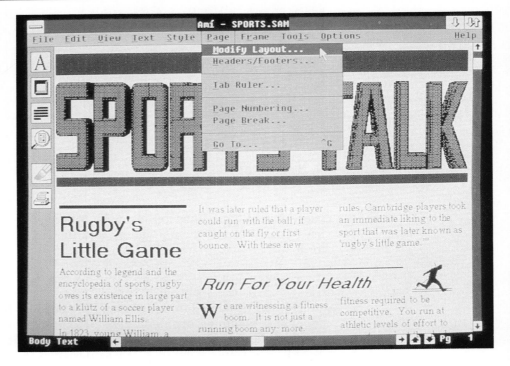

The advantages of bit mapping are important. First, graphs of all kinds can be displayed; even three-dimensional graphs can be produced with sophisticated software. For character or text display, more character types can be made available. For example, the popular word processor Microsoft Word is able to show italics, boldface, underlining, super- and subscripts, and other special character fonts that would be impossible to display without bit mapping (Figure 3–13).

Many new software packages that display text and graphics simultaneously on screen use bit mapping to achieve this result. Other software that use windows, such as Microsoft Windows, to view several applications at once may also use bit-mapping techniques, although other similar programs, such as Framework II, are able to use windows without resorting to the slower bit-mapping methods.

CHOOSING A DISPLAY SCREEN

Many computers, especially the clones, come with a screen, but here you do have many choices. Even a packaged system can often be redefined with a screen of your choice, although this may affect the price of the system. Choosing the right display for your work is important because you will spend much of your time looking at it.

Full-Page Displays

With the expansion of word processing into desktop publishing, the demand for screens that can display the entire contents of one page has grown. The average display screen shows 25 lines, and because of the software's needs for status lines or menus, this size may shrink by several lines. The end product is a display that shows only about one-third of a printed page at a time. To get the complete view of the page, the user must do page downs and page ups from the keyboard.

In contrast to the line limit of standard screens, **full-page display screens** show all lines of the page for a true "what you see is what you get" (WYSIWYG) display. Not all software will support these large screens, but some, such as Xerox's Ventura (Figure 3–14) and the Harvard Professional Publisher, are page composition packages that use the capability of these large screens.

Flat Displays

Developments in liquid crystal technology have led to the use of **flat display** screens that are as little as an inch in thickness. The liquid crystal display (LCD) is based on the same technology used in digital watches and calculators.

A liquid crystal substance is deposited between two sheets of a polarizing material that is then placed inside two glass panels carrying thin electrodes that act as conductors. Light is normally passed through the polarizing material and is reflected back to the viewer, but when the electrodes are charged, the liquid crystals are aligned so that the light cannot pass through, thus producing

---

[2] John Markoff, "Big Screens for Small Computers," *High Technology*, January 1987, pp. 56–57.

FIGURE 3–14

A full-screen display for use in desktop publishing.

Courtesy of Micro Display Systems, Inc.

FIGURE 3–15

A flat screen display is used on this Zenith Super Sport portable computer.

Courtesy of Zenith Data Systems.

a dark pixel. By controlling the area of charge, a character is formed as a series of dark pixels.

LCD flat displays are primarily used on portable computers (Figure 3–15) where the size is an important factor. LCD systems also consume much less power than other displays so that some portable systems, such as the Toshiba T1200, operate from a rechargeable battery and are truly portable. Flat displays also emit no radiation, which is of concern to some people who use regular monitors.

Flat displays are not without their problems. One difficulty is the rectangular shape of most screens. For text, this shape is not a great problem, but graphs, especially circular ones such as pie charts, do not form a true circle but are more of an ellipse. Some users also complain about the visibility of the LCD screen. In well-lighted areas the screen is usually quite readable, but in low-light situations, visibility is reduced. Some manufacturers circumvent this problem by providing a backlight that, of course, consumes more power. A more expensive solution (used by the GridCase 3 Plus computer) to the visibility problem is to use a glass plasma display that has a much brighter image.

CHECKLIST FOR CHOOSING A SCREEN

- Do you require text-only display? Then monochrome may be adequate. But do check the contrast and brightness controls to ensure that the two levels of black and white display distinctly. You will need to run software that uses two levels of brightness to determine this contrast.

- Do you expect to display graphs or use software that requires color? Then choose a color display.

- If you choose color, what quality of display is needed? Will a composite display do, or is RBG necessary? When choosing a color screen, look for a screen that displays true colors with good distinction between them. Color tends to be a subjective matter so choose a display that looks good to you. Try adjusting the color and tint controls to see if the results are within a range that you can accept. Try scrolling the text on the screen and check to see if there is color smearing as the display contents are changed. A good screen should not show any color smearing.

- What level of resolution is needed? You can select from CGA, EGA, PGC, or multi-scan. If your computer is a PS/2 or equivalent, check into the VGA screen. The level of resolution will depend on the type of software you plan to run. If you are only doing the usual word processing or spreadsheet work, then the standard resolution will be fine. For specialty graphics, desktop publishing, or computer-aided design, a higher resolution may be required.

- Check for display features such as boldface, underlining, italics, and reverse video.

- Check color displays for clarity of image, color trueness, and lack of smear.

- Check the glare on the screen from overhead lights and windows. Stores often position displays to minimize glare, and you should too when it is placed where it will be used. However, some locations may not eliminate all glare, and so a screen that reflects less light will be easier to read.

- Look for clarity of characters on the screen. Are all characters, especially at the corners and edges, clearly displayed without distortion?

- Some screens have a height and tilt adjustment, although most simply sit on the desk or on top of the processor. Some people with special needs may find an adjustable screen more suitable.

- For desktop publishing applications, look for full-page screens.

Video Display Terminals

Mainframe and minicomputers typically use **video display terminals (VDTs)** for interaction with the computer. These terminals are constructed from a **cathode ray tube (CRT)** and a keyboard with some electronic circuitry inside the enclosure. A VDT is similar to the screen and keyboard on a personal computer with one important difference. The PC has a microprocessor and memory while the VDT relies on the connecting mainframe computer for its processing.

Specifications for a VDT are similar to those for a PC's screen. Properties such as underlining, boldface, character highlighting, scrolling, page movement, and character density are all part of the options available. Both monochrome and color screens are available to satisfy different user needs.

Most terminals are classified as **dumb terminals** because they have no built-in processor. But for some applications, having some processing power available at the terminal can off-load some of the processing needs from the mainframe computer. Applications such as data entry often need to check data for errors before accepting the final input. For this purpose, **smart** or **intelligent terminals** are used that contain a microprocessor and sometimes a printer for local reports and a disk drive for temporary data storage. A smart terminal can edit the incoming data, while an intelligent terminal can be programmed to perform a variety of functions. After local processing, data are sent on to the mainframe or minicomputer, thus relieving the computer of some processing duties and creating a **distributed processing** environment.

Graphics display terminals are also used on mainframes when graphics design or the display of business graphics is needed. A graphics VDT terminal displays data by manipulating individual pixels on the screen to draw graphs, such as bar charts to show sales performance, buildings, or aircraft structures to show how the various components of a design fit together to produce the final product.

A monochrome visual display terminal for displaying upper- and lowercase alphabetics, numbers, and punctuation characters.

Courtesy of IBM.

A color VDT. By using color, items that require the user's immediate attention can be highlighted in one color, while secondary items can be in another color.

Courtesy of IBM.

An intelligent terminal used in a distributed processing environment.

Courtesy of DataPoint Corporation.

A graphics terminal used to display business graphics for sales forecasting, financial analysis, and production evaluation.

Courtesy of IBM.

Graphic display terminals are frequently used in computer-aided design and computer-aided manufacturing applications.

Courtesy of Apollo Computer, Inc.

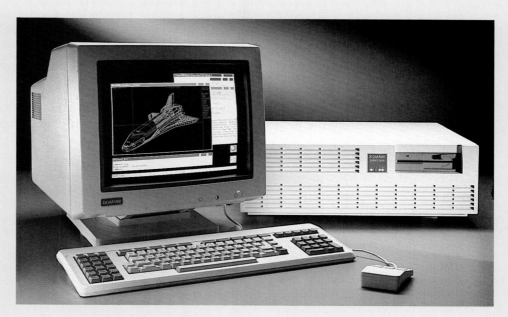

Graphics VDT terminals have been widely used for **computer-aided design (CAD)** in the automotive, aircraft, and ship design industries. Using graphics terminals makes the development of the design and model testing much easier and less costly than manual methods. Changes to the design can be easily incorporated at any time during the design stage. Resulting designs on the computer can be readily included in the manufacturing stage when **computer aided-manufacturing (CAM)** is used as for the construction of a car or aircraft.

SPECIAL-PURPOSE DEVICES

Most software is designed to use the keyboard and screen for user interaction. The screen may display the choices that are then made by entering a character or command at the keyboard. Movement of windows or pointers on the screen, such as that used in a spreadsheet program, is frequently done by using cursor keys. And, of course, data entry is done on the keyboard. But there are newer devices, and some not so new but becoming more recently popular, that can make some of these forms of computer interaction easier. In this section we will take a look at some of these devices.

Mouse

A mouse (Figure 3–16) is a device that attaches to the computer's serial port and replaces many of the functions of the Cursor and Enter keys in some software. The mouse is used by rolling it on the surface of the desk. As it is moved, a pointer on the screen moves in the same direction. Small movements of the mouse in any direction make for corresponding movements of the pointer on the screen.

A mouse has at least one button; some have two or three. Pressing a button causes a selection to be made on the screen such as choosing an option from a menu. In Microsoft Windows, the choice of software to run, such as a spreadsheet, filing system, word processor, communications, and so on, is made by pointing to the option with the mouse and pressing the button to indicate the selection. The mouse is also used to expand or contract the size of a window by pointing to a corner of the window and then pulling it in a direction that makes the window larger or smaller.

Keyboard advocates prefer not to use a mouse because it requires removing the hands from the keyboard, thus creating inefficiencies, while mouse advo-

FIGURE 3–16
A mouse is used with application software for making choices from the menu.

Courtesy of Apple Computer, Inc.

cates praise the ease of use of the mouse over the use of cursor keys. There are two basic types of mice: mechanical and optical. The main advantage of an optical mouse is that it has no moving parts and thus will not ordinarily require any maintenance. Some software, such as Lotus 1–2–3, Microsoft Word, or dBASE III Plus, requires a special software driver (usually provided with the mouse) to make the mouse active in the program.

Touch Screens

Some computers use touch-sensitive screens as opposed to the keyboard or mouse for selecting options. Instead of pressing a key or clicking a button on a mouse, the user points with a finger to a choice or command that is displayed on the screen (see Figure 3–17). Some proponents of the touch screen predict that it will replace the mouse because it is as easy to use but does not require another device to be attached to the computer.

Touch screens use one of three methods to function:

1. **Infrared light.** These invisible light beams criss-cross the surface of the screen and form a gridlike pattern. When a finger points to a location on the screen representing a choice from the software, the finger interrupts the beam of light, which is detected by the computer's circuitry. The resulting signal causes the choice to be made and the computer responds accordingly.
2. **Capacitance.** This method uses a technique that can sense the change in electrical capacitance when touched by a finger. Capacitance technology used in these systems is similar to devices used for biofeedback instruments for relaxation training.
3. **Pressure sensitive.** These screens have a built-in matrix of wires on mylar sheets. When the surface is pressed, two wires make contact, thus signaling the computer the location that was touched on the screen.

FIGURE 3–17
Using a touch-sensitive display screen.

Courtesy of Hewlett-Packard Company.

Light Pens

Another way of touching the screen is with a light pen. This device is a pen that is attached with a cable to the screen and senses light that is emitted at certain points on the screen. Light pens had a degree of popularity on mainframe systems but have not retained a high level of usage in recent years. Light pens have never been popular on personal computers.

Joy Stick

Everyone, it seems, is familiar with the joy stick. It was used originally on coin-opreated video games and soon became available for home computers as well. While the joy stick is still a favorite form of input device for the home computer, at least where games are concerned, it does not have much of a following in the business world.

Voice Recognition

Voice recognition systems (Figure 3–18) are slowly obtaining a following as these input devices are becoming more reliable. To use a voice system, the computer user speaks into a microphone that is attached to a compact electronic converter. The converter changes the voice impulses, which are in analog form, into digital impulses. Computer software then translates these digital impulses into meaningful words or phrases.

Most voice recognition systems require the user to train the system by speaking the required command words, such as Copy, Print, Sum, Move, and so on, into the microphone so the software can recognize the speaker's voice

FIGURE 3–18
Using a voice recognition system.

Courtesy of Texas Instruments.

pattern. A serious limitation with these systems is that they will not recognize anyone's voice but only the person who trained the system. In some circumstances this limitation might prove to be a benefit by offering a form of system security.

Most current systems only accept commands and cannot be used for large amounts of data entry as, for example, entering a letter into a word processing program. But, as voice detection software improves, recognizing plain English may soon be a reality.

PRINTERS AND PRINTED OUTPUT

When display screens first came into use, many advocates suggested that a major reason for using a screen was to reduce or eliminate paper output. While the use of screens may have reduced the quantity of printed output, or **hard copy,** as it is often called, printed reports are still a major need in information systems.

A printer is usually attached to the parallel port of the computer. Occasionally, it is attached to a serial port. Compared to some outputs, such as disk or screen displays, the printer is a slow device. Although some printers on a personal computer may print up to 700 characters per second (cps), speeds of 100 to 200 cps are more common.

The anatomy of a report. A detailed report with control breaks is commonly required in business. Data for this production report is in order by division and department number. As the report is printed, subtotals are given after each department and again at the end of a division. These total lines, called control breaks, are flagged with asterisks (*) to show whether they are a minor (*), intermediate (**), or major (***). Group printing is also used so that duplicate data, such as the division and department numbers, is shown only at the beginning of a common group of records.

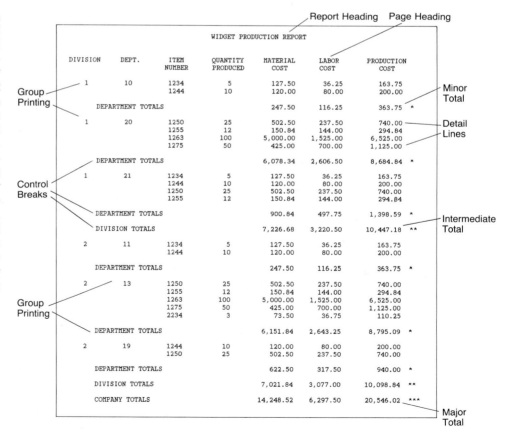

There are basically three printer groups and each satisfies a specific printing need, so much so that some offices will have a printer from at least two of the groups. Printer categories are

1. *Dot matrix*, which forms its characters from a matrix of dots.
2. *Daisy wheel*, which uses a fully formed character for letter- or typewriter-quality printing.
3. *Laser*, which uses laser technology to print full pages in a manner similar to that used by a copier machine.

A fourth type of printer is the ink jet, which forms a character by directing a jet of ink onto the paper to produce the character. Ink jet printers did not receive a wide following for personal computers but are in somewhat more widespread use on mini- and mainframe computer systems.

When a report or other output is printing, the operation ties up the computer so that no other tasks may be done until printing has finished. This is an obvious waste of the computer resource, so software companies have devised several solutions. Many full-featured word processors such as WordStar and WordPerfect permit the use of the word processor while simultaneously printing a report.

Another solution is to use print buffers that store the contents of a document in memory. Some programs, especially word processors, offer this as a built-in feature. While the document is printing from memory, other software may then use the computer. A third solution is to employ software that permits the simultaneous use of more than one program. Operating systems such as UNIX and OS/2 provide this capability on some personal computers.

Dot Matrix Printers

Personal computer users that want a good quality printer at low cost invariably select a dot matrix printer. **Dot matrix printers** are the most widely used printer with PCs, and they come with a variety of features and capabilities. A matrix printer contains a print head with a number of pins that are electrically fired against a fabric ribbon to make an impression on the paper (Figure 3–19). Pins are fired in a pattern to create different characters. Usually the better the printer, the greater the number of pins and the higher the print quality.

Because physical contact is necessary to create an image on the paper, the matrix printer falls into a category of printers called **impact printers.** Matrix printers are noisy and often require an acoustical printer cover when used in a quiet office environment.

Selecting a matrix printer can be confusing because of the many choices of printers and features. Printers generally come with a carriage that permits continuous stock paper that is 9½ inches wide, including the perforated edge for the tractor feed. This width will be useful for printing 80 characters per line at a density of 10 characters per inch. This density is commonly called pica type. Wider carriages of up to 19.5 inches are available on some printer models to accept wider paper.

Speed is another factor to consider when selecting a printer and is expressed in characters per second. Many matrix printers offer several choices of speed depending on the mode in which the printer is operating. Two commonly available modes are draft and near letter quality (NLQ), also called correspon-

FIGURE 3–19

The print head creates a pattern of dots to form specific characters when printing.

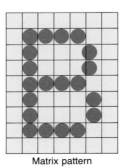

Matrix pattern

TABLE 3–1
A Comparison of Dot
Matrix Impact Printers

Printer	Price	Print Head Pins	Rated Speed (characters per second)	Type Pitch (characters per inch)
Seikosha SP-1000	$ 299	9	100 draft 15 NLQ	10.0, 12.0, 15.0
Olivetti DM 280	595	9	160 draft 27 NLQ	10.0, 12.0, 17.1
Epson EX-800	749	9	300 draft 43 NLQ	10.0, 12.0, 17.0 20.0
IBM Proprinter XL	799	9	200 draft 65 NLQ	5.0, 6.0, 8.6 10.0, 12.0, 17.1
Tandy DMP-2110	1,295	24	240 draft 62 NLQ	5.0, 6.0, 8.3 10.0, 12.0, 16.7
Mannesmann Tally 490	2,199	18	400 draft 123 NLQ	5.0, 6.0, 7.5 8.6, 10.0, 12.0 15.0, 17.1

dence quality. Draft mode is the higher speed and produces a readable but lower quality output than near letter quality.

Some printers also offer a graphics mode, the possibility of condensed or expanded type, and a variety of fonts and pitches. A final consideration in selecting a printer is its compatibility to certain standards. The two standards generally accepted are Epson and IBM. Most application software is designed to handle printers that conform to these standards, but if a printer is chosen that does not, the program may not be able to use all the printer's features.

A few dot matrix printers are capable of color printing, which is especially useful if graphs are printed. Table 3–1 shows several matrix printers and compares their prices and features.[3]

Daisy Wheel Printers

Daisy wheel printers create fully formed characters (Figure 3–20) for letter-quality printing; a thimble element is occasionally used in place of the daisy wheel. These impact printers produce output that is comparable to that from the best typewriters, and many such printers are produced by typewriter manufacturers.

Unlike a dot matrix printer, the daisy wheel always produces a high-quality print image. But it is much slower than a matrix printer. Daisy wheel printers usually operate at under 100 characters per second with 45 cps being the average speed. Most cannot print graphics.

Daisy wheels are interchangeable, so that different type fonts and pitches may be used. Many daisy wheel printers do single-sheet printing like a typewriter, in which case the program stops at the end of a page as the operator inserts a new page. Some printers have optional sheet feeders that eliminate manual insertion of the paper and speed up the printing of large numbers of

[3] See "Printers: The Third Annual Survey," *PC Magazine*, November 11, 1986, pp. 135–257, and "State of the Art in Dot-Matrix Impact Printers," *Byte Magazine*, April 1987, pp. 203–13.

FIGURE 3–20
A daisy wheel printer used
for letter-quality printing.

Courtesy of DataProducts Corporation.

pages. Because of the increasing affordability of the laser printer, the daisy wheel printer is quickly losing popularity with PC users.

Laser Printers

Until recently, laser printers (Figure 3–21) were available only for use with million-dollar mainframe computer systems. But now technology has made laser printing affordable for the office on almost any personal computer. Nonimpact laser printers for personal computers cost under $5,000, with a number of models available for $2,000 or less.

There are several reasons why the laser printer is becoming popular. Price, of course, is one, with lasers coming in at the price of a good daisy wheel

FIGURE 3–21
A laser printer.

Courtesy of Hewlett-Packard Company.

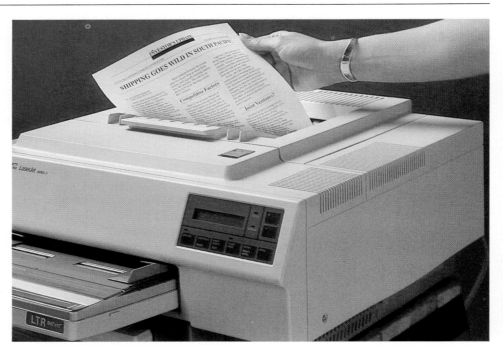

printer. Speed and print quality are also important. Laser printers operate like a photocopier and print a full page at a time. Thus, speed is quoted in pages per minute (ppm). Eight pages per minute is a common speed, which compares favorably with daisy wheel printer output of about one page per minute, and print quality is comparable to letter quality. Lasers also have font and pitch selections, and many are capable of graphics, which makes them a top candidate for desktop publishing applications.

Because laser printers are nonimpact, they are also quiet. Printing is done electronically, and the only noise generated is from the movement of paper through the machine. This makes them an attractive alternative to the much noisier daisy wheel in the office environment. Much software that was written prior to the availability of the laser did not provide support for this type of printer. But now, many upgraded software packages are providing printer drivers for some of the more widely used laser printers, such as the Hewlett-Packard laser jet printer.

CHECKLIST FOR CHOOSING A PRINTER

- Do you require draft quality or near letter quality or both? Then choose a dot matrix printer.
- Do you need letter-quality printing most of the time? Then choose a daisy wheel or laser printer.
- What is the volume of your printing? A dot matrix printer printing 400 words per page, at 100 characters per second will produce 3 pages per minute, or 180 pages an hour. At 20 characters per second (for NLQ), you get only 36 pages per hour.
- If you require graphics capability, then check your software to see what printers it supports and choose from this group.
- Do you print extrawide documents such as spreadsheets or other charts? A wider carriage might be the solution. Other approaches are to choose a printer with a suitable compressed mode or to use software that can print sideways on a matrix printer.
- Is your printer to be used in a quiet environment? How about choosing a laser printer? Or maybe an acoustical cover would be the solution.
- Will you be using desktop publishing software? Then a top-level matrix printer or a laser printer should be considered.

MAINFRAME PRINTERS

Printers on the mainframe computer serve the same purpose as on the personal computer, that is, producing hard copy for the user of the system. The difference in the two lies in the fact that there are considerably more users of a mainframe computer than there are of a PC. More users mean: more output. Thus the mainframe printer is called upon to produce more pages of output, at a faster speed, and often with higher quality than the printer on a micro.

Mainframe computers can use printers such as the daisy wheel or matrix printer, but generally these are for special-purpose use. More commonly the chain, band, or laser printer is used on the mainframe system.

A chain printer used by mainframe computers.

A mainframe computer uses a high-speed printer for high-volume production.

A type band used in a high-speed line printer.

Chain and Band Printers

This category of impact printer uses a chain or band formed into a circular loop. Because they both operate in essentially the same way, we will use the term chain to refer to both types of printers. The chain contains one or more sets (sometimes as many as five) of type characters along its surface. The chain rotates at a high speed in front of the paper, and as the correct character reaches the print position, an electromagnetic hammer is fired to make an impression through an ink ribbon on the page.

These printers are often called line printers because a line is printed at a time. The line can be up to 132 characters wide, and print speeds vary from 600 to 3,000 lines per minute. Because of their high speed, line printers often

A laser page printing system produces high-quality reports.

Courtesy of IBM.

have special attachments for stacking the paper as it comes out of the printer. Decollating or multipart forms may be done, as may bursting of the continuous form paper when printing is complete.

Page Printers

A common problem with all printers is that of speed. Compared to other devices such as disk or high-speed tape, the printer is relatively slow. By using electrophotographic and laser technology, full-page printers are now available on the mainframe that can print up to 20,000 lines per minute. Often speeds are quoted in pages per minute, which seems to be more meaningful. For example, one Honeywell page-printing system prints at 600 pages per minute.

Page printers use special paper similar to that used in a copier machine. Sizes are the standard $8\frac{1}{2}$ inches x 11 inches that is common in the office environment. Paper is supplied in individual sheets and is cheaper to purchase than is continuous form paper. One disadvantage is that multiple part forms cannot be used, but some printers can print on both sides of the page and others can print in color.

Who can benefit from the higher speeds of the page printer? A standard rule of measure in the industry is that a company printing more than a million lines of output a month can benefit even though the cost for a page printer may be up to $300,000.

PLOTTERS

Matrix printers have limited abilities to produce quality graphics that are suitable for reproduction into presentation graphic form. And lasers have yet to print in color. But plotters can draw line graphs, bar charts, pie charts, and other graphic images in four or more colors. Plotters (Figure 3–22) can take graphs generated by spreadsheet programs or specialty graphic programs and produce high-quality drawings.

FIGURE 3–22   A plotter used to prepare presentation-quality graphics.

Courtesy of Houston Instrument; CalComp, A Lockheed Company.

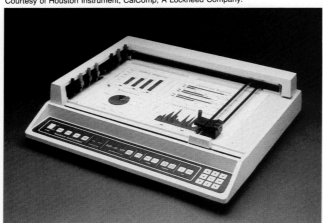

Typical plotters have a supply of pens, similar to colored ink markers, that are selected and used to draw the images sent from the computer. Some plotters select a different color pen automatically, while others require a manual change. Plotters draw lines rather than use dots, and as a result the density of the image is significantly greater than that produced by a matrix printer. Plotters can draw on paper, or for presentation graphics, a transparency master may be inserted and the image drawn directly on it.

Like most printers, plotters must also be compatible with the software that drives them. Most graphic software is provided with a set of drivers that can interface with a variety of plotter devices, but it is essential before choosing either a plotter or graphic software to ensure compatibility.

MAINFRAME DEVICES

Point-of-Sale (POS) Terminals

You have seen the automated checkout registers used in many food and department stores. These cash registers are called **point-of sale (POS)** terminals and are used to record purchases by reading the Universal Product Code recorded on each item purchased. POS terminals are attached to a computer that stores the prices of all items in the store. Storing prices in a central location ensures consistency in the price used by the cashier and allows for fast and easy updating when price changes occur.

Universal Product Code (UPC)

The **Universal Product Code (UPC)** is a bar code that is in widespread use by grocery chains for automatic recording of prices on checkout. The label on each item in the store is marked with the bar code that identifies the product. A store computer uses this data to look up the description and price of the item that is then printed on the cash register tape, supplying the customer with a complete record of the purchase.

POS terminal in supermarket.

Courtesy of Ralphs Grocery Company.

Grocery item with UPC bar code from a major supermarket chain store.

Courtesy of Teri Stratford.

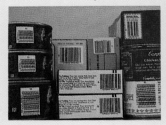

Wand Readers

The wand reader is another form of point-of-sale device that is used by department stores to read the price tag on clothes, household goods, and hardware. Items in the store are identified by a magnetically encoded price tag. Product identification that has been previously recorded magnetically on the price tag is captured by the wand for automatic data entry at the cash register.

Wand reader in department store.

Courtesy of NCR Corporation.

Teller machine at a major bank used for making deposits and withdrawals.

Courtesy of IBM.

Automated Teller Machine

Banks across the country have been providing customers with the option of using walk-in or drive-in **automated teller machines (ATMs)** to make withdrawals and deposits 24 hours a day. Customers are supplied with access cards, similar to a credit card, containing a record of the customer's account and credit limit on a magnetically encoded strip on the back of the card. As financial transactions occur at the ATM, the system uses **electronic funds transfer (EFT)** to update a computer record to reflect the current balance in the customer's account.

Optical Recognition

Optical character recognition (OCR) refers to a range of optical scanning procedures for the recognition of special codes, or characters, on a document. OCR machines read characters that conform to a special font character set. Variations of these devices recognize bar codes, handwritten characters (with some limitations), and machine-printed characters. OCR has been used for many applications, including payment processing by utility companies, medical claim forms, hospital registration, and attendance reporting. Although these devices originally gained attention on mainframe systems, low-cost OCRs are now available for personal computers.

Mark sensing is a form of optical device that senses the presence or absence of a mark on a document. You have probably written a test or filled out a questionnaire using a special marking sheet for your answers. This sheet has areas where a pencil mark is used to record an answer to a multiple-choice or true/false test question. A mark-sensing machine is used to read these marks on the answer sheet and converts them to digital codes to be read by the computer.

Magnetic Ink Character Reader

You have likely noticed that oddly shaped characters located at the bottom of a bank check. These are magnetic ink characters that are read into the computer by a **magnetic ink character reader (MICR).** The magnetic content and unique shape of each character are what allows them to be read by the reader as well as by humans.

MICR encoded checks are used by banks to speed the processing of financial transactions through the complex banking network. After you use a check to make a purchase, the check arrives at the bank's data processing center where the amount of the purchase is encoded on the check. Your check is then processed with thousands of other checks by the MICR device that not only reads the amount on the check, which will be deducted from your account, but also sorts the checks by account and branch so that the check can be routed back to your branch.

A check with the branch and account number coded in magnetic ink at the bottom.

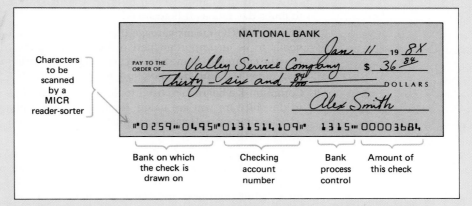

A magnetic ink character reader used to read and sort checks in a banking system.

Courtesy of Unisys Corporation.

In this chapter we have looked at the primary devices used for input and output. On the personal computer, the keyboard, screen, and printer are the most widely used primary input and output devices. We have seen that a variety of screens and printers are available to suit many different needs. Other devices for interaction include the mouse and touch screens. By contrast, the mainframe uses a display terminal that combines the keyboard and screen in a single package. Special-purpose devices are available for use in supermarkets, department stores, and the banking industry. In the next chapter, we will look at devices such as the magnetic disk for storing data in the computer to make it available for later use.

CHAPTER SUMMARY

1. Data entry refers to the entering of data at the keyboard or other input device into the computer for storage and processing.

2. A field refers to an item of data, such as an invoice number, whereas a record is a collection of fields or information that relates to one transaction.

3. Batch refers to a method where the data are collected over a period of time and entered into the computer as a group of records. Online data entry uses the computer to enter the data as it is received.

4. The term GIGO means garbage-in, garbage-out, which implies that error checking needs to be an important part of data entry to ensure that good data is entered into the computer. Some types of error checking are field missing, limit test, contents test, range test, and transposition error.

5. Computer keyboards are used to enter data as well as commands and instructions to the software you are using. Keyboards have alphabetic and numeric keys like a typewriter, as well as special-purpose keys such as Cursor control, Insert, Delete, and function keys.

6. A display screen is a TV-like device that displays text or graphics depending on the needs of the program. Screens can be monochrome or color. Color gives superior results for graphics, but except for the more expensive color screens, monochrome gives better sharpness and clarity for text.

7. Color displays can be either composite or RGB. Composite is a TV-like display while RGB gives significantly better results. A color display also requires a color board in an expansion slot. Five levels of color boards are CGA, EGA, PGC, multiscan, and VGA.

8. The resolution of the display determines the clarity of the character displayed for text and the precision of the image for graphics. Resolution depends on the number of dots or points of light, called pixels, on the display.

9. Bit mapping is a technique for displaying characters by controlling each pixel on the screen to determine the exact format of the character as needed for special fonts and graphics.

10. A full-page display shows the entire contents of a printed page on the screen, compared to a regular display screen, which only displays a maximum of 25 lines. The full-page display is especially useful for desktop publishing applications.

11. Flat display screens use liquid crystal display technology for a compact screen as used in portable computers. LCD displays are smaller and lighter in weight and consume much less power than do other screens.

12. A mouse is a device that replaces some of the functions of the cursor key. It is used by rolling it on the surface of a desk, which in turn moves a pointer on the screen. By pressing a button on the mouse, a software option may be selected.

13. A touch screen lets the user select options by pointing at them on screen with a finger. The touch screen requires a specially designed screen with infrared light beams, capacitance-sensitive, or pressure-sensitive technology.

14. Voice recognition systems may be used for limited data entry or the selection of program options. Most voice systems require the system to be trained to recognize an individual user's voice.

15. The three main printer groups are dot matrix, daisy wheel, and laser, with a distant fourth being the ink jet. Using a printer ties up the computer, but by using a print buffer, the computer can be used simultaneously with printing.

16. Dot matrix printers are the most widely used printers on a PC and have a variety of features. Features include a wide carriage, a range of speeds, near-letter-quality (NLQ) or draft mode, color, graphics, and condensed or expanded type. Dot matrix printers are a type of impact printer can be quite noisy.

17. Daisy wheel printers use fully formed characters to produce letter-quality results. They generally operate more slowly than dot matrix and do not have graphics capability. Daisy wheels are interchangeable and so can provide different fonts and pitches.

18. Laser printers are available in the price range of high-end daisy wheel printers. Lasers are quiet and operate faster than the daisy wheel printer. Print quality is of letter quality. Laser printers come with a variety of fonts and pitches and often include graphics, making them a suitable candidate for desktop publishing.

19. A plotter is used for graphic applications to produce a high-quality reproduction of a graph. Plotters are especially useful for preparing full-color presentation graphics on a transparency master.

IMPORTANT TERMS AND CONCEPTS

Batch
Bit mapping
Color graphics
 adapter
Composite
Cursor
Cursor control keys
Daisy wheel
Data entry
Display
Dot matrix
Error detection
Fields
Flat display

Full-page display
Function keys
Hard copy
Impact printers
Ink jet
Joy stick
Keyboards
Laser printers
Light pen
Monochrome
Mouse
Near letter quality
 (NLQ)
Online

Pixels
Plotters
Printer
Record
Resolution
Return or Enter key
RGB
Scrolling
Terminal
Touch screen
Voice recognition

REVIEW QUESTIONS

Fill-in Questions.

1. Items such as account number, name, and quantity are called _____.

2. A(n) _____ contains data that relates to a single transaction.

3. _____data entry refers to data that is entered at the keyboard as the data is received.

4. Two basic types of screens are composite and _____.
5. Screen _____ is determined by the number of pixels displayed. One such measurement is 320 × 200 pixels.
6. The flashing _____ on a screen shows where the next character to be typed will appear.
7. Daisy wheel and dot matrix are a form of _____ printer.
8. The _____ is a nonimpact printer that is becoming increasingly popular.

Matching Questions

Match each term with the description given below.
a. batch   d. CGA
b. bit mapping   e. near letter quality
c. mouse   f. scrolling

_____ 1. An input device that is used for selecting options from the screen. Moving this device on the desktop causes corresponding movements of the cursor on the screen.

_____ 2. A form of data entry where data is accumulated and entered at one time.

_____ 3. Dot matrix printers sometimes have this mode to produce documents that are similar to those printed with a fully formed character.

____*b*____ 4. This type of screen display controls individual pixels to form character fonts or graphic images.

____*CGA*____ 5. Using this level of color adaptor board the screen can display 16 colors at a resolution of 320 × 200.

____*f*____ 6. This term describes what happens when the screen is full and another line is displayed at the bottom.

Discussion Questions

1. Explain the term data entry. How do the terms field and record relate to a data entry screen?
2. What is the difference between batch and online data entry operations? Name some of the advantages and disadvantages for batch and online.
3. Describe the purpose of the keyboard for interacting with the computer. What are some of the more important keys on the keyboard?
4. Explain the characteristics of a monochrome and color screen.
5. What is meant by the term resolution? How does a pixel relate to this term?
6. Describe the purpose of bit mapping and explain its advantage over the use of predefined character display.
7. Why are full-page displays growing in popularity? Where are they best used in personal computing?
8. Flat displays are made using LCD technology. Why is this form of display useful and for what purpose?
9. Describe the function of a mouse discussing some of the pros and cons of its use.

10. A touch screen may be a possible replacement for the mouse. Discuss this statement.
11. What is the function of voice recognition systems in personal computing?
12. Name the three major printer groups briefly describing the type of printer.
13. Compare the main features of the three types of printers.
14. Discuss the usefulness of a plotter on a personal computer.

Secondary Storage Concepts

A VIEW OF THE CHAPTER AHEAD

After Reading This Chapter You Will Understand:

- The need for disk storage and its benefits to the personal computer user.

- The purpose of tape units for backing up disk files and for offline storage on mainframes.

- The different file organizations and why they are used.

D ata in a computer system often originates at the keyboard as a result of data entry operation. Other forms of entry, such as voice or document reading, may be used, but the end result is still the same. As data is entered into the computer, a place is needed for permanent storage. On most systems the storage device of choice is disk while some computers may also use tape for special purposes.

THE DIFFERENCE BETWEEN PRIMARY AND SECONDARY STORAGE

As data is entered, it resides in random access memory (RAM), which is also called primary storage. The problem with RAM is that it is temporary; as soon as the power to the computer is turned off, all data in RAM is lost. The solution is to have a **secondary storage** medium, such as disk, that can retain data permanently.

Figure 4–1 shows how data that is entered from the keyboard goes into RAM and from there is written, under program control, to disk storage. Writing to disk requires a separate operation by the program in addition to reading the source data from the keyboard. Often this requires the user to enter a command to save a file on disk before leaving the computer. Disk storage is nonvolatile, it does not depend on electrical power being present on the computer, and it usually has much greater capacity than RAM.

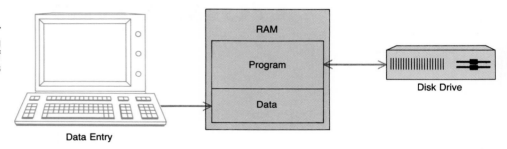

FIGURE 4–1

Data entry to a computer must also result in the saving of the data on some type of secondary storage such as a floppy disk.

WHY IS DISK USED?

On personal computer systems there are two basic forms of disks: **removable disk,** which includes floppy and disk cartridges (high-density or HD disk), and **fixed disk,** which is commonly called hard disk. Both types of disks are used for many of the same reasons. We have already seen that disk offers a permanent medium for storage, but disk is also a much faster form of storing and accessing data than other alternatives such as tape. Disk also offers both sequential and direct access to records stored on the disk surface.

Floppy disks or cartridges provide unlimited storage by using as many disks as necessary, but they must also be inserted and removed from the disk drive as new data is required. Fixed disks have large capacities ranging from 10M (megabytes) to over 100M and do not require any physical contact by the user. Floppies and cartridges are easily transportable and are a popular method for transporting data or programs from one location to another. Virtually all software companies use floppy disks for providing products to customers.

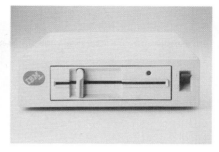

Disk drives come in compact 3½-inch size for portables and some newer computers such as the IBM PS/2 and 5¼ inches for most PCs and compatibles. Fixed or hard disk is popular because of its large storage capacity, compact size, and low cost.

Courtesy of IBM; Mitsubishi Electronics.

DISK CHARACTERISTICS

The 3½-inch micro floppy disk can store a minimum of 720K bytes, giving it double the capacity of most 5¼-inch floppy disks.

Courtesy of IBM.

All forms of disk use similar methods for recording data. The 5¼-inch floppy disk is made from a flexible mylar material, whereas the hard disk and the 3½-inch floppy or cartridge are made from a firm material, usually aluminum. The disk is coated with a material that can be magnetized and is the key to recording data on the surface of the disk.

The magnetic surface of the disk is organized into **tracks** as shown in Figure 4–2. Data bits are recorded magnetically, using positive and negative polarities to represent the zeros and ones of the ASCII code along these tracks. Disk surfaces on the personal computer are also divided into **sectors,** which aids the software in finding the data quickly and with a minimum of delay. On the 5¼-inch floppy the disk typically has 40 tracks and 9 sectors. The 3½-inch floppy uses 80 tracks and 15 sectors.

When the disk is in operation, a disk drive motor in the computer spins the disk while, at the same time, an **access arm** positions a **read/write head** on the disk surface (Figure 4–3). Some hard disk drives (particularly those

FIGURE 4–2
Tracks and sectors on the disk surface.

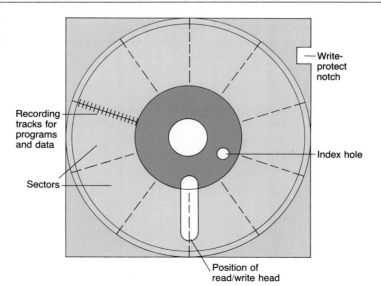

Recording tracks for programs and data

Sectors

Write-protect notch

Index hole

Position of read/write head

FIGURE 4–3

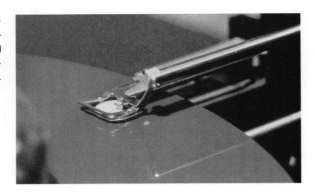

FIGURE 4–3

An access arm with a record-ing head is used for reading and writing data on the disk.

Courtesy of BASF Systems Corporation.

on mainframe computer systems) use compressed air to keep the head in close proximity to the disk surface. To write on disk, electrical signals from the computer flow to the head, which writes the data magnetically on the track. Reading is just the reverse. The head senses the magnetic spots on the track and sends the data these spots represent to the computer.

Floppy Disk

Characters (or bytes of storage)

K = thousand
M = million

5¼-inch

↓
160K
360K
1.2M

Oval cutout exposes actual disk surface.

The 5¼-inch floppy disk is widely used in PCs and PC compatibles for data storage.

The mainstay of the disk industry has been the 5¼-inch **floppy disk** with a capacity of 360K. It consists of a flexible mylar platter enclosed in a sturdy storage envelope that protects the recording surface from scratches, fingerprints, and dust. The oval slot in the envelope is where the read/write head accesses the data and is an area of the disk that should never be touched as it is placed in the disk drive.

The central hole is called the hub and is where the disk drive grips the disk so that it may be spun during reading and writing. The smaller circular hole is the sector hole, which identifies the location of the first sector on the disk while a read or write operation is underway.

The envelope is notched on the edge near one corner. This is the write-protect notch, which allows you to write data on the disk if it is open. By covering the write-protect notch with an adhesive-backed tab, writing on the disk is prevented and thus protects against unwanted recording or erasing of files.

DATA RATE

Data rate is the speed in bytes per second (bps) at which data is transferred to or from the disk. As a disk is being read or written, it revolves in the drive at about 300 RPM for a floppy or 3600 RPM for a hard disk. It is this speed which is a major factor in the rate at which data is transferred from the disk, the other factor being the density of the data on the track. Floppy disk is generally about one-twentieth the speed of a hard disk, although this is certainly not a hard and fast rule. An average hard disk has a data transfer rate of 625,000 (625K) bps with some operating up to 1M (million) or more bytes per second.[1]

---

[1] Heather-Jo Taferner, "Internal Hard Disks," *Personal Computing*, Vol. 11, no. 2 (February 1987), p. 135.

**AVERAGE
ACCESS TIME**

Data rate is an important measure of a disk's speed, but it only comes into play after the data you require from the disk has been found. Suppose a data base program requires a record for a specific item in inventory. There are two aspects to determining the time required for locating this record on the disk. First, the disk drive must position the head to the track containing the record: this is called seek time. Then the disk drive must wait while the disk rotates until the record required is positioned under the head: this is called rotational delay. After both these delays occur, the disk can read the record and transfer it to the program. Because the seek time and rotational delay can vary for each record, the average of these times is called the average access time, which refers to the time required to access a record. Average access times can be on the order of 30 to 100 milliseconds (thousands of a second), depending on the type of disk drive used.

When a query is issued on a data base several factors affect the amount of time taken to access the record: the data rate, seek time, and the average rotational delay all contribute to the waiting time experienced by the user after issuing the request.

Courtesy of IBM.

To identify the disk contents, an adhesive-backed label is placed on the surface of the envelope. Information about the disk's contents should be written on the label by using a felt tipped pen, rather than a ball point pen, to avoid damaging the disk.

A floppy that is designed to be recorded on both sides is a double-sided disk. The amount of data that can be packed on the disk is determined by the number of tracks and the density. The most widely used floppy disk is double density and has 40 tracks for recording data. A disk labeled as DSDD means double side double density, while SSDD is single side double density. Most PCs use DSDD floppy disks.

Floppies are inexpensive and quite durable. However, reasonable care should be taken to avoid bending or exposing the disk to foreign substances such as spilt coffee or dust. When disks are not in use, they should be placed back into their sleeve to minimize damage.

Newer PCs, portables, and IBM's PS/2 computers are causing the 3½-inch floppy disk to grow in popularity. In this construction, a floppy disk is contained

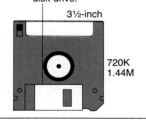

Metal cover automatically slides over to expose disk only when inside a disk drive.

3½-inch

720K
1.44M

Portables, laptops, and PS/2 generation computers mostly use the 3½-inch floppy disk.

A fixed disk resides permanently in the computer providing fast access to large quantities of data.

Courtesy of Microscience International Corporation.

in a rigid plastic enclosure. The exposed surface of the disk is covered by a sliding metal shutter that is opened only when the disk is accessed in the drive by the computer. A movable plastic tab is used to provide read only capability. A 3½-inch disk can store from 720K to 1.44M.

Hard Disk

Experienced computer users are moving more and more to the use of hard disks for their speed, convenience, and high capacity. **Hard disks,** also known as **Winchester disks,** or fixed disks have from 10 to 100M capacity with larger disk capacities on the way. To get this volume of storage, hard disks are manufactured with extremely close tolerances, which is why they are mounted in a fixed location in the computer and are not removable. The fixed disk is mounted in a sealed enclosure that protects the disk from environmental hazards such as dust and smoke particles, which can be damaging to the disk and its contents.

Many hard disks come as a half-height drive, which permits stacking two of them in one disk slot in the computer for extra storage capacity. Hard disks are noted for their reliability, and some portables now have built-in hard disks owing to their compactness and reliable operation.

Aftermarket hard disks are widely available and include a new item called a hard disk card. This fixed disk is mounted on a card that fits an expansion slot inside the computer. The hard card is especially useful in computers where floppy drives already occupy the location where the hard disk ordinarily is installed. But hard cards can require more space than other cards and thus present mounting problems, particularly if they are to be placed next to other expansion cards.

The hard card is a fixed disk that occupies one expansion slot thus using less space than other hard disk drives.

Courtesy of Plus Development Corporation.

Under ordinary conditions the hard disk requires no special care other than using it in a clean, dust- and smoke-free environment. To ensure the safety of the data, backing up the contents of the hard disk is an important operation that must be done at frequent intervals. See the section on disk backup for a discussion on this method.

Benefits of Disk

Both floppy and hard disk offer many benefits to the computer user. Some of these are summarized as follows:

- **Speed of access.** Data that is stored on a disk may be accessed quickly with a minimum of delay.
- **Access method.** Both floppy and hard disk offer sequential or direct accessing of data. With direct access only the record required by the user needs to be read, significantly improving the time needed for accessing disk records compared to tape which must access records sequentially.
- **Large storage capacity.** This is especially true of hard disk with capacities of from 10 to 100M and more, making a large amount of data available to the user at all times.
- **Storage cost.** While hard disk is more expensive than a floppy disk drive to install, the differences are not excessive. The larger storage capacity and faster speed of hard disk frequently outweighs the small difference in cost.

DISK DIRECTORIES

Using a disk requires that you know the names of the files that it contains. It is not usually enough to look at the label of a floppy disk and identify it as containing budget data, but rather, we will need to know the exact file that is required. On a hark disk, with its large capacity, there can be literally hundreds of files to choose from, while a floppy may have several dozen. For this reason a **directory** of files may be displayed by most programs or by using a DOS command prior to running the program.

Figure 4–4 shows a typical directory screen for a hard disk, displayed in this case, by the word processor WordPerfect. Other software packages will display a directory using some variation of this technique, frequently with less information than shown here. At the top of the directory screen, the date

FIGURE 4–4

A DOS command for display-ing a disk directory.

Disk in Drive A:

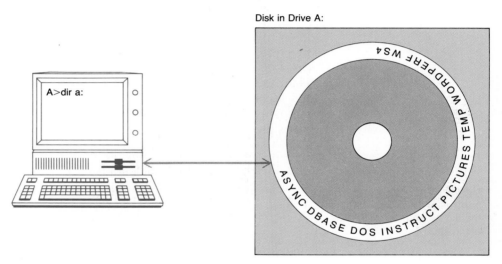

A WordPerfect screen dis-play of a hard disk directory containing both files and sub-directories.

```
04/17/87  15:47              Directory C:\*.*
Document Size:     8247                        Free Disk Space:   5218304

  . <CURRENT>    <DIR>                .. <PARENT>    <DIR>
ASYNC    .        <DIR>   11/20/86 02:42   BATCH    .    <DIR>   01/01/80 01:37
DBASE    .        <DIR>   11/20/86 02:48   DIAGS    .    <DIR>   01/01/80 00:01
DOS      .        <DIR>   01/01/80 00:04   FC       .    <DIR>   03/25/87 20:42
INSTRUCT.         <DIR>   03/19/87 06:34   LOTUS    .    <DIR>   01/01/80 00:52
PICTURES.         <DIR>   11/23/86 15:09   SYMPHONY.     <DIR>   11/27/86 09:14
TEMP     .        <DIR>   12/12/86 13:18   TERMINAL.     <DIR>   02/06/87 08:35
WORDPERF.         <DIR>   01/01/80 00:05   WS2000   .    <DIR>   11/21/86 19:17
WS4      .        <DIR>   03/24/87 18:54   AUTO2    .BAT     128  11/22/86 16:43
AUTOEXEC.BAK        256   04/04/87 11:23   AUTOEXEC.BAT     256  04/17/87 09:08
COMMAND .COM      17664   03/08/83 12:00   CONFIG  .OLD     128  11/20/86 04:19
CONFIG  .SYS        128   02/03/87 09:35   DOS     .MNU    3072  03/29/87 20:05
DOSCMND .HLP        506   07/20/84 24:00   INTRO    .       894  11/23/86 17:31
LEARN    .          995   10/25/85 13:33   MAINMENU.MNU     512  04/04/87 11:00
MASTMAIN.HLP      14211   07/20/84 24:00   MASTMENU.EXE   75492  07/20/84 24:00
MASTMENU.HLP      38437   07/20/84 24:00   MENUSYS .DAT     128  04/17/87 09:08
NULLSCRN.HLP        232   07/20/84 24:00   WS2PATH .BAT      22  04/04/87 10:01
```

and time are shown as are the directory name and the amount of free disk space still available.

The remainder of the screen shows the names of files available on the disk, the size of the file in bytes, and the date and time they were last revised. Entries with the <DIR> indicator signify that these are subdirectories that may themselves contain additional files.

Directories and Subdirectories

Fixed disks have capacities of 10M or more, which presents special problems when trying to find a file on the disk. Listing a directory of hundreds of files, let alone finding the specific file required, can be a difficult task. To resolve this problem, hard disks may be organized into subdirectories with each subdirectory serving as a separate minidisk. Floppies may also have subdirectories, but with their relatively small capacity, there is less need for this kind of organization.

Directory organization on the hard disk can be thought of as an upside-down tree structure as shown in Figure 4–5. The trunk is the **root** or **parent** directory, which contains several branches known as **subdirectories.** Each subdirectory may contain a number of files or may also contain lower-level subdirectories. Using this organization requires that files of a given type be located in a specific subdirectory.

For example, word processing files may go in one subdirectory while spreadsheets are in another. Within the word processing subdirectory, there may be

FIGURE 4–5

Using subdirectories on a hard disk simplifies finding the file needed for a specific application.

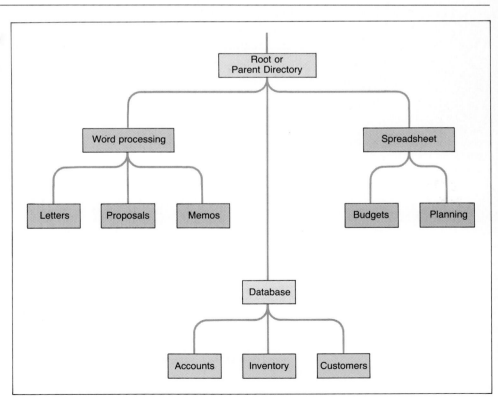

FIGURE 4–6

Using a software tool to manage and view the relationship between the root and its subdirectories.

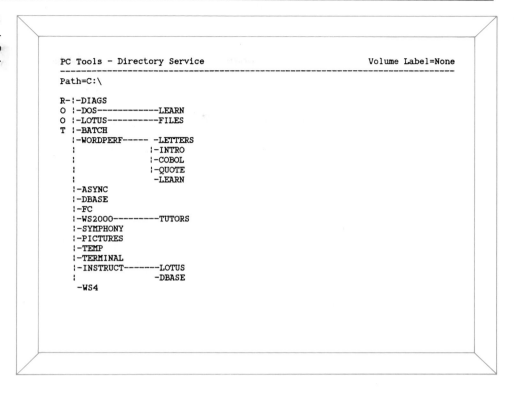

```
PC Tools - Directory Service                              Volume Label=None
-----------------------------------------------------------------------------
Path=C:\

R-!-DIAGS
O !-DOS------------LEARN
O !-LOTUS----------FILES
T !-BATCH
  !-WORDPERF----- -LETTERS
  !                !-INTRO
  !                !-COBOL
  !                !-QUOTE
  !                 -LEARN
  !-ASYNC
  !-DBASE
  !-FC
  !-WS2000---------TUTORS
  !-SYMPHONY
  !-PICTURES
  !-TEMP
  !-TERMINAL
  !-INSTRUCT-------LOTUS
  !                -DBASE
   -WS4
```

other subdirectories, such as one for letters, another for proposals, and a third for memos. Therefore, to find a letter to a client, you would first look under the word processing and then the letters subdirectory rather than look at all files located on the hard disk.

Some software, such as PC Tools, simplifies the use of subdirectories on the disk by showing graphically the relationship among the subdirectories on the disk. Figure 4–6 shows this graphic for the directory listing shown earlier.

ESTIMATING HARD DISK STORAGE SIZE

When purchasing a system a wide range of storage capacity is available for the hard disk drive. How is one to know the best size that is suitable for the needs of the application? Basically, there are two considerations when choosing the disk size. One is the amount of space required for the software to be used, and the other is the storage requirements for files.

Each software package has its own unique requirements, and so that figure will need to come from the specific packages to be used. File space will also vary according to the application. Word processing and spreadsheet files tend to accumulate and thus grow in space requirements over time, whereas data base files frequently begin with large requirements that can be computed in advance, but these calculations also need to allow for increasing requirements.

The following calculations demonstrate how disk space requirements are calculated. Consider a system that uses a 2M word processor, a 1M spreadsheet, and a 700K data base program. The data base consists of two files: the inventory file has 5,000 records with 200 bytes per record, and the customer file has 8,000 records with 120 bytes each. The word processing files are expected to require 3M and the spreadsheet files 1M after a year of use.

The calculations are as follows:

Word processor	2,000,000
Word processor files	3,000,000
Spreadsheet	1,000,000
Spreadsheet files	1,000,000
Data base	700,000
Inventory file (5,000 × 200)	1,000,000
Customer file (8,000 × 120)	960,000
	9,660,000

Consider that this total of 9.6M would almost fill a 10M hard disk. We have not considered backup files that will occupy some additional disk space. The data base will also require some space for index files, report files, and other support files. Finally, consider that figures such as these are always estimates and should allow for some expansion. Considering these factors, it seems that a 20M hard disk is the minimum size that should be used in this application.

DISK BACKUP

Most disk users agree that storing data using magnetic disks of all forms is a reliable storage media. But what about those times when something does go wrong and a file is accidentally erased or is damaged sufficiently that it cannot be retrieved? Losing a file can be a minor inconvenience at best or a major catastrophe at worst. To guard against inadvertant loss, experienced computer users regularly **back up** their disk files so that an alternate source is available if data is lost.

When using floppies or disk cartridges, backing up means making a copy of the disk on a second diskette. Usually the copy should be made after a file on the master disk has been changed. This file is then copied to the backup disk to create a second copy. If a problem occurs with the master, then the backup disk may be used to retrieve the data.

In the business environment, backup procedures should be done even more carefully. When important activities such as accounts receivable and payable are recorded on removable disk, a single backup may not be enough. In this situation the business needs to guard not only against loss of data but against loss of business. A single backup disk is adequate if the concern is only for losing a file, but what if the disk is lost or destroyed due to fire or other catastrophe? Then a third backup done at, say, weekly intervals is ideal. This third backup should be stored in another location, preferably another building for complete safety.

Figure 4–7 shows a series of backups proposed for many years in the information systems industry as being the ideal for accessing lost data. It is called the grandfather, father, son method. The son is the most recent backup, while the father and grandfather represent earlier backup files. When a new son backup file is created, the old son becomes the father, the father disk

114

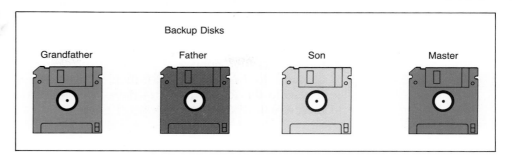

FIGURE 4–7

Three levels of disk backups for removable disks.

becomes the grandfather, and the old grandfather disk is no longer needed and may be reused for other data.

Hard disk can be backed up following the same procedure outlined for removable disks, but the large capacity of hard disk creates some unique problems. A 20M hard disk requires about 55 floppy disks for all its contents. But, if you maintain grandfather, father, and son backups, multiply that number by three. If the time comes to re-create a damaged hard disk from these floppies, the process is extremely time consuming. Loading these floppies onto the hard disk will take on the order of several hours of time.

While floppies are inexpensive, many businesses use a specialized tape backup system that has high capacity and a speed that is many times faster than floppy disks. These devices are discussed in the section on tape that follows in this chapter.

RAM DISK

Personal computer users are always looking for ways to speed up the operation of their software. Many programs exist on disk in parts, and only the parts that are needed are brought into RAM. This method is frequently used in word processing and data base software that have extensive features. Thus, the disk contains a main program and one or more overlay programs that are brought into RAM as needed. Help files may also be located on the disk.

As the program is used, disk activity is often necessary to bring into RAM the required features. This activity causes a delay in processing that can be mildly annoying to the experienced user and also results in lowered productiv-

Extra memory space can be allocated as RAM disk to improve the efficiency of some programs.

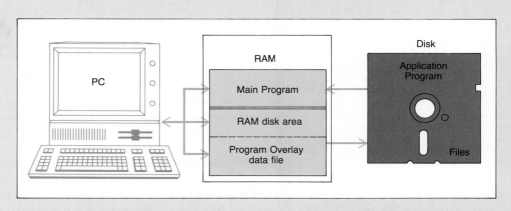

ity. One solution is to use a faster disk, but this can prove to be expensive. Another is to use a program that allocates a part of memory as a RAM disk.

For example, a 640K memory could have 256K allocated as a RAM disk area and still have enough memory available for other applications. Parts of the application, such as the overlay program or a frequently used file, are copied into this area of RAM; then, as the program requires this code or data, it goes to the RAM disk to retrieve it. Using RAM disk is significantly faster than a real disk whether floppy or fixed.

CD ROM OR OPTICAL DISKS

With compact disks (CDs) becoming the lastest audio craze, this technology is also beginning to impact the computer field. The attraction of CDs to the computer industry is enhanced by the CD's extensive storage capacity. While hard disks are capable of 20M, 40M, or 80M of storage, a CD can store from 540M to about 2 gigabytes (2 billion bytes) of data. This large storage capacity makes more information directly available to the computer than had ever been possible with previous technologies.

One application of the CD-ROM is Microsoft's Bookshelf (Figure 4–8). It is a single CD that contains ten commonly used reference works, including a dictionary, a thesaurus, the *1987 World Almanac and Book of Facts*, the *Chicago Manual of Style*, and *Bartlett's Familiar Quotations*. Bookshelf can run with a variety of popular word processors, making this information available to the user with a few keystrokes. Data found on the CD can be transferred directly to the document using a paste operation.

Like disk, the CD stores data along circular tracks. But data on a CD is stored as a bubble or flat spot, which represents a one or zero, respectively. The bubbles are smaller than a magnetic spot, and so more of them may be packed on the surface of the disk, resulting in the CD's greater storage capacity. A laser beam is used to read the data by reflecting its light off the bubble.

Current CD devices read only data that has been stored by the manufacturer; therefore users cannot write their own data. CDs are in the works that will permit one-time writing called **WORM** (write once, read many times), and, maybe in the future, CDs with read and write capability will be made available for the PC user.

FIGURE 4–8

Microsoft's Bookshelf CD, a CD-ROM for personal computer users containing ten reference works.

Courtesy of *PC Magazine*.

DISK USE ON MAINFRAME COMPUTERS

Disk drives on mainframe computers most closely resemble the PC's hard disk, but are usually constructed of more than one circular metal platter with a magnetic coating on both sides of the platter. The disk platter is mounted on a central hub, which is motor driven, to rotate the disk. When there is more than one platter, these are stacked one above the other on the central hub. Figure 4–9 shows a disk drive with six platters mounted on the central hub.

To read or write data on the surface of the disk, the entire disk is rotated on the hub. The data is read or written by the read/write heads that are mounted on access arms and positioned in close proximity to the surface of the disk.

WORMS FOR MASS STORAGE NEEDS

A WORM is an optical disk storage system based on a technology similar to CD ROMs. Both systems use optical disk storage techniques using lasers for reading the recorded data. Of course, a CD as we know it for music systems can only play back its recordings. We cannot record on it. A WORM can be recorded once and then played back any number of times. WORMs are intended for computer use and the storage of large amounts of data needed by the computer user.

WORM devices use a disk cartridge not unlike the 3½-inch disk but somewhat larger and of different design. To record data, a sliding shutter opens, giving the laser in the drive access to the disk. Data is recorded by the laser burning a small hole in the disk's substrate, thus making it a write once, read many times recording.

Because of the WORM disk's capacity, up to 400M, it can be used as a backup system instead of tape or disk systems. The large capacity makes it suitable for maintaining audit trails over long time periods. WORM records or files are stored in a manner similar to backing up a hard disk and for backup purposes the contents of an entire hard disk can easily be stored on the WORM with room to spare.

WORMs may also be used for recording data that needs frequent access. Some systems are designed for this use and, unlike a backup system, requires that the data be accessible from most programs on the PC. These WORM systems will permit files on the cartridge to be accessed like any other DOS file with speeds comparable to reading a disk file. As a read-only device WORMs have limited usefulness but they do fill a niche where large-capacity storage devices are needed.

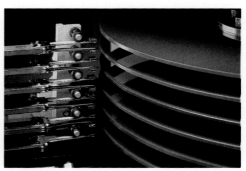

FIGURE 4–9

A disk drive and a drive assembly for a mainframe computer system.

Courtesy of Control Data Corporation; Amcodyne.

Usually there is one head per disk surface, although very-high-speed disks may have one head per track.

When several disks are stacked on a single drive hub, each surface will have a track and a read/write head that are accessible without head movement. If there are 10 surfaces that contain recording tracks, then each surface will have a track 0 located in a vertical column. Then when the head for one surface is positioned to track 0, all other heads will also be at track 0 on their respective surfaces. These stacked tracks form a **cylinder,** so-called because the shape of the tracks forms a cylinder-like object.

To save time when reading or writing sequential files, records are stored along a track until the track is filled. Then the data is stored on the next track in the same cylinder and so on until all tracks in the cylinder contain data. If the cylinder contains ten tracks, then all ten tracks of sequential data may be read or written without the need to move the heads. This approach to sequential access minimizes the seek time.

Timing considerations on mainframe disks are similar to other disk drives. There is the rotational delay determined by the speed of the disk's rotation. There is also seek time, which is the time taken for the head to reach the track containing the data. And then there is the data rate, which is the speed at which data flows to or from the disk to the central processing unit.

Access time is a term that refers to the time it takes to access a record on the file. Access time considers all aspects of the functions of the disk drive including the rotational delay, seek time, and reading time (data rate). Table 4–1 shows some representative specifications for several mainframe disk drives. This chart suggests why mainframe computers are still an important component of computing and information systems. The capacity of the mainframe disk drive begins at the top end of PC disk capacity. For example, the IBM 3340 has a capacity of 70M while the 3380 can store 1,260M. A typical mainframe

TABLE 4–1
Typical Mainframe Disk Drive Specifications Compared to a Hard Drive for the PC.

	IBM PC/XT/AT Seagate Hard Disk	IBM-Type Disk Drive					
		3330	3340	3350	3370	3375	3380
Disk capacity (bytes)	40M	100M	70M	318M	571M	820M	1,260M
Track capacity (bytes)	8,704	13,030	8,368	19,069	31,744	35,616	47,476
No. of cylinders	820	404	696	555	1,500	1,918	1,770
Tracks per cylinder	6	19	12	30	12	12	15
Avg. seek time	40 ms	30 ms	25 ms	25 ms	30 ms	19 ms	16 ms
Avg. rotational delay	—	8.3 ms	10.1 ms	8.3 ms	10.1 ms	10.1 ms	8.3 ms
Data transfer rate (per second)	625K	806K	885K	1,198K	1,859K	1,859K	3,000K

computer will have several disk drives that effectively multiplies these figures by the number of drives.

Speed of access and data transfer are important advantages of mainframe disks. Data transfer ranging from 806K (thousands of bytes per second) to 3,000K is a significant improvement over a PC hard disk and is of particular importance on the mainframe where many users require access to the same data on a centralized system. While the personal computer offers many benefits to the individual user, the mainframe must often serve hundreds of users with billions of bytes of data that can only be handled by large-capacity disk drives.

MAGNETIC TAPE

Early personal computers such as the Apple and the Commodore PET used magnetic tape for storing programs and data. These tape units were basically audio cassette recorders such as you would use for the recording and playback of music. While audio tape is an inexpensive means for storing data, it is many times slower than the slowest disk unit. Tape must be read sequentially from the beginning, causing an additional delay if the data required is located nearer the end of the tape.

For these reasons tape soon lost favor with personal computer users, and as disks and disk drives became less costly and more widely available, the disk was soon adopted in favor of tape. However, with disk came the problem of fast and efficient backup of the disk contents, as discussed earlier in this chapter. An important solution to the backup problem was the arrival of tape backups units that were designed to backup hard disk contents quickly and easily.

Using Tape to Back Up Hard Disk

The tape used for hard disk backup is often called a streaming tape because of its high-speed continuous movement as it is recording data from the disk. Tape backup systems are specialized hardware units that come with special software to ease the task of backing up hard disk contents. These systems are much different from the tape units used on earlier computers and cannot be used for data storage other than that required to backup the disk.

Most backup units use a tape cartridge (see Figure 4–10) that may be

FIGURE 4–10
A tape backup system and tape cartridge.

Courtesy of IBM.

replaced so that several levels of backup (grandfather, father, son) can be created. The cartridge contains a ¼-inch (0.635-cm) tape that can store up to 60M of data. Some units plug into a port and so may be shared between several computers in the office rather than purchasing a separate backup system for each PC. Backup tape units are also available with a built-in hard disk drive to offer a useful alternative to expanding disk storage as well as providing for file backup.

Some models permit backing up the disk by file so that only files that have been changed need to be copied to the tape. Other units back up the entire disk contents in one operation. Backing up the contents of a 10M disk can take from 3 to 30 minutes depending on the tape system used.

Tape Use on Mainframes

Mainframe tape drives, often called reel-to-reel tape drives, are quite different from those used for backup purposes on the PC. While the mainframe frequently uses tape for backup as well, it also relies on the large capacity available for data storage on tape. Magnetic tape on the mainframe is ½ inch (1.27 cm) in width and usually 2,400 feet (732 meters) long.

FIGURE 4–11

Data recorded along the surface of a nine-track tape using an 8-bit EBCDIC code and 1 parity bit for error checking.

Larry Long, *Introduction to Computers and Information Processing*, 2nd ed. (Englewood Cliffs, N.J.: Prentice Hall, 1988), p. 98. Reprinted by permission of Prentice-Hall, Inc., Englewood Cliffs, N.J.

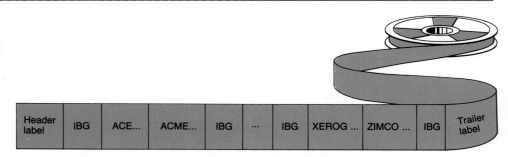

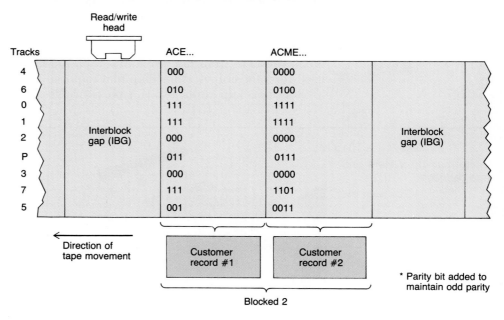

FIGURE 4–12　To reduce the amount of space lost between records, a group of logical records are combined into a block called a physical record. A physical record is written to the disk only after it has been filled with logical records by the program. Using this technique of blocking, the records require only one IBG per block and thus save space on the tape.

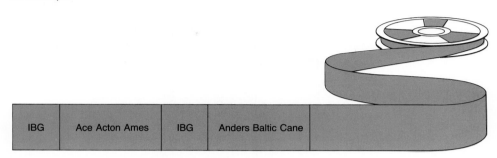

| IBG | Ace Acton Ames | IBG | Anders Baltic Cane | |

Tapes record mainframe data on nine separate tracks simultaneously, something like a nine-track stereo with all channels sounding at once. The nine tracks (Figure 4–11) correspond to 8 bits per byte in the EBCDIC or ASCII code plus 1 bit for error-checking purposes.

The amount of data that can be stored on the tape is largely determined by its density. **Density** expresses the number of bytes per inch (BPI) that can be stored on the length of the tape. A typical density on magnetic tape is 1,600 bytes per inch or 630 bytes per centimeter. To use an analogy, suppose each byte were a car on the thruway. Then 1,600 cars would form a line of about 5 miles (8 km) long. Quite a traffic jam! Other commonly used densities range between 800 and 6,250 bytes per inch.

This density suggests that we could store about 46M of data on one tape. However, tape on the mainframe is not quite this simple. Instead of moving continuously like streamer backup tape, the tape drive causes the tape to start and stop as each record is written so that processing in the CPU may occur between records. This start/stop motion causes a gap to be created between records called an **interrecord (IRG)** or **interblock gap (IBG)** (Figure 4–12). The presence of this gap reduces somewhat the total capacity of the tape.

Benefits of Magnetic Tape

- **High data rates.** Mainframe tape units have relatively high data rates with speeds on the order of 320,000 bytes per second not being uncommon.
- **Large storage capacity.** With lengths of 2,400 ft and densities up to 9,600 bytes per inch, tape has a high storage capacity. Tape is often used on the mainframe to store data that is not frequently accessed. Data such as personal tax records, aged accounts that are no longer active, and history files such as academic records for preceding years are all candidates for tape storage. These types of files can be stored on tape and then filed offline in a tape library until access to them is needed.
- **Low cost and ease of handling.** A reel of tape costs less than $20, making the cost per record only a fraction of a cent. Tape is reusable, and so when the data is no longer needed, other information may be recorded over it. A reel of tape is easily handled, and in large installations automated tape handling devices can select tapes from a library and mount them on the tape drive when they are needed.

Disks for computers come in a variety of sizes and capacities. Magnetic disks shown here range from a multi-level pack used on mainframe computers to the mini-floppy diskette for the personal computer.

Courtesy of BASF Systems Corporation; IBM.

Limitations of Tape

While tape would seem to be without any serious limitations, there is one major factor that limits its use. Data on a tape must be read or written sequentially from the beginning to the end of the tape. No direct access to an individual record is possible without reading all the records that precede the one required. For online and interactive systems this is unacceptable because the time required to find a given record would be too great. Thus disk is used whenever direct accessing of records is required.

FIGURE 4–13
The relationship of items in a data base. The smallest element of definition is the field. Records are composed of one or more fields that relate to a specific activity or transaction. All related records are recorded together in a file, and a collection of these elements is called a data base.

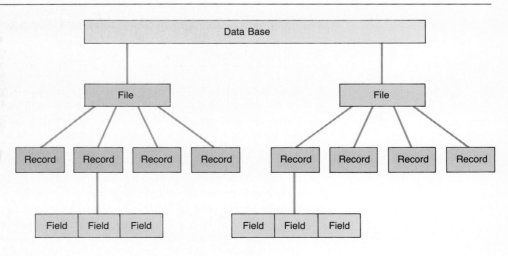

ACCESS METHODS

In any application, whether it is accounts receivable or payable, inventory or payroll, data needs to be stored on files in a manner that is easily accessible. As we have discussed earlier in the book, a file consists of a number of records as shown by the relationship in Figure 4–13 among a field, a record, and a file.

A field refers to items such as an account number, item description, unit cost, quantity, or date. A record contains a single transaction such as all fields that relate to the purchase of an item. At the next level is the file, which contains all records for a given application. There will be many files, including an accounts receivable file, an inventory file, a payroll file, and so on in a business system.

In general a collection of related files in a system is called a data base, but in some cases a data base will be a single file composed of elements of data that might otherwise exist in several files. A more complete discussion on this concept will be found in the data base chapter.

Sequential Files

Sequential tape or disk files are files whose records are stored in a consecutive order. Records in a sequential file are ordered one after the other from the beginning to the end of the file. The contents of each record do not need to bear any relationship to the order of these records because the term sequential refers to the physical order of the records. But, in reality, records are often stored in some order such as account number sequence or customer name sequence. Sequential files must always be read in this order whenever they are used by a program.

Sequence Fields

Records on a sequential file are often stored in a logical sequence. For example, accounting records would be stored in order by account number on the sequential file (Figure 4–14). The first record in the file would contain the lowest account number, the second record the next highest account and so on. The last record on the file would be the highest account number. The account number is called the sequence field. Notice that there are often gaps between the account numbers. Account number 120 is first but the next account on the file is account 122. This is a usual characteristic of sequential files and has some implications for programmers who write programs to handle these file types.

The previous example showed records in sequence by account number. Other files may use a customer number or an employee number. In some cases several fields may be involved in the sequence. If there are two sequence fields such as salesperson number within region we would have a major (region) and minor (salesperson) sequence. There could be more fields involved in the sequence depending on the type of data and the characteristics of the application.

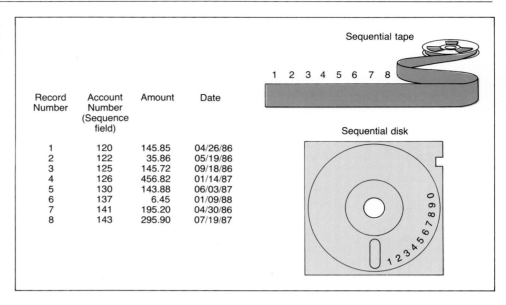

FIGURE 4–14
Records stored in sequence on account number in a sequential file.

Record Number	Account Number (Sequence field)	Amount	Date
1	120	145.85	04/26/86
2	122	35.86	05/19/86
3	125	145.72	09/18/86
4	126	456.82	01/14/87
5	130	143.88	06/03/87
6	137	6.45	01/09/88
7	141	195.20	04/30/86
8	143	295.90	07/19/87

When to Use a Sequential File

A significant disadvantage of sequential files is the need to read through the file from beginning to end, even if only a few records are required for processing. Some PC applications such as word processing or spreadsheets give you very little choice and almost always use sequential files.

Other software, particularly data base software, may give an option. Choosing to process a file sequentially will depend on the needs of the application. A payroll file may need to be accessed weekly to product paychecks and, of course, all employee records need to be read so that everyone will get paid. A high level of activity such as this would justify a sequential access method.

In other cases, using a sequential file would be inefficient and time consuming. For example, an employee personnel file may need to be accessed only occasionally to change an employee's address, or basic salary, a tax deduction, or a department. Because these changes seldom occur for most employees, in any given time period possibly less than 1 percent of the file will be affected. A low activity such as this will benefit from the use of a nonsequential file organization.

Nonsequential Files

Personal computers have a second form of file access known as **relative files.** This access method permits the direct access to any record in the file without the need to read any of the other records. An indexed organization is also used on some systems that uses an index to access a given record. This method has some advantages over the relative file as we will see shortly.

Relative files

Consider an application where 1,000 employee records are to be maintained on a disk file with direct access capability. For some uses the file needs to

FIGURE 4–15   Relative record organization on disk.

Record
Number

0001	Employee 1	0002	Employee 2	0003	Employee 3	0004	Employee 4
0005	Employee 5	0006	Employee 6	0007	Employee 7	0008	Employee 8
0009	Employee 9	0010	Employee 10	0011	Employee 11	0012	Employee 12
0013	Employee 13	0014	Employee 14	0015	Employee 15	0016	Employee 16
0017	Employee 17	0018	Employee 18	0019	Employee 19	0020	Employee 20
0997	Employee 997	0998	Employee 998	0999	Employee 999	1000	Employee 1000

be read sequentially, but most of the time only the record affected by the processing needs to be accessed due to a low file-activity ratio. Conveniently, these employees each have a unique employee number from 0001 to 1000 that could act as a key to identify the record. In such a situation a relative file would be an appropriate file organization method to use.

In a relative file, records are stored consequently as shown in Figure 4–15. Each record in the file has a key that identifies the record and permits direct access to it. The first record in the file has a key of 0001, the second record's key is 0002, and so on. Record one thousand would have a key of 1000. For random accessing of the file, the program supplies the key, and the record specified is supplied to the program.

Relative files on a personal computer's disk can be accessed quickly because each record can be read without the need to read other records in the file. In this inventory system the record for any item in stock can be referenced in seconds and updated immediately to show stock replenishment or the shipping of an in-stock item.

Courtesy of Sperry Corporation.

Pros and cons of relative files

Other than the benefits of the access method, a relative file uses disk space efficiently. Records are stored consecutively from the beginning of the file. Each disk address contains a record so there is no space wasted between records other than what the disk drive needs for its operation. This space efficiency, however, would not apply if some of the keys were not needed. Suppose there were no employees with numbers 0500 to 0549. These 50 records would still occupy space on disk, although they are not needed by the application. Thus relative files are most useful in applications where there are few gaps in the keys.

This is clearly a limitation. Relative files are fine if the application uses consecutive numbers such as the employee file mentioned already. But many applications do not fit so neatly into this pattern.

What about the organization that stocks parts from several suppliers and must record them under the supplier's number. These numbers may not be consecutive or may have many gaps between groups of numbers. Part numbers can also be alphanumeric, which creates other problems.

Even though the employee file, discussed before, looks foolproof, it could be changed over time. Employees quit, and their number is discontinued after a reasonable time period. New employees are hired and must be given new numbers, the company expands, and so on. Of course, we could suggest that employee numbers get recycled, but this may then cause excessive work to keep track of unused numbers.

Because of the inherent problems with relative files, other methods such as indexed files have become more popular and, in their own way, have resolved these problems with keys and storage efficiency.

Indexed Files

Many information system applications require the capability to access data from a file either sequentially or directly. Payroll is an excellent example of this type of requirement. On a weekly, biweekly, or monthly basis, a payroll file needs to be accessed sequentially to generate paychecks for each employee in the company. In this situation there is a high file-activity ratio, and direct accessing of the records would be inefficient and would not make it easier to generate the checks.

At other times new employees may be hired by the company and existing employees may require changes to their records such as an address change, income level, or the department in which they work. Because these types of changes are usually minor and represent a limited access requirement, direct accessing is a much more efficient way to access the records.

One method used for achieving the capability of both sequential and direct access to the same file is the use of indexed files, known as **indexed sequential access method (ISAM)** and a similar technique called **virtual storage access method (VSAM)** on mainframe computers.

Indexed File Organization

Records in an indexed file are stored sequentially, but an index is used to identify each record in the file. Every record contains a key that uniquely identifies the record and is used for directly accessing it. Because records are stored in record key sequence, ordered from the lowest key to the highest key in the file, the file can be read sequentially from the beginning to the end of the file.

Unlike relative files, indexed files do not require a record for each key value. If there is no record for a specific key, such as record 0003, it simply does not exist in the file, and the missing record will not occupy any space on the file. Thus gaps in record sequence have no adverse effect on storage efficiency in ISAM.

Figure 4–16 shows an indexed file that consists of the data organized much like a relative file. In addition to the data is an index. Some data base programs, such as dBASE IV, store this index as a separate file from the data. The index supplies information about the location of the record within the file, which is how records can be accessed directly instead of reading sequentially through the file. As records in the file are added or deleted the index is updated accordingly.

New records are added to the end of the file, and the index is updated to show the location of the record. For example, record 121 would be appended to the end of the file, but the index would record it in the second position to correspond with the sequence of other records (Figure 4–17). Using this technique requires that only the index needs to be maintained in order and, because the index is considerably shorter than the data file, this method results in more efficient file handling.

Other indexing methods can be much more complex than this. Mainframe indexed sequential organization (ISAM), which is also used on some smaller computers, uses several levels of indexes to provide for faster access to extremely large files. Recent mainframe systems use a virtual storage access method (VSAM), which is somewhat more involved than ISAM, but operates more efficiently, especially when many records are added to or deleted from the file.

Secondary storage in the form of disk or tape files is an important component of a complete computer system. Most primary-use data will be stored on disk

FIGURE 4–16
Indexed file organization on disk.

Index	120	1	122	2	125	3	126	4
	130	5	137	6	141	7	143	8

Record Number	Account Number	Amount	Date
1	120	145.85	04/26/86
2	122	35.86	05/19/86
3	125	145.72	09/18/86
4	126	456.82	01/14/87
5	130	143.88	06/03/87
6	137	6.45	01/09/88
7	141	195.20	04/30/86
8	143	295.90	07/19/87

FIGURE 4–17
Adding record 121 to the end of the indexed file causes a new entry in the index that identifies the record's location in the file.

Index	120	1	121	9	122	2	125	3	126	4
	130	5	137	6	141	7	143	8		

Record Number	Account Number	Amount	Date
1	120	145.85	04/26/86
2	122	35.86	05/19/86
3	125	145.72	09/18/86
4	126	456.82	01/14/87
5	130	143.88	06/03/87
6	137	6.45	01/09/88
7	141	195.20	04/30/86
8	143	295.90	07/19/87
9	121	165.23	06/15/88

with tape available for backup on the PC and some low-use data on the mainframe. When choosing the right disk drive, you will need to consider both speed and data capacity to suit the needs of the application. Then the data can be stored in either a sequential or some type of direct access mode. Many applications will benefit from using a data base that can access data either sequentially or directly depending on the need of the system.

CHAPTER SUMMARY

1. Data stored in RAM is temporary and is lost when the power is turned off, so a secondary storage medium, such as disk, is used to retain data permanently.

2. On personal computer systems there are two basic forms of disks: removable disk, which includes floppy and disk cartridges, and fixed disk, which is commonly called hard disk.

3. Disk surfaces on the personal computer are divided into tracks and sectors, which aid the software in finding the data quickly and with a minimum of delay.

4. The mainstay of the PC disk industry is the $5\frac{1}{4}$-inch floppy disk with a capacity of 360K. It consists of a flexible mylar platter enclosed in a sturdy storage envelope that protects the recording surface. The $3\frac{1}{2}$-inch disk is becoming increasingly popular.

5. Hard disks (also known as Winchester disks) are used for their speed, convenience, and high storage capacity of from 10 to 100M.

6. Disks in general offer high access speed, both sequential and direct accessing of data, high storage capacity, and low storage cost.

7. A disk directory lists the names of all files on the disk, the size of each file, the date and time they were last revised, and the amount of storage space remaining on the disk.

8. Directory organization on the hard disk can be thought of as a tree structure with the trunk as the root or parent directory containing several branches known as

subdirectories. Each subdirectory may contain a number of files or lower-level subdirectories.

9. To guide against inadvertant loss, experienced computer users regularly backup their disk files so that an alternate source is available if data are lost.

10. A backup system in widespread use in information systems is called the grandfather, father, son method. The son is the most recent backup, while the father and grandfather are previous backups.

11. Using RAM disk involves allocating part of memory for the use of disk files that reside there while running an application. Instead of going to disk for the program or files, the application can access these in the RAM disk area significantly improving access times.

12. CD ROMs are beginning to be used in the computer industry because of their large storage capacity of from 540M to 2G. CD devices use a laser beam to read data that has been stored as a series of bubbles on the surface.

13. Mainframe disks are useful because of their very high storage capacity of over 1G per drive. High access speeds also make these disks useful for systems where there are many users accessing the same data.

14. Tape units on personal computers are mainly used for backup of hard disk data while on mainframes tape is frequently used to store data offline that is not frequently needed. Tape is low cost, has a high data rate and large storage capacity, but is limited by its sequential only access method.

15. Sequential tape or disk files are files whose records are stored in a consecutive order. Records in a sequential file are ordered one after the other from the beginning to the end of the file and must be read in this order.

16. A sequence field is a field such as an account number that is used to determine the order of records within a file.

17. Relative files use an access method that permits direct access to any record in the file without the need to read any of the other records. Relative files are fine if the application uses consecutive keys but are inefficient when there are gaps in the key values.

18. An indexed file stores records sequentially, but an index is used to identify the location of each record in the file. Every record contains a key that uniquely identifies the record and is used for directly accessing it. Also, because records are stored in record key sequence, ordered from the lowest key to the highest key in the file, the file can be read sequentially from the beginning to the end of the file.

IMPORTANT TERMS AND CONCEPTS			
Access arm	File	Relative file
Access time	Fixed disk	Removable disk
Backup	Floppy disk	Root
CD ROM	Hard disk	Secondary storage
Data base	Indexed file	Sector
Data rate	Indexed sequential	Sequence field
Directory	access method	Sequential file
Disk cartridge	(ISAM)	Subdirectory
Field	RAM disk	Tape backup system
	Read/write head	Track
	Record	

Fill-in Questions

1. A(n) _____ disk generally has the capacity for 10M to over 100M in the larger personal computers.

2. The _____ disk drive uses removable disks that are placed in a protective sleeve when not in use.

3. A list of files contained on a disk is known as a _____. This list may be displayed by a DOS command or by user software.

4. The _____ _____ is positioned on the surface of the disk by the access arm to read or write data magnetically.

5. A(n) _____ allows several related files to be accessed either sequentially or directly.

6. A(n) _____ _____ provides a fixed disk drive that may be mounted in an empty expansion card slot in the computer.

Matching Questions

Match each term with the description given below.
a. root   d. ISAM
b. data rate   e. CD ROM
c. RAM disk   f. tape backup system

____*c*____ 1. One way to speed up the use of software is to place some of the program in memory. This method lets memory act like a disk drive.

____*f*____ 2. This is one way of creating a grandfather, father, son copy of the contents of a hard disk.

____*e*____ 3. This device provides storage of large amounts of data, but the computer cannot usually write data to the device.

____*a*____ 4. This is the first level of a hierarchical subdirectory from which other directories branch.

____*d*____ 5. A file access method that permits reading records either sequentially or directly.

____*b*____ 6. This term refers to the number of bytes per second that data are read from a disk drive.

Discussion Questions

1. Why is it necessary to have secondary storage devices such as magnetic disk available on computer systems?

2. Describe the characteristics of a disk drive distinguishing between floppy and hard disk.

3. Discuss the terms data rate and access time.

4. What are the benefits of using a hard disk over a floppy?

5. Discuss the need for a disk directory. When are subdirectories useful?

6. Explain why backup files are necessary. How are hard disks backed up?

7. What is meant by the term RAM disk? Explain how RAM disk is used on a personal computer.

8. Discuss the growing importance of CD ROM or optical disks on personal computers.

9. Identify some of the fundamental differences between disk on a mainframe and a PC.

10. Explain the use of tape on personal computer systems.

11. What is the fundmental limitation of tape? What use is tape on mainframe computer systems?

12. Discuss the characteristics and use of sequential files. Why are sequential files limited in their use?

13. Explain the organization of a relative file. What are the benefits and disadvantages of relative files?

14. Explain the characteristics of an indexed file as used on personal computers.

Computers and Communications

A VIEW OF THE CHAPTER AHEAD

After Reading This Chapter You Will Understand:

- The use of data communication between computers and the need for local area networks.

- The types of communications hardware required for transmitting and receiving data.

- The different types of online communications services.

Many forms of communication have been developed to help us humans exchange information and ideas more effectively. There is the most effective one-on-one verbal conversation, but, when we are farther apart, the telephone or a letter is used. Other, less intimate, ways of communicating are radio and television, sometimes using satellite relay of material, and there are also books and publications that relay information to the reader. Most of us have some familiarity with all these systems, but what about computer communication?

Serious use of computer communication began with mainframe systems back in the 1960s. At this time, mainframe computers were centralized systems with no means of communication between them other than physically moving data, in the form of tape or disk, from one computer to the other. As the need to share data increased, communications systems were developed so that computers could in effect talk to each other, usually over ordinary telephone lines.

Several types of needs were satisfied with the use of communications, and they have not essentially changed with the advent of personal computers. Although the circumstances may be different, the requirement for data communications is the same whether a large or small computer system is used. But due to increased availability, new markets and uses of communications systems have evolved. Some of these needs are the following.

- **Data sharing.** Computers sometimes need to communicate when one computer contains data that is needed by another computer system. For example, a stock analyst needs the daily stock quotations on her computer. Rather than going to the stock exchange and copying the data to a floppy disk and then taking the disk to her computer, the data can be received over communication lines from a stock service in a manner similar to using the telephone.

- **Inquiry.** Sometimes it is the computer user who requires the data that is located on a remote computer system. For example, the car dealer needs to know when a car will be delivered. Rather than physically go to the computer containing the data, the salesperson can make a remote inquiry and have the needed information delivered through the communication system.

- **Data entry.** An insurance agent needs to send daily sales to the company's head office computer. This data is collected during the day, and when the agent arrives at the hotel that night he can leisurely send the data over the telephone to the remote computer where it is stored for future use.

Data sharing.

Courtesy of Charles Feil/Stock Boston.

Inquiry.

Courtesy of Christopher Springmann/
The Stock Market.

Data entry.

Courtesy of Hewlett-Packard Company.

In each of these cases, data communication via a transmission line communicates information either to the user or to the computer. A personal computer could be used for all these examples, or in some cases, a mainframe may be used or a combination of the two. In the following material we will see examples of how both personal computers and mainframes use data communication.

HOW DOES DATA TRANSMISSION WORK?

When you pick up the telephone to make a call to a friend, you can take for granted that the technology will work and the only skill you need to master is dialing the number. Now that data communications is out of its infancy, using a computer on a communications line is almost as easy. But, as we will see before the end of the chapter, data communications can have its own complexities, and there are many choices of different types of networks for a variety of needs.

A simple, yet useful, communications system is shown in Figure 5–1 where a single personal computer communicates with another PC. The computers are linked together by a **communications line,** which is usually a telephone line, unless they are located in close proximity to each other, such as in the same room or in the same building.

Because computers use digital transmission of data (the human voice is analog) a device called a modem is located at each computer. The modem at the sending computer translates computer talk (digital code) into an analog signal that can be sent over the communications line. Analog code consists of a series of beeps that sound something like Morse code when you hear it. The modem at the receiving computer takes this analog signal and converts it back to digital form that the receiving computer can understand.

FIGURE 5–1   The sending computer transmits a digital signal that is converted to analog by the local modem. This analog signal that represents the data is transmitted over a communications line to the remote modem. At this end the signal is converted back to digital and read by the receiving computer.

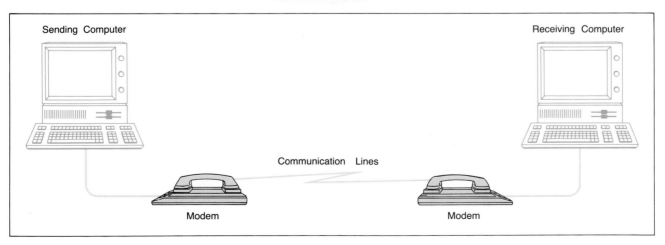

Sending Computer

Receiving Computer

Communication   Lines

Modem

Modem

A communications systems, such as this, might be used when one computer contains data on its disk that is needed by a second computer. Let's take an example of a franchise operation where the head office needs to have the sales figures sent to it each week from the branch office. The branch office computer becomes the sending computer and the head office computer is the receiving computer (see Figure 5–2). Data is transmitted over the telephone lines to the head office where it is received and stored on disk until needed for use.

Because a franchise typically has several branches, each branch may have its own computer and send its data in a similar manner to head office. In this example only one branch can transmit at one time. This situation is similar to three or four friends trying to phone you at one time. Only the one who gets you first will make contact, while the others will receive a busy signal and will need to try again later. With computer communcations there are networks and other devices that can get around this type of problem, but a simple communications system is not much different from a phone call.

Head office may also need to send data to the branches. Updated prices, information on new products, and other data can be transmitted to the branch from the head office computer. Then the head office becomes the sending computer and the branch the receiving.

Clearly there is extra hardware required when data communications is necessary between computers. In many instances there is a modem needed

FIGURE 5–2   A branch office for a franchise operation sends sales data weekly from its local computer to the head office computer over regular telephone lines. Each branch in the operation can send its data in a similar manner, but only one branch can send at a time.

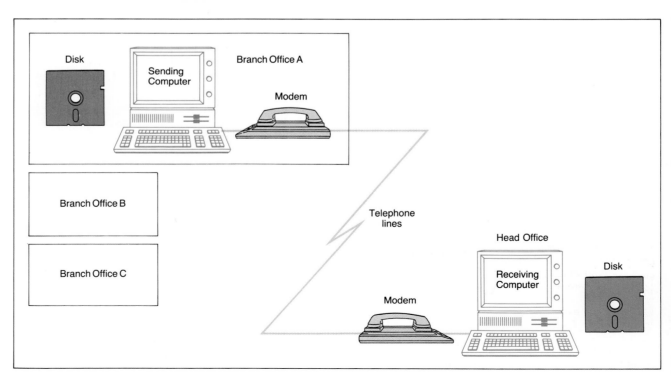

at each computer, while in other cases a special board in the computer may be required. In addition to hardware there are software requirements. A communications program will be necessary for many applications, while in other cases an existing program may provide communications capability. Some integrated packages such as Lotus Symphony, or word processors such as WordStar 2000, have a built-in communications section that makes it easy to transmit spreadsheets or word processing documents to remote computers and to receive data from these computers.

NETWORK TOPOLOGY

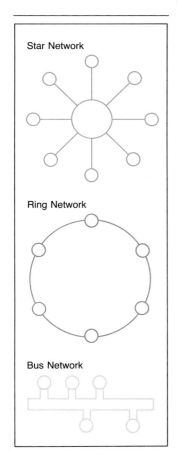

Star Network

Ring Network

Bus Network

FIGURE 5–3

Network topology. A star topology uses a central computer through which all other computers operate. Ring networks connect all computers together with each being of equal status. The bus network shares several computers or devices on the same network.

Networks are communications systems that provide a way for several computers to communicate with each other. Because communication needs vary, there are different types of networks available to satisfy the requirements of a variety of situations. Many networks connect a variety of computers, from micros and minis, to mainframes. Some connect several terminals with a central computer, while others use a more decentralized approach with several computers on the network.

Whatever the type of network, and mix of computers and terminals used, there are a few basic networks that form the core of communications systems. This physical organization is called **network topology,** and there are three basic types: the star, ring, and bus networks (Figure 5–3).

Networks such as these share the work load between several computers rather than having all the load on one central computer. Messages and data can be shared between users, and each user can manipulate their own data without the fear of destroying data needed by another operation.

Working at a local computer can be more efficient with fewer time delays than accessing a remote system. The user does not need to wait on an overloaded mainframe to answer her request but can get speedy responses from a local PC. Working on a local computer still gives easy access to remote data and programs located on the mainframe. And there is a sense of being in control when your work is done on a local desktop computer instead of some giant computer that no one really seems to understand.

There can also be a few disadvantages of networking computers. The extra hardware and software required can cost more than a single system, and there is the need for technical support at the remote location. Having copies of data bases on each computer can result in updating problems unless only a single, centralized data base is maintained. Then there is less control over security with many different computers and individuals who use them. But, in the view of most people, the benefits of networking computers far outweighs the disadvantages.

Star Network

A **star network** (Figure 5–4), such as AT&T's StarLAN network, is configured in a starlike pattern with a computer at the center of the pattern. The central computer is the **host** computer, which supplies information and computer resources to the other computers in the network. When the host is a mainframe, it often provides data base support to the other computers and supplies extra computing power when the node is a terminal.

A personal computer star network uses a PC as the host, which is called a **file server.** The central PC contains data bases and programs that are needed

These AT&T computers are linked together with the Star-LAN network. This network uses a star topology with a central host computer that acts as a file server to all personal computers on the network.

Courtesy of AT&T Archives.

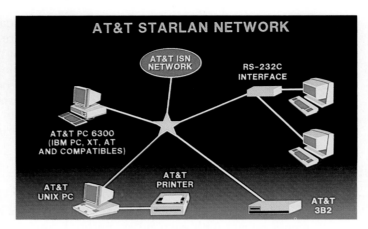

AT&T STARLAN NETWORK

AT&T ISN NETWORK

RS-232C INTERFACE

AT&T PC 6300 (IBM PC, XT, AT AND COMPATIBLES)

AT&T UNIX PC

AT&T PRINTER

AT&T 3B2

FIGURE 5–4 A star network used for a personal computing local area network. Each computer on the network shares data and software situated on the file server computer.

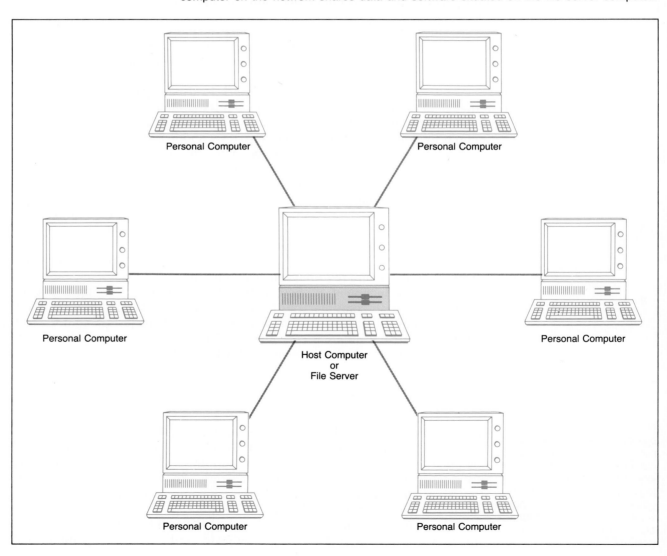

Personal Computer

Personal Computer

Personal Computer

Personal Computer

Host Computer or File Server

Personal Computer

Personal Computer

by the other computers. Rather than storing data and software on the local computer, the file server provides this service, thus eliminating duplication. Sharing programs can also reduce software cost by getting a network license rather than purchasing many separate copies of the program.

For personal computing, star networks are mainly used to connect a number of office's computers together and are also popular in educational settings for student use. The University of Waterloo's JANET Network is an example of such a configuration used by educational institutes, while AT&T's StarLAN is a network that is used in business settings. Coaxial cable or twisted-pair wire is used to attach each computer in the network, which makes movement of the computers to other locations difficult. Adding new computers to the network can also be disruptive to the existing network.

Computers on a star network cannot communicate directly with each other, which limits sharing of resources between them. Data can be passed to the central computer for subsequent sharing with other computers in the network, but this inhibits fast and efficient transmission of data where this procedure

A HIERARCHICAL STAR NETWORK

The central computer forms the hub of the starlike pattern to which other computers or terminals in the network are attached. In complex mainframe-based systems, such as those used by the banking industry, a node on the central hub can represent a computer located in a remote city. This node may itself be the hub of another star network to which other computers and terminals in that city are attached. The node in Boston is a computer that offloads much of the processing from the central computer in New York. Similar computer nodes in other centers take on local computing tasks, freeing the central system for major functions.

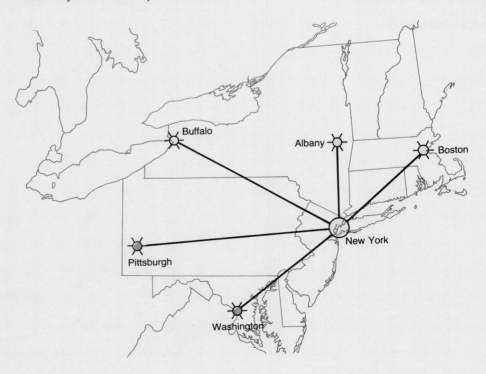

is frequently needed. A significant problem with star networks is the reliance upon the host computer. If this computer fails, all other computers on the network will either become nonoperational or be seriously limited in their operation due to lack of support from the host.

Ring Network

The **ring network** (Figure 5–5), such as IBM's Token-Ring network which is a variation of this concept, connects a number of computers to a continuous communication ring. There is no host computer, but each computer on the ring can communicate with all other computers. Data is passed along the ring from one computer to the next until it arrives at the receiving computer. All other computers simply pass the data along. In one form of ring network a nonfunctioning computer can cause an interruption of data traffic because it is unable to forward data.

A variation on this network permits a malfunctioning computer to be switched out of the ring, thus retaining communication with all remaining

FIGURE 5–5

A ring network ties all computers together on a single communication channel. A computer in the network can communicate with any other computer on the network by passing its data along the ring. Data not meant for a given computer is passed on until it reaches the system for which it is intended.

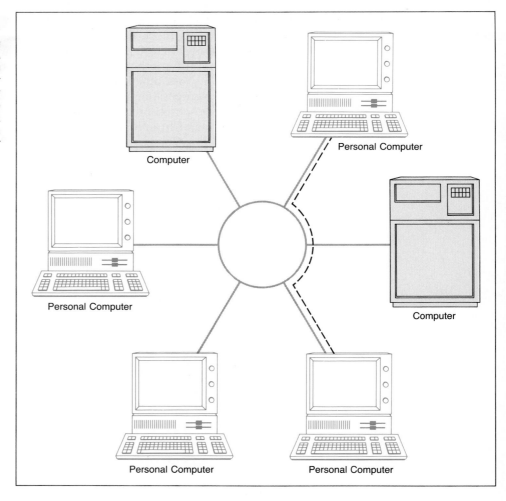

These personal computers are attached via IBM's Token-Ring network. This network combines the physical properties of a star network with the operational or logical qualities of a ring network. An electronic token is passed between the computers to determine who has transmission priority.

Courtesy of Sperry Corporation.

computers. This makes the ring network more reliable and not dependent upon any one computer in the ring. If one goes down, all the others can continue to operate.

The cost of communication lines in a ring can also be less expensive because lines of the shortest distance between adjacent computers can be used rather than longer lines usually required in a star. Being attached to a ring network also simplifies the passing of data between computers. The two communicating computers need only talk to each other, while other computers in the system ignore their transmissions.

This benefit also has its side effects. Because all computers use the same network special codes and communications, controllers are needed to ensure that data flowing between two computers does not get confused with other transmissions going on at the same time with other computers in the system. By having access to any computer in the network, potential security problems exist, requiring passwords and other software protection to ensure that the right users have access to legitimate data.

Bus Network

Many of the problems associated with star or ring networks are resolved by using a bus network. A **bus network,** such as 3Com's Ethernet, is a local area network that uses a cable to interconnect a series of computers and devices together. Often the cable is a coaxial cable, but twisted-pair wire or fiber optic cable can also be used. While this may seem similar to a ring network, the devices on the bus are each independent of the other.

Transmission on a bus network consists of messages that contain a device address as part of the data. Instead of a central computer, as in a star network, each device on the bus has its own CPU that recognizes when a message is sent to it. Additional devices may be added to the bus by attaching a new node to the cable at any point, and similarly a device is as easily removed. Failure on the part of any one device has no effect on other devices in the network.

A bus network simplifies the sharing of devices as shown in Figure 5–6. Several computers may share data resources as well as use a common printer, plotter, or remote mainframe system. The bus is not without some problems. Shared cabling means that when data is being sent to one device, the others must wait. So if printing is going on, disk access is impossible. A solution to this problem is to use memory buffers at the slower devices, such as a printer, to store data and thus free the channel for other messages. Many local area networks use this type of networking.

FIGURE 5–6

A bus network connects all nodes by a common cable. Messages are sent along the cable with a unique address for each device, so only the device recognizing the address receives the data.

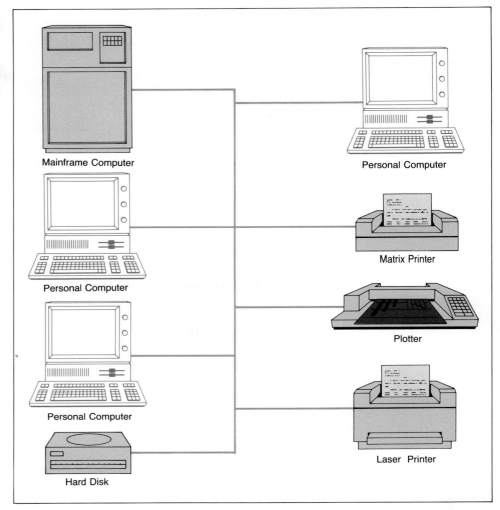

Mainframe Computer

Personal Computer

Personal Computer

Matrix Printer

Plotter

Personal Computer

Hard Disk

Laser Printer

LOCAL AREA NETWORKS

A **local area network (LAN)** can be likened to having your own private telephone network, but in this case we are referring to a computer network. A LAN might be thought of as the third utility in a building, after the telephone and electrical utilities. The term "local" means that the computers and devices are located in the same vicinity. Often a local area network serves computer devices within the same office space or in several adjacent offices. In other situations, the network can serve users several miles apart. IBM's PC Net can use a maximum coaxial cable length of 6.3 miles (10 kilometers) while Corvus Systems' Omninet uses twisted-pair wire to reach 0.8 miles. Speeds are up to 1 million bits per second (1Mbps). LANs are not intended for cross-country or international communcation.

LANs use different network topologies, but many have adopted the bus

IBM'S TOKEN-RING NETWORK

In theory, networks often seem to have simple topologies, but in practice more complexities are often found. The IBM Token-Ring network is one of these examples. Physically, the IBM Token-Ring network has a starlike topology with individual stations connected to a central access unit. But inside the multistation access unit the multiconductor cables are electrically connected like a ring.

To operate, the network uses an access method called token passing. An electronic token is circulated among the stations while they are waiting idly for some activity. When a station has a message to transmit, it waits until the token arrives at its location. It then takes the token, something like a relay runner taking the baton, and proceeds to send its message. All other stations must wait until the token becomes free again. In this way stations cannot interfere with one another's transmissions.

IBM's Token-Ring network comes as a starter kit, which includes one multistation access unit, with cables and interface cards for four stations. Cables can be either coaxial (Type 1 system) or twisted-pair wires (Type 2). Up to 260 stations can be connected together with data-grade coaxial cable by using multiple access units in the network. Seventy-two stations are possible when twisted-pair wire is used for the network.

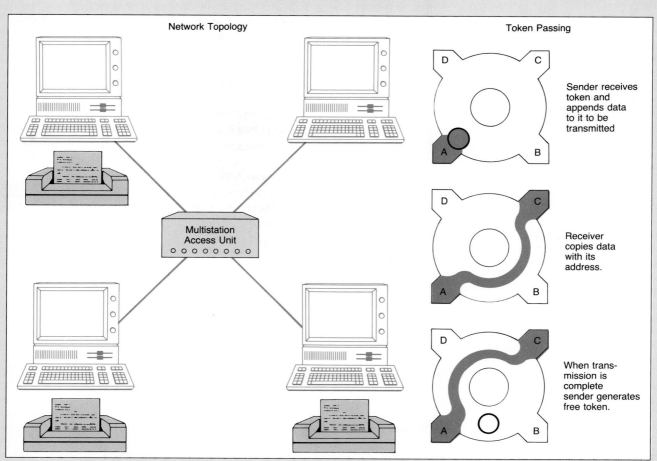

Network Topology

Multistation Access Unit

Token Passing

Sender receives token and appends data to it to be transmitted

Receiver copies data with its address.

When transmission is complete sender generates free token.

network concept described previously. Businesses use local area networks for a variety of reasons, including many of the following.

- Sharing common data located on a central hard disk.
- Sharing a common printer to reduce hardware costs or to make several types of printers such as a high-speed dot matrix and a laser printer available to all computers on the network.
- Simplifying communication with other computers in the business, as when electronic mail is used for internal management communication.
- Saving software costs by permitting the use of network licensing, which is less expensive than separate copies of the same program.
- Providing a backup of computer resources. If one computer in the network is down, the job can often be done by another computer on the same LAN by transferring tasks to the available computers.
- Helping to increase user productivity.

ONLINE COMMUNICATIONS SERVICES

When was the last time you stopped by the library at the last minute to look up a reference for a paper you're writing only to find that someone else beat you to the document or reference book? With the more than 3,000 online data services available today, you can now access a huge variety of information from your home computer. Services such as The Source, CompuServe, Dow Jones News/Retrieval, and Bibliographic Retrieval System (BRS) offer access to a wide assortment of data bases that accommodate many needs.

Some services offer special interest data or such features as electronic mail or an electronic bulletin board where you can advertise items for sale or purchase. Other services, such as The Source, provide access to many data bases to address the needs of a broad variety of users. Hundreds of subjects are available through online data bases, including such topics as airline schedules, investment, foreign news, sports, UPI news, and so on.

The costs for online services vary, but most charge a connect fee of from $0.08 to $2.00 per minute depending on the type of service supplied. Some have a minimum monthly charge. Some services have a reduced rate for non-prime-time users, usually for use after midnight.

There are three fundamental types of online communications services.

- **Videotext.** These services are the most widely used and provide a broad range of services fo home, education, business, and professional users. The Source, Compu-Serve, and Delphi are all videotex operations. Included in these services are serious applications such as data bases and communications as well as such fun things as games and chat features (discussed shortly).
- **Communications.** This type of service offers electronic mail, bulletin boards, and message services. Primarily designed for business users, this category is represented by Dialcom, EasyLink, and MCI Mail.
- **Data base.** BRG, Dialog, and Infomaster are all data base services. These are aimed at the business and educational research community by providing data on books in print, magazine bibliographies, the census, and stock futures.

Some online services provide access to fundamental types of information, while others give broad access. Some services give access to others that can

COMMUNICATION SERVICES

CompuServe was one of the first communication services for computer users. Here the subscriber is provided with services that include shopping and banking.

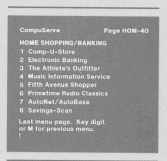

A CompuServe menu for home shopping and banking.
Courtesy of CompuServe.

Many communication services are text oriented. Viewdata is one of the few that combines graphic material with text such as used in this online encyclopedia.

Viewdata combines graphics and text.
Courtesy of Viewdata Corporation.

The Source is a popular communication service for business and professional people. Items ranging from up-to-date news to travel arrangements can be made by computer.

A menu of services from The Source.
Courtesy of The Source Information Network.

Using graphics and text in an online communication service makes it possible to offer some unusual services. Here a shop by computer service is made available.

A communications service sales screen.
Courtesy of General Instrument Corporation.

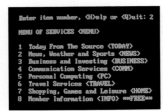

```
Enter item number, <H>elp or <Q>uit: 2

MENU OF SERVICES <MENU>

1  Today From The Source <TODAY>
2  News, Weather and Sports <NEWS>
3  Business and Investing <BUSINESS>
4  Communication Services <COMM>
5  Personal Computing <PC>
6  Travel Services <TRAVEL>
7  Shopping, Games and Leisure <HOME>
8  Member Information <INFO> **FREE**
```

FIGURE 5-7

A menu from The Source.

Courtesy of The Source Information Network.

save the expense of subscribing to several different services if the needs of the user are extensive. In the following section we will look at some of the online services.

The Source

Source Telecomputing Corp., a subsidiary of The Reader's Digest, provides an online information service that is popular with business and professional users. The Source might be considered an information utility because it offers so many different services such as online shopping, news services such as UPI, *The New York Times* Consumer Database, New York and American stock exchange quotations, and information desired by special interest groups. Business users may find the computer conferencing service of particular value. And hackers may find the chat mode useful, where they can connect directly with other users and exchange ideas and information in real time.

CompuServe

One of the oldest services, CompuServe was established in 1969 and now is one of the most diverse of the communications services available. Business, professional, educational, and other users have access to electronic mail, reference works, bulletin boards, travel services, electronic conferencing, and the Official Airline Guide.

Like The Source, CompuServe offers real-time access to other users, so they can chat about topics of similar interest. CompuServe also offers several services where messages can be forwarded to other users of the system. Electronic mail supplies users with a mailbox where mail can be received and forwarded electronically. There is also a bulletin board where messages can be posted for anyone to read. This service is used for getting help with technical problems, selling personal items, or advertising for items needed.

Infomaster

Infomaster is a service of Western Union Telegraph Co., which has access to over 720 online data bases. Rather than subscribing separately to these data base services, they are provided through this one system. Included in the array of offerings are BRS Information Technologies, NewsNet, VuText Information Service, and MedScan for searching medical data bases. Users of Western Union's EasyLink electronic mail are automatically supplied with InfoMaster service as well.

Using Infomaster gives a choice of three different search modes. The first lets Infomaster choose the data base, the second lets you choose the data base you want, and the third search is by the specific name of the company about which you want data.

Dow Jones News/Retrieval

As the name implies, this service is from Dow Jones & Co., Inc. Clearly this is a stock investment service. In addition to the expected stock information,

Dow Jones provides in-depth company reports from Disclosure, Investext, and Standard & Poor's. To compete with the many other services being offered, Dow Jones also offers weather reports and online shopping. Software is also available for users who want to combine the stock information from the Dow Jones with a spreadsheet such as Lotus 1-2-3.

Electronic Mail

E-mail is a generic name for a system based on a central computer with many PCs attached in a star network fashion (Figure 5–8). Special software in each computer provides a standard base from which communications proceed. Electronic mail replaces public mail only if both the sender and receiver subscribe to the same service. But a variation of E-mail prints out the letter at the receiving end, which is then delivered by the local postal service.

A user of E-mail sends a message by logging onto the network and entering a password to gain access. Then he proceeds by typing a letter on his computer. The letter includes a destination, which can be a name and address or a mailbox number, depending on the system. When the letter has been typed, it is stored in the central computer until the recipient logs onto her computer.

Most E-mail users check their "mailbox" several times a day and thus get messages within a few minutes or hours after they were sent rather than days or weeks by more traditional means. Some systems in place today are worldwide and have subscribers in Canada, the United States, Europe, South America, and truly remote locations. This type of system is particularly popular among universities where researchers in related disciplines can keep in touch with their colleagues.

FIGURE 5–8   An E-mail system uses a central computer to collect mail. Users dial in to send or receive mail, which is stored under their box number or by name and user identification.

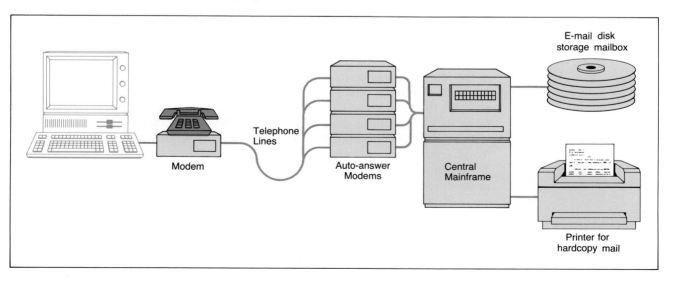

A personal computer used to send and receive electronic mail through a communications service.

Janet Wilson has given up licking stamps in favor of an E-mail system that lets her send mail electronically. When she has a letter or report to mail, she simply sits down at her home computer and, with her communications software, dials the number of MCI Mail, an E-mail service.

When MCI Mail responds to her call, Janet enters a password and a seven-digit mail ID. If there is mail waiting for her to read, MCI notifies her with an on-screen message. She then sends her mail either by typing it directly online or, in the case of a longer report that she would have typed earlier, by uploading the report to MCI.

After Janet has finished her session and signed off, the E-mail system sends the messages on to the various recipients. Depending on the urgency of a message, Janet could have coded it to be held until the recipient signed on to MCI and received the letter. If it was more urgent, and the recipient did not look at his mail, then the E-mail service could type a hard copy of the document and route it either overnight or by U.S. mail to the recipient.

E-mail services are generally substantially less costly than express mail such as Federal Express. The important consideration is that the recipient also subscribe to the same service; otherwise using the overnight hard copy service can result in comparable costs. Some E-mail services also provide access to other online data services as discussed in the text. Business E-mail services are also available for intracorporation mail. These are potentially the most widely used systems because of the need for fast mail delivery within the many branches and offices of a large organization.

Bulletin Board Services

Many organizations use a bulletin board service (BBS) because the system is installed easily and inexpensively. All that is required is a personal computer, a telephone line, a modem, and some software. Numerous colleges and universities have set up electronic bulletin boards for student and faculty access to announcement of new programs, tutorial help, message passing, and even student dating services.

Students wanting to sell an old car, or some textbooks, might find a purchaser through the BBS. Some bulletin boards also provide some entertainment in the form of games or software to help with academic needs such as statistical packages. Bulletin boards can also be used by business to provide needed services to customers. For example, *PC Magazine* uses this method to provide program code from its magazine to subscribers by downloading the program to the personal computer over the telephone. Special-purpose BBSs also exist for pharmacists and doctors to check on recent drug releases.

Because of the small investment required to install a bulletin board, many of them are free, while others have a minimal subscription rate.

MICRO-MAINFRAME LINKS

Many networks and message services involve a linkage between mainframe and personal or microcomputers. In most cases the central system is the mainframe with the data base and other features while the subscriber to the service uses a PC. These systems have a natural user interface, and often the user is unaware that a mainframe is even being accessed.

But there are many applications where the PC user needs access to data that is located on a mainframe: data that was not designed with personal computers in mind. Large corporate systems frequently have systems that were designed before the advent of micros and as a result do not link naturally with the PC. Rather special software often needs to be written to permit the linking of PCs with mainframe data.

One of the differences between micro and mainframe is the internal coding system used. Micros use ASCII while mainframes (at least IBM's) use EBCDIC. Thus the software needs to make a conversion between these coding systems if compatibility is to occur.

PC software also stores data differently. While both PCs and mainframes use data bases the method of storing data on the two systems is vastly different. Then PCs frequently use spreadsheets, but data on the mainframe is not often in a format that a spreadsheet can use. Thus extra software is needed to do the conversion from the mainframe format to the PC, or vice versa.

Sending data from the PC to a mainframe or other PC is called **uploading.** Receiving data from a mainframe or other PC to your computer is called **downloading.** Communications software is now available that assists in the uploading and downloading of data although there are many special cases on mainframes that would require unique programs to be written to download to the PC successfully.

TELECOMMUNICATIONS HARDWARE

Connecting a personal computer to another PC or to a large mainframe requires both software and hardware. Because computers are essentially digital devices and communication lines are analog there is a basic lack of compatibility between them. As Figure 5–9 shows there is a big difference between an analog and a digital signal. The analog signal varies in tone something like a musician playing a tune on a flute, or if you prefer, a synthesizer. Digital signals are more like the dots and dashes of Morse code. The same tone is always used, but the presence or absence of the tone and its length determines the differences in value.

FIGURE 5–9
The difference between an analog and digital signal explains why a modem is required to convert from one form to the other.

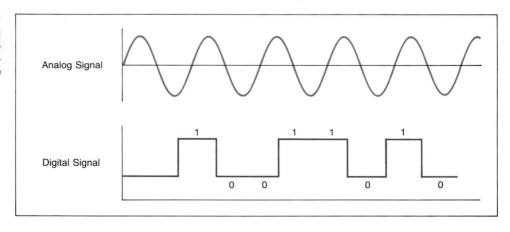

PCS DIRECTLY CONNECTED

Local area networks can be an exception to the rule of requiring a modem to connect two or more computers. Computers positioned near to each other are hardwired together with coaxial cable or by other means. In this case modems are not required because no external communication service such as telephone lines are required. Speeds may be in excess of 1 million bits per second.

While directly connecting two computers is economical when distances are short, using existing phone lines can be less expensive when distances more than a few hundred feet are considered.

FIGURE 5–10

A modem is a device for converting digital and analog signals.

Courtesy of Radio Shack, A Division of Tandy Corporation.

Modem

A **modem** (Figure 5–10) is an electronic device that converts a computer's digital signal to its analog equivalent. When receiving an analog signal, the modem converts it to digital form before sending it on to the computer. The name modem comes from the terms modulate and demodulate. **Modulation** is the process of converting digital signals to analog form, while **demodulation** is the opposite: converting an analog signal to digital.

When one PC communicates with another each one requires a modem as shown in Figure 5–11 (see the insert about exceptions to this rule). At the sending end, the computer transmits digital signals that flow as single bits into the modem. The modem converts these signals to analog form and sends them over the telephone line or other communication channel. At the receiving end, the analog signal arrives at the modem, and it converted to a sequence of digital bits. These are sent on to the computer that reads them as input data.

A communications program is needed with the modem to complete the link between remote computers. This Crosstalk Mark 4 screen shows some of the choices that are made when establishing computer communications over a telephone line. Communications choices are made by pointing at the options on the menu line at the top of the screen. Additional selections for each option are shown in the window below the menu.

Courtesy of Microstuf, Inc.

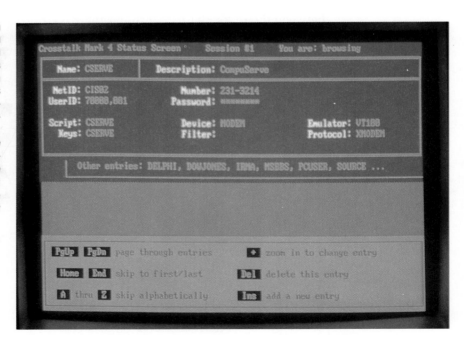

FIGURE 5–11   Transmitting data from one computer to another using a modem at each end. At the sending end, the modem converts digital code to analog signals that travel over the telephone lines. The receiving modem translates the analog signal to digital, which is accepted by the receiving computer.

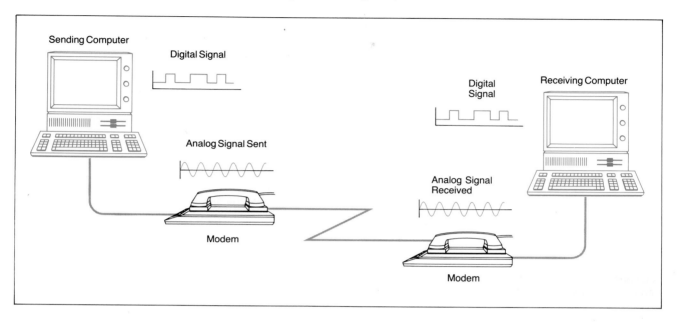

Bit rate

The rate or speed of transmission depends on the type of modem in use at each end of the communication line, the quality of the line, and the type of software used. Transmission speed is measured in **bits per second (bps).** Speeds of 300, 1,200, and 2,400 bps are in common use on personal computers, with some systems operating at up to 9,600 bps.

Modems are attached to the computer by an RS-232C serial connector. This is a standard connector used throughout the industry for serial data communications. The RS-232C standard is supported by the Electronic Industries of America (EIA) and is used when one bit at a time is transmitted between computer devices.

Types of modems

Modems come in several varieties. Early models were often **acoustic couplers** that made the connection to the telephone by placing the telephone receiver on rubber cups in the modem. Signals were audibly sent and received through the coupler. The advantage of the acoustic coupler is that no direct connection to the telephone line is necessary, and any standard telephone can be used to make the connection. Acoustic couplers are useful on the road for telephone connection such as in phone booths or motels rooms where direct connect is impossible. Although acoustic couplers are still available today, most other users prefer the direct-connect modem.

Direct-connect modems are plugged directly into the telephone line. With the move by phone companies to standard wall jacks the direct-connect modem can be attached permanently to the wall connector with the other end connected to the RS-232C port on the computer. A variation of this type of modem is the internal modem that is installed in an expansion slot inside the computer thus requiring no external component. With the popular use of designer phones and other multifunction business phones, the direct-connect modem is by far the most widely used.

A **smart modem** is usually a direct-connect modem with a built-in microprocessor. The smart modem was brought to popularity by Hayes Microcomputer Products, Inc., whose Smartmodem led the field in the use of these second-generation modems. A smart modem offers a number of features such as autoanswer capability where the modem will automatically, without human intervention, connect the line to the computer when a call comes over the phone. Smart modems can also dial the phone to make outgoing calls from the computer. To function fully, these modems are provided with software that gives

FIGURE 5–12   A multiplexor connects several slower-speed personal computers with one high-speed mainframe system. By allocating small amounts of CPU time to each PC, it appears that each user is getting total attention from the mainframe.

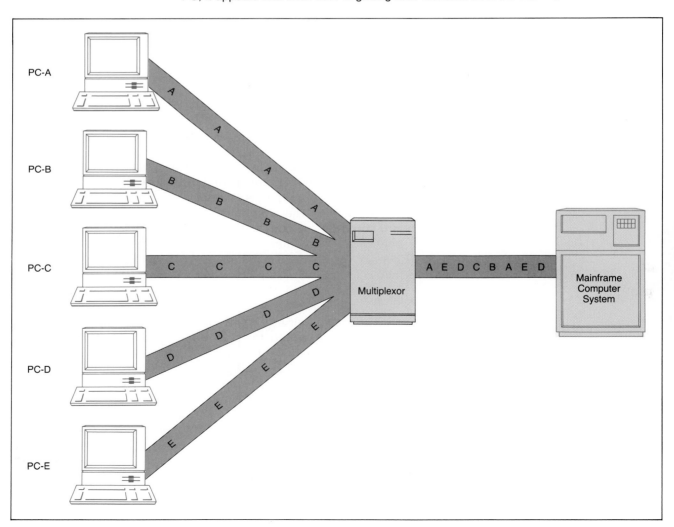

them the calling and autoanswering capability, including built-in telephone directories created by the computer user.

Multiplexor

Mainframe systems may need to service hundreds of personal computer users such as for online information systems discussed earlier. Connecting that many lines directly to the computer can be a problem because even mainframes have a limited number of ports, or channels, as they are called on the larger computers. A mainframe also operates at a much higher speed than does a single PC, and so it can service many different users simultaneously. To accomplish this seemingly magical feat, a **multiplexor** is used to combine several incoming lines into a single channel on the computer as shown in Figure 5–12.

As the relatively slow-speed signals arrive from each PC, they are combined by the multiplexor, which codes them so that their individual identities will not be lost. Each signal is then passed on to the mainframe at high speed where individual requests and inquiries are processed. Because of the mainframe's significantly greater speed, it appears to the PC that it is getting full attention. But in truth the mainframe is allocating small amounts of its time to each of the PCs to get the job done.

Front-end Processor

A **front-end processor** is actually another computer (often a minicomputer) that receives data prior to its being sent on to the mainframe. The purpose of the front-end processor is to take some of the processing load off of the mainframe, which may be overloaded with processing duties (see Figure 5–13). As requests are received from a remote computer, they are first interrogated by the front-end processor. This computer checks incoming data for errors and provides communications links with the outside world. Only acceptable requests are then passed on to the mainframe for processing.

FIGURE 5–13
A front-end processor relieves the mainframe of routine processing duties such as data validation.

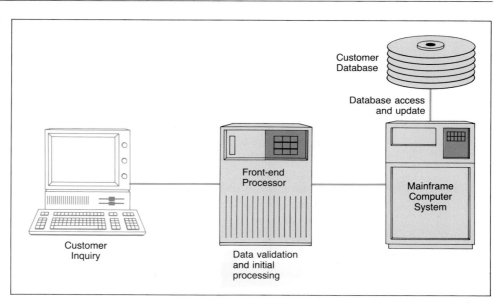

Customer Database

Database access and update

Front-end Processor

Mainframe Computer System

Customer Inquiry

Data validation and initial processing

CHOOSING A LAN

Making the right choice for a local area network can be a frustrating experience. Because there are dozens of networks from which to choose, these guidelines can help to pull together the various features and how they can address the needs of a specific installation.[1]

Security

There are two levels of security to consider. One is safeguarding against users getting into the wrong files either intentionally or unintentionally; the other is protecting the system from entry by unauthorized users. Network software provides protection for both these concerns by requiring a password for entry to the system. Some software also permits access to data based on a user profile so that only certain parts of the system are accessible.

Tapping into a system can be done more easily if twisted-pair or coaxial cable is used. Fiber optic cable, on the other hand, is difficult to tap into and discourages would be wiretappers.

Reliability

The concern over reliability depends largely upon the use of the network. Computer networks used for medical applications or robot control in process control manufacturing have a more critical level than does a network used in an office environment. Star networks are inherently more reliable because no one node of the system depends on the other, while a ring network has greater dependencies.

Some systems offer additional factors to improve reliability. For example, Proteon has a system with redundant cabling. If one cable fails, the other is used without an interruption in the process. Novell offers a system with extra hard disks and/or processors. If one fails, the other picks up without missing a beat.

Cost

If wiring is already in place (usually twisted-pair telephone cable), this can be a significant cost saver. A bus or ring network can require less wiring than can a star and so one of these will keep costs down. Software can be a significant part of the cost of a network. Networking software can run from a low of about $100 to several thousand dollars.

Network Performance

The performance of the network is affected by the number of stations, line speed, and the type of software used. Generally as more stations are added to a network, the performance is degraded. Using a faster file server such as an IBM AT (80286 processor) or even an 80386 based computer with a high-speed hard disk will improve performance.

Using the same kind of computer for each station is desirable for maximum performance. While other hardware can be used, mixing can require special connections and even conversion software to ensure compatibility. This problem is particularly evident when micros, minis, and mainframes are tied together in a network.

---

[1] Frank J. Derfler, Jr., "Making Connections—13 LANs in Perspective," *PC Magazine*, April 28, 1987, pp. 209–239.

1. Computers need to communicate with each other for several reasons, including sharing data, inquiring into a data base from a remote computer, and providing for remote data entry.

2. For simple data communications, two computers are linked together by a communications line. A modem at the computer is used to convert digital to analog at the sending end and analog to digital at the receiving end.

3. In addition to the communications line and a modem, communications software is necessary for data transfer.

4. Networks are communications systems that provide a means for multiple computers to communicate with each other.

5. Network topology refers to the three kinds of network configurations. These are the star, ring, and bus networks.

6. A star network is configured in a starlike pattern with a computer at the center of the pattern. If the central computer is a mainframe, it is called the host computer. If a PC is used, it is called a file server.

7. In a hierarchical star network, the central computer forms the hub of the starlike pattern to which other computers or terminals in the network are attached. A node can be the hub of another star to form a hierarchy.

8. The ring network connects a number of computers to a continuous communication ring. There is no host computer, but each computer on the ring can communicate directly with all other computers. Ring networks cost less than a star network because of the shorter lines required.

9. A bus network is a local area network that uses a cable to interconnect a series of computers and devices together. Transmission on a bus network consists of messages that contain a device address as part of the data that is recognized by the device to which it is sent.

10. A local area network ties together several computers in a nearby area such as within an office or between adjacent offices. A LAN is used to share computer resources such as common data or printer(s), or to transmit electronic mail, to reduce the cost of software, and to provide a backup of computer resources. Depending on the network, LANs may include devices up to 10 miles distant.

11. Online data services offer special interest data or services such as electronic mail or an electronic bulletin board where you can advertise items for sale or purchase; they can also provide access to many databases to address the needs of a broad variety of users. Hundreds of subjects are available through online data bases, including topics such as airline schedules, investment, foreign news, sports, UPI news releases, and so on.

12. E-mail is a system based on a central computer with many PCs attached in a star network fashion. Special software in each computer provides for communicating mail electronically between users who subscribe to the same service.

13. When micros and mainframes are linked together special software is frequently needed to ensure compatibility. Changing data formats, converting ASCII or EBCDIC code, and the ability to upload and download files are all part of the requirements for the micro-to-mainframe link.

14. A modem converts digital signals to analog by the process of modulation. Demodulation is the process of converting analog to digital. The modem is attached to the computer's RS-232C serial port.

15. Direct-connect PCs do not require a modem for data communication but are hardwired together with coaxial or other types of cable.

16. The rate at which data is transferred is expressed in bits per second (bps). Typical transmission rates are 300, 1,200, and 2,400 bps.

17. Modems come as acoustic couplers that use rubber cups to secure the telephone receiver, as direct-connect that are plugged directly into the telephone jack on the wall, or as a smart modems that have a built-in microprocessor and software to provide autoanswer and autodial features.

18. A multiplexor is used when numerous computers to terminals are attached to a mainframe. The multiplexor combines several low-speed incoming lines to the mainframe's single high-speed line.

19. A front-end processor is a computer that receives data prior to its being sent to the mainframe. The front-end processor takes some of the processing load off the mainframe to relieve it for other duties.

IMPORTANT TERMS AND CONCEPTS

Acoustic coupler	File server	Network
Bit rate	Front-end processor	Online data services
Bulletin board service (BBS)	Hierarchical Star network	Ring network
		Smart modem
Bus network	Host computer	Star network
Communication channel	Local area network (LAN)	Token passing
		Uploading
Direct-connect modem	Modem	
Downloading	Multiplexor	
Electronic mail	Network topology	

REVIEW QUESTIONS

Fill-in Questions

1. A communication line, usually a(n) _____ line, links two computers together for data communications.

2. _____ are communications systems that provide a means for multiple computers to communicate with each other.

3. The network topology that has a computer at the center of a starlike pattern is called a(n) _____ network.

4. A(n) _____ _____ or host computer is at the center of a network that provides each computer on the network with programs and data such as a common data base.

5. A(n) _____ network may connect many different devices, including computers, printers, and plotters.

6. A(n) _____ is an electronic device that converts a computer's digital signal to its analog equivalent.

Matching Questions

Match each term with the description given below.

a. The Source   d. E-mail
b. hierarchical star   e. LAN
c. ring network   f. downloading

_____ b _____ 1. This is a network that has a local network attached to a node of the main network.

_____ e _____ 2. This general term refers to a network that is used to connect computers in the same office space or other area where the computers are in close proximity to each other.

_____ d _____ 3. A system of this type uses a computer to collect and distribute mail for the users.

_____ a d _____ 4. This is one of the many online communication services available for computer users.

_____ c _____ 5. This network passes data from computer to computer around the net. A computer that is not receiving a message simply passes it on to the next computer in the network.

_____ f _____ 6. This is the process of receiving data from a mainframe computer and storing or processing it on the PC.

Discussion Questions

1. Describe a basic configuration for communicating data between two computers.

2. What is meant by network topology? Describe the three basic forms of networks.

3. Discuss the concept of local area networks and give some of the reasons they are used by business.

4. Describe IBM's Token-Ring network explaining how it is different from one of the three network topologies.

5. Review the need for online communications services and explain some of the more widely used types of services.

6. What is meant by E-mail? How is E-mail used? What are its advantages and disadvantages?

7. Describe what is meant by the terms uploading and downloading.

8. What is the purpose of a modem? What are three types of modems? Explain the meaning of bit rate.

9. When mainframe computers communicate with PCs a multiplexor and/or a front-end processor may be used. What is the purpose of these devices?

Operating Systems

A VIEW OF THE CHAPTER AHEAD

After Reading This Chapter You Will Understand:

- The different components of an operating system and how they function in the computer.

- The three basic operating system classes of single tasking, multitasking, and multiuser.

- The purpose and use of PC-DOS.

- Other popular operating systems and where they are used.

The operating system is the first program executed when the computer is turned on and the last one when the computer is shut down. Often the operating system is described as a computer traffic cop who directs the flow of activity in the computer. Early computers came without operating systems, and the operator or programmer would need to watch groups of flashing lights to determine what was happening in the computer.

Later, simple operating systems were included in the read-only memory (ROM) so that data could be read from external devices such as a keyboard or a cassette tape drive or written to a screen or printer. But using a ROM proved awkward because an operating system stored there could not easily be changed or upgraded as needs changed. Thus, by the time the IBM PC came on the scene, most operating systems were supplied on a floppy disk that was booted when the computer's power was turned on. This method is still widely used on most personal computers, except when the computer has a hard disk, in which case it will contain the operating system.

The **disk operating system (DOS)** that is used on IBM personal computers is called **PC-DOS.** It has a legacy that extends back to the early 8-bit microcomputers. Eight-bit systems that used the Zilog Z80 or Intel's 8080 microprocessor used **CP/M** (Control Program for Microcomputers). Apple computers used Apple DOS or Pro DOS, and Tandy Corporation's Radio Shack computers used TRS-DOS.

When the 16-bit computers came on the scene in the 1980s they primarily used Intel's 8088 chip and the **Microsoft Disk Operating system (MS-DOS).** It was MS-DOS that IBM adopted for its PC and renamed it PC-DOS when it

Operating systems perform the functions of input/output management, memory management, and command processing.

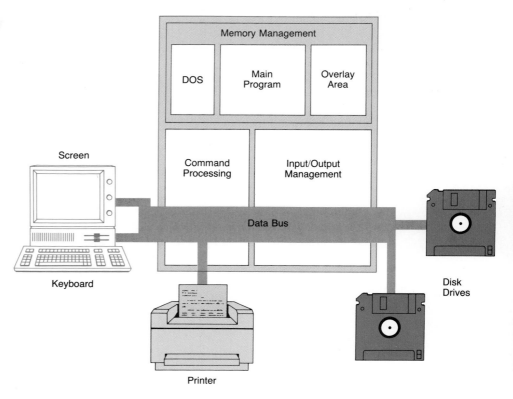

was marketed under its nameplate. This popular operating system has undergone many revisions since its inception and is widely used by other personal computer manufacturers. Most recently IBM has provided **Operating System/2 (OS/2),** also developed with Microsoft, for the top-line Personal System/2 computers.

FUNCTIONS OF THE OPERATING SYSTEM

There are many activities that occur during a session on the computer. Keyboard entries are made to call up a program. Entries are also made when text or graphic displays are needed on the screen, when data is read from a disk and is written back when it has been changed, or when external communication with another computer is needed.

While an application program will initiate most of these operations, it is the operating system that carries out its orders. To handle each of these operations, several components of the operating system provide for a variety of functions to be executed on the computer.

Input/Output Management

The component of the operating system for input/output (I/O) management takes care of the flow of data to and from the various devices attached to the computer. For example, when a key is pressed on the keyboard, the I/O manager interprets the code for that key and routes its signal to the appropriate part of memory. It also causes an image of the character represented by the key to appear on the screen.

Another function of the I/O manager applies when the program asks for data to be stored on disk. The I/O manager knows the right sequence of codes needed to send the data to the requested disk drive and controls the location on the disk where the data will be stored. It can also route data to the printer or accept directions from a mouse. All this is done without mixing up signals from different devices or confusing input with output.

Memory Management

With computers containing 640K of memory and more, good management of this memory space is essential for efficient operation. Memory management is another function of the operating system.

As we know, DOS resides in part of memory leaving space for an application program. The memory management function of DOS must remember exactly how much memory space is available and assign it to a program when we ask it to be loaded. If the program is another resident program, such as SideKick, then DOS needs to allocate its requirements and reserve the rest of memory for a word processing program or maybe a spreadsheet.

Application programs often come with main and overlay programs as we have already discussed in this book. Memory management also assists with the loading of program overlays and manages the link between the overlay and the main program that uses it. Eventually control is passed back to the main program, again with the assistance of the memory manager.

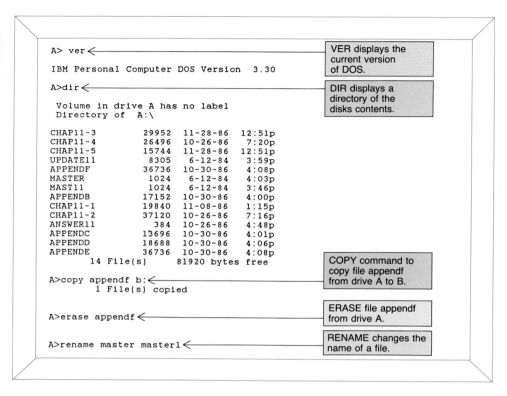

FIGURE 6–1
VER, DIR, COPY, ERASE, and RENAME are all PC-DOS commands that are acted upon when entered from the keyboard.

Command Processing

Another function of the operating system is the processing of commands that are entered by the computer user (Figure 6–1). Command processing is a function of the DOS program, COMMAND.COM, that is loaded into memory as a result of booting DOS. DOS provides a wide range of commands for copying, erasing or renaming files, defining and using subdirectories on hard disk, and listing the contents of a directory. All these activities begin by commands that are entered at the DOS prompt.

Until recently, the most widely used operating systems were command-driven programs and have their own language for use. PC-DOS Release 4.0 and OS/2 are the beginning of operating systems that depend more on menus than on commands for their operation.

Utilities

Utilities are operating system programs that can be run to perform disk maintenance activities. One of these is the FORMAT utility (Figure 6–2) that prepares a new disk for use. Other utilities can be used to copy the entire contents of one disk to another, check a disk for errors, sort a disk directory, or create a RAM disk in the computer's memory. Utilities reside on the DOS disk rather than in memory but are activated in the same manner as other DOS commands.

For hands-on work with PC-DOS, see the tutorial book that provides other examples and exercises using DOS commands.

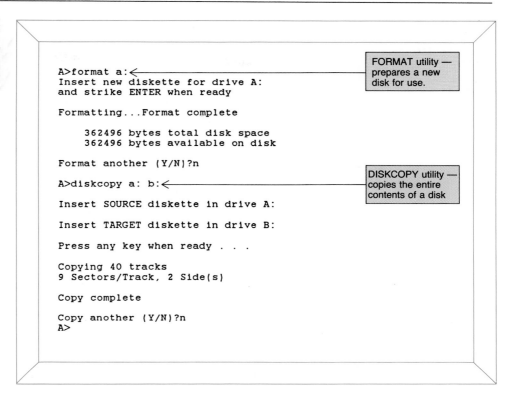

```
A>format a:
Insert new diskette for drive A:
and strike ENTER when ready

Formatting...Format complete

    362496 bytes total disk space
    362496 bytes available on disk

Format another (Y/N)?n

A>diskcopy a: b:

Insert SOURCE diskette in drive A:

Insert TARGET diskette in drive B:

Press any key when ready . . .

Copying 40 tracks
9 Sectors/Track, 2 Side(s)

Copy complete

Copy another (Y/N)?n
A>
```

FORMAT utility — prepares a new disk for use.

DISKCOPY utility — copies the entire contents of a disk

CLASSES OF OPERATING SYSTEMS

An operating system may be classified into one of three basic groups according to how it manages the user environment. These groups are single tasking, multitasking, and multiuser.

Single Tasking

Most personal computer operating systems fall into this category. A **single-tasking** operating system, as the name suggests, can work on one task at a time. The practical meaning of single tasking is that only one program can run on the computer at any one time. Thus if a spreadsheet is being run, the computer is not able to receive communications from a modem or print a report.

MS-DOS and PC-DOS are the most widely used single-tasking operating systems. CP/M and CP/M-86 are also single-tasking systems for 8- and 16-bit computers, respectively. For personal computing, PC-DOS has set the industry standard for single-tasking operating systems due to its vast user base.

Multitasking

When two or more tasks or programs may be run simultaneously this is called **multitasking.** In its simplest form, a multitasking operating system permits two programs to operate together on the computer, but only one instruction gets executed at a time. One program, such as a word processor, may be in direct use by the user and is therefore in the **foreground,** while a second program that may be printing a report is operating in the **background.**

UNIX is one of the most well-known multitasking operating systems that was originally developed for the minicomputer market. It is now available for personal computers under names such as XENIX and VENIX. Other operating systems that use a multitaskinglike environment are Concurrent CP/M, IBM's OS/2, and Microsoft's Windows.

These systems permit several programs to do **concurrent processing,** which permits switching from one application to another without the need to leave the current task. For example, in Windows, several different applications may appear in different windows on the screen. The user may switch between them with a few keystrokes and change tasks without having to discontinue work in any one environment.

Multiuser

Mainframe computer systems and many minicomputers have multiple users accessing the same central computer. Usually VDT terminals are used that have no processing capability and therefore rely on the central computer for all processing requirements. This type of computer system requires a **multiuser** operating system. The purpose of this operating system, in addition to functions already described, is to coordinate the processing needs of each terminal and ensure that each gets adequate access to the processor.

IBM's DOS/VS (Disk Operating System/Virtual Storage) and OS/MVS (Operating System/Multiprogramming Virtual Storage) are two examples of mainframe operating systems that provide multiuser capability. Digital Equipment Corporation's RSTS is one operating system used on its VAX minicomputer series of computers.

Personal computers in a local area network might seem to require a multiuser operating system. But this is really a special case because each user has a PC that contains its own operating system (usually single tasking). If there is a central computer on the LAN, it is frequently a file server and does not provide any processing power to the users on the network. Thus it may run a file serving program but does not require a multiuser operating system.

The advantage of a multiuser operating system is that several users can access data on a single computer and share the software resources. Users may access the central computer with either a personal computer or with a dumb terminal, depending on their individual needs.

Courtesy of Xerox Corporation.

When DOS was released by IBM for its first PC, it was known as DOS 1.1 to identify the first version of this product. Over the years DOS has evolved to handle new features such as hard disk, networking, and new high-density disks. As new features became available, the size of DOS grew, both in the disk space required to store it and the amount of RAM required to use it. The following are the PC-DOS releases up to 3.2 and their related storage requirements.[1]

DOS Version	Storage Requirements (bytes)	
	Disk	Memory
1.1	13,279	12,400
2.0	39,424	24,800
2.1	39,552	24,800
3.0	58,926	37,024
3.1	60,534	37,040
3.2	68,637	44,704

[1] *PC Magazine*, February 24, 1987, p. 278.

PC-DOS

In 1981 Microsoft was mainly known for its Microsoft BASIC, which was in use on many different brands of microcomputers. But in that year, Microsoft bought an operating system from a small hardware company called Seattle Computer Products. It did some reworking of the operating system and licensed it under the name MS-DOS, meaning, of course, Microsoft DOS.

One of the purchasers of MS-DOS was IBM, which released it on its personal computer as PC-DOS. When the IBM PC's sales took off, so did PC-DOS, and it is practically considered to be a standard in the business today. MS-DOS or PC-DOS is a necessary ingredient for every personal computer and must be used whenever a disk is part of the system.

Booting DOS

Booting DOS from a floppy disk

1. Place the DOS disk in drive A and turn on the power (drive A is the left drive if disk drives are full height or the top drive on stacked half-height drives). Wait for DOS to boot.
2. When DOS has booted, enter the date and time as requested.

DOS Prompt	**Type the Entry**
Enter new date:	**<month-day-year>** e.g., 10–12–90
Enter new time:	**<hours:minutes>** e.g., 14:35

DOS now displays the DOS prompt A>.

Now remove the DOS disk from drive A and replace it with the application disk. Close the drive door. Place a previously formatted disk into drive B>. For Lotus 1–2–3 software you would enter the following command.

DOS Prompt   **Type the Entry**

A>   **lotus**{enter}

Booting DOS from a hard disk

1. Be sure no floppy disks are in the disk drives. Turn on the power to the computer and wait for DOS to boot.
2. When DOS has booted, enter the date and time if requested. Many systems have a built-in clock and do not need date and time to be entered.

DOS Prompt   **Type the Entry**

Enter new date: **<month-day-year>**
                        e.g., 10–12–90
Enter new time: **<hours:minutes>**
                        e.g., 14:35

DOS now displays the DOS prompt C>.
To use Lotus 1–2–3 software you would enter the following command.

DOS Prompt   **Type the Entry**

C>   **lotus**{enter}

WARM OR COLD STARTS

Before using a PC it is necessary to boot DOS from either a floppy or hard disk drive. There are two ways of booting DOS on your PC: one is by turning the power on to the computer—a cold start—and the other is used when the power is already on—a warm start.

Cold Start

To do a cold start, insert the DOS disk into drive A: on a floppy disk system and turn on the power. On a hard disk system, when DOS is already on the hard disk, just turn on the power making sure that no disk is currently located in the A: drive. After a minute or two DOS will be loaded into memory. The reason for the delay is that the hardware does a self-test to make sure everything in the computer is working correctly before loading DOS.

Warm Start

This method is used when the computer has already been in use and you need to reboot DOS. Pressing the Ctrl, Alt, and Del keys together causes a warm start. To press these keys, hold down Ctrl and Alt with your left hand and then press the Del key. When this is done, booting takes only a few seconds as most of the self-checking features are not done. Warm starting is useful when a program stops running due to an uncorrectable program bug or the system locks up for no reasonable explanation.

THE DEFAULT DRIVE CONCEPT

After booting DOS the A> prompt—C> if you are using a hard disk—will appear on the screen. This is the default disk drive (also called the logged drive) and is the drive that will be affected by commands entered at the keyboard. For example, if you enter the DIRectory command, you will get the directory of drive A:. If you type the name of a program then DOS will expect to find the program on the default disk drive. The default drive can be changed by typing the name of the new drive. Typing b: will change the default disk drive to drive B: and the prompt will appear as B>.

default drive is a:	**dir** command gives a directory of drive a:	**b:** command changes default disk to drive b:	drive b: is now the default disk

Entering PC-DOS Commands

Because PC-DOS is a command-driven language, it is necessary to know the commands you wish to use and to be familiar with their format. All DOS commands are entered at the DOS prompt, either A> for the floppy A: disk or C> for the hard disk. A command is typed immediately following the prompt and the Enter key is pressed after typing the command. A few of the more commonly used DOS commands will be discussed here, but, for some practical exercises in their use, see the separate DOS tutorial.

Preparing a New Disk (FORMAT)

When you purchase a new diskette it is not yet ready to receive data. First, the disk must be formatted for the computer and operating sysem on which it will be used. Disks formatted for PC-DOS can be used on any IBM PC or compatible computer.

Using the FORMAT statement prepares the disk for initial use by writing data on it to assign tracks and sectors where your data will be stored. Systems using DOS 2.0 or later with 5¼-inch floppy disks use 40 tracks with 9 sectors per track giving a total of 360 sectors. Each sector is able to hold 512 bytes, giving a capacity of 184,320 bytes on one side of the disk. Since disks are double sided, there is a total of 368,640 bytes of storage on the disk. Some of this space (4 sectors) is used for a file allocation table (FAT) that DOS uses to keep track of the files stored on the disk. Seven additional sectors of the disk are used for a directory of filenames, dates, and other information.

There are several options available on the FORMAT statement. Either the statement may be typed by itself or it can be entered with one or more options as explained below.

FORMAT	The command used by itself formats a double-sided disk on the currently logged (default) disk drive.
FORMAT b:	Formats a disk on the B: disk drive. This is useful on a two drive system where the DOS disk is in drive A: and the new disk in drive B:.
FORMAT/S	Places a copy of the operating system on the disk making it bootable. This technique is useful for a disk that will contain a program you use a lot. By making it bootable, it is unnecessary to boot with a DOS disk and then switch disks for the application.

Basic DOS Commands

Internal and external commands

When a DOS command is entered at the prompt, it is basically one of two types of commands: internal or external (Figure 6–3). When DOS is booted the program COMMAND.COM is loaded into memory from the DOS disk. COMMAND.COM contains a number of frequently used DOS commands called

USING FORMAT

To use FORMAT it is necessary to have the DOS disk in drive A: or on the hard disk before typing the command. Then type **FORMAT** a: and the FORMAT program will be retrieved from the DOS disk. The screen prompt to insert a new diskette, shown below, requires that the DOS disk be removed and the new disk inserted in drive A:. Now press the Enter key to continue.

*** **WARNING** *** Formatting destroys the contents of the disk so be sure that only a new disk or one that contains no useful data is formatted.

```
A>format a:
Insert new diskette for drive A:
and strike ENTER when ready

Formatting...Format complete

    362496 bytes total disk space
    362496 bytes available on disk

Format another (Y/N)?n
```

FIGURE 6–3
Some DOS internal and external commands. Internal commands are brought into memory with the COMMAND.COM program when DOS is booted. Using these commands does not require the DOS disk to be present. External commands are located on the DOS disk, which must be present for their use.

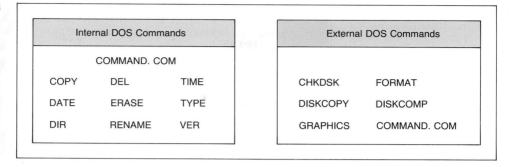

Internal DOS Commands		
COMMAND. COM		
COPY	DEL	TIME
DATE	ERASE	TYPE
DIR	RENAME	VER

External DOS Commands	
CHKDSK	FORMAT
DISKCOPY	DISKCOMP
GRAPHICS	COMMAND. COM

internal commands because they are located in memory and do not require any further disk access when they are used.

Because DOS commands mostly act on disk files, an internal command will often access a disk to carry out the command. For example, the DIR command is internal and does not require the DOS disk to be present when used. But, because it lists the directory of the default disk, it will need to access the disk drive for that purpose.

Other DOS commands are **external** because they reside on the DOS disk and require a disk access to be used. External commands require that the DOS disk be present in the default disk drive when the command is entered; otherwise a Not Found message will be displayed. When DOS is on hard disk, the external commands are essentially always present, but on floppy disk, it is not unusual for other disks to be in the drive, which then requires a swap of disks before using an external DOS command.

An example of an external command is FORMAT. It requires the DOS disk to be present for the FORMAT program to be read, then, as FORMAT executes the program requires a disk in the default disk drive that will be formatted as a result of the operation. Thus two disk accesses are required: one to read the FORMAT command itself, and a second to carry out the command.

Directory

The DIR command is an internal DOS command used to get a listing of a disk directory. DIR acts on the default disk drive unless a drive is specified in the command. The listing, as shown in Figure 6–4, includes the filename and extension (if one is used), the file size in bytes, and the date and time the file was created.

The DIR command has several options to make your task easier. In the directory shown, the lines that were displayed exceeded the number of lines on the screen and so scrolling would have occurred. Scrolling makes it difficult to read the screen contents, and so DOS has provided two options. One is the /p, which causes the directory to pause when the screen is filled; then by pressing a key, the displaying of the directory continues.

The second option shown in Figure 6–5 is the /w, which is for a wide display. Because five file names are displayed across the screen, no additional data about the file is given so that there is room for the directory of names.

FIGURE 6–4   Using the DIR command creates a scrolling list of files on the screen. By using the pause option/p, the display will stop temporarily when a screen fills. The user presses a key to continue the directory display.

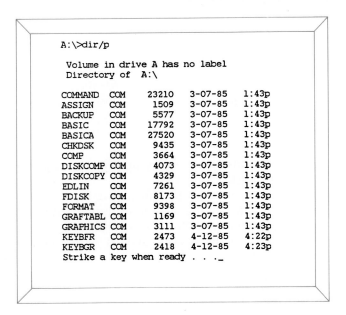

```
A:\>dir/p

Volume in drive A has no label
Directory of  A:\

COMMAND  COM    23210   3-07-85    1:43p
ASSIGN   COM     1509   3-07-85    1:43p
BACKUP   COM     5577   3-07-85    1:43p
BASIC    COM    17792   3-07-85    1:43p
BASICA   COM    27520   3-07-85    1:43p
CHKDSK   COM     9435   3-07-85    1:43p
COMP     COM     3664   3-07-85    1:43p
DISKCOMP COM     4073   3-07-85    1:43p
DISKCOPY COM     4329   3-07-85    1:43p
EDLIN    COM     7261   3-07-85    1:43p
FDISK    COM     8173   3-07-85    1:43p
FORMAT   COM     9398   3-07-85    1:43p
GRAFTABL COM     1169   3-07-85    1:43p
GRAPHICS COM     3111   3-07-85    1:43p
KEYBFR   COM     2473   4-12-85    4:22p
KEYBGR   COM     2418   4-12-85    4:23p
Strike a key when ready . . ._
```

```
KEYBIT   COM     2361   4-12-85    4:25p
KEYBSP   COM     2451   4-12-85    4:24p
KEYBUK   COM     2348   4-12-85    4:26p
LABEL    COM     1826   3-07-85    1:43p
MODE     COM     5295   3-07-85    1:43p
MORE     COM      282   3-07-85    1:43p
PRINT    COM     8291   3-07-85    1:43p
RECOVER  COM     4050   3-07-85    1:43p
RESTORE  COM     5410   3-07-85    1:43p
SELECT   COM     2084   3-07-85    1:43p
SYS      COM     3727   3-07-85    1:43p
TREE     COM     2831   3-07-85    1:43p
SETCLOCK COM     1079   9-26-83   12:12p
CONFIG   BAK      128   1-01-80   12:05a
VDISK    SYS     3307   3-07-85    1:43p
CONFIG   SYS      128  11-12-86    7:00p
     32 File(s)    126976 bytes free

A>
```

FIGURE 6–5
Using the /w option in the DIR command gives a wide listing of the directory.

```
A>dir/w

Volume in drive A has no label
Directory of  A:\

COMMAND  COM    ASSIGN   COM    BACKUP   COM    BASIC    COM    BASICA   COM
CHKDSK   COM    COMP     COM    DISKCOMP COM    DISKCOPY COM    EDLIN    COM
FDISK    COM    FORMAT   COM    GRAFTABL COM    GRAPHICS COM    KEYBFR   COM
KEYBGR   COM    KEYBIT   COM    KEYBSP   COM    KEYBUK   COM    LABEL    COM
MODE     COM    MORE     COM    PRINT    COM    RECOVER  COM    RESTORE  COM
SELECT   COM    SYS      COM    TREE     COM    SETCLOCK COM    CONFIG   BAK
VDISK    SYS    CONFIG   SYS
     32 File(s)    126976 bytes free

A>
```

Other File Operations

COPY

The COPY command makes a second copy of a file on another disk or on the same disk but with a different name. Using COPY requires the understanding of two terms.

- **Source disk.** Is the disk where the file(s) to be copied is found. Normally this is the default disk drive.
- **Target disk.** This is the disk that is to receive the copy of the file(s).

WILDCARDS IN FILENAMES

When you are specifying a filename in DOS, the ability to use a more general definition can be time saving. In the DIR command a wildcard may be used to reduce the directory displayed to a certain group of files. When using the ERASE command, a group of files may be erased at once by entering only one command instead of a separate command for each file. But with such power, care must also be taken, for obvious reasons, when using this feature for erasing files.

Wildcard characters are the asterisk (*) and question mark (?). An asterisk represents any number of characters. For example, using the entry D* would get a match on the names

```
DISK
DECK
DUCK
DINE
DITCH
DESTINY
```

In other words all names beginning with the letter D.

Using the question mark in the entry DI?? would get a match on the names

```
DISK
DINE
```

The entry D??K would match on the names

```
DISK
DECK
DUCK
```

In DOS the wildcard symbols can be used on both the file name and the three-character extension. Using an asterisk for the extension is useful when you want to see a certain type of file. For example, the command **dir *.sys** will list all files with the sys extension.

```
A>dir *.sys

 Volume in drive A has no label
 Directory of  A:\

VDISK     SYS      3307    3-07-85    1:43p
CONFIG    SYS       128   11-12-86    7:00p
        2 File(s)     126976 bytes free

A>
```

The command **dir key???.*** will list all files beginning with the letters key and having any extension.

```
A>dir key???.*

 Volume in drive A has no label
 Directory of  A:\

KEYBFR   COM     2473   4-12-85   4:22p
KEYBGR   COM     2418   4-12-85   4:23p
KEYBIT   COM     2361   4-12-85   4:25p
KEYBSP   COM     2451   4-12-85   4:24p
KEYBUK   COM     2348   4-12-85   4:26p
         5 File(s)    126976 bytes free

A>
```

Using COPY.

```
A>copy contents b:
        1 File(s) copied

A>copy *.bk! b:
CONTENTS.BK!
REFERENC.BK!
SCHED.BK!
END.BK!
FIGS4.BK!
TELE2.BK!
TELE1.BK!
        7 File(s) copied

A>
```

Remember that file names are not case sensitive in DOS commands: either upper- or lowercase letters may be typed.

ERASE or DEL

The ERASE command (DEL may be used in the same way) is used to remove a file from the disk permanently. Once erased, a file cannot be recovered unless a special utility program, such as Norton's Utilities, is available.

ERASE is used in a manner similar to copy except that only one file is referenced: the source file. More than one file may be erased by using wildcard entries in the file name. Unless a drive is specified, the default drive will be accessed for the erase.

Using ERASE.

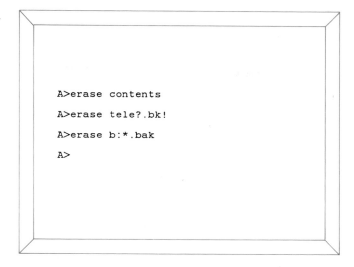

```
A>erase contents

A>erase tele?.bk!

A>erase b:*.bak

A>
```

RENAME

The RENAME command is used to change the name of an existing disk file. The file is found on the default disk drive unless a drive letter is specified in the command. Wildcard characters may be used in the file names to change groups of files with a single command.

In the RENAME command, the second file name given must not include a drive letter because the file to be renamed remains on the original disk where it was found.

Using RENAME.

```
C>dir

 Volume in drive C has no label
 Directory of  C:\

TOP              470    3-23-87   6:22p
DIR1             197    5-25-87   1:09p
DIR2              77    5-25-87   3:31p
DIR2     BAK     173    5-25-87   3:06p
      4 File(s)   4304896 bytes free
```

```
C>rename top begin

C>rename dir? new?

C>dir

 Volume in drive C has no label
 Directory of  C:\

BEGIN            470    3-23-87   6:22p
NEW1             197    5-25-87   1:09p
NEW2              77    5-25-87   3:31p
DIR2     BAK     173    5-25-87   3:06p

      3 File(s)   4304896 bytes free

C>
```

DISKCOPY

When it is necessary to copy the entire contents of one floppy disk to another, the DISKCOPY command is useful. If a single-drive system is used, DOS will prompt you when to place the source and target disk in the drive.

Using DISKCOPY.

```
A>diskcopy a: b:

Insert SOURCE diskette in drive A:

Insert TARGET diskette in drive B:

Press any key when ready . . .

Copying 40 tracks
9 Sectors/Track, 2 Side(s)

Copy another [Y/N]? n
```

DISKCOPY is an external command requiring the DOS disk to be present when the command is issued.

If DOS finds that the target disk is not formatted, then formatting will be done as the copy is made. The DISKCOMP external DOS command may be used after the copy is complete to ensure its correctness. DISKCOMP has the same format as DISKCOPY.

TYPE

The TYPE command lists or types the contents of a file on the screen or alternately on the printer. TYPE works best for files that contain ASCII characters. Other files such as COM or EXE files or certain spreadsheet files will appear as garbage or worse on the screen and should not be listed with this command.

Ctrl S may be used to stop and start scrolling, and Ctrl C may be used to abort the listing if you do not want it to continue.

Using the redirection command >PRN with TYPE will send the output to the printer. It is best to use TYPE to the screen first to be sure that what is later sent to the printer will be meaningful.

Using TYPE.

```
C>type wordstar.bat
echo off
cd \ws4
cls
ws
cls
echo
echo    END OF WS4 USE
echo
cd c:\

C>
```

Fixed Disks and Hierarchical Directories

In Chapter 4 we saw how a fixed disk could be divided into directories and subdirectories to make the large storage capacity manageable. Ordinarily, creating a hierarchical directory is done on the hard disk, which is usually the C: disk. But even floppy users can make a hierarchical directory on a floppy disk using drive A: or B: or any other floppy disk drive that is available. The only difference is in the default disk drive used in the operation.

There are three commands used for working with hierarchical directories. Each command may be written in full or as a two-letter abbreviation. These commands are

MKDIR (MD)   The MD command is used to *make* a new directory on disk.
CHDIR (CD)   CD is used to *change* from one directory to another.
RMDIR (RD)   The RD command is used to *remove* a directory from the disk.

Each of these commands will require an entry called a **path.** The path is an expression that defines the subdirectory you are working with. For example, the entry

C:\SHEET

means that you are referencing the subdirectory named SHEET on the C: disk. The back slash (\) character is important for identifying a subdirectory entry. You could use a path entry such as this in a DIR command.

DIR C:\SHEET

This entry would list the directory of files contained in the subdirectory SHEET. Now let's look at the rules for creating and using subdirectories.

MKDIR (MD)

The MKDIR or MD (make directory) command is used to create a new directory on the disk. To create a new directory, use the MD command followed by the path that describes the directory. Because subdirectories can be created on floppy as well as hard disk, the examples used here will refer to the floppy

---

RULES FOR DIRECTORY AND PATH NAMES

Directory names are like file names. They can have up to eight characters with an optional one- to three-character extension. For simplicity in naming directories it is usually best to avoid the extension and also to keep the directory name reasonably short yet descriptive.

Path names consist of one or more directory names beginning with the back slash (\). The maximum size for a path name is 63 characters. If necessary a drive name (like A: or C:) may precede the path name.

C:	this path refers to the root directory.
C:\SHEET	refers to the subdirectory SHEET.
C:\SHEET\BUDGET	this path refers to the sub-subdirectory BUDGET contained in the subdirectory SHEET.

disk in drive A:. If you are trying these commands on the hard disk in drive C:, change all references of A: to C:.

To create a directory called SHEET on drive A: the command

MD A:\SHEET

is used. To create a subdirectory called BUDGET within SHEET, the command

MD A:\SHEET\BUDGET

is used. A second subdirectory is created with the command

MD A:\SHEET\PLAN

When a directory listing is called up on the screen, only files in the current directory are shown. This list also includes subdirectories. The entry

SHEET   <DIR>   5-27-87   8:34a

in the directory listing shows the presence of the subdirectory SHEET in the current disk directory (the root). However, directories within SHEET are not shown at this level. To see the contents of SHEET, we need to use the CHDIR command to change the directory currently in use.

CHDIR (CD)

Use the CHDIR or CD (change directory) command when you want to work in a directory other than the current one. Assuming that you are in the A: root directory, to change to the SHEET subdirectory use the command

CD\SHEET

Now we can see the contents of SHEET by using the DIR command. This subdirectory is now the default disk drive, and any DOS activity will take place in this subdirectory.

Making a new directory.

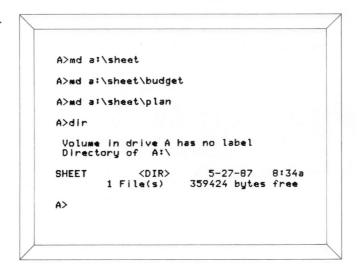

```
A>md a:\sheet

A>md a:\sheet\budget

A>md a:\sheet\plan

A>dir

 Volume in drive A has no label
 Directory of  A:\

SHEET        <DIR>        5-27-87    8:34a
        1 File(s)    359424 bytes free

A>
```

```
A>cd\sheet

A>dir

 Volume in drive A has no label
 Directory of  A:\SHEET

.               <DIR>        5-27-87    8:34a
..              <DIR>        5-27-87    8:34a
BUDGET          <DIR>        5-27-87    8:35a
PLAN            <DIR>        5-27-87    8:36a
        4 File(s)    359424 bytes free

A>
```

```
A>cd\sheet\plan

A>dir

 Volume in drive A has no label
 Directory of  A:\SHEET\PLAN

.               <DIR>        5-27-87    2:08p
..              <DIR>        5-27-87    2:08p
        2 File(s)    359424 bytes free

A>cd\

A>
```

Changing directories.

To get to the BUDGET subdirectory in SHEET, use the command

CD\SHEET\BUDGET

When listing the directory at this level, two entries are shown: one with a single period (.) and another with a double period (..). The single-period entry represents the current directory, and the double-period represents the parent directory. The parent, of course, is the directory that created (contains) the current directory.

To return to the root directory from any current subdirectory, use the command

CD\

Removing a directory.

```
A>rd\sheet\plan

A>dir

 Volume in drive A has no label
 Directory of  A:\SHEET

.               <DIR>        5-27-87    8:34a
..              <DIR>        5-27-87    8:34a
BUDGET          <DIR>        5-27-87    8:35a
        3 File(s)    360448 bytes free

A>
```

A subdirectory is used in the same manner as other directories: files can be copied to it, they can be renamed, erased, or typed. When a subdirectory is the current directory, then copying a file to it is easy. First, set the directory using the change directory command.

CD\SHEET\BUDGET

To copy the file DOC12 from the B: drive to the subdirectory \SHEET\BUDGET on the A: drive, the following command is used.

copy b:doc12

Because the BUDGET subdirectory is active on the A: drive, it will receive the result of the copy. But, what if BUDGET was not currently active and for some reason you would prefer not to change directories? Then use the following command.

copy b:doc12 a:\sheet\budget

The first entry, **b:doc12,** is the source file, and the second entry, **a:\sheet\budget,** is the target.

This format may be necessary when a file in one subdirectory needs to be copied to another subdirectory. Since you can't be in two different subdirectories at one time at least one of the entries will need to be a full path name. For example, to copy the file **trial88** from the directory **\sheet\plan** to the directory **\sheet\budget** use the following command.

copy a:\sheet\plan\trial88 a:\sheet\budget

With this command it doesn't matter which directory you are currently in because the source and target are completely defined. If you had already been in the PLAN directory, then the following command could be used.

copy trial88 a:\sheet\budget

When in doubt use a complete path name to avoid errors or even sending the file to the wrong directory.

Other DOS commands can be used in a similar manner. To type the trial88 file from the budget directory, use the following command.

type a:\sheet\budget\trial88

However, for the easiest use of a directory, it is better first to change to the directory in which you plan to work and then issue the commands from that directory. The foregoing command is greatly simplified after changing to the directory containing the trial88 file.

cd\sheet\budget

type trial88

DOS VERSION 4.0

In 1988 PC-DOS Version 4.0 was released with a number of upgrades not included in previous releases of DOS. Two significant features of release 4.0 are the DOS Shell and the support of fixed disk volumes that exceed 32M of storage capacity. In addition a number of minor improvements have been made to some existing DOS commands, and several new commands have been supplied. Error messages have been improved for added clarity.

The DOS Shell provides menus with a variety of options for DOS operations. Instead of typing commands at the old DOS prompt, the user of DOS 4.0 selects an operation, such as directory, by using the cursor keys or a mouse, from the menu. The disk directory then displays in a window on the screen. Familiar DOS operations, such as type, copy, rename, delete, and format, are available. Activities such as sorting the contents of a directory can also be selected from a menu. Moving a file from one directory to another can be done in one step instead of several steps required in previous DOS releases.

Another feature of release 4.0 supports large-capacity fixed disks. Under previous versions of PC-DOS, fixed disks up to 32M were supported. Disks larger than this needed to be divided into a 32M primary partition and one or more extended partitions. Release 4.0 will handle disk volumes in excess of 32M without requiring any special consideration.

Some of the new DOS commands include DOSSHELL, which starts the Shell program from the DOS prompt and lets you alternate between DOS prompt and Shell commands. INSTALL is a program to assist in the installation of DOS features to be used on your system, and MEM is a new command that displays the amount of used and unused memory and programs currently in memory.

A number of former DOS commands have been changed for more effective use. For example, the ERASE command provides an option that prompts you before a file is erased and requires user verification before the file is removed. FORMAT provides an option to enter a volume label when entering the command. The GRAPHICS command now supports CGA, EGA, VGA, and several other display formats and supports more printers than previous DOS releases.

DOS 4.0 still permits the user to escape to the familiar DOS prompt. Experienced DOS users may be comfortable entering their own DOS commands, but new PC users will likely find the menus of the Shell to be much more user friendly and less intimidating until they get up to speed on DOS operations.

RMDIR (RD)

When a directory is no longer required, it can be removed from the disk, providing two conditions are met. The first condition is that the directory must contain no files, and the second is that the full path name be used. To ensure that no files are present a DIR command could be issued first and any files deleted prior to removing the directory.

To remove the subdirectory PLAN from SHEET use the command

RD\SHEET\PLAN

and the directory will be removed. A DIR can be listed at this time to verify that the PLAN directory is no longer present.

OS/2   When IBM announced the new Personal System/2 computer, a parallel announcement of Operating System/2 (OS/2) was made by Microsoft. OS/2 is an operating system that is designed to move us into the world of 32-bit microprocessors and harness the power of Intel's 80286 processor chip and the faster but similar 80386. OS/2 requires a minimum of 1.5M of RAM and a hard disk to run on the PS/2.

Microsoft's goal in designing OS/2 was to create a system that would be suited to an automated office environment. As such, OS/2 is a multitasking, single-user operating system that incorporates windowing, such as that used by the Macintosh, integrated data base functions, and mainframe communications protocols.

Users of OS/2 will soon forget about the old A> prompt so familiar in PC-DOS. Instead, a presentation manager is used that contains many of the features of Microsoft Windows. Icons and menus make the choice of operating system options much simpler than knowing a multitude of commands and parameters.

OS/2 supports several partitions for multitasking: a real-mode that will run a single application program written for the 8086/8088 processor so that programs used on the PC can be run on the PS/2 and a protected-mode that can run a theoretically unlimited number of tasks from RAM. The number of tasks will be limited by the size of RAM and the performance of the system.

Providing a real-mode offers compatibility with older systems already in use with little or no revision to the software. Protected-mode offers many new features such as software protection, virtual memory management, and task management. Software protection is necessary when several programs are running together. If an error or program bug occurs in one program, it is isolated from other programs on the system to ensure that further errors are not created. Applications can use up to 16M of real memory and a gigabyte of virtual memory space on disk.

OS/2 uses the concept of screen groups to manage multiple tasks on a single computer. A screen group can be thought of as a separate computer,

OS/2 memory allocation.

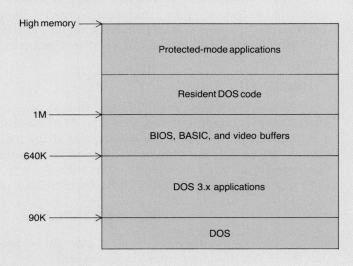

High memory

Protected-mode applications

Resident DOS code

1M

BIOS, BASIC, and video buffers

640K

DOS 3.x applications

90K

DOS

IBM's Presentation Manager.

Courtesy of IBM.

and several of them may be regarded as several PCs all in the one computer. Each screen group can run a separate application. To switch between applications there is a session manager that displays a menu of current screen groups. You rotate through the menu and select the group required by pressing the Enter key. Eventually a mouse will be used to make this selection.

Another concept used on the OS/2 is one of threads. Sometimes it is necessary to have several streams of execution within one task. This might happen when you are waiting for a calculation to be done on a spreadsheet and you could be entering new data or displaying a graph at the same time. OS/2 sets up separate threads of execution in this situation, and each executes independently of the other. Threads may also be assigned different priorities so that the graph might be displayed quickly while the calculation carries on at a more leisurely pace.

Tasks running together may need to communicate with each other and so OS/2 provides pipes, similar to UNIX pipes, to provide a communications channel. A pipe allows an exchange of data between processes. As processing continues, an application can send data as a stream of bytes through a pipe to another task using a process similar to reading and writing a sequential file.

OS/2 also includes a LAN manager to manage local area networks. The assumption seems to be that LANs will become a standard feature of computers that use this operating system. Any computer in the network will be able to function as a file server as well as a work station at the same time. The LAN manager will provide for file and print sharing, user security features, and powerful network administration tools. It also allows a mix of stations running OS/2, MS-DOS, and Xenix.

With the move to 32-bit processing, OS/2 is a new operating system that opens the window to more sophisticated applications in the world of office computing and eases the transition to larger and more capable systems.

Batch Files

A **batch file** is a disk file containing a series of DOS commands. Instead of typing frequently used DOS commands repetitively, they can be stored on an ASCII file with an extension of .BAT. The file can be created with a word processor, such as WordPerfect or WordStar, that can produce an ASCII file, with DOS's COPY CON or with DOS's EDLIN program. EDLIN is a line editor that can create, change, or delete text files from DOS.

Each line in the batch file is a separate DOS command and may include commands that are not ordinarily entered from the keyboard. An example of this type of command is CLS, which clears the screen either before or after other operations. The batch file in Figure 6–6 assumes that there is a subdirectory named \LOTUS that contains the Lotus 1–2–3 program. This batch file is executed by typing the name SS (for spreadsheet) at the DOS prompt at which time the directory is changed to the \LOTUS subdirectory and the Lotus program is executed.

FIGURE 6–6   The batch file SS.BAT is used to start up Lotus 1-2-3 so that the user does not need to enter the commands to change directories each time it is used. The command **echo off** stops DOS from displaying all the commands in the batch file as they are executed.

Next, the entry **cd\lotus** changes to the \LOTUS directory and then a message is echoed to the screen to welcome the user. The **pause** command waits for the user to press any key before it continues at which point the screen is cleared **(cls).** Next **lotus** is run.

Now the usual Lotus 1–2–3 commands will be in effect until the user leaves Lotus in the normal manner. Finally, the batch command **cd** is issued to return DOS to the root directory before leaving the batch file.

```
A>dir

 Volume in drive A has no label
 Directory of  A:\

SHEET          <DIR>       5-27-87   8:34a
LOTUS          <DIR>       5-28-87  10:41a
SS       BAT        81     5-28-87  10:44a
        3 File(s)     355328 bytes free

A>type ss.bat
echo off
cd\lotus
echo
echo       Welcome to Lotus 1-2-3
echo
pause
cls
lotus
cd\

A>
```

UNIX

UNIX is a multiuser multitasking operating system developed in the late 1960s at the Bell Laboratories that gained prominence under AT&T's leadership. It is a large and complex operating system that is loaded with features and used by many university computer systems. Because of its extensive nature, UNIX takes a long time to learn but users who have made the commitment are generally enthusiastic about the software.

Computers ranging from personal computers to minis to mainframes can run UNIX, and it is easily adaptable to new systems. Because PCs have not generally been multiuser systems, the need for an operating system such as UNIX has been minimal and as a result few versions have been developed for the PC. An exception is the XENIX operating system by the Santa Cruz Operation (Figure 6–7). With larger-capacity systems such as the IBM PC/AT and the PS/2, the need for a multiuser multitasking operating system is becoming more apparent.

UNIX is attractive to software development programmers because it contains many supporting features that simplify the task of writing programs. Included in UNIX are more than 200 utilities that take away much of the drudgery of coding from the programmer. However, detractors say that UNIX is too big,

UNIX operating system. Courtesy of *High Technology* magazine.

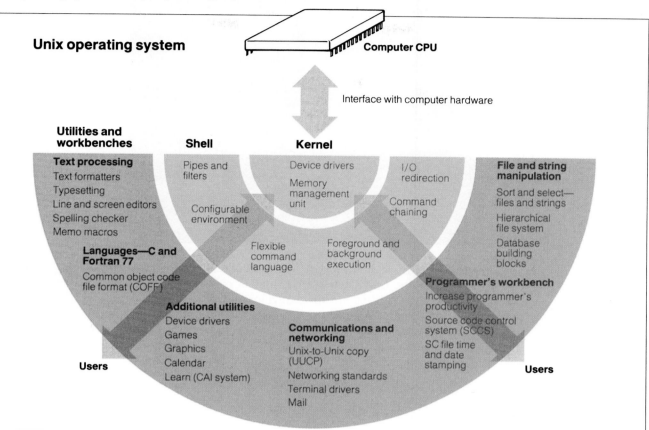

Unix operating system

Computer CPU

Interface with computer hardware

Utilities and workbenches   **Shell**   **Kernel**

Text processing
Text formatters
Typesetting
Line and screen editors
Spelling checker
Memo macros

Pipes and filters

Configurable environment

Flexible command language

Device drivers

Memory management unit

Foreground and background execution

I/O redirection

Command chaining

File and string manipulation
Sort and select—files and strings
Hierarchical file system
Database building blocks

Languages—C and Fortran 77
Common object code file format (COFF)

Additional utilities
Device drivers
Games
Graphics
Calendar
Learn (CAI system)

Communications and networking
Unix-to-Unix copy (UUCP)
Networking standards
Terminal drivers
Mail

Programmer's workbench
Increase programmer's productivity
Source code control system (SCCS)
SC file time and date stamping

Users

Users

The multiuser, multitasking Unix operating system from Bell Labs is a a layered system. The **kernel** interfaces directly to the computer's central processing unit (a microprocessor chip, in the case of super-micros) and is modified to run on different CPUs and to alter hardware-related operations such as memory management. Because Unix is written in C, a high-level language, it is less hardware-dependent than operating systems written in lower-level

machine language. This trait makes Unix easy to transport from one system to another. Surrounding the kernel is the **shell**, which serves as a programming language and as a command language interpreter, reading lines typed by the user and interpreting them as requests to execute certain programs. Around the shell are various **utilities** and **workbenches** such as text processing and support for the C and Fortran 77 languages. Some parts of Unix,

such as the **programmer's workbench**, which helps software developers, aren't required by all users and are sometimes dropped in Unix-derived systems sold by companies that license the operating system. These firms also modify parts of Unix to meet different requirements. The kernel might be changed to run on different chips, for instance, or menus might be added to help novice users interact with the system.

it requires 15 disks for the IBM PC, is too slow, and is too hard to use. It is interesting to observe that when IBM brought out the second-generation PC, the Personal System/2, it did not adopt UNIX as its operating system.

The part of UNIX that communicates with the user is called the **shell.** It is distinctive from DOS in that it can be customized in any environment to meet the users' needs. By modifying the shell, UNIX can be very user friendly, and as a result the complexities of the system can be reserved for the professionals.

Because UNIX is developed for different systems and under different names, there needs to be some consistency in its implementation. This consistency

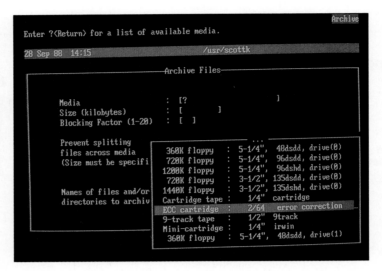

FIGURE 6–7

A screen shot of the Santa Cruz Operation's XENIX multiuser multitasking operating system based on AT&T's UNIX. XENIX offers multiscreen capability, a system administration shell, use of high-capacity Winchester disks, clock support, multiple printer support, a software development tool, and a text processor, among many other technical features.

Courtesy of XENIX, Santa Cruz.

is ensured through the heart of the UNIX system called the **kernel.** This is the part of the operating system that is essentially the same on all versions of UNIX. All utilities are then developed external to the kernel and can vary from one system to another. Because AT&T continues to provide UNIX with its PCs, and given its popularity on a variety of minicomputers, UNIX is likely going to be around for a long time.

OTHER OPERATING SYSTEMS

CP/M

CP/M (Control Program for Microcomputers) was developed by Digital Research Corporation as an operating system for 8-bit microcomputers. It initially gained popularity on computers based on the Zilog Z80 processor chip and was an option on early Apple computers where a second processor was required if CP/M was to be used.

Many other 8-bit computer manufacturers adopted CP/M because it was less expensive than developing their own operating system. CP/M's popularity on 8-bit systems led to a large variety of software being developed for most of the traditional business applications and some not so traditional. When 16-bit computers became available, a new version called CP/M-86, for the new family of 8088/8086 processors, was developed. Although CP/M was a leading operating system, and is still in use today on existing 8-bit systems, it has taken a back seat to MS-DOS/PC-DOS.

Macintosh Operating System

Unlike other operating systems that are procedural in nature, the Macintosh operating system uses an object-oriented language. Object-oriented means that the user concentrates on the task to be done and not on the commands needed to do the job. This feat is accomplished by using icons on the screen that

POPULAR OPERATING SYSTEMS

PC-DOS from IBM (MS-DOS from Microsoft) is the most widely used operating system on personal computers today. Whether the PC is from IBM or is one of the many compatibles, this operating system is likely the one to be in use.

MS-DOS/PC-DOS on the PC/AT.
Courtesy of IBM.

Operating System/2 (OS/2) was released for the IBM PS/2 and other 80286 or higher level computers. OS/2 provides the advanced computer user with the Presentation Manager, multitasking, and LAN management features.

OS/2 on the PS/2.
Courtesy of IBM.

The UNIX operating system is a serious competitor for users requiring a multitasking environment. Originally developed for minicomputers, variations of UNIX are now available for a variety of personal computers.

UNIX on an AT&T PC.
Courtesy of AT&T Archives.

Operating systems originated with mainframe computers and many of the features used historically on the mainframe for several decades are just now becoming available in the personal computing environment.

OS/MVS on an IBM mainframe system.
Courtesy of IBM.

(Continued)

The Macintosh operating system uses an object-oriented approach. Users select activities by pointing to icons on the screen that represent tasks to be done.

Macintosh on the Apple MAC II.
Courtesy of Apple Computer, Inc.

represent tasks. For example, a file folder is used to represent opening a file and is selected by pointing to it with a mouse and pressing a button.

The advantage of using icons for an operating system is that the system is easy to use, often requiring little or no training for its use. Rather than needing to know specific commands such as DIR, or ERASE, the user simply needs to recognize a few common symbols.

An offshoot of using icons in the operating system has been application programs that take the same approach. Using icons in a word processor or spreadsheet makes it easier to learn, and the user becomes productive very quickly. Because of IBM's dominance in the PC marketplace, the Mac has had a long struggle to carve out its own niche. Slowly but surely it has been able to find a market for this product, and there is no doubt that the Macintosh operating system will be around for many years to come.

Apple's Macintosh uses an object-oriented operating system. Here we can see the use of icons to select system functions, thus letting the user see what is to be done rather than memorizing a series of commands.

Courtesy of Apple Computer, Inc.

OPERATING SYSTEMS TODAY

We have seen that operating systems for personal computers have developed separately from those for mainframes. But as PCs have grown in power and capacity, they have begun to adopt features formerly available in the mainframe. The ability to do multitasking and to serve multiusers originated with the mainframe but are now becoming available on personal computers with operating systems such as OS/2. Although these developments are becoming more widespread, the single-user, single-tasking operating system, such as PC-DOS, is still in common use among PC users.

CHAPTER SUMMARY

1. The disk operating system (DOS) that is used on IBM personal computers is called PC-DOS based on Microsoft's MS-DOS.

2. The component of the operating system for input/output (I/O) management takes care of the flow of data to and from the various devices attached to the computer.

3. Memory management is a component of the operating system that controls where programs are located in memory and whether there is room for application and resident programs and the loading of main and overlay programs.

4. The operating system also processes commands that are entered by the computer user such as commands for copying, erasing or renaming files, preparing new disks for use, defining and using subdirectories on hard disk, and listing the contents of a directory.

5. Utility programs are another component of operating systems that can be run to perform disk maintenance activities such as formatting, copying the entire contents of one disk to another, checking the disk for errors, sorting a disk file, or creating a RAM disk in the computer's memory.

6. An operating system may be classified into one of three basic groups: single tasking, multitasking, and multiuser. Single tasking works on one task at a time, multitasking performs two or more tasks simultaneously in foreground and background, and multiuser permits more than one user to have access to a single computer from separate terminals.

7. DOS may be booted with either a cold or warm start. A cold start occurs when the power is turned on and a full self-test of the hardware is done before DOS is booted. A warm start of DOS occurs by pressing the Ctrl-Alt and Del keys. Only a few of the self-checking features will be done following a warm start.

8. PC-DOS commands are always entered at the DOS prompt, which is usually A> for a floppy disk or C> for hard disk.

9. The DOS prompt currently showing on the screen also identifies the default disk drive. DOS actions will take place on this disk drive unless otherwise requested in the command.

10. A new disk must always be formatted with the FORMAT command before the disk can be used.

11. DOS contains both internal and external commands. Internal commands are contained in the COMMAND.COM program, which is loaded into memory when DOS is booted. Commands such as COPY, DATE, TIME, DIR, ERASE, and TYPE are internal commands. External commands are contained on the DOS disk as separate files. Commands such as CHKDSK, FORMAT, and DISKCOPY are external.

12. A hard disk benefits from the use of a hierarchical directory so that files may be organized in several subdirectories. Commands used with hierarchical directories

are MKDIR (MD) to make a new directory, CHDIR (CD) to change to a different directory, and RMDIR (RD), which removes a directory from the disk.

13. Path names consist of one or more directory names beginning with the back slash (\). The maximum size for a path name is 63 characters. If necessary a drive name (like A: or C:) may precede the path name. A path name could be as simple as C:\ for the root directory, or more complex such as C:\SHEET\BUDGET when a sub-subdirectory is in use.

14. A batch file is a disk file containing a series of DOS commands stored in ASCII format with an extension of .BAT. Each line in the batch file is a separate DOS command. Commands can be those normally entered at a DOS prompt such as cd\ or a program name or other DOS commands such as cls, pause, or echo.

15. UNIX is a multiuser multitasking operating system developed in the late 1960s at the Bell Laboratories. Computers ranging from personal computers to minis to mainframes can run UNIX, and it is easily adaptable to new systems. UNIX is attractive to software development programmers because it contains many supporting features that simplify the task of writing programs.

16. The part of UNIX that communicates with the user is called the shell. The shell can be customized to meet user needs.

17. Because UNIX is developed for different systems and under different names, there needs to be some consistency in its implementation. This consistency is ensured through the heart of the UNIX system called the kernel, which is the part that is essentially the same on all versions of UNIX.

18. The Macintosh operating system uses an object-oriented language rather than a procedural one like other operating systems. Object-oriented means that the user concentrates on the task to be done and not on the commands needed to do the job by using icons on the screen that represent tasks.

IMPORTANT TERMS AND CONCEPTS		
Batch file	Hierarchical directory	Path
CHDIR (CD)	Input/output	PC-DOS
Cold start	management	RENAME
Commands	Internal commands	RMDIR (RD)
COPY	Kernel	Shell
CP/M	Memory management	Single tasking
Default disk drive	Microsoft disk	Source disk
DIR	operating system	Target disk
DISKCOMP	(MS-DOS)	TYPE
DISKCOPY	MKDIR (MD)	UNIX
DOS (disk operating	MS-DOS	Utilities
system)	Multitasking	Warm start
ERASE	Multiuser	Wildcard
External commands		
FORMAT		

REVIEW QUESTIONS

Fill-in Questions

1. The term DOS is an abbreviation for _____ _____ _____.

2. A(n) _____ operating system permits two or more tasks to function at the same time.

3. The _____ command is used in PC-DOS to provide a list of files contained on a disk.

4. New disks are prepared by using the _____ command.

5. Names such as \SHEET\BUDGET are called a(n) _____.

6. The _____ disk drive is the disk that DOS will operate on unless instructed otherwise.

Matching Questions

Match each term with the description given below.

a. CD   d. OS/2
b. RENAME   e. single tasking
c. UNIX   f. utility

_____ *e* ___ 1. The class of operating system, such as PC-DOS, that permits only one task at a time.

_____ 2. This DOS command is used to change the name of a file on disk.

_____ *c* ___ 3. A multitasking, multiuser operating system used primarily on mini-computers.

_____ 4. A DOS command that is used when you want to switch to a different subdirectory.

_____ 5. An operating system program, such as FORMAT, that is used to perform disk maintenance activities.

_____ 6. This operating system was developed by Microsoft for the IBM Personal System/2 and other 80286 and 80386 computers.

Discussion Questions

1. Name and describe the four basic functions of an operating system.

2. There are three classes of operating systems in use on today's computers. What are they? Describe their main function.

3. Describe two different methods for booting DOS.

4. What is meant by the default disk drive? How do you know which drive is the default?

5. Discuss the difference between DOS's internal and external commands. What effect does this difference have on the way they are used?

6. Explain how one of the following commands works. Give at least two examples of its use. COPY, ERASE, RENAME, DISKCOPY, or TYPE.

7. Explain what is meant by a path name. Write the path name for the file TEST2 which is located in the subdirectory EXAMS on the C: disk.

8. Name three commands used for hierarchical directories and explain how and why they are used.

9. What is a batch file? Why are batch files useful?

10. Why is UNIX likely to become a more popular and widely used operating system? What are its basic strengths and weaknesses?

11. Discuss the characteristics of OS/2.

Application Software

A VIEW OF THE CHAPTER AHEAD

After Reading This Chapter You Will Understand:

- How application software is used on a personal computer.

- The different types of user interfaces used by computer programs.

- Why it is necessary to install software before it can be used to its full capacity.

No matter what your reason for using a computer it will require the use of software. Whether you are a businessperson doing accounts receivable, a manager doing sales forecasting, or a technician repairing computers, software will be used to assist you in your activities on the computer. In many cases two or more levels of software will be used on the computer. This chapter will discuss ways of using software and the basic skills required to begin the process of learning different software packages.

DISK OPERATING SYSTEM

All activity on the computer comes from the underlying operating system. We saw in Chapter 1 that the disk operating system (DOS) controls the input and output activity from active programs in the computer. Before a program is run it is important that DOS first be **resident** in the computer's memory. Figure 7–1 shows how DOS is the primary resident program used for running a variety of different software packages. Only one of these programs can be active with DOS at any one time, but, when one is finished running, another can take its place in memory.

DOS is first booted on the computer when the power is turned on as described in Chapter 6. After DOS has been loaded, the DOS prompt is displayed (see Figure 7–2) on the screen. DOS 4.0 may display a Shell menu instead of a prompt.

All users of personal computers require the disk operating system to be used with their application software. DOS handles input and output activities required when working with disk files or using the printer.

Courtesy of IBM.

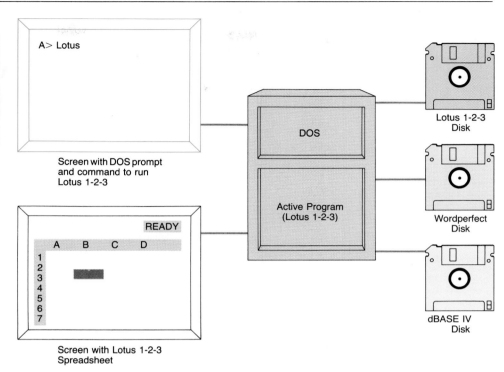

FIGURE 7–1
DOS is always resident when other programs are run on the computer. At the DOS prompt the name of the program is entered, which causes the program to be loaded and run. When you are finished using one program, another may be loaded in a similar manner.

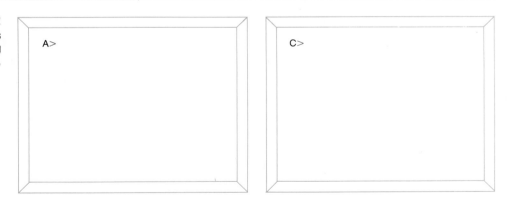

FIGURE 7–2
Two types of DOS prompts that can appear after booting DOS on an IBM PC, PC/XT, AT, PS/2, or compatible.

DOS Prompt Commands

There are many commands that may be entered at the DOS prompt, some of which are DOS commands for working with disk files such as DIR, COPY, or ERASE as described in the previous chapter. A number of these commands are explored in detail in the DOS tutorial that accompanies this book. Others are commands for loading and running programs or software. Table 7–1 shows

TABLE 7–1

Commands for Starting a
Variety of Software from
DOS.

Command to Enter at the DOS Prompt	Software Package
BASICA	Advanced Disk BASIC
DBASE	dBASE III Plus or dBASE IV
HAL	Lotus HAL
HPG	Harvard Presentation Graphics
LOTUS	Lotus 1–2–3
RBSYSTEM	R:BASE System V
SC4	SuperCalc 4
WP	WordPerfect
WS	WordStar Professional

a few commands that are used for running some of the more popular software packages. Commands may be entered in either upper- or lowercase. Also included is the command for running BASIC, which is one language used for writing your programs.

The rules for using a specific software package are unique to that program. Rules of use that have been learned for one program may not necessarily apply for another. Even some simple things such as the use of a key on the keyboard may take on different meanings. So in this chapter we will discuss general principles. For specific details on a given software package, see the tutorial for that software.

APPLICATION PROGRAMS

What the majority of users see when using the computer is the application software. Much of the work by computer training companies goes into teaching the user an application package and then training them to become productive with it. Application packages include hundreds of programs in several different major groups (see Figure 7–3). Some of the best known of these are the spreadsheets Lotus 1–2–3 or Excel, data base software dBASE IV or R:BASE System V, and word processors such as WordPerfect and WordStar. Of course there are many more programs available in each of these categories, and you may well have some favorites that are not mentioned here.

Software Packages

Applications software consists of more than just the disk on which the software resides. As Figure 7–4 shows, a software package often comes in a neatly packaged carton (thus the origin of the name software package) suitable for storing the material supplied for easy reference.

FIGURE 7–3

The seven major categories
of application software.

Photos courtesy of (a) IBM; (b) Apple
Computer, Inc.; (c) IBM; (d) Home Shopping
Network; (e) GNF Robotics; (f) Apple
Computer, Inc.; (g) Apple Computer, Inc.

Software Category	Specific Applications	
Productivity	Graphics Spreadsheet Word processing Presentation graphics Integrated software Desktop publishing	
Business systems	Accounting Payroll Decision support systems Industry specific	
Data base management	Flat file databases Relational databases	
Communications	Local area networks Online services Micro-mainframe link	
Artificial intelligence	Knowledge-based systems Robotics	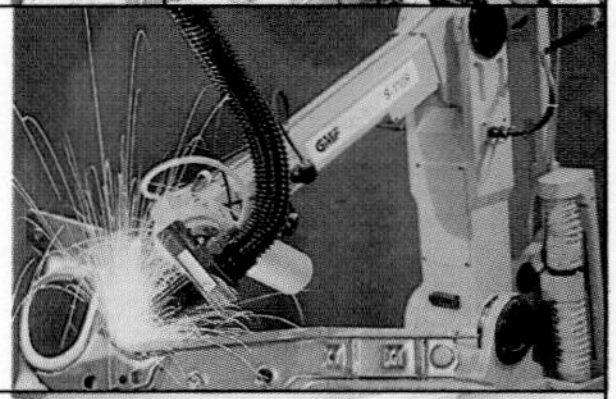
Education	Tutorial Administration Languages	
Home Systems	Entertainment Record keeping	

THE VARIED USES OF SOFTWARE

Communication lines.

Courtesy of Western Union Corporation.

The software on these Western Union computers is used for network management of communications lines across the country. The program finds the optimum route for calls from one area of the country to another. As a call is made, the program looks for available channels, finds the most direct route, and makes the connection.

Desktop publishing.

Courtesy of IBM.

Interleaf is IBM's top level desktop publishing program. It is a powerful publishing tool originally developed for mainframe computers and now available on 80386 based personal computers. Interleaf is a graphics based word processing program with charting and text capabilities. With its extensive features only the most demanding applications will require a program of this character.

Music applications.

Courtesy of IBM.

Computers are making inroads into the world of music. Although synthesizer hardware has been available to musicians for some time, new software is now integrating the computer with the instrument. This PS/2 Model 30 is being used to compose, record, and play back music with an attached synthesizer.

Instructional software.

Courtesy of Mindscape, Inc.

Computer graphics have made new inroads into the field of instructional software. In this Body in Focus application, the graphics software is used to study the muscle structure of the body.

(*Continued*)

Automotive guidance system.

Courtesy of Chrysler Corporation.

Using a system such as this NAVSTAR guidance computer can help to keep you from getting lost when in unfamiliar surroundings. The software in this system refers to a data base of maps and compares this data to the movement of the car. Advanced automotive guidance systems also use satellite communication to help determine the car's location at any time.

A complete software package makes it easier both to install the program on your computer and to learn how to use the software. Packages typically include the following components.

- **Diskettes.** Included with the package are one or more diskettes containing the program and other necessary data. Typical packages contain five or six disks; some have many more. If $3\frac{1}{2}$-inch disks are provided then only half as many disks are needed. In addition to the main program, diskettes may also include help information, an on-screen tutorial to demonstrate the use of the program, an install program to install the software on your unique computer system, printer drivers, and conversion programs to convert data prepared by other software.

- **Manuals.** Most important is the instruction manual that explains the use of the software. Some of the more complete packages also include a separate installation manual, and an overview manual or lesson that quickly and easily introduces the owner to the more commonly used features of the program without getting into all its complexities. A few of the more complex packages may also have a separate manual that explains the advanced features of the software.

FIGURE 7–4

A complete software package includes diskettes, one or more instruction manuals, a quick reference guide, a keyboard template, and a warranty card.

Courtesy of Lotus Development Corporation.

- **Keyboard Template.** Much of today's software makes use of the function keys provided on the computer's keyboard. The plastic template fits over the function keys and lists all the function key commands for easy reference at the keyboard.

- **Quick Reference Guide.** This is a handy reference to all the commands in the software. Once the contents of the reference manual has been mastered, most users find a reference card to be an easier way to look up instructions.

- **Warranty Card.** This card is similar to one you might get with a new stereo or camera and is filled out and mailed to the manufacturer. Registering your software gives coverage in the event that a failure occurs with the software or its disk. This does not necessarily cover bugs in the program but may entitle you to free or low-cost updates if a revised program is made available in the near future.

Main and Overlay Programs

Complex application software such as data base, spreadsheet, or word processing programs contain a considerable amount of program code. For example, the code for dBASE IV listed in the directory in Figure 7–5 contains a total of over 2.2M bytes on disk. If all this code were required to reside in RAM at one time, a 2M computer could not handle it. Many 80286 or 80386 computers are not equipped with this amount of RAM.

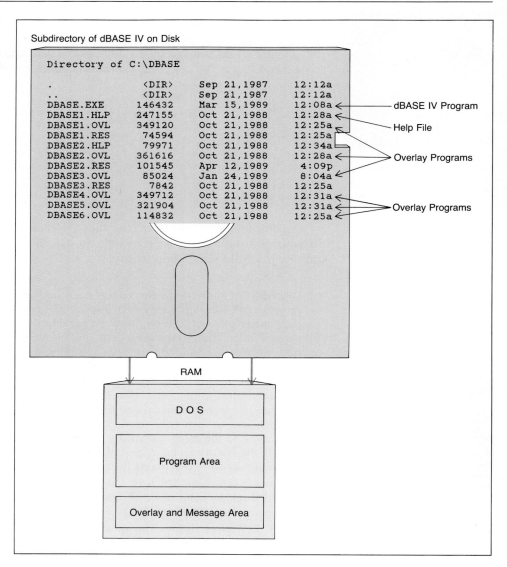

FIGURE 7–5
Using overlays in RAM to reduce the total memory requirements for an application program.

To solve this problem, software is often developed in parts: the main program and one or more overlay programs. The main part is the controlling program called the .EXE (pronounced exec) for an executable program. For dBASE this consists of about 146K of code. The rest of the program is stored in parts on disk and are called into memory as they are required. dBASE has six overlay (OVL) files as shown in the directory. As certain features of the program are required, the code for executing those features is temporarily brought into the overlay area of RAM. When a new program feature is required, it replaces the code formerly in the overlay area thus minimizing the amount of memory required to run the program.

Other program overlays are also handled in this manner. Overlays for help files, messages, and assistant menus are also provided and brought into memory only as they are needed.

FIGURE 7–6

Location of a drive A on full- and half-height disk drive systems.

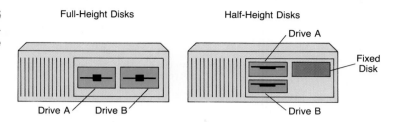

Running a Program

To run a program such as dBASE, Lotus 1–2–3, or WordPerfect, it is first necessary to have DOS booted on your computer as explained earlier in the chapter. The next step is to insert the disk containing the software you wish to run into drive A (unless the program is already installed on the hard disk, drive C). Drive A is the left drive on a dual-drive full-height system or the top drive of a dual-drive half-height system (Figure 7–6).

After inserting the system disk for the application, the program name is typed at the DOS prompt. If the DOS prompt was displayed as

A>

then typing the command DBASE would show on the screen as

A>DBASE

after which the Enter key would be pressed. The program now loads into memory.

Some programs—dBASE is one of them—require a disk to be changed after the program has been loaded. A message on the screen gives instructions for this step. Refer to the appropriate tutorial with this book for specific instructions for each software package.

To Program or Use Application Software?

Pioneers in computing were required to write a program for each application that was needed on the computer. But, during the four generations of computer use, an abundance of software has accumulated for an almost unlimited variety of applications. Does this widespread availability mean that it is no longer necessary to write programs? Or even to learn a programming language such as those in the following table?

Programming Languages for PCs	
Assembler	Forth
BASIC	FORTRAN
C	Pascal
COBOL	Prolog

For many computer users writing a program will be unnecessary, and even learning to program might be a questionable activity. Before writing a program, you need to ask a few pointed questions.

1. Is there a program available that will do the task required? Will it run on my computer?
2. Would it be less costly to purchase the program than to write an equivalent one?
3. Can an existing program be adapted to my needs? Will it take less time and money than writing a completely new program?
4. Can the application be implemented with spreadsheet or data base software instead of using a traditional programming language?

Many applications have already been developed and can be used as is. Most programs for personal computers cost a few hundred dollars; some cost considerably less. Writing a complex program can require hundreds of hours, which far exceeds the cost of buying a program. In other cases, some changes will need to be made to an existing program, but this is much easier and less costly than writing a completely new program.

Sometimes, the only option is to write a program that will do your unique job. If this is necessary, following an orderly, well-planned approach is vital to successful program development. Hacking together a "quick and dirty" program is rarely a satisfactory solution.

Another approach that is becoming more and more popular is to implement the solution to a business problem using a spreadsheet or data base software package. Because these are general-purpose packages, a wide variety of applications can be developed with them. Using a spreadsheet or other general-purpose package can speed up application development many times over using a programming language. And, because they are not programming languages, almost anyone can master their use.

However, learning to program does have its advantages. To use software, such as a spreadsheet like Lotus 1–2–3, or a database such as dBASE IV, to its greatest advantage requires the use of programminglike tools. Thus having some programming knowledge can pay dividends when developing applications on many different types of software packages.

Writing a program from scratch can also be useful if the user requirements are not suited to application packages. Although packages are generally flexible, they do have some limitations that can often be easily overcome with a program in Assembler, BASIC, Pascal, or C language. Writing your own program, or having a professional write it, offers the most flexibility if you are prepared to wait and to pay the price for a custom job.

USING THE KEYBOARD

Using any software requires that you have an understanding of the keyboard. In this section we will discuss the primary keys and their use for most software packages. The box "Using the PC Keyboard" explains the purpose of the keys for commonly used keyboards. If you are using some other keyboard on a PC compatible or a PS/2, there will likely be some differences, but they will be

The most widely used keyboard is found on the IBM personal computer. Other keyboards may be used and will likely differ only slightly from this one. Even more recent IBM keyboards such as the AT or the Personal System/2 have many similarities. So if you master one, then adapting to another keyboard will be quite easy. Most keys are autorepeat, meaning that if you hold them down, the character or action will be repeated until the key is released.

IBM Personal System/2 Keyboard.

Courtesy of IBM.

Function Keys

The function keys are assigned for special duties in each software package. In Lotus 1–2–3, F1 is used for help information while F10 is used to draw a graph.

 to

Main Keyboard

The Escape key is used to escape from an operation before it is completed.

The Tab key is used to move the cursor to preset tab stops across the screen. Reverse Tab is used with the Shift key to move to a previous tab stop.

The Ctrl (control) key is used with another key (usually a letter) to issue a command to the software. Holding down Ctrl and pressing the S key will stop scrolling in DOS.

The shift keys are used to select uppercase letters or to type the character found at the top of a key such as the $ above the 4.

The Alt (alternate) key is used like Ctrl with another key. In WordPerfect, holding down Alt and pressing F2 starts the search and replace operation.

Backspace Delete is used to delete the character to the left of the cursor position.

The Return or Enter key is used to complete an entry. In DOS, after typing the name of a program, Enter is pressed to enter the command and load the program into memory. The name Return comes from the carriage return key on a typewriter.

Print screen can be used to print the entire contents of the screen on your printer. To use this key, hold down shift and press PrtSc.

When pressed all alphabetic keys will type capital letters. Press again to return to lowercase.

Ins (insert) is used to turn insert mode on or off. In a word processor, this mode will let you insert letters or words in existing text.

The Del (delete) key is used to delete a character at the cursor position.

Numeric Key Pad

Pressing Num Lock causes the numeric keypad to go into number mode. Keys pressed will enter numbers. Pressing Num Lock again will return to cursor mode.

In some software, such as Lotus 1–2–3, pressing Scroll Lock will permit lines on the screen to move but not the cursor.

The Home key moves the cursor to the top left corner of the screen.

The End key moves the cursor to the bottom of the screen.

The Page Up key moves the screen contents up one page to the previous page.

The Page Down key moves the screen contents down one page to the following page.

Cursor Up moves the cursor up one line.

Cursor Down moves the cursor down one line.

Cursor Left moves the cursor left one character.

Cursor Right moves the cursor right one character.

In most software this key enters a minus sign.

In most software this key enters a plus sign.

few. Regardless of the keyboard you are using there are three basic categories of operation that it provides to the computer user. These are

1. Entry or changing of characters.
2. Cursor movement.
3. Entry of program commands.

While much of the use of the keyboard is common between application programs, there are differences. Categories 1 and 2 are often quite similar from one software package to another while category 3 can be totally different, although the same keys are used but for different purposes.

Keyboard Templates

Because application software packages each have different uses for the function keys, a method is needed to reference the use of these keys easily. Many software packages, such as Lotus 1–2–3, provide a plastic keyboard template that fits directly over the function keys on the keyboard (Figure 7–7). Each key's function is clearly identified on the template, and by pressing that key the specific action will occur. In Lotus 1–2–3 Release 2 ten different functions are provided.

Other software, such as WordPerfect, provides 40 different functions by combining the Crtl, Shift, and Alt keys with the function keys. Ten functions are available with the function keys alone, ten with the Ctrl and function keys, ten more with Shift, and another ten with Alt.

Remembering 40 different functions is no mean feat, so WordPerfect provides a color-coded template (Figure 7–8) with all the functions on it. Pressing the appropriate combination of keys activates the required function. For example, pressing F3 by itself calls up the help screen. Pressing Ctrl and F2 activates the spelling checker.

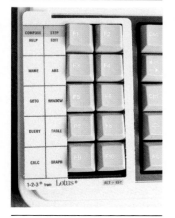

FIGURE 7–7
A function key template used in Lotus 1–2–3.

Courtesy of Christie Tito.

USING SOFTWARE

Once a program has been loaded into memory, by entering its name at the DOS prompt, it is ready for use. Software often begins by displaying an opening screen that presents copyright information and an agreement for use. Most programs will clear this information from the screen after a few seconds, but others, such as dBASE III Plus, ask you to press the Enter key to assent to the agreement. Other software may ask you to insert a key disk at this point, if you are running from a hard disk drive.

Following these preliminaries, the program presents the first screen that you will need to understand to use the programs. What is presented at this

FIGURE 7–8

WordPerfect's color-coded function key template. Entries in black use the function key by itself. Red entries require the Ctrl key, green uses the Shift key, and blue the Alt key for a total of 40 different function key combinations.

Courtesy of WordPerfect Corporation.

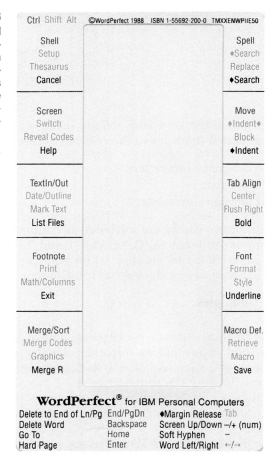

Ctrl Shift Alt	©WordPerfect 1988 ISBN 1-55692-200-0 TMXXENWPIIE50	
Shell		Spell
Setup		◆Search
Thesaurus		Replace
Cancel		◆Search
Screen		Move
Switch		◆Indent◆
Reveal Codes		Block
Help		◆Indent
TextIn/Out		Tab Align
Date/Outline		Center
Mark Text		Flush Right
List Files		Bold
Footnote		Font
Print		Format
Math/Columns		Style
Exit		Underline
Merge/Sort		Macro Def.
Merge Codes		Retrieve
Graphics		Macro
Merge R		Save

WordPerfect® for IBM Personal Computers

Delete to End of Ln/Pg	End/PgDn	◆Margin Release	Tab
Delete Word	Backspace	Screen Up/Down –/+ (num)	
Go To	Home	Soft Hyphen	–
Hard Page	Enter	Word Left/Right	←/→

Pop-up menus are used in Top-View for making selections in the application program.

Courtesy of IBM.

time varies considerably from one program to another and depends to a large extent upon the way the user interface to the program was designed. There are several software techniques that users may use to interface with programs.

1. Menu software driven
2. Function key driven software
3. Prompt driven software
4. Command driven software
5. Form filling software
6. Icon interface software

User Interfaces

Menu-driven software

You are certainly familiar with menus, at least those you might find in a restaurant where you make a choice of several appetizing alternatives. It is much the same way with a software menu. A list of choices is presented on the screen (Figure 7–9), and the user makes a selection from this list.

A menu, such as that used by WordStar, requires that you type a letter that identifies the selection. In WordStar's case typing the letter will immediately activate the command. For example, pressing the letter D will cause a document to be opened. When a letter describes the operation, such as D for Document, P for Print, and M for Merge, then the command is called **mnemonic.**

Some menu systems require that the Enter key be pressed after the selection is made. The advantage with this method is you can change your mind if you want a different option or if a typing error was made.

Cursor Pointing. While menus have been around since the first microcomputers, a more recent development in thinking led to the use of cursor pointing to make a selection. This concept was made popular by Lotus 1–2–3 with its menus displayed on the top line, called a command line, of the screen (Figure 7–10). The menu is displayed by first pressing the slash (/) key. Then, pressing the right or left cursor keys causes the highlighted bar, called a pointer, to move from one option to another. When the pointer is resting upon the required option, say, the Worksheet option, the Enter key is pressed to make the selection.

To make the software even easier to use, the first letter of any option in the menu may be pressed instead of moving the pointer. Simply pressing / W causes the Worksheet option to be chosen. By a clever choice of names, each option begins with a different letter and therefore also has a mnemonic meaning.

Multilevel Menus. Many application software programs use several levels of menus in their operation. Both Lotus 1–2–3 (Figure 7–11) and WordStar (Figure 7–12) use multilevel menus although in quite different ways. A multilevel menu means that once a choice has been made from one menu, it can lead to further choices on a second menu and so on. Multilevel menus generally

FIGURE 7–9

A pull-down menu screen displayed from WordStar Professional Version 5. Typing the command from the menu activates the related operation.

Courtesy of Micropro

FIGURE 7–10

Menus in Lotus 1–2–3 use cursor keys to move the cell pointer to the option required in the menu.

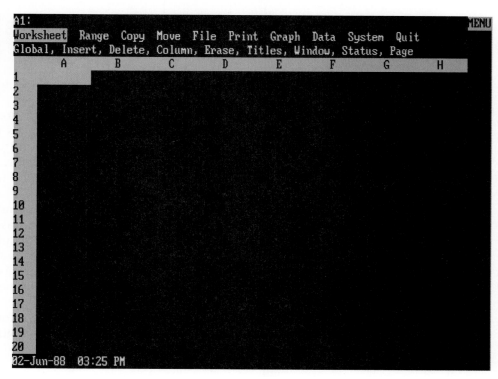

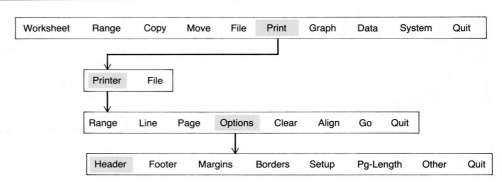

FIGURE 7–11
The use of multilevel menus in Lotus 1–2–3. A choice of Print at the top-level menu leads to a choice of Printer or File at the second level. Selecting Printer gives a third-level menu with a number of choices. Choosing Options at this level gives a further list of activities relating to printing.

FIGURE 7–12   Multilevel menus used in WordStar Professional. Menus present an average of 16 choices from which the user can select.

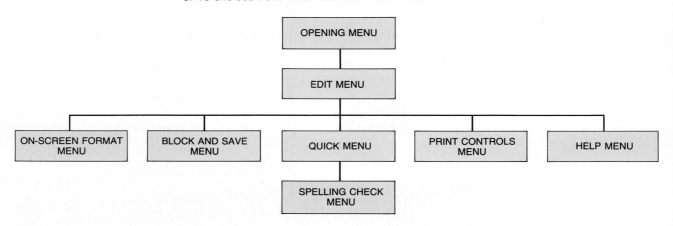

begin with a single main menu that branches out to one or more subsidiary levels where further choices are made.

The benefit of multilevel menus is that they present the user with fewer options at any one time. Then, when an option has been selected, the user is presented with further choices that pertain to only the option chosen. This greatly simplifies the use of the software and helps to make it user friendly. For more detail on using menus of this type, refer to the tutorial package on Lotus 1–2–3.

Pull-down and Pop-up Menus. These menus are an alternate method of presenting a multilevel menu where several entries need to be made to take a specific action. Pull-down menus frequently require fewer keystrokes than do multilevel menus. As a choice is made from a menu at the top of the screen, a submenu drops down to show the lower-level choice to be made. These are selected by pointing with the cursor keys or typing the first letter of the choice.

An example of a pull-down menu is shown for dBASE IV in Figure 7–13. When Set Up at the top of the screen is highlighted, the pull-down menu

FIGURE 7–13
Pull-down menus are used in dBASE IV and Framework for selecting program options. As each option in the menu at the top of the screen is highlighted, a new pull-down menu will appear below it.

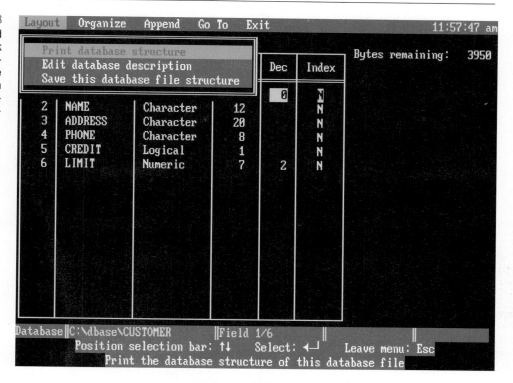

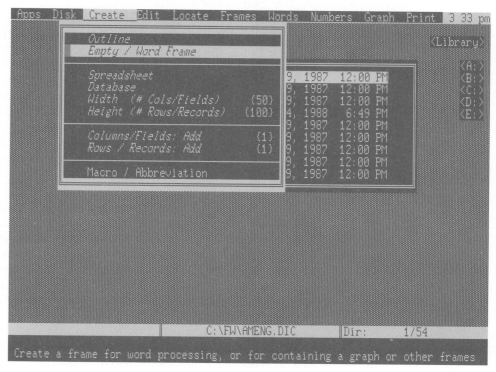

FIGURE 7–14
SideKick Plus uses a pop-up menu that appears over existing work on the screen. When the activity selected in SideKick Plus has been completed, the screen returns to normal.

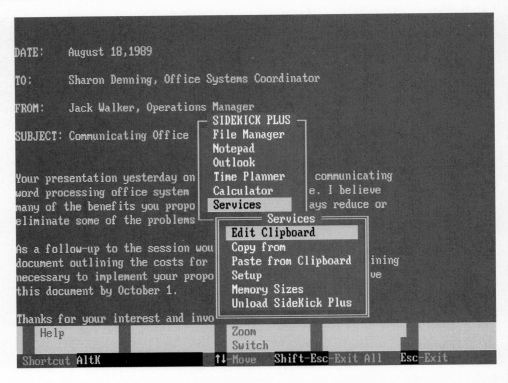

shows the six choices that may be made if you choose Set Up from the main menu. By pointing down to any one of these with the cursor key and then pressing Enter, the choice is made. Other choices are identified at the bottom of the screen.

A pop-up menu is one that appears somewhere in the middle of the screen. This menu is activated by some predefined keystroke on the keyboard. For example, the memory-resident program SideKick is activated by pressing the Ctrl and Alt keys together. As shown in Figure 7–14 when such a keystroke is entered, the main SideKick menu pops up on the screen and a choice is made, in this case, by pressing the appropriate function key.

Function key driven

Early office computers, such as Micom, Wang, and AES stand-alone word processors, were designed with one purpose in mind. That purpose was for word processing, which gave rise to the name **devoted computer.** To make these computers easy to use and the commands easy to learn, special-purpose function keys were included for most of the major operations thus making the programs function key driven. This type of user interface permitted the operator simply to press the appropriate key to print a document, read a file, or underline a word.

With the trend to using general-purpose personal computers in the office, function keys also became general purpose, thus the numbering from F1 to F10 on most machines. Some software designers have recognized the wisdom of providing the commands for the program on the function keys. In a manner similar to the techniques used on the devoted computers, the function keys

FIGURE 7–15
WordPerfect 5.0, a word processing program, is function key driven for 40 different operations. By pressing the function key either alone or in combination with the Ctrl, Shift, or Alt key, a specific operation is begun.

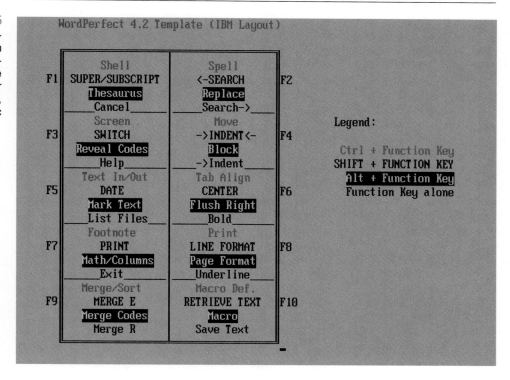

FIGURE 7–15
WordPerfect 5.0, a word processing program, is function key driven for 40 different operations. By pressing the function key either alone or in combination with the Ctrl, Shift, or Alt key, a specific operation is begun.

are given specific duties. By either pressing the function key alone or with the Ctrl, Shift, or Alt keys, up to 40 different functions are available with a single key press (Figure 7–15).

Prompt driven

Prompts are used by programs to query the user about an operation to be done by the program (Figure 7–16). Usually one prompt is issued at a time, and the user responds to it by typing Y or N for Yes or No, entering a number such as the position of the right margin or the name of a file to be saved. Single-character responses often do not need to be followed by the Enter key, but entering several characters such as the name of a file requires the Enter key to be pressed after the name has been typed.

Prompts are considered a useful form of user interaction because a specific question is asked of the user. Unlike menus, which are often short entries, the prompt can be self-explanatory. On the down side, prompts take more time to read, and the response often takes longer to enter.

Command driven

Command-driven programs require that the user know exactly what operation is to be done and the command required to invoke the action. PC DOS is an example of a command-driven program. Figure 7–17 shows a screen where the DOS prompt is all that the user sees. To cause any action to occur, the user must know the command and its precise format. There is no help, prompting, or list of choices presented on the screen.

FIGURE 7–16
These prompts ask a Word-Star user about the requirements for printing a document.

```
P                        WordStar Professional Release 4

To skip further questions, press the Esc key at any point. Press ⏎
at any question to use the default answer.

Document to print? book1
  ⏎ done  ^U cancel ^R repeat ¦ ^S left  ^D right ¦ Del char  ^G char  ^Y all
  ^X directory         ^P literal¦ ^A wd lf ^F wd rt ¦  ^H left  ^T word


            Number of copies? 1
   Pause between pages (Y/N)? N
      Use form feeds (Y/N)? Y
            Starting page? 1
             Ending page? 12
         Nondocument (Y/N)?




DIRECTORY    Drive C:\WS4  1.0M free
  11k ANOREXIA        10k ANOREXIA.BAK    8.4k BOOK1        .4k BOX
  2.3k BREPORT        10k BREPORT.BAK     3.6k COND.OP     8.5k DESIGN
  2.0k ELEPHANT       1.9k ELEPHANT.BAK   2.4k ESTHERBR    2.3k ESTHERBR.BAK
  3.1k HISTORY1       2.4k JAPAN.H        3.1k OUTPUT2.WS   80k PATCH.LST
```

FIGURE 7–17
PC DOS is an example of a command-driven program. On the left is the screen with the DOS prompt waiting for a command to be entered. The screen on the right shows the copy command that has been given to copy the file expenses from the A to the B disk.

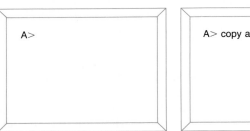

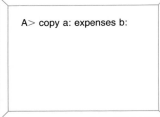

Some DOS Commands
dir a:
date
diskcopy a: b:
erase b:memo5.bak
rename sample fig. 1.2

The second screen in the figure shows a command entered by the user for copying a file from drive A to drive B. The user must know the name of the command (copy) and the format of the entries for the source file (a:expenses) and the drive to receive the copy (b:).

Command-driven programs are more difficult to learn to use but are considered to be more direct and faster to use once the commands are known. Because of the longer learning time, fewer programs today are command driven. Even IBM's new operating system OS/2 is menu driven. Some programs, such as dBASE IV, offer a pull-down menu for the new user and a command mode for the experienced user.

FIGURE 7–18
A form-filling screen used in dBASE IV to create a data base file. At each entry line in the form a field name, type, width, and number of decimal positions is entered. When a field is complete, the program automatically moves the pointer to the next empty field in the form.

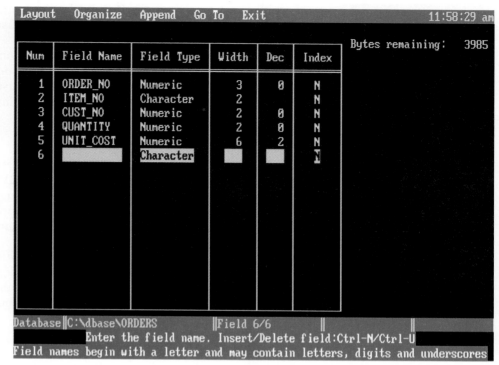

Form filling

You have no doubt filled out a form as an application for college or to apply for a driver's license. Software form filling is a type of user interface where a screen is presented with empty spaces and used something like a blank paper form. Each space may have some identifying label, so that the user will know what data is to be entered on the form. As data is entered, the cursor, under program control, moves from field to field in the form indicating what is to be entered next.

Business software for accounting or payroll frequently uses this type of interface for data entry. Some software also uses it for user interaction. Figure 7–18 shows a dBASE IV screen that is used for defining the fields when creating a file.

Icons

The use of icons on the screen for user interfacing was made popular by the Apple Macintosh computer and is now used on other systems. An **icon** is a graphic image on the screen that represents a file, notepad, disk, printer, or other object. By pointing to the icon, often by using a mouse, you can select the operation you wish to do. For example, pointing to an icon of a printer suggests that you wish to print the document.

Microsoft Windows is a software package that provides access to many programs written for the PC varying from data base to desktop publishing and expert systems to computer-aided design. Windows also provides some

FIGURE 7–19

The Apple Macintosh is a computer that uses icons for user selection of program options.

Courtesy of Apple Computer, Inc.

basic functions and uses icons to show the DOS executive (a floppy disk symbol), a calculator, notepad, clock, and other features. Icons work best with a mouse. An option is selected by pointing the mouse to the icon and clicking the button to make the selection.

The Apple Macintosh is a computer that has been using icons and a mouse interface for some time. Figure 7–19 shows a situation on the Macintosh where icons are used to make program choices. The mouse moves a screen pointer to the appropriate icon and a button is pressed to make the choice.

Multiinterface Programs

Many programs make use of several types of user interfaces and not just one exclusively. Although a program such as dBASE IV may primarily use pull-down menus, it also uses prompting, cursor pointing, function keys, and command-driven interfaces. Each of these methods is appropriate at different times during the use of the program, and the switch from one to the other occurs quite naturally when a program is well designed.

Many of the leading programs for word processing, spreadsheets, and data bases will use several types of interfaces and not depend on just one for their operation. Although icon-driven systems may depend less on other forms of interaction, they too will use more than one approach for user interfacing.

Help Screens

What do you do when using a software package and you can't remember how a command works? One solution is to find the manual, look up the command in the index, and then read the instructions on its use. A faster solution is to use the Help system built into the software. By pressing a key, you can access a screen of information about the use of the program.

There are basically two types of help systems. One is general in nature and requires multikeystrokes to get to the information you require. This type of help is shown in Figure 7–20 for WordPerfect. To get help in WordPerfect, you first press the Help key (F3) and then press the key for the command you require help on.

The second type of help system is called a **context-sensitive** system. Context-sensitive help systems take a look at what you are doing in the program and then give you help on that specific type of operation. Lotus 1–2–3 is an example of this system as Figure 7–21 shows. On this screen help was requested when using the graph command.

INSTALLING SOFTWARE

Software meant for the IBM PC or compatibles should run on all these computers without any user modification. True or false? In many instances, this statement is false because the software needs to be **installed** on a specific computer system configuration before it can be used. Software often depends on the memory size of the computer, the type of screen whether monochrome or color, low or high resolution, whether a mouse will be used for interaction,

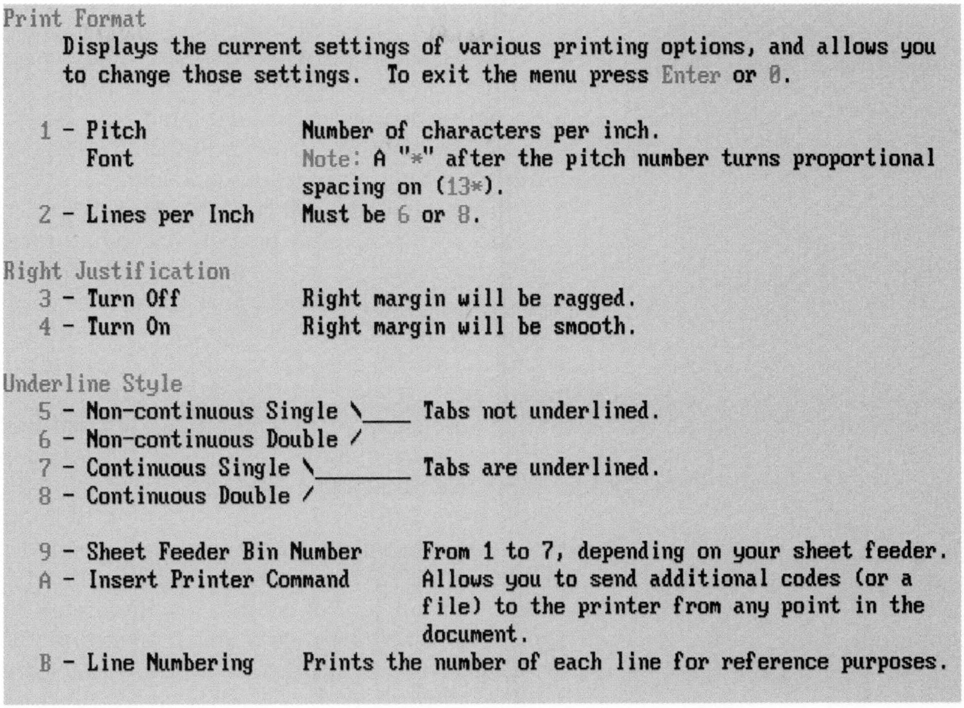

FIGURE 7–20
A help screen with printing instructions displayed in WordPerfect.

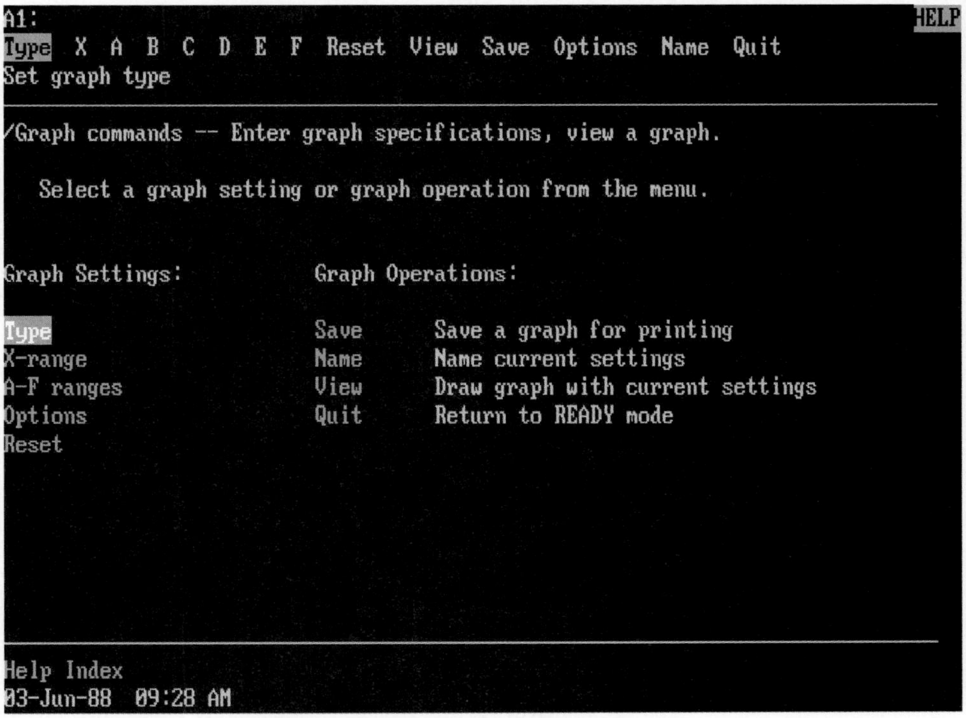

Print Format
        Displays the current settings of various printing options, and allows you
        to change those settings. To exit the menu press Enter or 0.

        1 - Pitch   Number of characters per inch.
            Font   Note: A "*" after the pitch number turns proportional
                             spacing on (13*).
        2 - Lines per Inch   Must be 6 or 8.

Right Justification
        3 - Turn Off   Right margin will be ragged.
        4 - Turn On   Right margin will be smooth.

Underline Style
        5 - Non-continuous Single ___   Tabs not underlined.
        6 - Non-continuous Double /
        7 - Continuous Single _____   Tabs are underlined.
        8 - Continuous Double /

        9 - Sheet Feeder Bin Number   From 1 to 7, depending on your sheet feeder.
        A - Insert Printer Command   Allows you to send additional codes (or a
                                      file) to the printer from any point in the
                                      document.
        B - Line Numbering   Prints the number of each line for reference purposes.

FIGURE 7–21
A context-sensitive help screen for graphics commands in Lotus 1–2–3.

A1:   HELP
Type X A B C D E F Reset View Save Options Name Quit
Set graph type
───
/Graph commands -- Enter graph specifications, view a graph.

    Select a graph setting or graph operation from the menu.

Graph Settings: Graph Operations:

Type   Save   Save a graph for printing
X-range   Name   Name current settings
A-F ranges   View   Draw graph with current settings
Options   Quit   Return to READY mode
Reset

───
Help Index
03-Jun-88 09:28 AM

**MEMORY-RESIDENT
SOFTWARE**

SideKick Plus

Memory-resident software refers to a range of programs that reside in memory along with other applications. By hitting a special key combination, the memory-resident program is activated and available for use. SideKick was the grandfather of resident tools that provided a notepad, calculator, calendar, and dialer in a neat, easy-to-use package.

As you are working with your word processor, spreadsheet, or other application program, SideKick may be activated by pressing Ctrl-Alt and a note written, an appointment noted, or a calculation done. You can even write a memo while you are in a spreadsheet and import the memo later to a word processing document. All these tasks are done very efficiently and naturally using SideKick. Since 1984, over a million copies of SideKick have been sold by Borland International.

Like all good software companies, Borland has been hard at work revising SideKick to provide more features and tools for the computer desktop. In 1988 SideKick Plus was released with many enhancements. First, SideKick Plus includes all the features of SideKick with many improvements of these features, plus a number of new features.

One new feature is Outlook: the Outline Processor. With Outlook you can develop an outline of a report or document you are preparing to write. It provides up to nine outline windows, an automatic table of contents, an organization chart of the headlines, headline numbering, and an attached notepad for making additional notes. After an outline has been prepared, you may view any level of the outline. By pressing the Minus key, only the essential

points of the outline are displayed. Pressing Plus causes successive levels of detail to appear.

Another new feature is the file manager. The manager comes up automatically when an incomplete file name is specified, or you can call it with a simple command. With the file manager the functions of copy, delete, move, rename, print, and view may be done from SideKick Plus without having to go to DOS. It can also format disks and move directories.

The text editor used in SideKick Plus is based on WordStar commands but has nine different notepads. That way you can switch quickly between any of these notes without the need to save and retrieve files. Notes may be saved in different disk directories depending on their application. Notes may also be attached to other SideKick Plus applications such as the phone dialer or the appointment scheduler.

Using the appointment book provides a calendar and a daily schedule for making half-hour entries. Appointments may be viewed by opening a schedule window on the screen. A nice feature of the appointment book is the ability to set a reminder alarm. The alarm is set to go off at a specific time and is given a default amount of time prior to the appointment. When the alarm goes off (even if you are working on something else), a window opens to the appointment. You can then close the window, open the appointment book, or even choose a snooze setting, and the alarm will go off again shortly.

The calculator in SideKick Plus now has four different options. There are business, scientific, programmer, and formula calculators available. The business calculator has standard math and business functions modeled on a popular Canon calculator. Entries made on the calculator are recorded on a simulated tape so that you can retrieve them for reuse or editing.

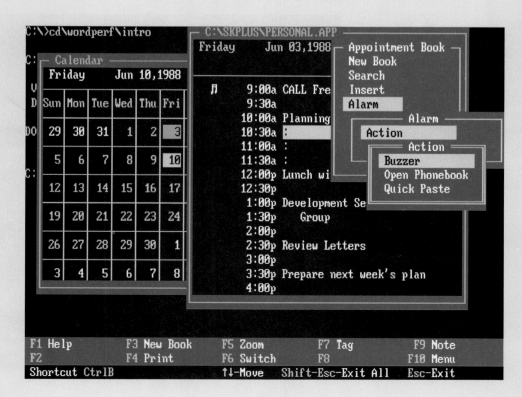

215

The phone dialer has a pop-up screen for making new phone number entries. All that is necessary is to fill in the entries. To use the dialer, just point to the number you want to call and press Enter.

A trade-off with SideKick Plus is that it is simply much slower than the original SideKick, and it uses considerably more disk and memory space. With all the features it contains this is bound to be the result, but there is a solution. By installing SideKick Plus with a limited number of features, it can be made to operate more efficiently than the complete package. Most users will not need all the features, so by customizing SideKick Plus, a more efficient memory-resident program is produced.

and the type of printer to be used for reports or graphs. Until the program has been installed, many of these features will either not work or will function incorrectly.

Install Programs

Many software packages come with an **install program** that helps the user to identify the unique features of his or her computer. By typing the command INSTALL, or some similar name, at the DOS prompt the procedure for installing the software on your computer is begun. Figure 7–22 shows a screen from Lotus 1–2–3's install program. Programs such as this one take the user step

FIGURE 7–22
An install screen for use when installing Lotus 1–2–3 on a personal computer. This screen provides options for first-time installation and for updating the program if the computer's configuration has been changed.

```
                    M A I N   M E N U

  Use ↓ or ↑ to move menu pointer.          Select First-Time Installation
                                             for a guided path through the
                                             installation procedure.  This
    First-Time Installation                  path lets you select drivers
    Change Selected Equipment                for screen display and for
    Advanced Options                         printers.
    Exit Install Program



  ↓ and ↑ move menu pointer.           [F1] displays a Help screen.
  [RETURN] selects highlighted choice. [F9] takes you to main menu.
  [ESCAPE] takes you to previous screen. [F10] shows current selections.
```

by step through the installation procedure. The better written install programs require very little technical knowledge on the part of the user. By using prompts or menus, each step is outlined by the program, and the user merely needs to select the options that apply to the computer in use.

Some programs, such as WordPerfect 5.0, have many of the install options built into the software so that a separate program is not needed. Changes to the defaults or other features can be easily changed because it is not necessary to run the install program each time: just select the changed feature, and the program modifies itself according to the new specifications.

Backup copies

When installing a new piece of software, it is wise first to create a backup copy of the new program. In many cases the software will exist on several disks so each disk will need to be backed up before proceeding to install the program. A blank disk will be required for each of the original disks. Instructions for creating the backup disk will come with the software and usually use the DOS COPY command. In some cases it will not be possible to make a backup disk because the original is copy protected.

Device drivers

Some input or output devices are so different from one another that software companies must provide a **device driver** with the install disk to give information about the device. To some extent, screens have this problem. There are both monochrome and color screens, and a variety of resolutions in each category and different graphic adaptor boards may be used for these screens. Thus a device driver is needed to provide all the data required by the program to display information correctly on the screen.

Plotters, and especially printers, are even more notorious for having differences. With the widespread capabilities for draft or letter quality, enhanced or compressed printing, italics, graphics, super- and subscripts, line drawing, and so on, printers must be precisely defined in the program. To make matters worse, printers often use different commands from one another to activate the same feature. Recently there has been some standardization such as the Epson standard and the IBM standard, but even these companies don't follow their own standards absolutely.

Software packages, especially word processors that use many printer features, must provide drivers for a variety of printers. WordStar Professional Version 4 supplied drivers for over 50 printers while WordPerfect 4.2 provided two floppy disks containing over 250 printer drivers. Figure 7–23 shows a screen of printer drivers available in WordPerfect when installing a printer.

Default Settings

Sometimes a software publisher will supply the software with the programs preset for a certain set of specifications. It may, for example, assume that the program will be run on a computer with a monochrome screen, use two floppy disk drives, and have an Epson-compatible printer. These **default settings** may permit the software to be used immediately without the need to go through a special installation procedure unless your computer system differs from this norm.

A second meaning for default settings refers to features inside the software.

FIGURE 7–23
A screen of printer drivers that may be chosen when installing WordPerfect.

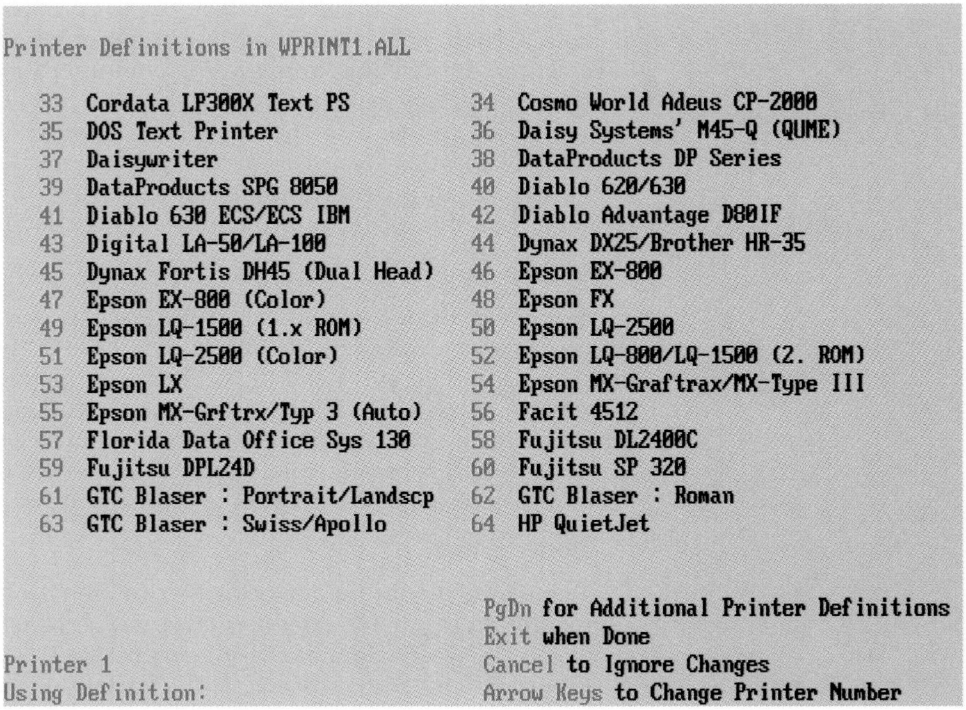

```
Printer Definitions in WPRINT1.ALL

   33  Cordata LP300X Text PS        34  Cosmo World Adeus CP-2000
   35  DOS Text Printer              36  Daisy Systems' M45-Q (QUME)
   37  Daisywriter                   38  DataProducts DP Series
   39  DataProducts SPG 8050         40  Diablo 620/630
   41  Diablo 630 ECS/ECS IBM        42  Diablo Advantage D80IF
   43  Digital LA-50/LA-100          44  Dynax DX25/Brother HR-35
   45  Dynax Fortis DH45 (Dual Head) 46  Epson EX-800
   47  Epson EX-800 (Color)          48  Epson FX
   49  Epson LQ-1500 (1.x ROM)       50  Epson LQ-2500
   51  Epson LQ-2500 (Color)         52  Epson LQ-800/LQ-1500 (2. ROM)
   53  Epson LX                      54  Epson MX-Graftrax/MX-Type III
   55  Epson MX-Grftrx/Typ 3 (Auto)  56  Facit 4512
   57  Florida Data Office Sys 130   58  Fujitsu DL2400C
   59  Fujitsu DPL24D                60  Fujitsu SP 320
   61  GTC Blaser : Portrait/Landscp 62  GTC Blaser : Roman
   63  GTC Blaser : Swiss/Apollo     64  HP QuietJet


                                 PgDn for Additional Printer Definitions
                                 Exit when Done
Printer 1                        Cancel to Ignore Changes
Using Definition:                Arrow Keys to Change Printer Number
```

For example, a word processor may have defaults for single-line spacing, a left margin at column 1 and a right at 65, automatic right margin justification, and so on. If the user wants different settings, then a command in the program will need to be entered at the time the setting is to be changed.

But some users may not find the default to be appropriate for their use of the software. Writers would prefer a word processor that starts with double-line spacing, which is the requirement for most manuscripts. Thus, during the install procedure, an entry can be made to change this default setting so that the program always starts with double spacing instead of the usual single. Changing defaults such as these allow users to customize the software to their own needs.

APPLICATION SOFTWARE AND YOU

We have seen that to run application software, you must first boot the computer with the operating system. Then an application program may be loaded for your specific needs. Using a program requires that you know the specific commands or procedures for that package. These commands may be found in the documentation that comes with the software, by the use of menus, function keys, icons, or other form of user interface or through the program's Help system. Because each computer has a different mix of components, software must first be installed to match the specifications of the system. In the next chapter we will look at some of the application software packages used on personal computers today.

1. DOS is a resident program that occupies memory while another program is running on the computer.

2. DOS is booted from a floppy disk or hard disk whenever the computer's power is turned on.

3. DOS commands, such as COPY or ERASE, or commands for running a program, such as LOTUS or DBASE are entered at the DOS prompt.

4. Seven major software categories are productivity, business systems, data base management, communications, artificial intelligence, educational, and home systems.

5. Software packages typically include one or more of the following: diskettes, manuals, keyboard template, quick reference guide, and a warranty card.

6. A large program often exists in several parts. There is the main program and one or more overlay programs. There may also be overlays for help files, messages, and menus.

7. Using an application program can be considerably less costly and less time consuming compared to writing your own. Spreadsheet or data base packages can also be a better way of implementing a solution rather than using a traditional programming language.

8. Keyboard templates fit over the function keys to tell the user of a software packages how each function is identified. Functions may also be available with the Ctrl, Shift, and Alt keys.

9. Menu-driven software offers a list of choices on the screen from which the user makes a selection by typing a number or character. A mnemonic character has built-in meaning such as P for Print.

10. Cursor pointing, in software such as Lotus 1–2–3, is used to make a selection from a menu.

11. Multilevel menus are used to narrow the number of choices and to group them into meaningful categories.

12. Pull-down menus come down from the top of the screen and pop-up menus appear in the middle of the screen. Their use can require fewer keystrokes to make a choice.

13. Function key–driven software, such as some word processors, use the function keys as a primary means for making program selections.

14. Prompt-driven programs query the user about an operation and often require a yes or no response or an entry such as a file name. Prompts can be self-explanatory but do take longer to read than menus.

15. Command-driven programs require the user to know and enter the command needed for a specific action. There is no help, prompting, or list of choices presented. Command-driven applications are harder to learn but can be faster to use after the commands are known.

16. Form-filling software presents a screen that looks like a form where empty spaces are filled with data. As data is entered, the cursor moves from field to field to prompt for the next entry.

17. Icons present a graphic image on the screen that represents a file, notepad, disk, or printer and represents an action that will be taken when selecting that icon. Icon software works best with a mouse.

18. Help screens may be accessed by one or more keystrokes to get information about a program feature. Context-sensitive help gives information directly about the operation you are working on at the time that help is requested.

19. An install program is run to identify the unique features of a user's computer and to adapt the software to the screen, printer, and other user needs.

20. Device drivers are files that provide information during installation about specific screens, printers, and plotters.

21. Default settings refer to options that will ordinarily be used when software is run. For example, defaults may be used for single spacing or right justification unless the user requests otherwise.

Application package	Help system	Overlay program
Booted	Icon	Pop-up menu
Command driven	Install program	Programming
Context sensitive	Key disk	language
Default setting	Keyboard template	Prompt
Device driver	Main program	Pull-down menus
Disk operating system	Manual	Quick reference guide
(DOS)	Menu	Resident
DOS prompt	Mnemonic	Software package
Form filling	Multilevel menus	Warranty card
Function key driven		

Fill-in Questions

1. It is necessary to _____ DOS before application software can be run on the computer.

2. A software _____ is usually supplied with a manual, disks, reference card, a warranty, and a keyboard template.

3. _____-driven software, such as WordStar, provides a list of options from which a selection is made.

4. Software such as Lotus 1–2–3 lets you use the _____ key either to point at a specific choice or to type the first letter of the entry.

5. A(n) _____ menu, such as in dBASE IV, shows two levels of choices: a main menu at the top of the screen and one that drops down to show a submenu.

6. _____ key–driven software often supplies a template to show the options available on the keyboard.

7. A(n) _____ shows a graphic image of the choice to be made.

8. Running a(n) _____ program is often necessary to have access to the full features of a program and to customize it for your computer's screen, printer, and other devices.

Matching Questions

Match each term with the description given below.
a. context sensitive   d. template
b. Help   e. icon
c. menu   f. prompt

_____ 1. A message or query that asks the user for a response or a specific command.

_____ 2. A list of options from which one is selected.

_____ 3. Help information that relates directly to the operation being done when help was requested.

_____ *e* _____ 4. A symbol used on the screen to select certain features of the program.

_____ d _____ 5. This plastic device is a useful tool for identifying the various operations on the keyboard's function keys.

_____ b _____ 6. Usually a function key that is pressed to get more information about the operation of the program.

Discussion Questions

1. Explain what is meant by the expression "booting DOS."
2. Describe some types of commands that are entered at the DOS prompt.
3. What is meant by the term application program? Name the seven major categories of software for which application programs have been developed.
4. Describe briefly the various items that may be included when you purchase a software package.
5. What is the difference between a main program and an overlay program? Why are both needed for complex applications?
6. Discuss the pros and cons of writing your own program versus buying an existing software package.
7. Why do some programs come with copy protection? What are the solutions to this problem if the company using the software has several computers or a network of computers requiring the same software?
8. What is the purpose of a keyboard template? How does software, such as WordPerfect, resolve the problem of using function keys for up to 40 different operations?
9. Name and briefly describe six different methods used for user interfacing with programs.
10. Describe the different forms of menus that are used in some software?
11. Why are help screens a useful component of a program? Explain the meaning of context-sensitive help.
12. Discuss the purpose of the install program and the use of drivers when installing a software package.

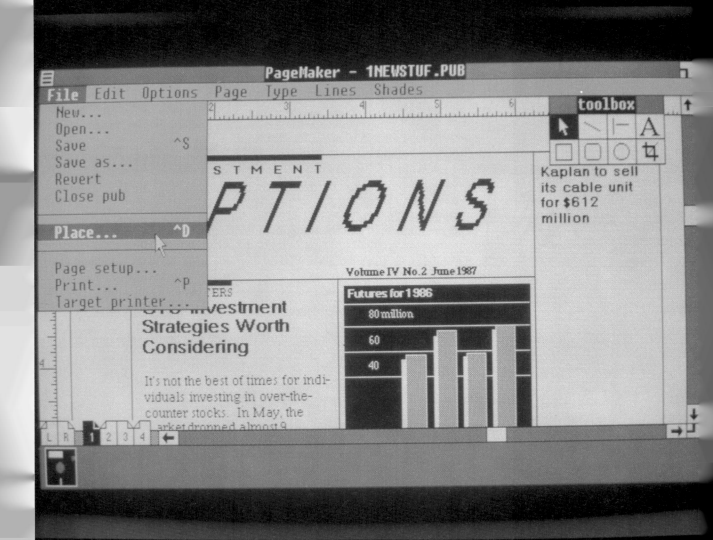

Word Processing and Desktop Publishing

A VIEW OF THE CHAPTER AHEAD

After Reading This Chapter You Will Understand:

- The concepts and uses of word processing.

- The stages of word processing from text entry to printing a document.

- The basic features available in word processing software packages.

- The concepts and uses of desktop publishing.

W ord processing is considered to be the number one use of personal computers and is frequently the main application that prompts the purchase of a first computer. While the typewriter has not yet met its demise in the modern office, the PC, with word processing software, is fast becoming the productivity tool of choice in today's modern business.

THE BENEFITS OF WORD PROCESSING

Improvement over the Typewriter

Whether you are typing a 1-page application for a job, a 25-page report, or several hundred pages of a manuscript, it is unusual to get it right the first time. Using a standard typewriter you would need to retype some pages in their entirety or use white-out to make corrections on others. You might also cut and paste other pages to get the final version of the document. In some applications, such as the legal office, the only solution is to retype the page completely if there is a typing error.

Enter word processing. With a word processing package, a draft copy of the document can be made, corrections and changes noted on the page (Figure 8–1), and then the changes are made to the original by using the word processor. A new copy is then printed by the computer without the need for the user of the system to retype words or lines that were originally correct. The time saving over using a typewriter can be dramatic.

Form Letters

The business that frequently requires a form letter to be sent to its clients can also benefit immensely from word processing. First, text that is the common letter to be sent to each client (Figure 8–2) is prepared as the primary file in the word processor. A secondary file of names and addresses is also typed.

To create the form letters, the merge feature of the word processor is used, which automatically combines the text of the letter from the primary file and the names and addresses from the secondary file, thus producing a personalized letter for each client. Only one original letter was manually typed and the computer does the rest of the work thus saving many hours of laborious typing by the office staff.

Camera-Ready Copy

With today's sophisticated word processing systems and letter-quality printers, **camera-ready** text can be prepared directly on the personal computer. This text is suitable for photographing and using the results directly in a publication without the need for typesetting, which can be time consuming and costly.

While the quality of camera-ready copy is not as good as a typeset page, it is usually quite readable and more than acceptable for many types of publications. For example, books on computer programming frequently use camera-ready copy of program listings. Not only does this method reduce costs, but the errors that can be introduced when typesetting a complex document such as a computer program are eliminated. With the rise of desktop publishing

FIGURE 8–1

A draft copy of a document is printed from the word processor. Changes are noted in writing on the document and then keyed into the word processor. Correct text does not need to be reentered, only the changes need to be typed. Finally, the computer prints a copy of the new version of the document.

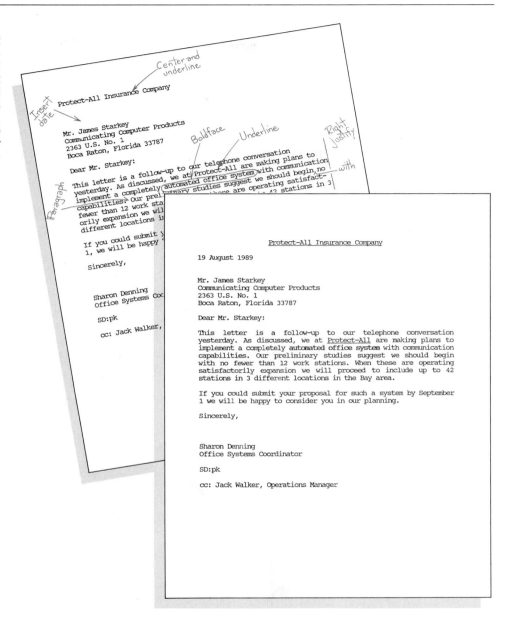

systems, this approach to publishing will be used more widely by business and industry.

Electronic Mail

We saw in the chapter on communications that electronic mail facilities were being provided by information organizations such as The Source and MCI Mail. Text that is prepared for E-mail is generally first developed in a word processor and then sent to the remote location using a communications program.

The Primary Form Letter File

```
^F1^
^F2^
^F3^

Dear ^F4^:

     We at Protect-All are making plans to implement a completely
automated office system with communication capabilities. Our
preliminary studies suggest we should begin with no fewer than 12
work stations. When these are operating satisfactorily expansion
will proceed to include up to 42 stations in 3 different
locations in the Bay area.

If you could submit your proposal for such a system by September
1 we will be happy to consider you in our planning.

Sincerely,



Sharon Denning
Office Systems Coordinator

SD:pk

cc: Jack Walker, Operations Manager
```

The Secondary Merge File

```
Mr. James Starkey,^R
Marketing Representative,^R
Communicating Computer Products,
2363 U.S. No. 1,
Boca Raton, Florida 33787^R
Mr. Starkey^R
^E
Mr. William Best,^R
Sales Manager,^R
Best Computers,
2501 Almedas Drive,
Los Angeles, California 76887,^R
Mr. Best^R
^E
Mr. Ted MacDonald,^R
VP Computer Sales,^R
Personal Office Computers,
401 Seabreeze Dr.,
Boston, Massachusetts 12045,^R
Mr.MacDonald^R
^E
```

```
Mr. James Starkey,
Marketing Representative,
Communicating Computer Products,
2363 U.S. No. 1,
Boca Raton, Florida 33787

Dear Mr. Starkey:

     We at Protect-All are making plans to implement a completely
automated office system with communication capabilities. Our
```

```
Mr. William Best,
Sales Manager,
Best Computers,
2501 Almedas Drive,
Los Angeles, California 76887,

Dear Mr. Best:

     We at Protect-All are making plans to implement a completely
automated office system with communication capabilities. Our
```

The Resulting Form Letters

```
Mr. Ted MacDonald,
VP Computer Sales,
Personal Office Computers,
401 Seabreeze Dr.,
Boston, Massachusetts 12045,

Dear Mr.MacDonald:

     We at Protect-All are making plans to implement a completely
automated office system with communication capabilities. Our
preliminary studies suggest we should begin with no fewer than 12
work stations. When these are operating satisfactorily expansion
will proceed to include up to 42 stations in 3 different locations
in the Bay area.

If you could submit your proposal for such a system by September 1
we will be happy to consider you in our planning.

Sincerely,



Sharon Denning
Office Systems Coordinator

SD:pk

     cc: Jack Walker, Operations Manager
```

FIGURE 8–2

Text is created in a primary file so that form letters may be printed easily from the word processor. A secondary file containing names and addresses is merged with the form letter to produce the letters automatically.

The advantage of using a word processor for E-mail is primarily due to the editing capabilities that it offers. A second benefit is that the sender automatically may retain a copy of the document using the file-saving capability of the word processor.

STAGES OF WORD PROCESSING

The user of a word processing system soon recognizes a pattern of activities or a cycle that is followed. These stages are essentially the same for every word processor, although the specific actions taken may differ. The stages (Figure 8–3) are entering text, editing, print formatting, printing, and saving or recalling the text to or from disk.

■ **Text entry.** The first stage in the process is to enter the text of the document into the word processor. This is usually done by typing the contents on the keyboard, making minor corrections as you go.

■ **Editing.** The next stage is to edit the document until it is in the final form desired. Depending upon how close the original text was to the final result, editing can be a major task. To edit the document you may rewrite parts of the text, **delete** sections that are no longer required, or **insert** new words, sentences, or paragraphs. A good word processor will save text you delete in a buffer, so it can be easily restored if the deletion was done by mistake or you have a change of heart.

Most word processors will also permit you to **move** text from one location to another called a **cut and paste** operation. A paragraph or section, or just a sentence or two, can be removed from one location and quickly moved to another with a few keystrokes. Similar to the move is the ability to **copy** text. This editing operation can save a lot of typing if the same material is required several places in the text. Using the **search and replace** feature automates the replacement of many occurrences of the same word such as replacing all uses of the word "document" with the word "text."

■ **Print formatting.** Print formatting is preparing the text for printing and has a significant effect on how the document will look when it is printed. In some word processors, this step will be much the same as editing while in others there will be distinctive commands entered for formatting that are quite different from editing.

Formatting determines line spacing (single or double spacing), left and right margin settings, page length, and indenting of text from the margins. Programs will also let you select from a ragged right margin (letter style) or **monospace** right margin justification (book style). Sophisticated word processors will also provide for **proportional** spacing where each letter occupies a different width similar to that in a typeset document.

Formatting typically provides for underlining and boldface of characters and different typefaces such as condensed or expanded print. Many word processors now provide for access to laser printers with the many type fonts that they provide. Another feature is the ability to include header and footer lines automatically on each page as well as automatic page numbering.

Because of the extensive nature of page formatting not all the format changes will appear on the screen of the word processor. Some will exist only as a command. For example, most state-of-the-art word processors show underlining and boldface directly on the screen. But few have the ability to show compressed print or headers and footers on the screen. These will be evident only when the document is printed.

As more advanced word processors are announced, more formatting features will show directly on the screen, and the program truly becomes a WYSIWYG (what you see is what you get) system.

The stages of word processing from original text entry to the final printing of the document.

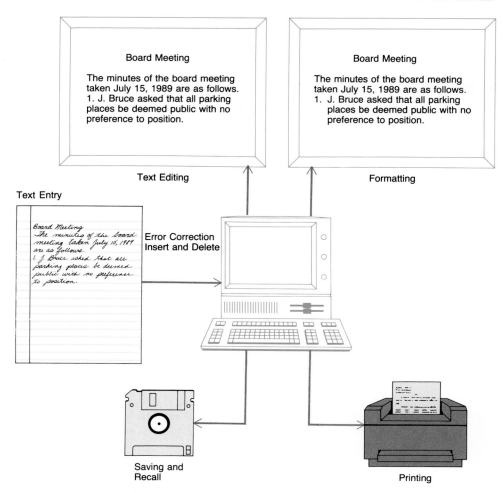

Text Editing

Formatting

Text Entry

Error Correction
Insert and Delete

Saving and
Recall

Printing

■ **Printing.** When the document has been developed to the satisfaction of the user, then it is ready for printing. Usually this is a simple command that activates the printing operation. On some systems it is necessary to save the document on disk before it can be printed, but most let you print a document from the screen.

Many users like to print a draft copy (sometimes using the high-speed draft mode of the printer) before all formatting is complete. The draft copy is then marked with changes that are made in the word processor prior to printing the final copy.

■ **Saving or recalling text.** When the document has been typed, then it is usually saved on disk so it may be recalled at a later time for reference or changes. Saving a document is simply a matter of entering the save command, which is usually one or two keystrokes, and then giving the document a file name that will identify it on the disk.

At a later time, the document may be recalled from disk by entering the retrieve command. You are then prompted to type the name of the file or to point at it from a list of file names. The document is retrieved from disk and presented on the screen where additional editing, formatting, or printing may be done before it is once again saved on disk.

THE LANGUAGE OF WORD PROCESSING

Part of the task of learning to use a word processor effectively is to become familiar with its language. This is true of any skill, isn't it? Even learning to drive a car requires us to know the meaning of such terms as yield, caution, one way, and so on. These are familiar terms to most people, and we often understand them intuitively because of our constant exposure to them.

Some terms in word processing are likewise familiar, but many are unique to word processing software and need to be understood to use the package successfully. In this section we will discuss the concepts by using WordPerfect, one of the leading word processors today. Once we know the terminology and gain some experience in one word processor, it is fairly easy to learn a second or other word processing language.

The screen displays in Figure 8–4 show a letter that has been typed on WordPerfect. This letter occupies three screens but when it prints it will require only one full page and part of a second. Because computer screens generally show only 25 lines, even one page of printout will require two or more screens.

These screens show a number of features used in word processing. First, is the difference between **single spacing,** which is useful for letters, and **double spacing,** which can also be used in letters but more often is used for reports or manuscripts. **Word wrap** is an automatic feature of most word processors. As a paragraph is typed, the cursor will automatically move to the next line as soon as the current line is filled. A word that may have started on the previous line, but is too long to fit, will automatically be brought (wrapped) to the next line.

Line centering is used to automatically center a heading on the line as it is typed. **Underlining** and **boldface** is done directly on screen in some word processors as shown here. Others mark the text in color or with special characters for these features, but only do the underlining or boldface when printing occurs.

At the bottom of the screen is a **status line** that shows the name of the document being edited, the document number (for split screen use), page number, line number, and cursor position. Some word processors show a status line at the top of the screen while others display a menu that includes status information.

The double line across the screen represents a **hard page break,** meaning that the user forced the page break to occur at a specific line. If a hard break is not requested, the word processor will create a **soft page break** automatically when a page is full. In WordPerfect a soft break is shown by displaying a single line across the screen.

Left and **right** margins are set automatically to columns 10 and 74 leaving room for blank margins on both sides of the paper. WordPerfect 5.0 leaves 1-inch margins on both sides of the page. These settings can be changed at will to either narrower or wider settings. The width of the paper and the printer carriage must be kept in mind when changing margin settings. Normal $8\frac{1}{2}$-inch by 11-inch letter-size paper can print a maximum of 80 characters per line at 10 characters per inch; the usual printing density.

Some text, such as the list of four points on the second screen, look better if indented. **Indenting** is a feature on a word processor where the text word

FIGURE 8–4

Screens showing parts of a letter as it appears in Word-Perfect. This screen shows some of the basic elements of a text created with a word processor.

Line centering

```
            Protect-All Insurance Company
                  410 Bay Drive
              Clearwater, Florida 36546


     19 August 1989


     Mr. James Starkey
     Marketing Representative
     Communicating Computer Products
     2363 U.S. No. 1
     Boca Raton, Florida 33787

     Dear Mr. Starkey:

     This letter is a follow-up to our telephone conversation
     yesterday. As discussed, we at Protect-All are making plans to
     implement a completely automated office system with communication
     capabilities.
C:\WP\LETTERS\DENNING                        Doc 1  Pg 1  In 24  Pos 12
```

Double spacing

Underlining

Word wrap

Single spacing

Bold face

Status line

Left margin

Right margin

```
        Our preliminary studies suggest we should begin with no fewer than
        12 work stations. When these are operating satisfactorily
        expansion will proceed to include up to 42 stations in 3 different
        locations in the Bay area.

        Obviously, such a system will require considerable training for
        our office personnel. What facilities and provisions can you make
        for such training. How long will it take? Will this training be
        included in the cost of the system?

        As far as hardware and software is concerned our current studies
        have indicated a need for the following minimum configuration:

          1. Software to provide for word processing, filing, spreadsheet
             and communication capabilities.

          2. A central processor at each work station with the following
             attributes:
               - 128K memory
               - green phosphor screen
               - dual drive diskettes
C:\WP\LETTERS\DENNING                        Doc 1  Pg 1  In 44     Pos 10
```

Word wrap

Tab setting

Indenting

Tab setting

Continuation of page 1

wraps to the indent position that is normally defined several columns past the starting position of the first line.

Tab settings are preset on most word processors to every five columns. Tabs are like the tab setting on a typewriter and use the tab key to move to a preset tab stop quickly. Tab settings may be removed or reset by entering a few keystrokes.

These features, or others similar to them, are provided by most word processors. But many go well beyond these basic features, providing a higher level of productivity for the user, but also a longer training time is needed to learn to use the software.

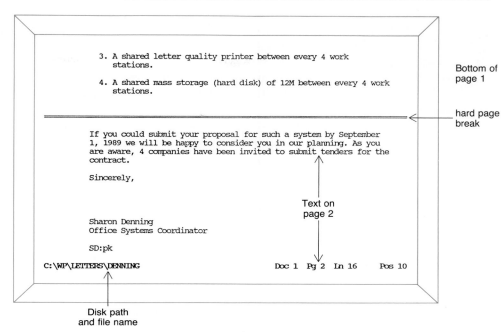

FIGURE 8–4 (Cont.)

Software, WordPerfect 5.0, courtesy of
WordPerfect Corporation.

CHOOSING A WORD PROCESSOR

The word processor against which most are compared today is WordPerfect
because of its many and varied features as well as its excellent performance
for most operations. When choosing a word processor, there are several considerations, including features, performance, and price. For some, price will be
important because it can vary from less than $50 to almost a thousand for a
full-featured system.

Most word processors are either **function key driven,** such as WordPerfect,
or **menu driven,** such as WordStar, although WordStar is moving to more
extensive use of function keys. The preference of users today seems to be
favoring function key–driven software, where commands are given by pressing
a function key by itself or in combination with another key. A menu is a list

SOME OF THE MANY WORD PROCESSORS AVAILABLE FOR THE PERSONAL COMPUTER			
Bank Street Writer	MultiMate Advantage II	StarWriter Plus
DisplayWrite 4	Nota Bene	Volkswriter
Easy Extra	OfficeWriter	Webster New World Writer
Einstein Writer	Paperback Writer	
Easywriter	PC-Write	WordPerfect
Final Word II	Perfect Writer	WordPerfect Executive
Leading Edge Word	PFS: Professional Write	WordStar
Lotus Manuscript	Q&A Write	WordStar Version 5
MacWrite	R Word Plus	WordStar 2000
Microsoft Word 5.0	Samna Plus IV	WyWrite III Plus

WORDPERFECT 5.0

WordPerfect Corporation released version 5.0 of its popular word processing program in early 1988. WordPerfect 5.0 contains all of the features of the previous version 4.2 with a number of significant improvements as shown here.

Text and graphics figures may be combined in a document similar to that done in desktop publishing packages. First, the text and a figure box are created on the screen to show the relative location of the contents in the document.

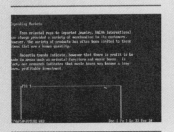

Text and graphics

Although version 4.2 had a document preview, this latest release provides significant improvements. A full page preview of the page with integrated text and graphics is shown. To get all the content on the screen, text is reduced to give a sense of how it would appear on the printed output.

Document preview

A 100 percent preview of the page zooms in to give a closer view of the page contents.

100% preview

Previewing at 200 percent zooms in to show the smallest detail of the text and graphics. Cursor keys are used to move to any location on the page. Edit screens are available in WordPerfect to make changes to either text or graphics.

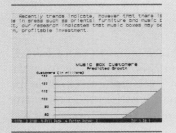

200% preview

WordPerfect's style feature combines text and codes to give a specific appearance to a document. In this case a letterhead is produced using both different fonts and containing a graphic image.

Style feature

(*Continued*)

Newspaper style

Although WordPerfect contained newspaper-style text in previous versions, the latest edition combines fonts and graphics with newspaper-style formatting. First the text is prepared on screen with the usual word processing features.

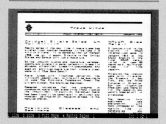

Preview feature

Using the preview feature, the complete text, including graphics, fonts, and columns is viewed.

of options where you select a command by pressing a key often in combination with the Ctrl key.

Major attention should be given to the features that you require in a word processor. Some features, such as merging form letters, may be nice, but will form letters be an important activity for you? On-screen display of page formatting is also nice, but do you need to spend the extra hundred dollars for this feature? Of course the answers might be yes to these and many other questions, but asking them will help to rule out some word processors and include others.

Another basis for your decision is to know who developed and markets the software. This will have some bearing on the amount of support you can receive from the company should you run into difficulty. Some of the lesser known and usually inexpensive programs will not come with much in the way of manufacturer support, although some are well supported. In contrast, the larger companies typically provide toll-free lines with personnel who can answer most of your questions when you encounter difficulty.

Finally, a decision for an office or company should consider compatibility with other word processors that may already exist in the company. If you intend to share files and documents with other employees, then either the same word processors should be used or ones that have utility programs to convert from one word processor to another. Similar concerns apply if electronic mail is used, if documents are to be uploaded or downloaded to or from a mainframe computer, or if data from spreadsheets or data bases is to be used in the word processor.

COMPARING WORD PROCESSOR FEATURES

Word processors are available with many different strengths indicated by the type of features they contain. Some features, such as a spelling checker or mail merge, will help to determine if the program contains everything that is required of a word processor for your needs. Others, such as page or document orientation, are a matter of personal preference and operating style. This list is not meant to be absolutely complete but to give a flavor of the features that you can find in full-featured word processors.

Today's full-featured word processors.

Courtesy of WordPerfect Corporation.

Courtesy of MicroPro International Corporation.

Courtesy of Microsoft Corporation.

Courtesy of Microsoft Corporation.

Standard Features

Cursor control

Insert—character, word, sentence, line, paragraph.

Delete—character, word, sentence, line, paragraph.

Block move

Block copy

Word wrap

Margin settings

Tabs settings

Margin justification

Page or document orientation

Print Enhancement

Boldface

Underlining

Subscript

Superscript

Overprint

Pitch change

Italics

Alternate fonts

Advanced Text Handling

Search

Search and replace

Go to page number

Headers and footers

Cursor—by word, line, page, document

Automatic paragraph reform

Macros

Math

Column blocks

Advanced Features

Outliner

Footnotes

Automatic figure numbering

Graphics

Utilities

Spelling checker

Thesaurus

Mail merge

Indexing

Line and box drawing

Word processor conversion

Importing from spreadsheets or data bases

UTILITIES

Utilities are programs that supplement the operation of a word processor and generally render it more useful to a broader range of needs. Utilities are often provided with a word processing package but in some cases are extra cost options from either the word processing software publisher or from an independent publisher.

Spelling Checkers

A **spelling checker** is virtually considered a necessity on today's word processors. Most of the leading word processing programs include a spelling check feature as part of the package. For others, the spell check is an option or can be purchased separately from software publishers, such as Webster's New World Spelling Checker, that specialize in word processor utilities.

Spelling checkers usually consist of a dictionary disk containing 80,000 to over 100,000 words. Most will allow the user either to add words to the existing dictionary or to create a personal dictionary of additional words (Figure 8–5). Some even adapt the spelling to the country where the checker is sold so that the United States, Canadian, or British user will get the correct spelling for the appropriate country. In many cases a specialized dictionary is available containing legal, medical, or other terms relating to a specific profession.

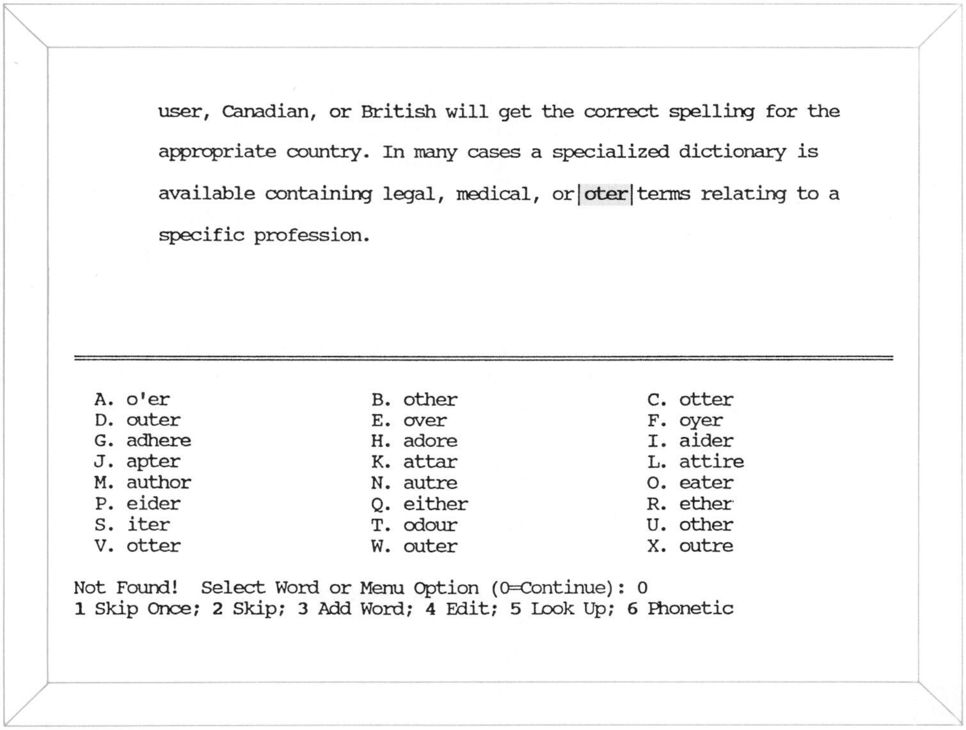

FIGURE 8–5

WordPerfect's spelling checker finds the word "oter" is misspelled or mistyped and offers a number of suggestions for the correct spelling. To select the correct spelling of "other," the user simply presses the B key, and the word in the text is replaced with the correct one.

```
          user, Canadian, or British will get the correct spelling for the

          appropriate country. In many cases a specialized dictionary is

          available containing legal, medical, or|oter|terms relating to a

          specific profession.


     _____

          A. o'er              B. other             C. otter
          D. outer             E. over              F. oyer
          G. adhere            H. adore             I. aider
          J. apter             K. attar             L. attire
          M. author            N. autre             O. eater
          P. eider             Q. either            R. ether
          S. iter              T. odour             U. other
          V. otter             W. outer             X. outre

     Not Found!  Select Word or Menu Option (0=Continue): 0
     1 Skip Once; 2 Skip; 3 Add Word; 4 Edit; 5 Look Up; 6 Phonetic
```

FIGURE 8–6
WordPerfect's thesaurus is activated by the command Alt F1. The word at the cursor position is checked for synonyms that are then displayed in the first column on the screen. If there are more synonyms, a second column will be used if necessary. A word from the first list, such as "relevant," may also be looked up as shown here in the second column. The process may be repeated until a suitable word is found.

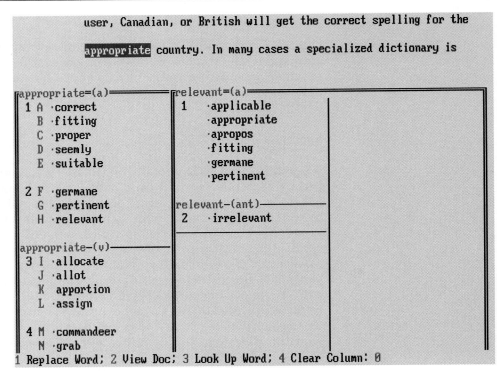

Thesaurus

A **thesaurus** is a program that provides synonyms for words in the text. The most popular of these in printed form is Roget's *Thesaurus*, which is used by most college students. When a thesaurus is provided for a word processor, it typically contains over 100,000 synonyms. Some also contain antonyms. For word processors that do not contain a thesaurus, an add-on one may be installed from several suppliers. Some of these are Random House's Reference Set, Microlytics' Word Finder, and Webster's New World On-Line Thesaurus from Simon & Schuster, which has 20,000 root words and 120,000 synonyms.

Using a thesaurus is easy. If you have a word in the text that you would prefer to replace with one that has a similar meaning the command to activate the thesaurus is entered when the cursor is resting on the word you want to change. The program then presents a list of words that have a similar meaning as shown in Figure 8–6. The user then selects the new word that replaces the original in the text.

Outliners

While an **outline generator** may not be very useful to an office secretary it can be an immense aid to writers who use the computer for developing ideas and writing about them. An outliner such as Ready! or ThinkTank permits the writer to create a general outline of the material to be written. This is a process that many writers use to collect their thoughts and to create a plan for their work.

RIGHTWRITER[1]: THE INTELLIGENT GRAMMAR, STYLE, USAGE, AND PUNCTUATION CHECKER

Most word processors now provide a spell check capability and many also make a thesaurus available to help with your writing. How often have you found a sentence that was badly constructed or grammar that just did not seem to be correct? With this new software product more help is on the way for computer users who need assistance with the presentation of their letters, memos, or reports.

RightWriter is a writing aid that helps you create strong, clear documents. It examines the text and analyzes it for problems with the grammar, style, word usage, and punctuation. Inserts are placed within a copy of the document to identify potential problems. A summary is included at the end to rate the text's readability, strength of delivery, use of descriptive language, and use of jargon.

The problem is not the same as a human. It will not find certain subtleties in the use of language or the exercise of literary license. RightWriter cannot find all errors and in some cases may point out an error which is a correct use of the language.

But RightWriter can identify words or phrases that should be replaced by simpler or more common words. It can also identify sentences that are too long which may be potentially confusing. It also flags the use of the passive voice where a stronger sentence or phrase could be used for more effective writing.

RightWriter is meant to be an aid for business or technical writing. Its 4,000 rules (similar to rules used in expert systems) are based on mistakes commonly made by business writers. Other writers of material such as fiction, technical reports, articles, proposals, and manuals can change the rules that RightWriter uses to correspond to their type of writing.

Original document.

```
There is a problem of a severe nature in widget production.
It is clear that our current system will not cut the mustard.
We may possibly need to move on this reasonably quickly.  To
start, it would be advantageous to see if a new design is doable.
(This should be looked into at once.
```

RightWriter flags errors and problem areas in the document.

```
    <<* U12. WORDY. REPLACE BY severe problem *>>
It is clear that our current system will not cut the mustard.
        <<* S14. CONSIDER OMITTING: It is clear that *>>
            <<* S16. CLICHE: cut the mustard *>>^
We may possibly need to move on this reasonably quickly.  To
     <<* U13. REDUNDANT. REPLACE may possibly BY may *>>
            <<* S17. WEAK: reasonably quickly *>>^
start, it would be advantageous to see if a new design is doable.
   <<* S13. REPLACE advantageous BY SIMPLER helpful or good? *>>
         <<* U16. NOT A WORD. REPLACE doable BY can be done *>>^
(This should be looked into at once.
 ^<<* P11. IS THIS PARENTHESIS CLOSED? *>>
              ^<<* S1. PASSIVE VOICE: be looked *>>
```

---

[1] RightSoft Incorporated, 4545 Samuel Street, Sarasota, Florida 34233–9912.

RightWriter is an example of the new and interesting software packages that are making the computer a truly helpful device. With software developments such as this the computer is going beyond the level of a productivity tool and becoming an electronic assistant to those who communicate with words.

```
                    <<** SUMMARY **>>

Overall critique for: C:\RIGHT\TEST.DOC
Output document name: C:\RIGHT\TEST.OUT

READABILITY INDEX:  5.23

    4th        6th        8th       10th       12th       14th
    |****|*    |    |    |    |    |    |    |    |    |    |
    SIMPLE    | ------ GOOD ----- |            COMPLEX
    Readers need a   5th grade level of education.


STRENGTH INDEX:  0.00

    0.0                   0.5                         1.0
    |*    |    |    |    |    |    |    |    |    |    |
    WEAK                                          STRONG
    The writing can be made more direct by using:
                    - the active voice
                    - fewer weak phrases
                    - fewer cliches
                    - more positive wording


DESCRIPTIVE INDEX:  0.50

    0.1                   0.5                   0.9     1.1
    |****|****|****|****|    |    |    |    |    |    |
    TERSE   | ------------ NORMAL ------------ |   WORDY
    The use of adjectives and adverbs is normal.


JARGON INDEX:  0.00

SENTENCE STRUCTURE RECOMMENDATIONS:
    2. Few compound sentences or subordinate
       clauses are being used.

                << WORDS TO REVIEW >>
Review this list for negative words (N), jargon (J),
colloquial words (C), misused words (M), misspellings (?),
or words which your reader may not understand (?).
    advantageous(M)  1              doable(J)  1
            not(N)  1              severe(N)  1
        widget(?)  1
            << END OF WORDS TO REVIEW LIST >>
                <<** END OF SUMMARY **>>
```

FIGURE 8–7

FIGURE 8–7
An outline created using WordPerfect's Outline feature. Level numbers are generated automatically as new entries are made in the outline. If an entry is deleted or a new one inserted, the outline feature automatically updates the level numbers to maintain the sequence.

```
        I. Application Development
            A. Conventional Applications Development
                1. Work Load and Overload
                2. Labor Cost
                3. Time Requirements for Applications Development
            B. User Applications Development
                1. Systems Concepts
                2. PC Software Tools
                3. Query Languages and Report Generators
                4. Decision Support Systems
            C. Information Centers
                1. User Training
                2. User Assistance
                3. Standards Administration


    Outline                              Doc 1 Pg 1 Ln 20  Pos 10
```

After the general outline has been developed (Figure 8–7) more detail may be added, steps may be deleted, and text may be moved or expanded. As these revisions are made, the outliner automatically updates the numbering system with new numbers or subcategories as necessary to keep the outline in order.

DESKTOP PUBLISHING

With the advent of more powerful computers, laser printers, and sophisticated software, desktop publishing has become a natural step up from word processing. **Desktop publishing** takes the concept of WYSIWYG to its limit by providing the software that can display a page on the screen in exactly the format it will be printed. Unlike the majority of word processors, desktop software can display different fonts and graphics integrated together on the same document as they will be printed (Figure 8–8).

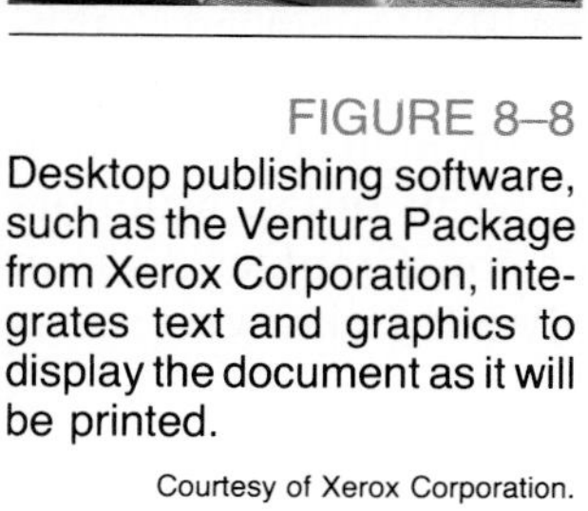

Using desktop publishing is a definite advantage for the small business. By eliminating typesetting costs and artist fees, publications can be created for considerably less expense than with previous methods. An example of this was the startup of *Personal Publishing* magazine. Page masters for the magazine were produced on an Apple Macintosh with PageMaker software and printed with an Apple LaserWriter.[2] Many of the concepts of desktop publishing began with the Apple Macintosh, which had the high screen resolution and fast processing speed needed for the page composition software. But with faster PCs, such as the IBM PC/AT and now the Personal System/2, more publishing software is available for these and compatible products.

For successful desktop publishing, a system requires five or six main components: page composition software, a personal computer, a high-resolution display, a keyboard and preferably a mouse, and a suitable printer. In the following sections we will look at each of these requirements for desktop publishing.

FIGURE 8–8
Desktop publishing software, such as the Ventura Package from Xerox Corporation, integrates text and graphics to display the document as it will be printed.

Courtesy of Xerox Corporation.

[2] Steve Ditlea, "Homegrown Publishing," *Science Digest*, March 1986, pp. 76–77.

Page Composition Software

Page composition software is the heart of the system. This name refers to the desktop publishing software that is used to create pages of text. The software, such as PFS: ClickArt Personal Publisher or Xerox's Ventura Publisher, is the program that brings graphics and text together on the screen. Page composition software provides the tools to format the text and lay out the content, with columns, boxes, lines, headings, and so on.

Software for the PC generally runs in the $200 to $800 range or at the top end of the word processor market. Formerly, comparatively expensive systems for minicomputers were used by typesetting professionals and offered considerably more power and features than the PC software. But as micros have grown in capability, this software is being redesigned for the PC. An example is the $7,000 SuperPage page composition system from Bestinfo that offers professional-quality composition and typesetting features for the PC.[3]

Frequently, a word processor such as WordStar or WordPerfect is used with the page composition software to aid in the creation of text. Because of this marriage of the two software packages, compatibility is an important concern when choosing software for desktop publishing. Choosing the right package can reduce training time and enhance operator efficiency.

Ideally the page composition software should show on screen exactly what will be printed (WYSIWYG). Because most screens are less than a full page in length, scrolling is usually necessary to see all the page. Many packages will also show a reduced text view so that you can see all of the page at once on the screen. This technique will result in some loss of legibility and in some cases the software does not show actual words but just illegible symbols to represent the words.

The Computer

Many of the page composition packages are available for the IBM PC with 640K and a hard disk. But to operate effectively, a computer the speed of the AT or the PS/2 will be much more satisfactory. Some sources recommend at least an 8-MHz processor and 1 megabyte of memory for desktop publishing.[4] The need for a fast processor and large memory is dictated by both the size of the program used for page composition and also the use of bit-mapped graphics for the display. Because text and graphics are displayed together bit mapping is required to create the display.

The Screen

Because users of desktop publishing systems need to see on the screen what will be printed, a high-resolution display is required. The IBM Enhanced Graphics Adaptor (EGA) or equivalent is a minimum level of resolution acceptable for page composition. The screen can be monochrome, although some desktop software now supports color so a color monitor may be in order. Monitors that display a full page, such as one from the Princeton Graphics System (Figure 8–9), are now available and give a true WYSIWYG (what you see is what you get) format.

---

[3] Thom Holmes, "Make My Page," *Byte*, May 1987, pp. 159–166.
[4] Stewart Alsop, "Desktop Publishing Without Hype," *PC Magazine*, February 10, 1987, pp. 111–115.

FIGURE 8–9

Full-page displays such as the one shown here make desktop publishing easier by presenting the entire contents of a page at one time on the screen without resorting to a reduced size required by some displays.

Courtesy of Princeton Graphic Systems.

The Input

The primary input device for desktop publishing is, of course, the keyboard. Much of the input will be text and is often entered through a full-featured word processor, which also uses the keyboard. But for formatting text, entering graphics, choosing options from the page composition software, and so on, a mouse (Figure 8–10) can sometimes function more effectively than the keyboard.

FIGURE 8–10

A mouse is an effective input device for working with a page composition software package. Using a mouse simplifies the selection of options in the software, formatting the document, and even creating your own graphics.

Courtesy of Brosan Studios.

Here's What You Desktop

BALLOON LIFE

May, 1986 $3.50

Magazine by Tom Hamilton, Balloon Life Magazine, Inc.

78   KICK WHEELS - KICK / MOTORIZED / KITS

BRENT STEEL KICK WHEELS

Brent Model J Steel Kick Wheel
This steel framed kick wheel is designed both for form and function. The flywheel is a full 135 lbs. of concrete with steel reinforcement. It is rough on top near the 1" shaft for kicking, and smooth near the rim for braking. The shaft is supported by high quality ball bearings with cast iron housings. The head is 14" dia. and the seat can be adjusted to fit any potter. A motor kit is available to convert the Model J to a Model EJ motorized wheel. Splash pan (BSPAN) optional $30.00.
Brent J -$555.00 (FOB In) Ship wt 325 lb

Brent Motor Kit for Model J Kick Wheel
This motor kit can be added to make a Model J into a Model EJ motorized kickwheel. See information on Brent EJ below.
JMOTR -$285.00 Ship wt 52 lb

Brent EJ Motorized Steel Kick Wheel
This is the Brent J wheel motorized. It combines the quiet, strength, and control of a steel frame kick wheel with the power of a 1/3 hp,110V AC motor attachment. The 9" diameter solid rubber wheel is driven by the motor through a small steel driving wheel and is engaged by a foot lever. A motor switch shuts the motor off when the foot lever is released. The head is 14". For 220V, add $45.00.
Brent EJ -$795.00 (FOB In) Ship wt 375 lb

BRENT WOOD KICK WHEEL KITS

Brent Metal Parts Kit for Kick Wheel
Makes a good project for schools, hobbyists, and studio potters who need an inexpensive wheel. All of the metal parts are included: 12" aluminum wheel head, shaft, first quality ball bearings, flanges for the flywheel, nuts, bolts, and 9 pages of illustrated instructions on how to build the kick wheel. Supply your own wood to build frame or order the complete wood parts BKWWK. See below.
BKWK -$160.00 Ship wt 20 lb

Brent Wood Parts Kit for Kick Wheel
Separate wood kit providing all of the wood pieces, precut, drilled, and ready for assembly. The unique frame design uses a 1/2" exterior plywood stressed skin which is as rigid as most steel designs. The flywheel is a sandwich structure using bricks held between plywood disks, so the amount of weight can be varied (up to 110 lbs) by the number of bricks used. The seat is easily adjustable by sliding it out of one slot and into another. When you order the wood kit with the metal parts kit, all you need to complete the kick wheel are a drill, hammer, nails, glue and bricks.
BKWWK -$175.00 Ship wt 90 lb

RANDALL STEEL KICK WHEELS/ optional MOTOR

Randall Kick Wheel
All parts are precision machined. This sturdy steel wheel is designed with welded tubing. It is fitted to receive a Work Table and a Splash Guard which are optional. Removable tractor type seat is adjustable in height and nearness to wheelhead. The 23" dia. flywheel is an iron casting machined to true balance and weighing 115 lbs. There is a 1 1/2" true-level track cast in the rim for power attachment. Bearings require no lubrication. Wheel can be assembled without special tools.
RANDK -$545.00 Ship wt 165 lb

Work Table (as illustrated)
Wood, 3/4" X16" x 32". Optional.
RKWT -$55.00

Splash Guard
A strong plastic half circle. Optional
RKSG -$42.00

Randall Motor Kit
This motor kit is 1/3 hp, single phase, 60 cycle, 110 volt, AC; enclosed and rubber mounted to minimize noise and vibration. The complete motor unit is easily and quickly attached to the kick wheel unit by U-bolts. Alignment is made quickly and accurately by the small pin on the wheel frame. No special tools are required. Starter switch is a 6-amp plunger type, activated by a foot lever which controls the power unit in starting and stopping the motor and engaging the drive wheel.
RMOTR -$215.00 Ship wt 36 lb

Drive Wheel
Replacement 2 3/4" dia. wheel is made of composition rubber to minimize noise and vibration.
RDWH -$24.95

Catalog by Judith Baldwin, Ceramic Supply of New York and New Jersey.

The DUCK Inn

This summer discover Pacific Northwest style...

Brochure by Kristen Ransom, Communique, for the Duck Inn.

COOKS HEADQUARTERS

jackie winkel
owner

COOKS HEADQUARTERS

151 west twenty fifth
san mateo, ca 94403
415/345 7668

Letterhead, Business Card by Kristen Ransom, Communique, for Cooks Headquarters.

HEALTHNEWS

Thorek Hospital celebrates 75 years of service

The best defense is right inside

Your immune system protects you from a very

Tabloid by Bill Bosler, FDR Publications, for Thorek Hospital and Medical Center.

FRANK'S MONTHLY GARDENER

JUNE, 1986

Tips on office plant care, growing tomatoes & roses, and on managing plants raised in clay soil.

The Corporate Plant

Frank's Nursery & Crafts

SPRING SALE!

Small Business Communications by Lisa Menders for Frank's Nursery and Crafts, Inc.

Can Do With Publishing.

A LAKEWOOD PUBLICATION

TRAINING DIRECTORS' FORUM
N E W S L E T T E R
A Forum for Leaders and Managers of Training

Volume 2, Number 4   April, 1986

Protecting a training budget when finances are tight requires timing, sales skills and corporate perspective

[body newsletter text]

continued on page 2

If management isn't sold on training you might as well stay home to bake cookies.

INSIDE STORIES...
- The Editors' Forum...p.3
- Hiring Consultants...p.3
- How to Select a CBT Authoring Program...p.4
- Problem Column...p.5
- Profile—Melinda Bickerstaff American Express...p.6
- Eye on Training—a column by Ron Zemke...p.7
- Directors' Notebook...p.8

Contributors to this issue...p.5

An Alternative View

ELECTRONIC CERAMIC MATERIALS BUSINESS

For use in the production of ceramic capacitors, varistors, thermistors and piezoelectrics, Transelco produces high quality raw materials often developed and formulated in close cooperation with customers to meet increasingly stringent specifications.

[brochure body text]

Automated computer testing supports research and quality assurance.

Research and development kiln for firing multilayer ceramic capacitors.

Jim Arthur, Sales Manager, Electronic Ceramic Materials

"My job is equivalent to being the customer's representative at Transelco. From something as simple as making sure labels are printed the way a customer requests them to participating in the development of a new product, I feel that it's my responsibility to see that the customer is satisfied."

"We have built Transelco to being responsive and working with customers. Whatever customers need — customized material," ... rush shipments or running additional tests — we'll bend over backwards to meet their demands. For Transelco to be successful in an industry as intensely competitive in price and quality as ours, we have to do our job right every time."

Newsletter by Brian McDermott, Lakewood Publications.

Brochure by Joanne and David Lenweaver, Lenweaver Design, for Transelco Division, Ferro Corporation.

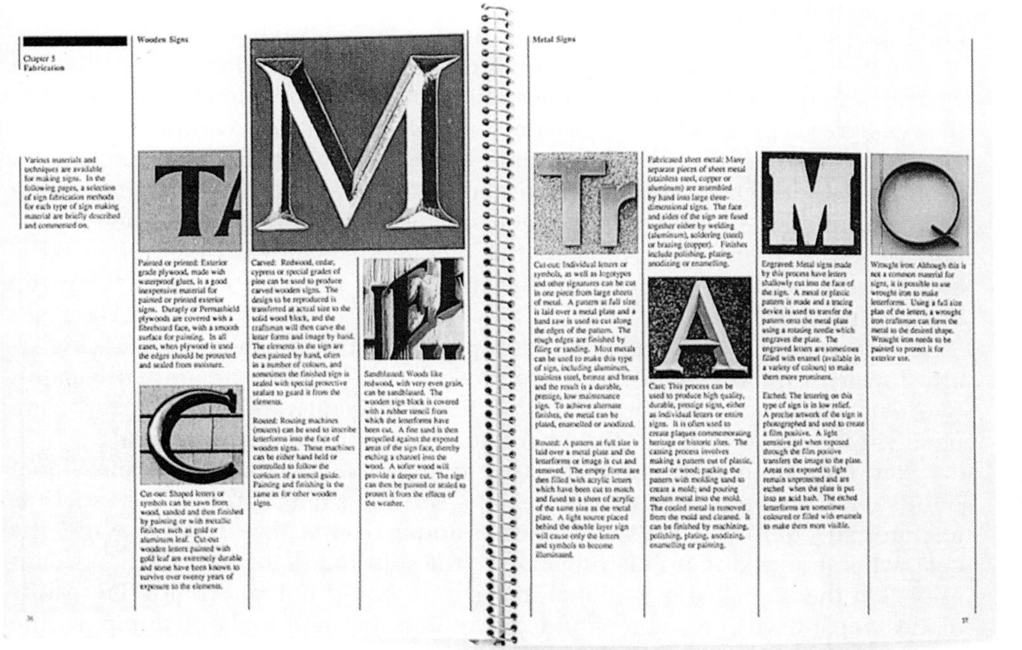

Chapter 5 — Fabrication — Wooden Signs — Metal Signs

Various materials and techniques are available for making signs. In the following pages, a selection of sign fabrication methods for each type of sign making material are briefly described and commented on.

Painted or primed; Carved; Sandblasted; Routed; Cut-out (wooden signs)

Cut-out; Cast; Engraved; Etched; Wrought Iron (metal signs)

1986 - 87 SEASON

Pegasus Players

Your Ticket to Magic and Excitement!

Book by Denise Saulnier, Communication Design Group Ltd., for the City of Halifax, Nova Scotia, Canada.

Program by Eda Warren, Eda Warren Design, for The Pegasus Players.

Some software supports both a mouse and keyboard for all functions, but users find that when a mouse is used to enhance the keyboard's function, software is much more effective.

Clip Art Software

For graphics, users generally do not create their own art because that is too time consuming. Instead, so-called clip art software is available that provides a library of graphic images for use in page composition software. Required images are extracted from the clip art software and are inserted into the document as it is prepared using the desktop publishing program.

The Printer

Effective desktop publishing requires the use of a laser printer. The laser offers not only a higher resolution for good-quality printing, but a variety of type fonts are available to satisfy the needs of a diversity of publishing requirements. Although laser printers do not match the quality results available from professional typesetting and graphic artists, the results are suitable for all but the most demanding applications.

Dot matrix printers can also be used for desktop publishing, but they present a compromise on quality. Although a matrix printer can create the images developed with page composition software, it cannot produce the higher resolution of the laser printer. Serious users will need to consider an investment in a laser printer for an effective desktop publishing system.

Is Desktop Publishing for Everyone?

Desktop publishing may seem to be the solution for many business problems. No longer is it necessary to send out manuscripts to a typesetter, which is time consuming and costly. Even the graphic artist is not required because graphics can be developed along with the text, again saving time and money.

These would seem to be the arguments for using a desktop publishing system, and they are persuading ones. But there is another side to the argument that designers, professional typesetters, and graphic artists would make.

There is some concern that users of desktop publishing systems are not professional designers and therefore may actually spend far more time doing a second-rate job of creating documents. The professional who knows his or her job is far more effective than the businessperson who has other skills and training and can actually do the job in less time for less cost than the businessperson.

A second argument against desktop publishing is that the results are generally lower in quality than those produced by graphic artists and colleagues. Because desktop publishing is a new field, the software and the hardware have yet to evolve to the point where quality results are the standard.

Naturally both sides have effective arguments. Certainly the professional publishers can produce superior results, but for some applications, such as an internal company newsletter, professional results may not be worth the cost, whereas desktop publishing may be the solution that keeps the newsletter alive. On the other hand, national magazines would not yet accept the results of desktop publishing, nor would the writers be happy about doing all the composition, and so there are many applications where the professionals are irreplaceable. However, as software and hardware improves and users become more knowledgeable, there is no doubt that desktop publishing is going to have a major impact on the publishing business.

<table>
<tr><td>CHAPTER
SUMMARY</td><td>

1. Word processing is considered to be the leading use of personal computers and is frequently the main application that prompts the purchase of a first computer. Early word processors were dedicated systems that had word processing as their only function. By the mid 1980s dedicated word processors were in the minority as the more powerful and flexible personal computer took its place in the business office.

2. With word processing a draft copy of a document can be made, corrections and changes noted on the page, and then the changes are made using the word processor without the need for retyping the document.

3. Form letters are produced easily with a word processor by creating the letter in a primary file and names and addresses in a secondary file. A merge program combines the contents of these files producing the letters.

4. Publishers frequently benefit from word processing by using the printout, called camera ready copy, directly in the publishing process. Text that is prepared for electronic mail is generally first written in a word processor and then sent to the remote location using a communications program.

5. The stages of word processing are entering text, editing, print formatting, printing, and saving or recalling the text to or from disk.

6. When choosing the hardware for a word processor consideration should be given to memory size, the keyboard layout and feel, screen display characteristics, disk capacity, and type of printer.

7. Word processors use a variety of terms to describe their operation. Users should be familiar with the terms word wrap, line spacing (single or double), line centering, underlining, and boldface. The status line gives information about the page and the word processor operation. Other terms used are left and right margins, soft and hard pages breaks, indenting and tab settings.

8. The search command is used to find the occurrence of a word or phrase that has been used in the text. This is a useful method for getting to a specific location where you know of some unique word that is used at that place in the document. Search and replace not only finds the word or phrase but replaces it with another. A wildcard may be used in the search string so that a range of words may satisfy the search.

9. Blocks may be defined as words, sentences, paragraphs, or other sections of text. In most word processors, a block may be moved, copied, deleted, or written to disk. A column block is a rectangle of text or a column of numbers or characters.

10. Formatting a document can create numerous effects depending on the choice of features available in the word processor. Formatting features include line spacing, margin settings, right margin justification, and tab settings. In addition a choice of printer fonts, printers, settings for headers and footers, and the insertion of page numbers may be available.

11. A WP utility may include a spelling checker, thesaurus, mail merge, and an outliner.

12. Desktop publishing takes the concept of WYSIWYG to its limit by providing software that can display a page on the screen in exactly the format it will be printed including different text fonts and graphics. Page composition software is the desktop software that is used to create pages of text and provides the tools to format the text and lay out the content, with columns, boxes, headings, and so on.

13. Desktop hardware will include a fast PC such as an IBM PC/AT, PS/2, or compatible, a keyboard and mouse, and laser printer or high quality matrix printer. Clip art software may also be useful for generating graphics.

</td></tr>
</table>

Camera-ready copy
Clip art software
Copy
Desktop publishing
Editing
Electronic mail
Form letter
Formatting

Function key driven
Insert
Mail merge
Menu oriented
Move
Outline generator
Page composition
  software
Print formatting

Printing
Recalling text
Saving Text
Search and replace
Spelling checker
Thesaurus
Utilities
Word wrap

REVIEW QUESTIONS

Fill-in Questions

1. The process of _____ is used for making changes such as inserting or deleting text in the document.

2. _____ _____ occurs when typing a line of text and a word that will not fit at the end of the current line is moved automatically to the next line.

3. Text that is aligned on the right margin is called _____.

4. _____ a document from the word processor causes it to be stored as a disk file.

5. The _____ and _____ command is used to look for a word that has been used in the text and change it to another word.

6. A(n) _____ and _____ operation would be used to move a paragraph from one location in the document to another.

7. Programs such as a spell checker and thesarus are _____ programs that enhance the use of a word processor.

8. Using _____ _____ software is one way to combine both text and graphics into the same document.

Matching Questions

Match each term with the description given below.

a. spelling checker
b. word wrap
c. function key driven
d. hard page break
e. search and replace
f. formatting

_____d_____ 1. This is caused when the user forces a new page to occur at a specific line in the text.

_____e_____ 2. This command is used to find a word and change it to some other word or phrase.

_____a_____ 3. A utility program that checks for errors in the user's typing.

_____f_____ 4. This operation is used to change margins or line spacing.

_____c_____ 5. Some word processors, such as WordPerfect, are given commands in this manner.

_____b_____ 6. This action occurs when typing a sentence that contains too many words for a line.

Discussion Questions

1. Discuss some of the benefits of using a word processor over the typewriter. Include in your discussion some of the areas where word processing is used.

2. What are the five stages of word processing? Give a brief explanation of the activities associated with each stage.
3. What are some of the features you might consider when looking for a word processor?
4. Identify some of the basic terminology used with word processing systems.
5. What is meant by a cut and paste operation? How can it be used when editing a document?
6. Explain the use of formatting in word processing.
7. What is the purpose of a utility program in word processing? Describe three common utilities available for word processors.
8. What is meant by desktop publishing? What role does page composition software play here?
9. Discuss the hardware requirements for a desktop publishing system.

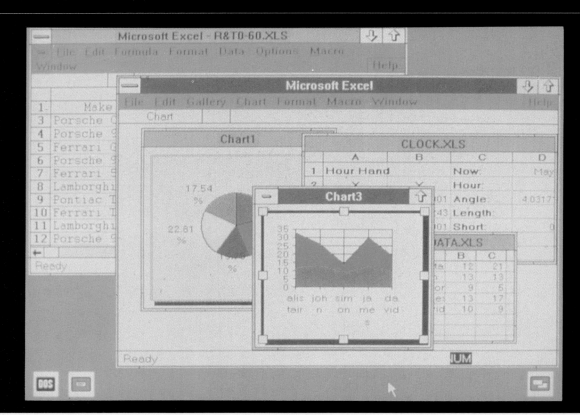

9

Spreadsheets, Integrated, and Other Software

A VIEW OF THE CHAPTER AHEAD

After Reading This Chapter You Will Understand:

- The use of spreadsheets in business and their strengths when asking "what if" questions.

- The basic components of a spreadsheet such as cells, values, labels, and formulas.

- Some of the basic operations of a spreadsheet such as the use of functions, formatting, ranges, and graphing.

- Why integrated packages are a useful alternative to several specialized programs.

- The use of other software such as project management, presentation graphics, and CAD/CAM.

S preadsheets are relative newcomers to the computer software club. The first spreadsheet, VisiCalc, was released in 1979 for the Apple computer and represented a new way of thinking about computing that had not previously been considered. The concept was so revolutionary that it was claimed to have sold users on purchasing a microcomputer on the strength of the software alone.

SPREADSHEETS

Soon other companies created their own versions of the spreadsheet, including Lotus 1–2–3, Multiplan, and SuperCalc. Of these, Lotus 1–2–3 has become the uncontested leader (Figure 9–1) by virtue of its ease of use and wide range of features, but mostly because it was one of the first full-featured spreadsheets available for the IBM personal computer.

FIGURE 9–1

The clear leader in the spreadsheet software industry is Lotus 1–2–3. Lotus has done much to legitimize the personal computer market and is a software package used by the majority of PC users. Here Lotus 1-2-3 Release 3 is used to display sporting goods sales in three dimensions (top). A graph displayed with the spreadsheet gives an immediate picture of sales in each quarter (bottom).

Courtesy of Lotus Development Corporation.

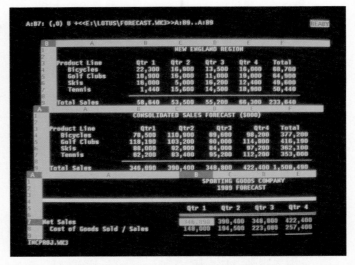

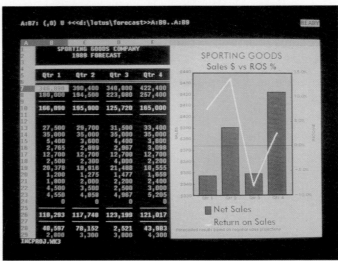

Typical Spreadsheet Applications

Spreadsheets are frequently used as a convenient method for recording numerical data, taking advantage of the automatic calculations that can be done efficiently with a spreadsheet program. Users of spreadsheets find them useful for hundreds of applications, some of them quite widely used such as

- Preparing and analyzing financial statements to show the assets and liabilities of the company.
- Forecasting sales by analyzing previous trends and projecting future growth based on trends and sales objectives.
- Controlling inventory and updating the data when shipments are made or items are received.
- Pricing of goods based on purchase cost, cost of storage, the cost of processing an order, and other factors unique to the product.
- Analyzing product performance on factors such as cost of production, amount of sales, and customer satisfaction.
- Create graphics for easier spreadsheet analysis and presentation of business data.
- Other applications such as investment alternatives, cash flow projections, and rate structure analysis.

"What If" Questions

Spreadsheets today generally provide three major areas of capability: spreadsheet, graphics, and data base. The fundamental component of these three is the spreadsheet, which is used for creating models and asking "what if" questions. Some of the discussion in this chapter will concern the use of a spreadsheet to create a model (Figure 9–2) and ask questions about what happens if certain values are changed.

FIGURE 9–2

A budget planning model is built into a spreadsheet to show total expenses per year in five different categories. The question "What if we spend less for travel?" can be asked by changing the travel expense of $1,200.00 in 1988 to some other value such as $1,000.00. The effect of the change will be shown in all the travel values for the following years and in the spreadsheet totals for those years.

B13: (,2) @SUM(B7..B11)   READY

	A	B	C	D	E	F	G
1			Budget Spreadsheet				
2							
3	Budget	Projected	Values ══════════════════════════>				
4							
5	Type	1988	1989	1990	1991	1992	1993
6							
7	Supplies	150.75	162.81	175.83	189.90	205.09	221.50
8	Travel	1,200.00	1,296.00	1,399.68	1,511.65	1,632.59	1,763.19
9	Phone	300.00	324.00	349.92	377.91	408.15	440.80
10	Xpress Mail	425.00	459.00	495.72	535.38	578.21	624.46
11	Periodicals	290.00	313.20	338.26	365.32	394.54	426.11
12							
13		2,365.75	2,555.01	2,759.41	2,980.16	3,218.58	3,476.06
14							
15							
16							
17							
18							
19							
20							

As soon as a new value is entered, the new value for travel expenses takes its place on the screen. Immediately the spreadsheet program recalculates totals or other formulas. Automatic recalculation of formulas is a unique feature of spreadsheets and is one of its major strengths. In the example we could just as well have asked the question "What if travel increased to $1,400.00?" or possibly "What if periodicals were reduced to $150.00?"

There are clearly many alternatives that the manager could seek an answer for. It is also possible to make several changes and view the results. So within a few minutes many possible combinations of budget values can be considered and the results seen immediately on the screen.

Spreadsheet Components

Spreadsheets, like the one in Figure 9–3, consist of a number of cells arranged in rows and columns. This organization is similar to the ledger pad used by accountants to assist in recording and calculating all the values needed for financial planning. In a computer spreadsheet, a value, label, or formula can be stored in each cell.

The number of rows and columns depends on the spreadsheet used and even on the version of the spreadsheet. For example, Lotus 1–2–3 Version 2 has 256 columns and 8192 rows. The original Lotus 1–2–3 Version 1A had 256 columns and 2048 rows. Thus version 1A has 524,288 cells, and version 2 contains 2,097,152 cells.

While the number of cells available in version 2 may seem extravagant, they were provided at the demand of Lotus's customers who found version 1A to be too restrictive for their applications. Whether or not a computer can use all this space depends on the amount of memory installed. In some cases special memory expansion boards are required to take advantage of the extensive capability of a spreadsheet program.

FIGURE 9–3

A spreadsheet display has rows identified with numbers and columns with letters. A cell is the area found at the intersection of a column and row. Cell C5 is identified here. At the top is a control area where messages are displayed. Some spreadsheets have the control area at the bottom of the screen.

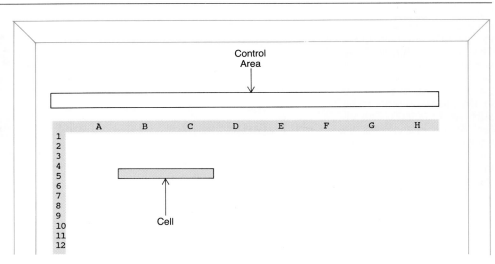

Cells and addressing

A **cell** is located where a row and column meet on the screen. At the intersection of column A and row 1 is a cell where a value may be placed in the spreadsheet. The address of this cell is composed of the column and row number and for this cell is address A1. Cell A1 is also called the **Home** address. Moving one cell to the right is cell B1 and so on. A spreadsheet like Lotus 1–2–3 goes all the way out to column IV for a cell address of IV1.

Moving down from the Home address is cell A2, then A3, and so on. Lotus 1–2–3 Version 2 goes all the way down to address A8192.

The control panel

Spreadsheet programs use a **control panel** or **status line** to communicate with the user. One or more lines are used to display menus, prompts, cell contents, current cell address, and mode. Not all of this information will display at one time as it depends on the operation being done. Figure 9–4 shows the contents of the control panel for Lotus 1–2–3.

The **cell pointer** is the highlighted bar that points to the current cell where a value or formula may be entered or edited. The **cell address** refers to the cell where the pointer is currently positioned. The **cell contents** are shown in the control panel. In the event that the contents are too extensive to be displayed in the cell itself, the control panel will show all the cell contents when the pointer is located on that cell.

The **menu line** appears only when the slash (/) key is pressed. By pressing the slash Lotus 1–2–3 displays a list of options that may be selected. A **submenu** shows additional options when the bar is positioned on the menu line. These are options available if the main option, such as Worksheet, is selected.

The **mode indicator** identifies the current mode or status that the program is in. Modes determine the types of actions that may be taken or the type of data entered.

FIGURE 9–4

Contents of the control panel for Lotus 1–2–3 when a menu has been accessed.

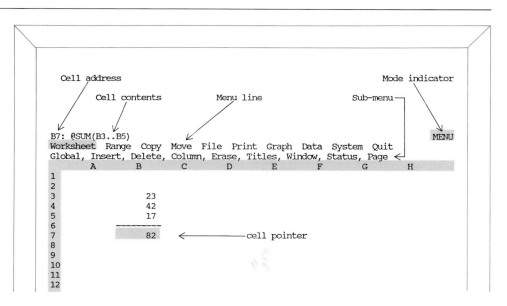

Creating a Spreadsheet

To create a spreadsheet it is first necessary to have a basic understanding of the results we require. A mental image or even a rough paper image of what the spreadsheet will look like is a good planning step. Ideas for rows and columns, where the labels will go and what cells will contain values or formulas are necessary first steps in our planning.

Assume that we are planning a spreadsheet for first quarter expenses, but a reasonable guess would suggest that eventually there will also be second, third, and fourth quarter values. So a good analyst would lay out the cells so that additional quarters can be easily added. Figure 9–5 shows how we want the spreadsheet to appear when it is finished.

Three types of entries can be made on most spreadsheets: labels, values, and formulas. **Labels** are entries such as names, descriptions, and titles. **Values** are numeric data such as quantity, costs, and percentages. Labels and values may be entered interchangeably on the spreadsheet. Each label is entered by first positioning the pointer on the cell, typing the entry, and then pressing a cursor key to get to the next cell. Values are entered in the same manner and include decimal points or minus signs if needed.

A **formula** is an arithmetic expression or formula that does a calculation using values on the spreadsheet. The calculation of a value such as the sum of all budget values (Figure 9–6) requires the use of a formula in cell B12. There are several ways this can be done. One method is to use the expression +B6+B7+B8+B9+B10. But in the example a function @SUM(B6 . . B10) is used that defines the range of the cell that are summed for the total. Because the values we want to add are cells B6 to B10, the formula

@SUM(B6 . . B10)

is used, which is simpler than writing an arithmetic expression. This formula is placed in the cell where we want to see the sum, in this case cell B12.

A result of typing a formula is that the result of calculating the formula appears in the cell. Thus cell B12 will display the sum of cells B6 to B10 and not the formula that was typed. By placing the pointer on the cell containing the formula, the contents of that cell will appear in the control panel at the top of the screen.

FIGURE 9–5
A spreadsheet plan prior to making the initial entries. Developing a plan saves time and ensures that entries made will represent the model effectively.

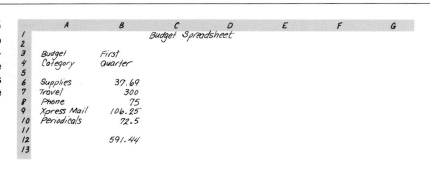

FIGURE 9–6
The entry of labels, values, and a formula on the spreadsheet. When a formula is entered into cell B12 the result of calculating the formula is displayed in the cell. The formula contents will display on the control panel when the pointer is positioned on cell B12.

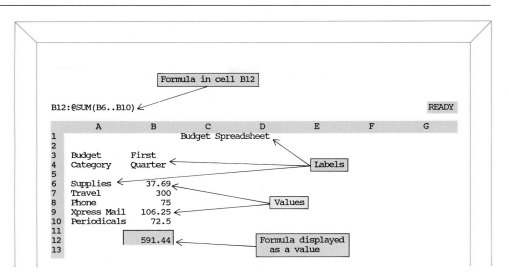

Ranges

To simplify entries, such as those used in formulas, spreadsheets provide a **range** definition that includes one or more cells in a simple expression. Figure 9–7 shows different ways cells can be included as a range. Notice that in every case the range is either rectangular or square in shape. This is a primary requirement of a range definition.

Ranges are always identified by the first and last cell in the range. A range may be a single cell or many cells. The range B6 . . B10 refers to cells B6, B7, B8, B9, and B10. A rectangular range always specifies the addresses of the upper-left and lower-right corners of the range. Thus the range D3 . . F5 would refer to cells enclosed in a rectangle with these upper left and lower right coordinates.

FIGURE 9–7
Several ways in which a range may be defined in a spreadsheet. A range is always identified by the first and last cell in the range such as A1 . . A10, which includes all cells in column A from row 1 to row 10.

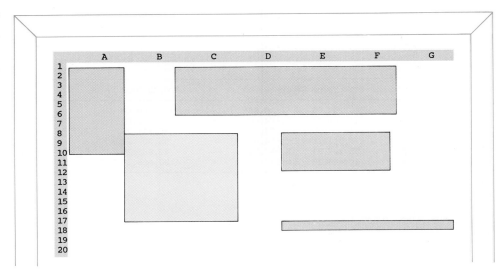

Using Ranges in the Spreadsheet

Ranges are used in two basic ways in a spreadsheet. One use is in a formula that requires a range of cells such as finding the sum of a column of numbers. The other use of a range is when giving a spreadsheet command (slash command) that requires a range of cells for the operation, as when copying formulas or values from one range of cells to another.

Formatting the Spreadsheet

As a variety of data is entered on a spreadsheet the appearance of the values may not be exactly as desired. This is especially true when formulas have been used to develop some values and the results go into several decimal places. In such a case, values may have differing decimal positions and will not align in the column.

Other times there may be large numbers that could benefit from the use of commas to set off the thousands position. Dollar values sometimes look better with a dollar sign. A percentage such as 0.25 would be more readable if it were displayed as "25%."

The appearance of one or more cells may be changed by using a **format** command. Figure 9–8 shows a depreciation spreadsheet where currency, date,

---

FIGURE 9–8

A variety of formats used in a depreciation spreadsheet developed in Lotus 1–2–3.

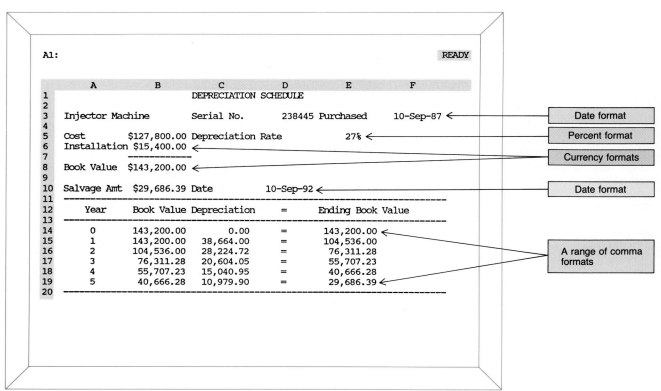

comma, and interest formats have been used. Both single cells and a range of cells are formatted in this spreadsheet indicating the variety of formatting needs in a business application.

For exercises in formatting, see the spreadsheet tutorial that accompanies this book.

SPREADSHEET TEMPLATES

Applications, such as invoices, use a common format for the spreadsheet, while the data entered will be different for each order. Instead of recreating the spreadsheet for each new invoice, a template is prepared and saved on disk until it is needed. The empty template is then read into memory and filled with the data unique to the customer's order. The filled template then becomes a permanent record of the order that can be printed, saved on disk, and used for follow-up with the customer. The next order begins with the empty template and the process is repeated.

An empty template used for a customer invoice.

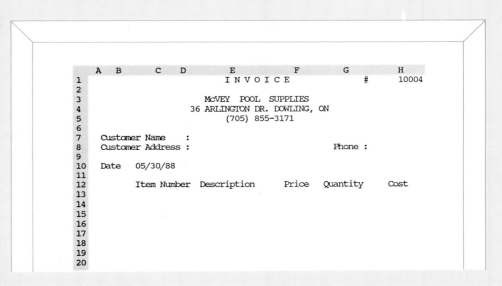

The invoice template filled with data.

FIGURE 9–9
Relative addressing causes the formula in each cell to be addressed relative to the position it occupies in the spreadsheet.

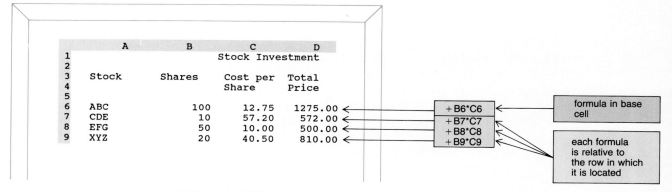

Relative Addressing

Figure 9–9 shows a formula used in a stock investment spreadsheet that uses relative addressing. When the formula in cell D6 is copied to the second cell (D7), its addresses are adjusted so that the correct row and column will be referenced. The figure shows how this affects each row number in subsequent cells affected by the copy. Because the row (in this case) or column is adjusted when the formula is copied, it is called relative addressing. In other words the address used in the formula is relative to its position in the spreadsheet. A formula located in cell D7 will reference other cells in row 7, while a formula in cell D8 references cells in row 8.

FIGURE 9–10
The use of absolute addressing in a formula where the depreciation rate is taken from a single cell.

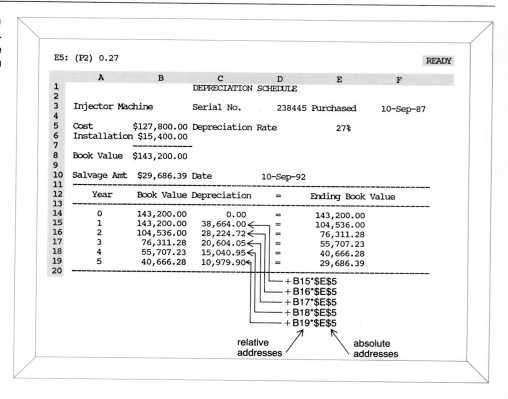

Absolute Addressing

When absolute addressing is used, an address in the formula is not to be adjusted when a formula is copied. From the previous example, this may seem to be undesirable, and it is, but in some cases using an absolute address is a necessity. Let's take another look at the depreciation spreadsheet in Figure 9–10, which uses a depreciation rate in cell E5. Every time this rate is used, it must be taken from cell E5. Therefore, when a formula is copied that uses the address E5, it must be treated as absolute and the row or column may not be adjusted.

To use a cell as an absolute address, it is necessary to enter it with dollar signs. Cell E5 would be entered as E5 to be treated as an absolute address. Either the row or column can be treated as absolute by entering a dollar sign in front of just the row or the column.

Graphs

When data is shown on the spreadsheet, it is sometimes difficult to understand the meaning of the numbers and their relationship to each other. By doing arithmetic or other operations on the data, we can sometimes produce helpful results, which can greatly enhance our understanding of the data. All this is well and good, but there are many times when a graph or chart can convey significantly more meaning and in a more concise form.

Business reports frequently include bar charts, pie charts, or line graphs to present information in a pictorial form rather than as raw data. These graphs, when used appropriately, can have a much greater impact on the reader than mere numbers alone. By using graphs, the manager or businessperson can make immediate observations, such as salaries that represent well in excess of half the budget, or that sales in region 3 have been steadily declining over the past three years.

Types of graphs

Most spreadsheet software will produce a variety of graphs, some with more types than others. Lotus 1–2–3 has five graph types available as shown in Figure 9–11. These graph types are selected by the user of the software depending on the type of data to be represented. The five graph types are

1. *Line graph.* This graph plots points on a grid and connects them with a line. This is a suitable graph for representing a frequency distribution of a set of values. A line graph can also be used for comparing several sets of values, such as the trend of different stocks over a period of time.
2. *Bar graph.* This graph represents values in bar form. Values, such as individual sales amounts for five different regions, will each be represented by a single bar.
3. *XY graph.* The XY graph is similar to the line graph, except that the data is represented by both *X* and *Y* coordinates. This is useful for charting one value against another, such as revenue against advertising costs. It can also be used for mathematical graphs, such as for plotting sine waves.
4. *Stacked bar.* This is similar to the bar graph except that each bar shows an accumulation of values. For example, sales for four quarters within a region would be shown on a single bar to show accumulated sales for the year.

5. *Pie graph.* The fifth form of graph is the pie chart. Using a pie chart automatically represents the data in terms of percentages. For example, if the data for sales in five regions were displayed as a pie instead of a bar chart, then each region would represent a wedge of the pie. Each wedge would show the sales for the region as a percentage of total sales.

FIGURE 9–11

Five graphs produced by Lotus 1–2–3. A line graph, bar graph, XY graph, stacked bar, and a pie chart.

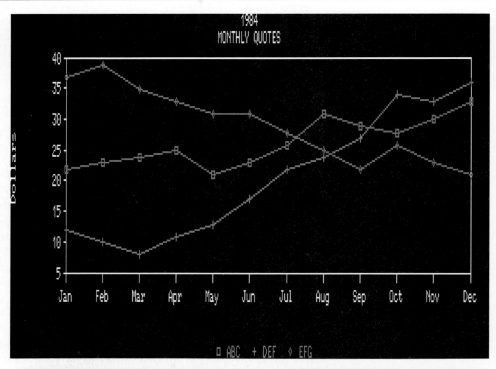

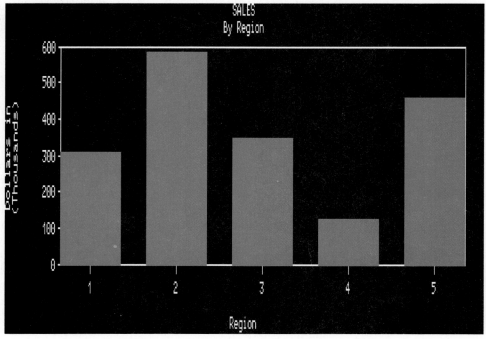

FIGURE 9–11
(Continued)

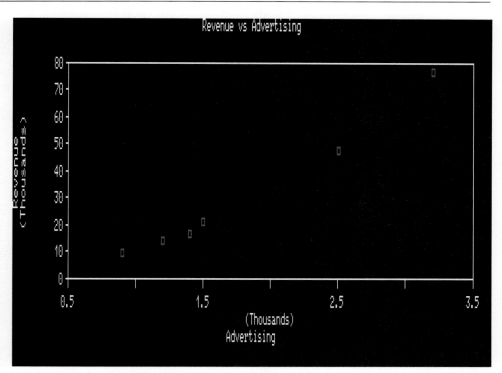

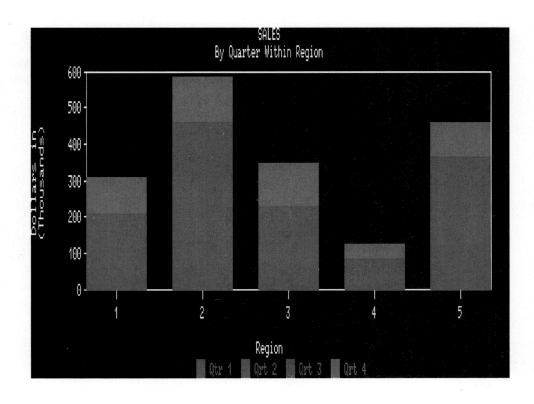

FIGURE 9–11
(Continued)

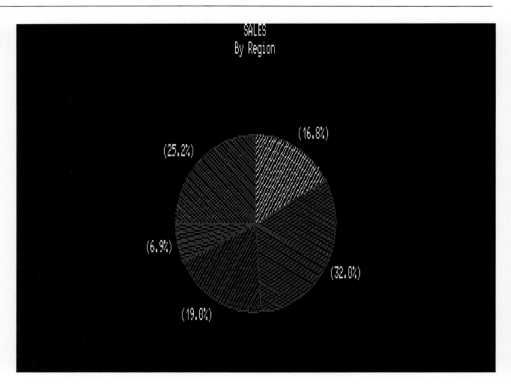

Macros

Most spreadsheets provide a macro facility to help automate the use of the spreadsheet. Macros can be written at two levels. The first simply records the keystrokes used to operate the spreadsheet. This can include operations such as saving or retrieving a file, displaying a graph, accepting data, or issuing

FIGURE 9–12
Part of a macro using Lotus 1–2–3's command language. Lines such as MENU1 and TYPE define menus that are displayed and used in the same manner as Lotus commands. Other commands, such as {GOTO}A142~ and {RIGHT}{?}~, represent keyboard macros that automate the use of the spreadsheet.

	J	K	L	M
1		MACROS		
2				
3	\0	{GOTO}S1~		
4	\z	{MENUBRANCH MENU1}		
5				
6				
7	MENU1	Expenses	Car	Office
8		Daily Expenses	Maintenance Costs	Office Expenses
9		{BRANCH EXPENSES}	{BRANCH CAR}	{BRANCH OFFICE}
10				
11	EXPENSES	{GOTO}A142~{DOWN}/wth{END}{DOWN}{DOWN}		
12	REPEATEX	@today{edit}{calc}~{right}		
13		{MENUBRANCH TYPE}		
14				
15	TYPE	Supplies	Meals	Postage
16		Press Enter	Press Enter	Press Enter
17		Supplies~	Meals~	Postage~
18		{RIGHT}{?}~	{RIGHT}{?}~	{RIGHT}{?}~
19		{RIGHT}{?}~	{RIGHT}{?}~	{RIGHT}{?}~
20		{RIGHT}{?}~	{RIGHT}{?}~	{RIGHT}{?}~

a recalculation of the spreadsheet. All these steps can be done manually, but they require some knowledge of the use of the spreadsheet commands. By automating the commands a simple keystroke can activate them letting the user concentrate on the data.

The second form of macro lets the spreadsheet developer create applications with spreadsheetlike commands. Using the Lotus 1–2–3 command language (Figure 9–12), a program is written that creates its own menus. These menus are used like Lotus menus, but they are specifically developed for the application. Thus choices, such as Expenses, Car, and Office are made available. With a command language the user only needs to know the application and is relieved from the need to know spreadsheet commands.

Three-Dimensional Spreadsheets

Traditional spreadsheets display data in two dimensions using row and columns. Now software such as Lotus 1–2–3 Release 3, Boeing Calc or McDonnell Douglas Communication's microCUBE offers spreadsheet programs with three-dimensional capability. This does not mean that the spreadsheet displays with a 3-D image on the screen, but rather that there is a third dimension, called a page, to the spreadsheet.

Using a two-dimensional spreadsheet, a budget might be displayed with budget items down the first column with additional columns side by side showing amounts for each month of the year. A three-dimensional spreadsheet can show the items and amounts for one month on the screen as the first page. A second page (behind the first) with a similar format is used for the next month. A total of 12 pages would be used for an annual budget. Only one page is visible at a time, and so the 3-D spreadsheet appears similar to a two-dimensional one.

Three-dimensional spreadsheets tend to display data in a simpler fashion because less data needs to be visible at any one time. This makes for less crowded displays and easier design. True three-dimensional applications can be developed more easily whereas a two-dimensional spreadsheet requires some ingenuity. For example, a sales application with sales for each product by region and month is awkward to manipulate on a two-dimensional spreadsheet but is quite natural on a three-dimensional one.

A 3-D spreadsheet, such as Boeing Calc, uses a page number in its cell addressing. The upper left cell in Lotus 1–2–3 Release 2.01 has an address of A1, while in Boeing Calc, it is 1A1, the first number referring to page number 1. Boeing Calc also uses a virtual memory technique to hold the spreadsheet on disk if memory space fills up. The worksheet of 16,000 rows by 16,000 columns by 16,000 pages can use up to 32 megabytes of disk space. Only the parts of the spreadsheet that are needed at the time are kept in memory. The rest is on disk until needed by the program.

While 3–D spreadsheets may seem to be a natural evolution for spreadsheet programs they have not received a great deal of attention. One reason may be that spreadsheets like 1–2–3 and SuperCalc provide more capability than many users need, and so there is little reason to use a three dimensional.

Another reason may be the seeming complexity of the 3–D software. In some cases the three-dimensional spreadsheet may be quite different to use than a traditional spreadsheet. This is true of microCUBE. But other software, such as Boeing Calc, uses Lotus 1–2–3 like commands and is relatively easy to learn if the user already knows 1–2–3.

MICROSOFT EXCEL:
A NEW GENERATION SPREADSHEET

When you define a range as a data base, Excel automatically uses column headings as field names in the data base. The contents of the cells become the entries.

Courtesy of PC Magazine.

The edit menu is displayed in this Excel screen, which shows a spreadsheet in the right window and macro script in the left one.

Courtesy of PC Magazine.

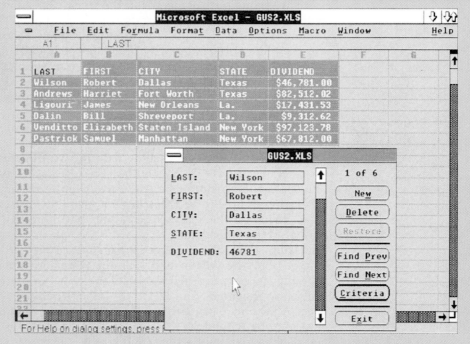

(continued)

Excel, the leading spreadsheet on the Apple Macintosh, was released by Microsoft in 1987 for use on the PC/AT. This is a state-of-the-art spreadsheet program that uses graphics, colors, icons, and menu bars. By displaying everything on the screen as graphics you can have spreadsheet, graphics, and menus all displaying at the same time in different areas of the screen. Choices are made from the screen with either a mouse or the keyboard.

Although Excel is designed to run on any PC/AT or faster system, it gets bogged down because of its graphics when run on a system less than a 80286 processor. Its graphic display really needs at least the resolution of an EGA to be effective, although a CGA display will work. So Excel is a new generation program that is really intended for 386 machines typified by the top end of IBM's new Personal System/2 series of computers.

Excel offers all the fine features that users have come to expect from Lotus 1–2–3 but goes well beyond this standard. Numbers can be displayed as boldface, italic, underlined, color, or even with a shaded background. Both column widths and row heights can be adjusted to suit the user's needs.

There are 131 functions available compared to 1–2–3's 89, and you can even write your own functions if what you need is not supplied. Display formats provide good flexibility with 21 standard formats including one for a telephone number with parentheses for the area code. In addition you can design your own display formats.

Formulas are copied in a simple manner. Instead of typing the formula and then issuing the copy command, in Excel first you highlight the cells to receive the formula and then you type it. Finish the entry by pressing Ctrl-Enter, and the formula is copied into all the highlighted cells.

When developing a spreadsheet the user might want to make a note about the contents of a given cell to remember how it was developed or how it works.

Excel makes it easy to transfer data. Here a range was cut from the spreadsheet on the left of the screen and pasted into the spreadsheet on the lower right.

Courtesy of PC Magazine.

(continued)

The preformatted line chart type in reverse video has been selected as the format for the active chart. In the background are different Excel charts, all displaying the same data.

Courtesy of *PC Magazine*.

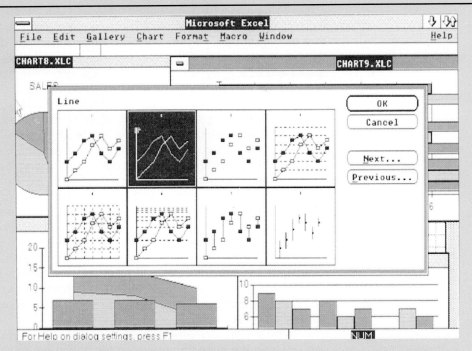

With most spreadsheets this cannot be done unless an add-on note-making program is being used. Excel has a built-in note feature so that notes can be posted to any cell.

Excel provides 7 different graphs including bar, line, pie, and high-low with 44 variations on how these are displayed. The program can tell the difference between data labels and values and automatically allocates the two ranges in the graph accordingly. Editing the graph provides for entering titles and other text using a variety of fonts and colors. As the graph is developed it can display in a window in one corner of the screen while the spreadsheet occupies another area of the screen simultaneously (Lotus Symphony style). This eliminates the need to switch back and forth between spreadsheet and graph.

While Excel is a superior product to 1–2–3 and costs about the same, it is primarily useful to those who have the faster 286 or 386 computers. Those of us who are still using PCs and XTs will have to wait until our systems are upgraded to use Excel effectively.

INTEGRATED SOFTWARE

Integrated software generally provides a combination of spreadsheet, data base, word processing, graphics, and communications in a single package. Integrated packages try to provide a smooth transition from one application to another on the computer with a minimum of change in the mode of operation. In a certain sense Lotus 1–2–3 achieves the spirit of integration by providing spreadsheet, graphics, and data base capabilities in a single environment. The

An integrated software package such as Framework III offers the user a choice of modes. Word processing, spreadsheet, graphics, data management, and data communications are all components of the software. Data can be readily transferred between windows as needed by different parts of the application.

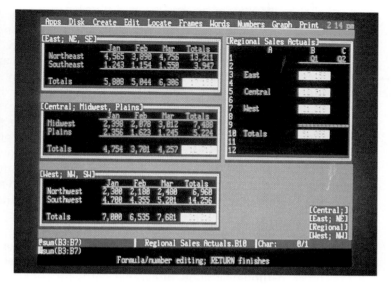

command structure for each component of the package is the same; they even use the same data organization.

This is the essence of integration: several applications are combined into one software package, and they are used in a similar manner within the software. While 1–2–3 might be considered integrated, it is mostly an excellent spreadsheet program. Its graphic or data base components do not compare to the features available on a stand-alone graphics package, such as Harvard Presentation Graphics, or compared to a full-featured data base, such as dBASE IV.

Thus there is a range of integration in software. Integrated software, such as Lotus Symphony, combines more features with more power than does Lotus 1–2–3 and so Symphony might more truly be considered an integrated package.

Why Are Integrated Packages Useful?

There are several reasons why computer users are attracted to integrated packages. Although different packages may offer an assortment of features there are some common reasons stated for choosing an integrated software package. Some of these reasons are

1. They reduce the number of software packages that the user needs to learn.
2. They are less costly than buying many separate programs.
3. It is easier to switch from one mode to another.
4. Data can be readily transferred between applications.

Let's look at each of these benefits of integrated packages in more detail.

Reducing the number of packages to learn

A computer user that requires a variety of software such as a spreadsheet, data base, word processor, and communications will typically buy four different programs. After buying this software, the next step is to learn each package, which no doubt will take some time. It may take several weeks to have a good command of one program.

This user will also soon realize that each program is quite different from the other. So once the spreadsheet has been mastered the learning process starts over again with the data base package. Few software packages adopt their commands from other software unless they are doing the same thing. So a package such as Lotus 1–2–3 may have many similarities to SuperCalc (another spreadsheet) but will have no similarity to dBASE IV (a database package).

An integrated package can help to reduce the time it takes to learn the capabilities of the software. A well-designed integrated program will use a similar command structure for all its features. So once you know how to use the spreadsheet, learning the word processor will not be so difficult or time consuming. Naturally, some integrated packages have succeeded at incorporating this similarity among its features better than others.

Reducing the cost of software

Another benefit of using an integrated package is cost. It is simply less expensive to buy one integrated program than three or four or more separate ones. Although a good integrated software package will be quite expensive, often in the $500 range, it will be much less costly than buying four major packages.

Changing environments

Because an integrated package offers several modes of operation, a keystroke is usually all that is necessary to change from one mode to another. If the user is in the data base environment, a simple command can switch instantly to the spreadsheet or word processor environment.

Compared to separate programs this speed of change is attractive to users who require a frequent change of software environment to do their work. With stand-alone packages the user must first save the current file in the data base, exit from the program to DOS, then load the spreadsheet program. Finally, a file would be retrieved in the spreadsheet. All this might take a minute or more, a long time in computer terms.

Data transfer

Integrated packages generally store their data in a common format. Thus data from the data base can be read by the spreadsheet or the word processor or even transmitted to another computer over the telephone. With separate packages this data transfer process can range from quite simple in some cases to extremely difficult or virtually impossible in other situations.

Exporting data from a dBASE IV data base and **importing** it into a Lotus 1–2–3 spreadsheet is possible but requires some technical knowledge on the part of the user or the use of a separate program to translate from one form to the other. However, an Enable user can easily transfer data from an Enable data base environment to the Enable spreadsheet with a few keystrokes.

Thus PC users who have the need to move data from one environment to another on a frequent basis will find that an integrated package will handle this operation with little difficulty.

Problems with Integrated Packages

While it might seem that integrated packages are the answer to all the needs of most users, they are not without limitations. By trying to cover all the bases by offering uniformity among its features, there are obvious drawbacks. A command structure that works well for a spreadsheet may not be as appropriate for the word processor.

The way data is stored in an integrated package may not always be suitable for the different components. A spreadsheet with rows and columns and cells with formulas does not lend itself well to a word processing document or to a database with fields and records. Thus the concept of data transfer between the applications may not always work so simply in real life.

Integrated packages seldom offer the full range of features seen in single application programs. Until recently most programs have had limits on size to run efficiently in 640K of memory, thus an integrated package must have some compromises. Even though program overlays can overcome some of the limitations of memory size an integrated package is usually somewhat restricted compared to a separate word processor or data base program.

OTHER SOFTWARE PACKAGES

Resident Applications

Resident applications are programs that occupy memory while other applications are running. In this category are desktop managers such as SideKick or Lotus Metro, RAM disk, and print spooler programs. Most of these programs are sold for under $100 and add many useful features to the personal computer.

Many of these programs reside in memory, invisible to the user, until a certain keystroke pattern brings them into action. Then the existing application is temporarily interrupted while the resident program is used. In the case of print spoolers and keyboard enhancers, they run in the background while other applications are performed by the user.

Desktop managers

Desktop managers are programs that replace traditional office tools with an electronic equivalent. Some of the items that may be found in a desktop program are

- Appointment book
- Calendar
- Clock
- Note pad
- Phone book and dialer
- Stop watch
- Text editor

Depending on the program more or less of these features will be found. Borland's SideKick Plus is a desktop manager.

RAM disk

Using an area of RAM (memory) to act as a disk file space is a technique that speeds up the operation of programs that frequently access disk. As Figure 9–13 shows, an area of memory is set aside to act as a RAM disk. Either program code or data is loaded into the RAM disk space, which is called by a disk name such as drive C:.

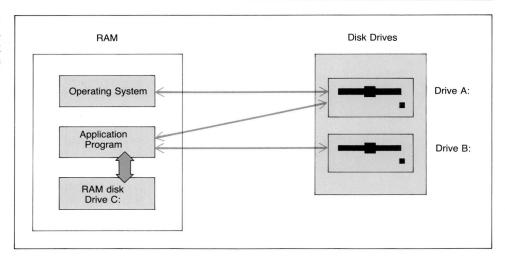

FIGURE 9–13
RAM disk is an area of memory set aside to reduce disk activity, which results in faster program operation.

RAM disk software, such as the VDISK program on the IBM PC DOS 3.3 disk, is used to access drive C: as though it were a real disk drive. Because the data is in reality coming from memory, the transfer time is at memory speed that is considerably faster than accessing a disk drive. With RAM disk, the computer user decides what files should go into the RAM and needs to ensure that the space reserved will not interfere with memory needed for application programs.

Prior to the use of hard disks, RAM disk was a commonly used method of improving the access speed of disk. With hard disk, and its much greater speed, using a RAM disk space does not offer as significant improvement as was the case with a floppy disk–based system.

Newer PC operating systems are using a technique called **virtual storage,** which automatically uses RAM and disk for the storage and access of files and programs. Virtual storage is not really new because it has been used for years on mainframe computers. But with PCs using a megabyte or more of memory, these techniques are now possible on the PC resulting in more effective use of the RAM.

Print spoolers

A **print spooler** is a program that will let you print a document or other material while you continue to work on the computer. Usually the spooler reserves an area of memory for the material to be printed, but some use disk space so that larger documents may be spooled. The main advantage of a spooler is that your work does not need to be interrupted until printing is finished.

A good spooling program will let you begin several printing tasks. It then builds a queue with each item in line to be printed. If a given print job is urgent, then you can give it a higher priority even though others were earlier in the queue. Jobs can also be canceled or held for later printing.

The spooler acts as a background program that executes while the main application is also in process. The main program may experience a slight slowdown in operation or there can be a temporary halt when a disk access is needed, but essentially you can continue with little interruption.

Spoolers are ideal for programs, such as spreadsheets where a built-in spool operation is not normally available. Many of the leading word processors, however, do have their own spooling ability and do not require a spooling program. Offices that do primarily word processing may find that their own word processor will already handle the task.

Project Management

An important function of management is planning. Planning new projects, scheduling the necessary activities, and doing follow-up to keep everything on schedule. Computer-age managers are beginning to use computer software (Figure 9–14) to aid in the management of ongoing projects.

Project management software typically produces a chart that helps the user to manage the project effectively. One type of chart is the PERT chart (Program Evaluation and Review Technique), which shows the relationships between tasks. It uses a critical path method to show the order in which tasks must be done and identifies those tasks that are critical to the timing of the project and must be completed in a given time frame to ensure that other dependent tasks are completed on schedule. Other noncritical tasks may be done at any time without an untoward effect upon the project.

Another type of chart is a Gantt chart, which shows the timing of each task. By comparing the timing on the Gantt chart to the current status of each task, it is possible to determine if a task is on schedule.

FIGURE 9–14
This output from the Harvard Total Project Manager shows how software is used for project management. Software can identify critical tasks and show dates when specific tasks must be completed.

Courtesy of Software Publishing Corporation.

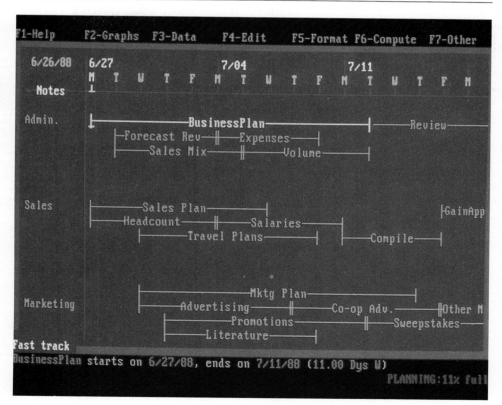

LOTUS AGENDA

With the growing popularity of desktop managers, many other software products are competing with SideKick and SideKick Plus for a piece of the market. Lotus Corporation has addressed this market segment with Metro, a memory-resident desktop management program, and Agenda, a personal information manager. Metro has more features than SideKick but at the price of using almost double the memory. Agenda is a program that needs 640K of RAM to run and so is not intended to be used with other programs unless a 386-based PC is used with a multitasking operating system.

Agenda is used to collect information about any task that requires the organization of ideas and knowledge. For example, a manager may use Agenda for help in preparing a report on a new product. Over the next few weeks all ideas and information she may have about the product would be typed into Agenda. Possible names for the product, the types of markets that benefit from the product, and an idea from a business magazine would all be typed into Agenda. Even the name of suppliers and distributors could be included.

After a few weeks a solid body of information would be gathered in the file. Now Agenda can be used to process the information by chopping it into compartments, filtering it for specific components, and organizing it into different sections. In other words the program becomes an idea processor instead of a word or data processor.

Agenda has three basic building blocks: an item, a category, and a view.

- **Item**—is a single piece of information such as a phrase, "sell the product in upscale neighborhoods." It can be as many as 350 characters in length, and a note of up to 10K may be attached for storing additional information.

- **Category**—is the way you file or organize data. Items that are entered into Agenda are assigned to categories. As the information entered grows in size and variety, Agenda will attempt to assign items to a category automatically based on other available data in the data base.

Lotus Agenda is a personal information management program that provides a method for organizing information. Items contain information in a variety of categories and can be filtered, divided, or grouped in different ways to provide a new view of the data.

Courtesy of Lotus Development Corporation.

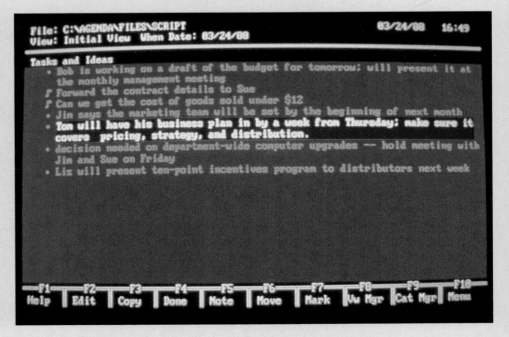

- **View**—is the way you look at the information. After data has been filtered and organized, the view is how it is presented on screen to the user. The filter is a set of conditions that define how the data is to be selected for viewing. A hierarchy may also be used to attach a priority to items that are selected.

Agenda is also useful as a time manager. It can keep track of appointments, to-do lists, track projects, and delegate tasks. Another of its abilities is as an outliner with categories that may be nested up to 12 levels deep. Agenda can also be used as a text retrieval system by importing documents and searching for the use of certain phrases. Clearly Agenda is an interesting and powerful new trend in the processing of information that goes well beyond the traditional processing of words or data.

Presentation Graphics

A pie chart created with Chart-Master using art from its extensive symbol library. Chart-Master outputs to a variety of devices such as printers, plotters, and film image recorders.

Part of any business requirement is the need to communicate effectively. Whether the manager is presenting the plans for a new operation or reviewing the results of past accomplishments, effective communication tools are needed to make the presentation both interesting and informative. Now presentation graphics computer software, from under $100 to over $500, is available to help to prepare and present quality graphics.

Using a software package, such as Harvard Presentation Graphics or Lotus Freelance Plus, charts or graphs can be prepared on the computer for use in a business presentation. A chart is something that contains text, while a graph contains analytical data presented as a pie, bar, line, or other form of graph. Either of these can be prepared as masters for an overhead transparency or as color slides. Some graphics packages can also be used to display the chart or graph on a screen using a projector system attached to the computer.

A presentation graphics program is used to design the chart using a variety of type sizes (Figure 9–15). Large type can be used to emphasize important

FIGURE 9–15
Two charts produced using Harvard Presentation Graphics.

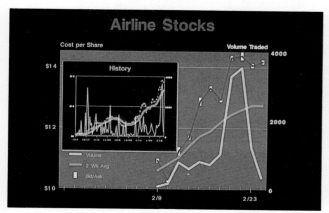
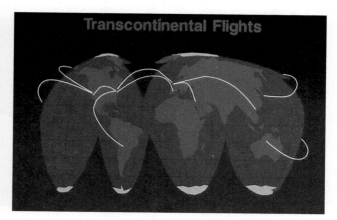

Courtesy of Software Publishing Corporation.

273

points or topics and smaller type for the finer details. Different type styles or fonts also contribute to the effectiveness of the chart. Some systems permit italics, boldface, underlining, or even color for extra emphasis.

Presentation graphics programs can also produce graphics from data that either is entered into the program itself or is imported from a spreadsheet. Many graphic programs accept data from Lotus 1–2–3 or other spreadsheet software, thus eliminating the need to retype data that is already available on the computer.

Output from a graphics program is initially on a color or monochrome monitor, although color is usually best for this type of application. Once the graph or chart has been developed, it can be printed on a graphics printer. Many matrix printers have a graphics mode and can print graphic data. Alternatively, a plotter can be used to create high-quality drawings of the chart or graph using color as required for exceptional results.

A few of the presentation graphics packages provide for film output. Using a special interface, a device such as the Polaroid Palette or MAGICorp slide service can be used to produce color slides from the program. This form of output gives the highest-quality results, but the camera device is an expensive attachment. A less costly alternative is to use a service company to produce the slides from your files.

A package such as Lotus's Freelance Plus (Figure 9–16) offers many of the features described here but also has a large clip art library that can be used to dress up the charts. Using clip art is much easier than is trying to draw your own images, which is very time consuming. However, Freelance Plus also permits the user to draw or paint images of their own on the screen if the exact art required isn't available.

As presentation graphs software becomes more sophisticated, additional features are emerging. Not only do these newer packages create good graphs or charts, they can now do animation. IBM's PC Storyboard is a good example of this class of software. It combines a paint program, a graphics package, and an image editor for manipulating the images. Animated shows are displayed on the screen as a series of slides and are useful for business presentations.

This Polaroid Palette is an attachment for producing color graphic slides from a personal computer. The Palette is frequently used with presentation graphics software to produce high-quality images of graphics on 35mm film.

Courtesy of Polaroid Corporation.

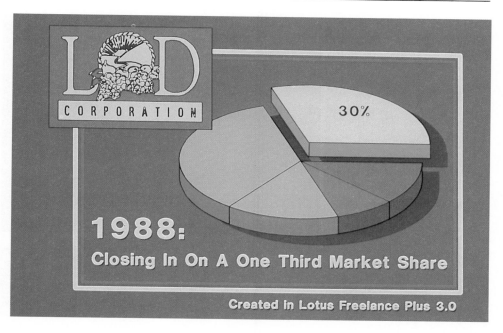

CAD/CAM

The twins CAD and CAM are acronyms for computer-aided design (CAD) and computer-aided manufacturing (CAM). CAD usually refers to software run on a personal or larger computer system that is used for drawing designs for new products. CAD is the computer-age equivalent of the drafting board and is to images what word processing is to words. CAM normally refers to using a computer to run machine tools that shape parts on the shop floor.

A CAD image on the computer screen typically consists of lines, arcs, or circles that represent the design of a product. The leading software for CAD is AutoCAD (Figure 9–17) with competitors VersaCAD and CAD-plan. These are expensive programs, costing $1,000 or more, but less costly software, such as EasyCAD, is now on the market for $500 and less.

CAD software is attractive to engineers and designers because of the productivity gains it offers over manual systems. It is particularly productive when repetitive tasks are done, but speed isn't the only reason for using CAD: the program can store drawings on disk, output them when required, and edit the contents, resulting in a quality gain—an important consideration.

Because drawing is an important component of CAD software, the programs interface with a mouse or digitizer pad. Keyboard entries are used to access functions or to type descriptions on the drawing. A CGA or EGA resolution screen or better is used to give a high level of resolution needed for drafting. Hard copy output is usually on a plotter although a graphics printer may be used with some software.

Until recently, drawings that were produced on a CAD system would be reentered into a CAM system for manufacturing. Because the two systems were not compatible, the specifications for manufacturing would be entered into the shop floor computer as a separate operation. Now newer CAD/CAM

FIGURE 9–17
AutoCAD is the leading computer-aided design software for the IBM PC and -compatible computers.

Courtesy of AutoDesk, Inc.

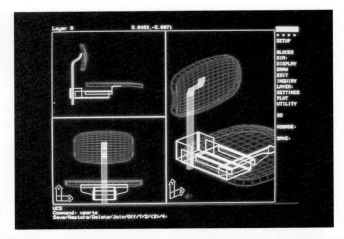

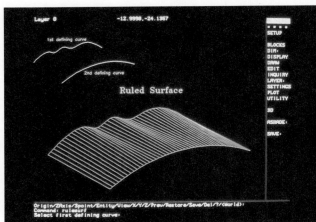

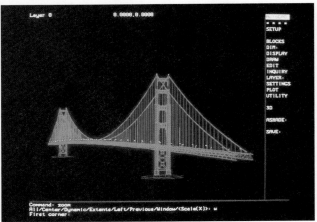

systems, such as Rocketdyne's linked with Allen Bradley's automation control, allow CAD data to be linked directly with the CAM computer for manufacturing of the product. Systems of this type are of the minicomputer variety but will soon be possible with PC-level systems.

Many new software packages continue to appear on the market, which will date this chapter early on. Word processors, spreadsheets, data bases, integrated packages, and resident software are appearing regularly as are upgrades to existing products, and the new user needs to know what is available and which package will best meet his or her needs. Interested users should subscribe to a computer magazine or other publication to keep informed of these latest products.

CHAPTER SUMMARY

1. Spreadsheets are frequently used as a convenient method for recording numerical data, taking advantage of the automatic calculations that can be done efficiently with a spreadsheet program.

2. The spreadsheet is usee for creating models and asking "what if" questions such as "What if we spend less for travel?" by changing the value of travel expenses in the spreadsheet to some other value.

3. Spreadsheets consist of a number of cells arranged in rows and columns. This organization is similar to the ledger pad used by accountants to assist in recording and calculating all the values needed for financial planning. In a computer spreadsheet, a value, label, or formula can be stored in each cell.

4. A cell is located where a row and column meet on the screen. At the intersection of column A and row 1 is a cell where a value may be placed in the spreadsheet. The address of this cell is composed of the column and row number, and for this cell is address A1.

5. Spreadsheet programs use a control panel or status line to communicate with the user. One or more lines are used to display menus, prompts, cell contents, current cell address, and mode.

6. The mode indicator identifies the current mode or status that the program is in. Modes may be one of READY, LABEL, VALUE, MENU, CMD, HELP, POINT, EDIT, or ERROR.

7. A range is a rectangular or square grouping of cells. Ranges are identified by the upper left and lower right cell addresses of the range.

8. Formatting may be used to set values to display in different ways. Some formats display dollar signs, commas, dates, or interest rates.

9. Business reports frequently include bar charts, pie charts, or line graphs to present information in a pictorial form, rather than as raw data. These graphs, when used appropriately, can have a much greater impact on the reader than mere numbers alone.

10. Most spreadsheet software will produce a variety of graphs, some with more types than others. Five common types of graphs are line, bar, XY, stacked bar, and pie.

11. Three-dimensional spreadsheets are used to manipulate data in three dimensions. Data on the 3-D spreadsheet often tends to appear simpler and easier to read than on a two-dimensional spreadsheet. True three-dimensional applications are easily developed, whereas they are quite awkward on a two-dimensional spreadsheet.

12. The essence of integration is combining several applications such as spreadsheet, word processing, data base, and communications into a single software package.

13. Integration reduces the number of software packages that a user needs to learn.

14. Using integrated software is less costly than purchasing separate programs.

15. Switching from one mode to another, such as from word processing to spreadsheet, is easier to do in an integrated package.

16. Data stored in one form, such as a data base, in an integrated package can readily be transferred to another, such as a word processor.

17. Integrated packages may not have the same power that a single program has. Thus a word processor may have greater capabilities than the word processing component of the integrated package. A common command structure has its own inherent weakness because commands for a spreadsheet may not be suited for the word processor component of an integrated package.

18. Desktop managers, such as SideKick and Lotus Metro, are memory-resident programs that include a range of features. Some of these are an appointment book, calendar, clock, note pad, phone book and dialer, stop watch, and text editor. These features may be brought up on the screen and used while other application programs are in memory.

19. RAM disk is an area of memory that is used like a disk drive. A program or data is loaded into the RAM disk area and then accessed from memory by other programs. Using RAM disk can speed up disk operations, especially with floppy disks.

20. A print spooler is a program that will let you print a document while you continue

to work on the computer. The main advantage of a spooler is that your work does not need to be interrupted while printing is going on.

21. Project management software produces a PERT chart or a Gantt chart to aid in the development and management of projects. The PERT chart provides critical path analysis of the tasks to be completed, while a Gantt chart show task timing to determine if tasks are completed on schedule.

22. Presentation graphics software, such as Harvard Presentation Graphics or Lotus Freelance Plus, assists in the preparation of charts or graphs for use in a business presentation. These charts can be printed, plotted, or recorded on film in black and white or color.

23. Computer-aided design (CAD) and computer-aided manufacturing (CAM) are used by engineers for the design and manufacturing of products.

24. CAD usually refers to software run on a personal or larger computer system that is used for drawing designs for new products. CAD is the computer-age equivalent of the drafting board and is to images what word processing is to words.

25. CAM normally refers to using a computer to run machine tools that shape parts on the shop floor.

IMPORTANT TERMS AND CONCEPTS

Address	Gantt chart	Print spooler
Absolute addressing	Graph	Project management
Cell	Integrated software	RAM disk
Column	Label	Range
Computer-aided design (CAD)	Macro	Relative addressing
Computer-aided manufacturing (CAM)	Menu	Row
	Mode	Spreadsheet
Control panel	PERT chart	Template
Desktop managers	Pointer	Value
Format	Presentation graphics	"What if" question
Formula		

REVIEW QUESTIONS

Fill-in Questions

1. A budget planning _____ can be built into a spreadsheet showing total expenses per year using a number of different categories.

2. A(n) _____ is the area found at the intersection of a column and a row.

3. The _____ _____ or status line is where the program communicates with the user of the spreadsheet.

4. A mode indicator of _____ in Lotus 1–2–3 indicates the user is entering a numeric value or a formula.

5. An entry on the spreadsheet such as +B6+B7+B8+B9+B10 is called a(n) _____ .

6. An entry such as @SUM(B6 .. B10) is called a(n) _____ .

7. A(n) _____ , such as A1 .. A10, refers to a group of cells specified by the address of the first and last cell in the group.

8. A(n) _____ format would be used to cause the number 0.125 to be displayed as 12.5% on the spreadsheet.

9. When a formula is copied into a new cell, the _____ will be adjusted to correspond to the new location.

10. A formula such as +B15*E5 contains a(n) _____ address because of the entry E5.

11. Overhead transparencies and color slides may be prepared by graphics programs called _____ graphics.

Matching Questions

Match each term with the description given below.

a. range
b. "what if" question
c. integrated software
d. cell
e. formatting
f. menu

_____e_____ 1. This is the process of giving a cell a fixed, currency, or percentage notation.

_____f_____ 2. Options, such as Wordsheet, File, or Copy, are selected from this item.

_____b_____ 3. This term expresses the process of entering different values to observe the results on the spreadsheet.

_____a_____ 4. Using this term refers to a group of cells that may be formatted, copied, or moved.

_____d_____ 5. This refers to the intersection of a row and column where a value or formula is stored.

_____c_____ 6. Software in this category combines the features of several stand-alone packages, such as word processing, data base, spreadsheet, and graphics.

Discussion Questions

1. Discuss the uses for a spreadsheet in the business environment.
2. Explain the nature of a "what if" question and its purpose in a spreadsheet.
3. Describe the fundamental components of a spreadsheet.
4. Explain the function of a cell and the items it may contain. How are cells addressed on the spreadsheet?
5. What is the purpose of the control panel? What are some of the items it may contain?
6. Discuss the purpose of five different modes that may be identified on the control panel representing spreadsheet operations.
7. Explain the idea of a range. What are ranges used for in a spreadsheet?
8. Compare the difference between relative and absolute addressing and the effect they have on the spreadsheet.
9. Discuss the five different types of graphs that can be produced by Lotus 1–2–3.
10. Discuss what is meant by the term integrated software.
11. In a paragraph each, give four reasons why some users prefer an integrated software package.
12. A desktop manager is an example of a memory-resident program. Why is a program such as SideKick useful to a PC user?
13. Discuss the benefit and use of presentation graphics software.
14. Discuss the use of CAD and CAM software in industry.

Data Base Systems

A VIEW OF THE CHAPTER AHEAD

After Reading This Chapter You Will Understand:

- The concept of a data base and know why it is more effective than a sequential file for data storage.

- The differences between a flat file data base and a data base management system.

- Some of the methods for creating and using a data base.

- The unique problems with a local area network that uses a data base.

Applications such as word processing and spreadsheets use disk files to store documents and data. These are sequential files that require the reading of all data in the file from beginning to end. Sequential processing is necessary for such applications and provides a fast and efficient means of reading data. However, sequential files are only useful when data has a high level of activity; otherwise, excessive time is spent reading data that is not required by the application.

Data base software provides a means of recording and recalling data without the need to process every record in the file each time. This method is beneficial when applications such as inventory or customer orders are processed and only a few of the records on file need to be accessed. The data base can then find only the records that are required and ignore all the others for a much faster data retrieval method. A data base is useful when data has a low level of activity because only active records need to be accessed.

But, because of their flexibility, today's data bases can also be used effectively for files with a high level of activity. This access would occur when a report is generated that contains most or all of the records in the data base.

A library card catalog is an example of a manual filing system. Such a system is accessed directly but often requires some sequential searching. An equivalent computer system is faster to use and easier to update.

Courtesy of Tom Tracy/The Stock Market.

A personal computer is used to access a data base by a user in the National Park Service.

Courtesy of National Park Service/ M. Watson.

As orders are received by phone in a mail-order business, they are entered on the computer where a data base provides both customer and product information and is updated by the order.

Courtesy of American Airlines.

WHAT IS A DATA BASE?

A **data base** is a collection of logically related files and records. A customer order data base (Figure 10–1) may have a file of customer records containing data about the customer's name, address, date of last order, and so on. The data base may also contain a file showing the items that each customer has ordered. Thus the two files are related due to common information between them, which might be the customer number. A third file may contain unique data about the items ordered by the customer such as the item's description and quantity in stock. This file is accessed by the item number.

FIGURE 10–1

A data base consisting of customer, order, and item files. Using separate files reduces data redundancy, simplifies updating, and provides faster access to the data needed.

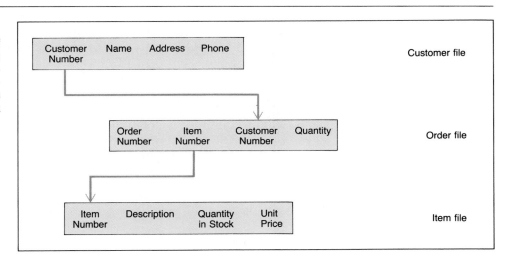

Data entry in supermarkets is done on this hand-held device as the operator reviews the shelf contents. After data entry is complete, the portable unit is attached to the store's main computer where the data base is updated with current information.

Courtesy of Memorex Corporation, a Subsidiary of Burroughs Corporation.

Data bases vary from simple packages called **file managers** to the more complex and sophisticated ones known as **data base management systems (DBMSs)**. File managers generally work with only one file at a time. A DBMS can work with several files at once for more intricate applications.

A data base has many uses. Customer records, order entry, inventory control, mailing lists, data analysis, and accounting are a few of the ways in which a data base can be used.

Data base software packages are used to create a data base. PC data base software usually costs a few hundred dollars for a complete package. Some packages, such as PFS:file, are simple to learn and require very little training or experience to use. Others, such as PC/FOCUS, are more complex and can require a course or training session with an expert user or instructor.

Once the data base has been created, many kinds of activities can be done with it. There is the usual updating of records, such as changing the customer's address or phone number, adding new records, or deleting old ones. Reports can be generated, bills printed, and reminders sent. But the data base can also be used to do searches for specific data, such as who ordered the disk controller card, or queries, such as how many customers live in Detroit. Data base records can also be sorted, extracted, or combined with other records.

dBASE III PLUS

In 1978 Wayne Ratliff, an engineer with Martin Marietta working on NASA's Viking space program, created a data base program in his spare time that he called Vulcan. By late 1979 he was marketing the software through *Byte* magazine and received an encouraging response of 60 sales over a nine-moneth period.[1]

To concentrate on software development Ratliff joined forces with George Tate of Ashton-Tate who took over the marketing responsibilities. The first major change suggested by Tate was the name. Vulcan became known as dBASE II implying an upgrade to the program. In the next three years dBASE II sold more than 140,000 copies.

dBASE II, the first programmable relational data base, was introduced in late 1980 offering a wide range of features, which caused it to quickly become the leading data base package. dBASE II was originally written for 8-bit CP/M-based microcomputers and was limited to 64K of RAM. This memory limitation continued to apply even when used on the much larger IBM PC. When competing packages, such as MDBS's KnowledgeMan and MicroRim's R:BASE 4000 came on the market, dBASE began to decline in market share and was thus ready for a new release with major improvements.

dBASE III represented a complete rewrite of the software to take advantage of the 16-bit computer generation. Ashton-Tate used the C language when developing dBASE III to improve the speed and efficiency of the new program. Using C also eased the conversion of dBASE to other operating systems such as UNIX-based computers.

---

[1] "From Basement to Boardroom," *PC Magazine*, February 7, 1984, pp. 131–35.

By early 1986, another release, dBASE III Plus, offered further enhancements. The ASSIST menus provided pull-down menus for easy selection of program features, thus improving the user interface. Support for local area networks and file locking opened the door to a broader use of LANs with dBASE III Plus applications. Originally, dBASE was a software package tailored for the single-user environment. With dBASE III Plus, files created for single users can be used in a network with little trouble.

dBASE's most powerful feature is its extensive programming language. It is easily as complete as many popular programming languages and is a favorite of software developers and PC consultants. Programming in dBASE has been available from the beginning and no doubt was a major factor in pushing this product to the top of the database software market.

dBASE III Plus can handle up to 1 billion records per file. However, the total file length must not exceed 2 billion characters. Records can consist of a maximum of 128 fields or 4,000 characters. And dBASE can work with up to ten files simultaneously. With these capabilities dBASE III Plus can handle all but the most demanding tasks.

dBASE IV

In 1988 Ashton-Tate announced a much improved data base called dBASE IV. This edition supports both OS/2 and MS/DOS systems with improved interfaces for program development. A new applications generator is included to make applications development easier for programmers and nonprogrammers alike. dBASE IV includes improved networking capability over III Plus and a new dBASE/SQL language, which combines IBM's Structured Query Language used on mainframes with dBASE's query capabilities. dBASE IV is another example of a successful product that has gone through another release to continue to meet or exceed the competition's software products and user requirements.

The enhanced dBase IV features a user interface geared toward nonprogrammers.

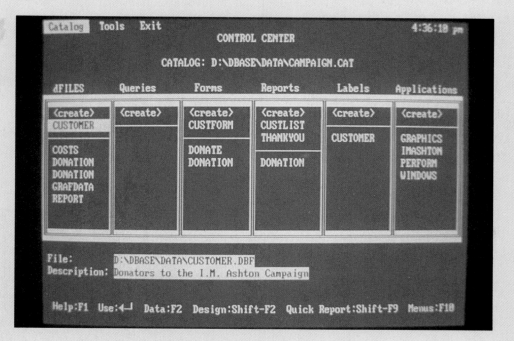

FILE MANAGERS AND DBMS

A file manager can work with only one file at a time. This is a useful form of data base for applications such as keeping a mailing list or an inventory of items such as a record or book collection. This type of file organization is acceptable for storing data and permits some useful analysis or reporting from the data. It can be used to create mailing lists, envelope labels, or a customer listing, and some can be used to generate form letters.

The main problem with the file manager is its restriction to a single file. A customer order system would be difficult to implement and inefficient to operate with a single file system. However, a DBMS could keep the customer data in one file and the order data in another as discussed previously.

Moving from a file manager software package to a DBMS helps to minimize several problem areas that are a concern with the file manager. The following are a few of the major problems that DBMS can help to eliminate.

1. **Data redundancy.** File managers tend to store a lot of duplicate data among different files. A customer's name and number might be stored in the customer file and in the order file and again in the accounting file. Because a file manager does not have ready access to these files at one time some duplication is necessary.

2. **Data dependence.** When the same data is stored in several different files, any updating on this data must be done on each file when a change occurs. A DBMS can store the data in a common file and thus reduce dependence by updating only the one file.

3. **Excessive manual operations.** A DBMS can usually be programmed so that frequently used activities in the data base can be automated. This avoids the need for a user to be trained in the technical aspects of the data base, because the program does all the difficult parts. Many file managers do not have programming capabilities, and therefore the user must learn the command language of the software package and do these operations manually.

DESIGNING A DATA BASE

To design a relational data base we need first to collect the type of data that will be needed in the data base. Figure 10–2 shows an example of the data needed in a Customer file that will become part of our data base. Other files such as an order file and an item file may also be included as development of the data base progresses.

FIGURE 10–2

A preliminary design of a customer data base. The credit field signifies whether credit is granted the customer or not. In the design only three sample customers are shown, but the actual file will contain more.

Customer Number	Name	Address	Phone	Credit	Credit Limit
12	A. Bow	15 Maple St.	452-6745	Y	500.00
13	C. Down	18th Avenue	451-7457	N	0.00
14	E. Holt	12 Wade St.	551-6346	Y	1299.99

When designing the data base we need to consider the kinds of questions it will be used to ask and the kinds of reports that it will generate. Some of the questions our data base could be called upon to answer are

- Which customers do not have credit with the company?
- What is C. Down's phone number?
- Which customers have a credit limit of $500.00 or more?

In choosing the data to be included in a data base, it is necessary to consider the kinds of questions that might be asked. Leaving out this step could result in a data base that cannot provide important information. For example, the customer data base shown could not be used to ask the question, "Which customers have a zip code of 33540?" because the code is not part of the record.

CHARACTERISTICS OF THE DATA BASE

A PC data base is usually based on a **relational** data structure. This structure is organized in rows and columns similar to a spreadsheet (Figure 10–3). Each **row** represents a record that contains facts about one customer. A **column** is equivalent to a field and contains the same type of data for each customer. The first column contains the customer number and, although it is a different number for each customer, the value in the column is always a customer number.

In the relational data base, the customer file is searched to get address information about the customer. The relation, customer number, is used to search the item file to find out which items the customer ordered.

To help organize and control a complex data base environment, a **data dictionary** may be used to document and maintain the data definition. Among other details the data dictionary records the types of data and their relationships within the data base.

A **data base administrator (DBA)** is a position in the organization responsible for the control of the data base. In large corporations one or more people may have this function. The DBA establishes data definitions, defines the data base standards for the company, and maintains the integrity of the data relationships.

FIGURE 10–3

A PC data base uses a relational structure. Data is organized into rows containing one customer record and columns that contain the same type of data for each customer.

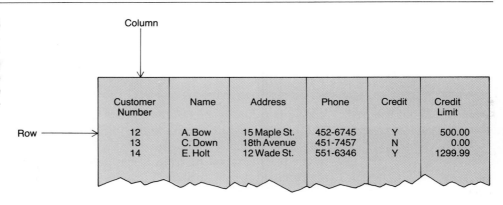

Column

Customer Number	Name	Address	Phone	Credit	Credit Limit
12	A. Bow	15 Maple St.	452-6745	Y	500.00
13	C. Down	18th Avenue	451-7457	N	0.00
14	E. Holt	12 Wade St.	551-6346	Y	1299.99

Row

Data base software permits a variety of field types to satisfy the needs of different applications. Depending on the software used for the DBMS, the field types may vary slightly or the terminology may be different. The field types discussed here refer to those available in dBASE III Plus.

J. Jones

SL-3189 CD System

(519) 858-2301

Character fields are fields that store text, including letters, numbers, special characters, and spaces. This type of field is often used for names, addresses, descriptions, and even phone numbers.

2139.75

35   .015

−79.89

Numeric fields are those that store numbers. Numbers may be either integer or decimal and may be positive or negative. Numeric fields are generally those used in calculations and include quantities, costs, and rates. Sometimes a numeric field is not used for calculations such as those used for customer numbers or account numbers.

.T.

.F.

Logical fields are fields that can be either true (T) or false (F), indicating two alternatives. A field such as sex could use T to represent male and F for female. A customer with a credit account would be coded as T, but one without credit would be F.

10/25/89

Date fields store a date. Date is usually in the form of mm/dd/yy representing month, day, and year. In dBASE III dates cannot be manipulated numerically.

Learning dBASE III

Plus in Ten Easy

Lessons

Memo fields are like character fields except they may contain substantially more data. Memo fields are stored separate from the data base.

R:BASE

R:base is a family of relational data base management system software from Microrim Corporation. Since the forming of Microrim, R:base 2000, 4000, and 5000 and System V have emerged. Each version represents significant advances in the package ranging from a stripped-down, low-cost version 2000 to a full-featured multiuser System V. By 1987 R:base 4000 and 5000 and the newly released System V were being actively marketed.

Microrim was founded in 1981 by Wayne Erickson who was a software developer with the Boeing Computer Service Company. Like Wayne Ratliff of dBASE fame, Erickson developed a mainframe data base management system for a NASA project. R:base software products evolved from this project, and in 1983 R:base 4000 was introduced.

One premise behind the development of R:base was its recognition of the expansion of user needs as applications were developed. To meet this demand, more features were included than in the leading DBMS software, which was dBASE II at the time. R:base also provided prompting so the user could be guided through the commands rather than depending on the user's memory and command of the language.

R:base 5000 was released in 1985. Some new marketing strategies were used such as selling R:base to certified accountants for as little as $95. A later two-for-the-price-of-one offer brought greater attention to this software product. Although Microrim was able to grab second place in the data base software market it still lagged considerably behind dBASE, despite reviews that placed it ahead of dBASE in features and overall capability.

R:BASE System V was released in 1986 as a full-featured, fully integrated, and easy-to-use DBMS package. One of its strongest features is the built-in application generator, Application Express, which has been adopted from R:base 4000. This is a menu-driven utility something like dBASE's Assist. Application Express goes beyond dBASE in that you can design menus and allocate tasks to each menu selection. Express then creates the command file (program) to implement the design.

Three other features supplement the Express in System V. These are the Definition Express, Forms Express, and Reports Express. Using these Express

R:base System V is a PC-based DBMS software package from Microrim Corporation.

Courtesy of Microrim Corporation.

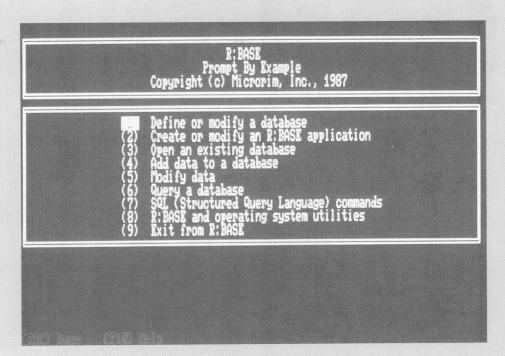

289

programs helps the user to develop data base structures, screen formats, and report layouts without the need for a complex command language. All these programs are accessible from within R:base System V's main menu for ease of use.

The best recognized add-on program for R:base is Clout. Clout is a conversational language program that uses a limited form of artificial intelligence to permit the use of plain English statements to access R:base data bases. Clout comes with a dictionary of commonly used words and permits the user to add more words to customize it to specific language uses.

R:base System V can have an unlimited number of records per file. A record can contain up to 4,096 characters and up to 800 fields. Up to 80 different files can be opened simultaneously in System V. One of the problems with comparing data base software is that of rating the software by these specifications. In reality most applications require no where close to the limits of a package such as R:base System V. Thus the package features are a much more important area where these comparisons need to be made.

CREATING A DATA BASE

A data base file is set up in dBASE IV by selecting the appropriate options from menus and pull-down menus presented on screen by the software. Figure 10–4 shows the entries made to create a data base for the customer file.

FIGURE 10–4

When the file name has been entered, dBASE IV presents this screen. On it, each field in the data base is defined with a field name, type of field, its width, and the number of decimal positions where applicable.

Layout	Organize	Append	Go To	Exit			2:44:52 pm

Bytes remaining: 3950

Num	Field Name	Field Type	Width	Dec	Index
1	CUST_NO	Numeric	2	0	Y
2	NAME	Character	12		N
3	ADDRESS	Character	20		N
4	PHONE	Character	8		N
5	CREDIT	Logical	1		N
6	LIMIT	Numeric	7	2	N

Database C:\dbase\CUSTOMER   Field 1/6

Enter the field name. Insert/Delete field:Ctrl-N/Ctrl-U
Field names begin with a letter and may contain letters, digits and underscores

A data entry screen used to enter data into a data base file. The screen is designed to simplify the entry of data so that a data entry operator can enter the data efficiently and accurately.

Courtesy of Microrim Corporation.

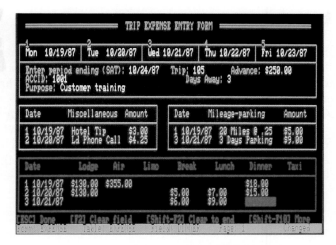

An invoice such as this one is often the source document for providing data to create a data base. After the structure of the data base has been defined the data is supplied for entry from the form.

D. G. Dologite and R. J. Mockler, *Using Computers*, 2nd ed. (Englewood Cliffs, N.J.: Prentice Hall, 1989), p. 335. Reprinted by permission of Prentice-Hall, Inc., Englewood Cliffs, N.J.

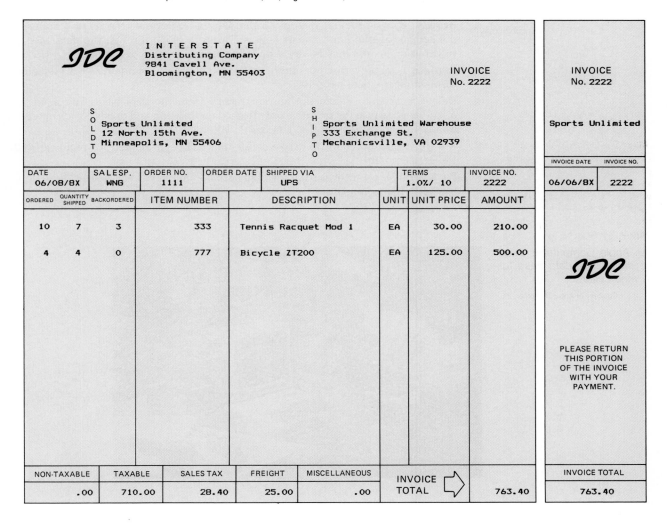

Defining the File

First the Create option is selected from a menu. Then a name is given to the file that will be used throughout its life as a data base. The last step is to define each field in the data base. Each field must have a name composed of a beginning letter and followed by other letters, digits, or underscore characters. Other data base systems may have different rules for field names.

The type of field is also specified, as is the width of the field and the number of decimal positions it contains if it is a numeric field. Decisions about field sizes and types must be taken seriously at this stage of the implementation because changes are not easily made once the data base is created.

UPDATE ACTIVITIES IN dBASE

- **Append** adds a new record at the end of the current data base file. After appending new records, it is sometimes necessary to sort the file to maintain a required sequence of records, such as customer number sequence.

- **Edit** presents the contents of record so that changes may be made to it. Fields may be revised or deleted in edit mode.

- **Display** provides a means for showing the contents of the current record on the screen.

- **Browse** lets you look at records in the data base. Several records will appear on the screen together, and cursor keys are used to move through the data base file. In Browse, records may be revised, deleted, or appended to the file.

- **Replace** is a powerful operation that can change the contents of a given field throughout the data base file.

- **Delete** is used to delete the current record from the data base. The name is a misnomer because the record is only flagged for deletion and needs a Pack operation finally to remove it from the data base.

- **Recall** restores a record to active status that has been marked for removal by the Delete command.

- **Pack** removes all records from the data base file that have been marked for deletion by the Delete command.

An Apple Computer is used to maintain a data base for a wine cellar.

Courtesy of Apple Computer, Inc.

SORTING THE DATA BASE FILE

Over time, as the data base is maintained, the records can lose their original order. As records are appended and deleted, the file that might have originally been in customer number sequence may now be in a more or less random order. One solution to this problem is to sort the file.

Although sorting may seem to be a useful operation, in some data base software, such as dBASE IV, it is time consuming and requires double the disk space for file storage. The larger the data base file becomes, the less efficient sorting will be. As a result, another technique, called indexing, is used, that is more effective than the sort.

USING AN INDEX

Because sorting takes a lot of time and requires disk space for the sorted file in addition to the original unsorted file indexing, using the INDEX command, is an often-used alternative. Indexing a file is an operation that also creates a second file called an index file. But the index file requires only the key field that identifies the data base file sequence and a record number that is used as a link to the original record in the data base.

Figure 10–5 shows the customer file as it might appear as an unsorted file. There is no sequence on the desired field customer number. By creating an index file as shown, the data base can be treated as if it were in customer

FIGURE 10–5

An index file is used to access the data base file in customer number sequence. Rather than sorting the entire data base file, only the index is sorted on the key field and the record numbers are used as a link to the data base file.

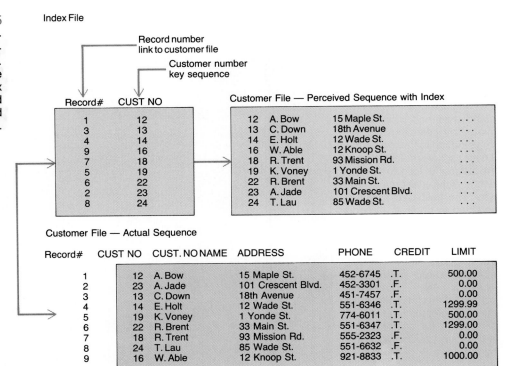

number sequence. The index file contains the customer number that is the key field. The index also contains the record number of the record in the data base. Because the index retains the data in customer number sequence, the data base can be accessed in that order by reading each record according to the record number in the index file.

Indexing a data base is also more useful than sorting because a data base file can have several indexes describing different sequences. One may index on the customer number, another may be in name sequence, and yet another by address. Thus a data base may be easily accessed in any number of sequences, depending on the needs for processing in a given application.

DATA BASE QUERIES

A **query** is a request for information or an inquiry into the contents of a data base. One of the benefits of having a data base is that inquiries can easily be made of it. Companies using a data base may want to ask questions such as: "What orders do we have from customer number 19?" or "We have a problem with reliability on item number 27—what are the orders in the data base for item 27?"

Menu-Driven Queries

Software such as dBASE III Plus provides a series of menus for the user to identify the conditions of the query. When asking a question about the orders for customer 19, a sequence of menus and submenus is presented on the

FIGURE 10–6
A query to display all orders for customer number 19 is built. The top screen shows the beginning of the command sequence, which is activated by selecting the Retrieve option in the top menu. Then Display is selected from the submenu, followed by the option Build a search condition. The field CUST_NO is selected to begin the condition. In the bottom screen, additional submenus are selected to create the command CUST_NO = 19. No more conditions are needed, and so the entry, execute the command, from the first submenu is selected, and the list of records for customer 19 is displayed as shown at the bottom.

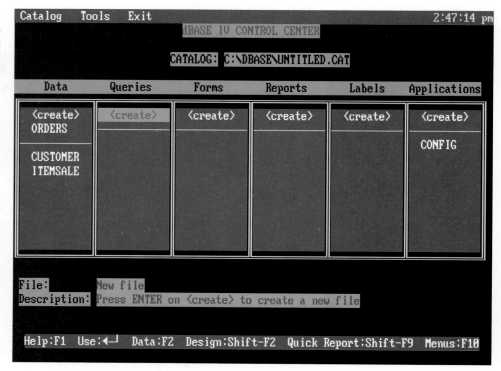

screen where a search condition is built to access records that meet the requirements of the inquiry.

Figure 10–6 shows the menus used to display all orders for a customer. Prior to this time the data base file must be set up and then a Retrieve operation is begun. Using the Display option, a search condition is built that asks for

FIGURE 10–6
(Continued)

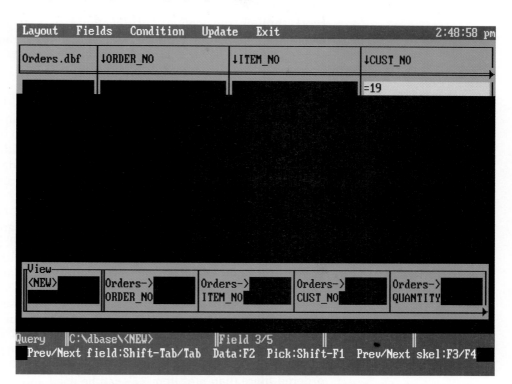

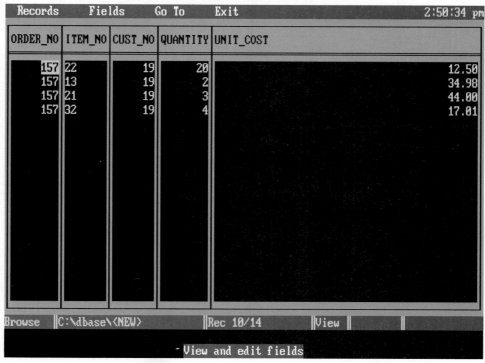

records with a Customer Number equal to 19. As the query is constructed, the equivalent command is displayed on the screen. Finally, the records that meet the conditions are displayed.

Menus, in this setting, have the advantage of directing the user through each step of building a condition. If the next step is uncertain, the menu always presents the choices to follow. Very little experience is needed to work through the menus and develop a successful query. Although menus may take a little time because of all the choices, they are easy to use and all the information needed is presented on the screen.

Query Languages

Complex queries frequently require several conditions or relations to be satisfied in a search of the data base. A question such as list all orders for item number 27 with a quantity greater than 5 requires two conditions. Figure 10–7 shows the relational operators that can be used in stating a condition. In addition to these operators, the .AND. and .OR. operators can be used to combine two or more conditions.

Figure 10–8 shows a condition in dBASE IV command mode that asks for a list of item number 27 that have a quantity greater than 5 in the order. dBASE uses this type of command, which is called a nonprocedural query language. Languages such as COBOL or BASIC would require a complete program or procedure to be written to accomplish the same result and are therefore called procedural languages.

A data base package such as Microrim's R:Base also uses nonprocedural queries for accessing the data base. But Microrim has available a software tool called CLOUT that permits a conversational style of making inquires. CLOUT uses techniques from artificial intelligence to provide a natural language interface with R:Base. Thus a query such as "Tell me the customers who ordered more than 5 of item 27" can be used and understood by the software.

FIGURE 10–7

These operators are used to describe the relation between two fields or a field and a value.

Operator	**Meaning**	
	=	Equal to
	<=	Less than or Equal to
	<	Less than
	>	Greater than
	>=	Greater than or Equal to
	<>	Not Equal to

FIGURE 10–8

Using a nonprocedural query language in dBASE IV simplifies making an inquiry.

```
.LIST FOR ITEM_NO = '27' .AND. QUANTITY > 5


Record#    ORDER_NO ITEM_NO CUST_NO QUANTITY UNIT_COST
      2       123 27          12       17      5.75
      8       156 27          16       10      5.75
```

Natural language interfaces, such as Clout or IBM's SQL, require a dictionary of words that are used to understand the use of common word. Thus the words "Tell me" could mean "List," which translates it to the nonprocedural form before the command is processed. Natural language is becoming a more widely used tool in computer software and will no doubt become the language in favor by new users of sophisticated computer systems.

PC/FOCUS

PC/FOCUS is a relational data base program that has been developed from a mainframe software product. FOCUS was originally a mainframe computer data base program developed by Information Builders, Inc., of New York. Users were large-scale mainframe systems, but in 1985 Version 1.5 of PC/FOCUS was released to IBM PC users.

It is unlike most other PC data base products in that it can upload and download data from the mainframe. As a stand-alone system, PC/FOCUS is too complex, owing to its ability to handle complex files and data structures. It is almost an exact duplicate of the mainframe software. But users of the mainframe product find PC/FOCUS a good solution to transferring some of the mainframe tasks to the PC.

Because of this compatibility with the mainframe, the PC version tends to be less user friendly than other DBMS packages. Usually, technical support is needed from the MIS department to implement applications in PC/FOCUS unless the user is particularly competent in computer applications development. Users of PC/FOCUS tend to be companies that are already using the product on the mainframe. For them it is a natural step to place some of the applications on the PC.

PC-FOCUS includes a report writer, text editor, file editor, a screen manager, data base manager, and a financial modeling language. Graphics and a statistics

PC/Focus is a relational data base program for personal computers.

Courtesy of Information Builders.

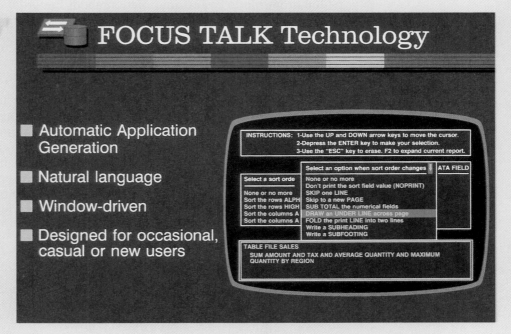

package are also included. Version 1.5 added a screen painting utility. Data bases in PC/FOCUS can be relational, hierarchical, or networked for greater flexibility than other software packages.

The lastest addition to PC/FOCUS is TableTalk, a window-driven data base and application development tool. Using principles from artificial intelligence, TableTalk allows the user to create FOCUS requests without the usual typing of commands. Instead, options are presented on the screen in a series of overlapping windows where choices are made using a mouse or with the cursor keys. Selecting from the available options results in logically developed requests that work the first time.

TableTalk is fully integrated with PC/FOCUS so that all the FOCUS features continue to be available to the PC user. New users of PC/FOCUS find that TableTalk is an easier way to begin using the power available with this extensive software package.

MULTIPLE FILE DBMS

Data base management systems such as dBASE IV and R:Base permit the use of more than one file in the data base. This offers much greater flexibility in the applications of the software and provides for greater efficiency in data storage and retrieval. Multiple files provide for the linking of data between different applications so that activity in one may influence the other.

The application used throughout this chapter of the customer and order files demonstrates this principle. When a customer places an order, information about the customer such as the name, address, or credit rating can be retrieved from the customer file. At the same time the data base application can access the order file to record information about the order, such as the item number and quantity ordered. Queries can also use data from both files in a multiple file data base application.

Normalizing Files

When a multiple file data base is designed, the process of normalizing is essential if efficient operation is to result. **Normalizing** is the process of eliminating redundant or duplicate data from each file. Including the customer's name in both the customer file and the order file would be an example of redundancy.

An order file contains a unit cost field for an item. However, if an item file was designed for the data base, then the unit cost would be stored there and would be redundant if it also appeared in the order file. Effective design ensures that the files used in the data base are normalized before filling them with data.

Relations

A relational multiple-file data base is designed with fields that are used to establish a relation between the files. The customer file in Figure 10–9 uses the customer number to form a relation between it and the order file. An

FIGURE 10–9
A relation is established on the customer number field between the customer file and the order file.

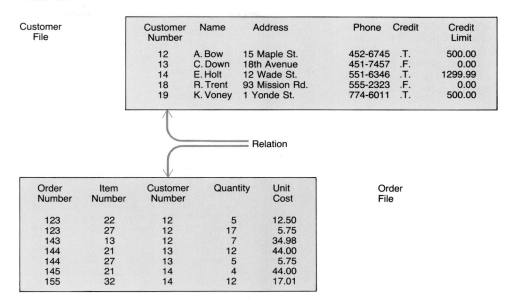

Customer File

Customer Number	Name	Address	Phone	Credit	Credit Limit
12	A. Bow	15 Maple St.	452-6745	.T.	500.00
13	C. Down	18th Avenue	451-7457	.F.	0.00
14	E. Holt	12 Wade St.	551-6346	.T.	1299.99
18	R. Trent	93 Mission Rd.	555-2323	.F.	0.00
19	K. Voney	1 Yonde St.	774-6011	.T.	500.00

Relation

Order File

Order Number	Item Number	Customer Number	Quantity	Unit Cost
123	22	12	5	12.50
123	27	12	17	5.75
143	13	12	7	34.98
144	21	13	12	44.00
144	27	13	5	5.75
145	21	14	4	44.00
155	32	14	12	17.01

order is always made for a given customer so the order file contains an order number field that establishes a relation between it and the customer file. Without a field forming a relation between files in a data base, the file will operate in isolation, which is essentially how a single file data base operates.

When more than two files are established in the data base, the third file will require a relation to be established with only one of the other two files. Thus an item file could establish a relation with the order file through the item number. The item file does not require a customer number because it can access the customer number in the order file. Obviously large data base applications can become very complex and require considerable planning to design and implement.

Joining Files

Data from two or more data base files may be joined to create a composite file or report. Figure 10–10 shows a Join operation using the customer and order files. First, a relation is set between the customer numbers. In this example the application requires a list of orders for customer number 12.

The record for customer 12 is joined with the records in the order file that match the customer. Specific fields in each file are accessed to create the joined file. Not all fields are needed so in this application only the customer number, name, and address are extracted from the customer file. The order file provides the order number, item, quantity, and unit cost. Although the result of the Join is shown for only one customer it could be done for any number or even all customers in the file.

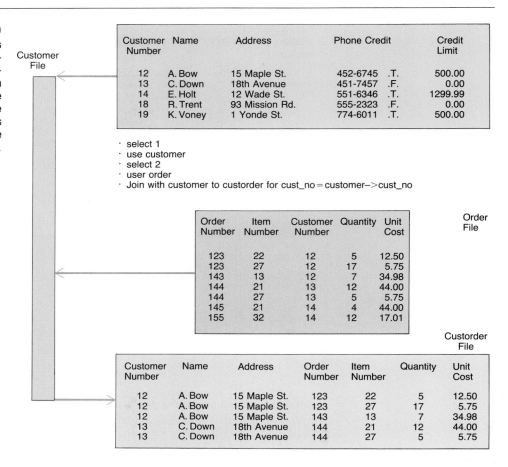

FIGURE 10–10
Data from two data base files are combined in a Join operation. A Join defines the relation on which the operation occurs, such as in this case for customer number 12. The Join also defines the fields from each file that are to be included in the resulting file.

Customer File

Customer Number	Name	Address	Phone	Credit	Credit Limit
12	A. Bow	15 Maple St.	452-6745	.T.	500.00
13	C. Down	18th Avenue	451-7457	.F.	0.00
14	E. Holt	12 Wade St.	551-6346	.T.	1299.99
18	R. Trent	93 Mission Rd.	555-2323	.F.	0.00
19	K. Voney	1 Yonde St.	774-6011	.T.	500.00

```
· select 1
· use customer
· select 2
· user order
· Join with customer to custorder for cust_no = customer–>cust_no
```

Order File

Order Number	Item Number	Customer Number	Quantity	Unit Cost
123	22	12	5	12.50
123	27	12	17	5.75
143	13	12	7	34.98
144	21	13	12	44.00
144	27	13	5	5.75
145	21	14	4	44.00
155	32	14	12	17.01

Custorder File

Customer Number	Name	Address	Order Number	Item Number	Quantity	Unit Cost
12	A. Bow	15 Maple St.	123	22	5	12.50
12	A. Bow	15 Maple St.	123	27	17	5.75
12	A. Bow	15 Maple St.	143	13	7	34.98
13	C. Down	18th Avenue	144	21	12	44.00
13	C. Down	18th Avenue	144	27	5	5.75

DBMS PROGRAMMING

Full-featured data base software such as dBASE III Plus, dBASE IV, and R:Base System V provides a programming capability for more advanced users. Programming of data base software is also frequently done by microcomputer consultants and application software developers. dBASE in its several releases since 1980 has become the favorite software package for developing data base application programs and is in widespread use in the industry.

Programming a data base is done for two fundamental reasons:

1. A program provides a way of storing frequently used command sequences so that they do not need to be typed on the keyboard each time.
2. A program permits the development of complex applications in the data base making use of a wide variety of features not readily available with the menus.

Programs themselves may also call other programs. Thus a program can be developed that consists of many modules, each of which concentrates on doing a single task such as updating a record or adding a new record to the data base. This method of using different modules is a structured programming technique, which will be discussed later in the chapter on programming.

NETWORKS AND DATA BASE SYSTEMS

Using a data base on a local area network presents some unique problems that do not occur on stand-alone systems. A LAN permits several stations (usually PCs) to communicate with each other or with a file server on the network. Data base files and commonly used software are often situated on the file server so that public access may be had by all users in the system. Other devices such as printers, plotters, or modems may also be shared by stations on the local area network.

File Locking

One of the problems on a network is two or more stations attempting to access the same data base or worse the same record. For example, an order system may receive an order at one station for 25 lamps. The system may show 25 in stock so the order is placed. Simultaneously, a second station receives an order for 20 lamps. If the station looks at the stock record before the first station has recorded the order, then the record will continue to show 25 in stock. Thus, unknown to both stations, orders will be placed for a quantity that exceeds the stock.

To get around this problem networked data base software uses a file-locking technique. File locking is a feature of data base software that will not let a second station access the data base while it is in use by another station. There will be a slight delay at the second station until the first has finished with the data base, but this avoids the problem just outlined. Some data base software also provides for record locking. With record locking only access to the record is denied if it is already in use.

A DBMS used in a local area network permits several users to share the same files.

Courtesy of AT&T Bell Laboratories.

File Security

As more users have access to data on a network, there is an increased possibility of unauthorized access to data. LAN-based data base software provides for several types of data security. The most common is the use of passwords to ensure that only authorized users will have access to specified data bases. Changing passwords on a regular basis helps to maintain continued security over time.

Another level of security gives users either read-only or write capability. Some users will be able to view only the contents of a data base (read-only) while others will have a security code that permits both reading and updating (write) of the data base contents.

Data Base Networking Software

Using a data base on a network often requires a different version of the software. Some data base software is not written for use on a network and can create serious security and data integrity problems if used in this environment. Other software, such as dBASE III Plus, has a network version that provides additional features necessary for installation on a LAN.

Figure 10–11 shows how dBASE III Plus handles a local area network environment. There are two types of programs in use. One is the dBASE Administrator, which goes on the file server PC. This program provides for the file and record locking of the data base to ensure data integrity. A PROTECT

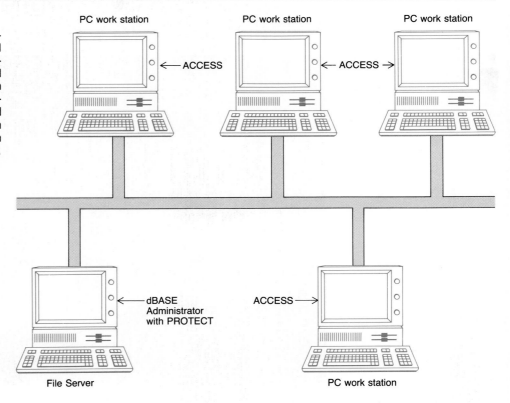

FIGURE 10–11
Ashton-Tate's local area network version of dBASE III Plus uses Administrator software on the file server and ACCESS software on each work station. The Administrator offers file security and password protection when stations access the common data base files on the LAN.

program is also available for use with the Administrator to provide password and access security.

Individual PC work stations that use dBASE III Plus also use a program called ACCESS, which provides the link between the station and the Administrator. In addition to the dBASE programs the communication software for the network is also required such as the IBM PC network program or Novell Advanced Netware.

CHAPTER SUMMARY	1. Data base software provides a means of recording and recalling data without the need to process every record in the file each time. 2. A data base is a collection of logically related files and records. Using separate files reduces data redundancy, simplifies updating, and provides faster access to the data needed. 3. Data bases vary from simple packages called file managers to the more complex and sophisticated ones known as data base management systems (DBMS). Data base software can be either command driven or menu driven. 4. A file manager can only work with one file at a time. This is a useful form of data base for applications such as keeping a mailing list or an inventory of items such as a record or book collection. The main problem with the file manager is its restriction to a single file.

5. A DBMS helps to minimize several problem areas that are a concern with the file manager. One is data redundancy, which refers to duplicate data stored among different files. Another is data dependence, which occurs when the same data is stored in several different files; then any updating on this data must be done on each file when a change occurs. A DBMS also helps to minimize excessive manual operations.

6. A data base is created by selecting the appropriate options from program menus and pull-down menus presented on screen by the software.

7. Software such as dBASE III Plus provides for update activities such as append, which adds records to the end of the data base; edit, which provides a screen to change the contents of a record; display, which shows the contents of a record on a screen; browse, which displays a series of records and permits changes to them; and replace, which provides a means for changing field contents in a group of records with a single command. Delete permits the temporary deletion of a record, recall can make it active again, while pack makes the delete permanent.

8. Sorting a data base creates a new data base file that has been ordered into the sequence requested.

9. Indexing a file is similar to sorting but is more efficient. It is an operation that creates a second file called an index file. The index file requires only a key field that identifies the data base file sequence and a record number that is used as a link to the original record in the data base.

10. A query is a request for information or an inquiry into the contents of a data base. A query in dBASE III Plus can be either menu driven or command driven.

11. Query languages are generally nonprocedural as in dBASE III Plus. A few DBMS packages, such as Microrim's CLOUT used with R:Base, use a natural language interface.

12. A multiple-file DBMS provides for the linking of data between different applications so that activity in one may influence the other.

13. Programming a data base management system provides a means of storing frequently used commands in a file to be used as needed without the need to type them

each time. A DMBS program also permits the development of complex applications making available more powerful features of the software.

14. Using a data base on a local area network presents some unique problems that do not occur on stand-alone systems. If several users try to access the data base simultaneously, the data base software uses a file locking technique to permit only one access.

15. Security of access is maintained by the use of passwords to ensure that only authorized users will have access to specified data bases.

16. Some users will be able only to view the contents of a data base (read-only), while others will have a security code that permits both reading and updating (write) of the data base contents.

IMPORTANT TERMS AND CONCEPTS

Append	Edit	Normalizing
Data base	File locking	Passwords
Data base	File manager	Query
administrator	Indexing	Read-only files
(DBA)	Join	Redundant data
Data base	Natural language	Relational
management	queries	Sort
systems	Nonprocedural query	
(DBMS)	language	
Data dictionary		

REVIEW QUESTIONS

Fill-in Questions

1. Using separate files in a data base helps to eliminate _____ or duplication of the data.

2. In a(n) _____ data structure, used primarily on personal computers, data are stored in the form of tables with relations established between each item.

3. A(n) _____ field type in a data base stores data such as quantities, costs, and rates.

4. When changes are necessary against a data base, such as changing an address or phone number, a(n) _____ operation is done to make the modifications.

5. The _____ command creates a new data base that is in a different sequence from the original data base.

6. A(n) _____ might be done to find all orders for customer 19 rather than looking through all of the other customers.

Matching Questions

Match each term with the description given below.

a. DBMS   d. data base
b. query   e. index
c. data dictionary   f. append

_____ 1. This is a collection of fields, records, and files relating to a specific application.

_____ 2. Used to document and maintain the data definition for a mainframe data base.

_____ 3. This operation is done to add records to the end of the data base.

_____ 4. This is a file that is used to reference the records in a data base in a specific sequence.

_____ 5. The acronym for data base management system.

_____ 6. This is the process of examining the data base to find a record that meets a specific requirement.

Discussion Questions

1. Describe a data base and the relation between two or more files in the data base.
2. What is the difference between a flat file database and a data base management system (DBMS)?
3. What is data redundancy? How does a data base management system help to reduce redundancy?
4. Define the five field types used in dBASE III Plus or dBASE IV. Give an example of each.
5. There are eight possible update activities in a data base manager such as dBASE III Plus. Name and describe four of them.
6. Describe the difference and compare the advantages of indexing a data base to sorting it.
7. Discuss the two basic forms of queries used in a data base system.
8. Why is a relation important with a multiple file data base? How is the relation used in the Join operation?
9. What are some of the advantages of programming a DBMS?
10. Describe some of the problems that are unique to a DBMS on a local area network.

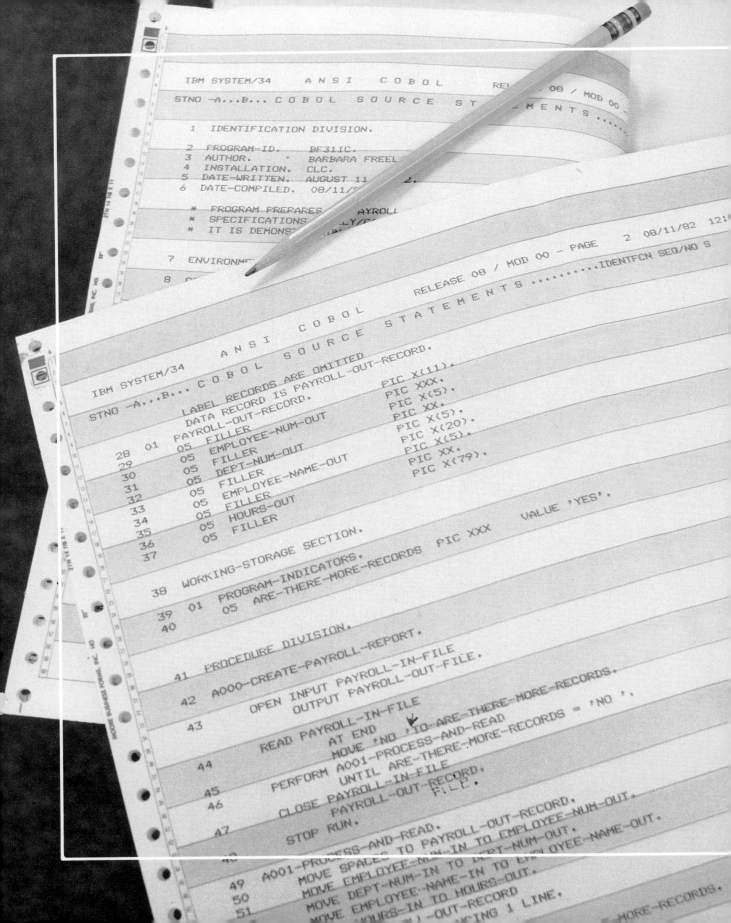

IBM SYSTEM/34   A N S I   C O B O L   REL... 08 / MOD 00 -

STNO -A...B... C O B O L   S O U R C E   S T A T E M E N T S ......

```
    1   IDENTIFICATION DIVISION.

    2   PROGRAM-ID.        BF31IC.
    3   AUTHOR.            BARBARA FREEL...
    4   INSTALLATION.      CLC.
    5   DATE-WRITTEN.      AUGUST 11 ...2.
    6   DATE-COMPILED.     08/11/8...

    *   PROGRAM PREPARES ... AYROLL
    *   SPECIFICATIONS ... LY/C...
    *   IT IS DEMONS... ...LY ...

    7   ENVIRONME...

    8   ...
```

A N S I   C O B O L   RELEASE 08 / MOD 00 - PAGE   2 08/11/82 12:...

IBM SYSTEM/34

STNO -A...B... C O B O L   S O U R C E   S T A T E M E N T S ....IDENTFCN SEQ/NO S

```
            LABEL RECORDS ARE OMITTED
            DATA RECORD IS PAYROLL-OUT-RECORD.
   28  01   PAYROLL-OUT-RECORD.
   29   05   FILLER              PIC X(11).
   30   05   EMPLOYEE-NUM-OUT    PIC XXX.
   31   05   FILLER              PIC X(5).
   32   05   DEPT-NUM-OUT        PIC XX.
   33   05   FILLER              PIC X(5).
   34   05   EMPLOYEE-NAME-OUT   PIC X(20).
   35   05   FILLER              PIC X(5).
   36   05   HOURS-OUT           PIC XX.
   37   05   FILLER              PIC X(79).

   38  WORKING-STORAGE SECTION.

   39  01   PROGRAM-INDICATORS.
   40   05   ARE-THERE-MORE-RECORDS  PIC XXX   VALUE 'YES'.


   41  PROCEDURE DIVISION.

   42  A000-CREATE-PAYROLL-REPORT.
            OPEN INPUT PAYROLL-IN-FILE
                OUTPUT PAYROLL-OUT-FILE.
   43       READ PAYROLL-IN-FILE
                AT END
                MOVE 'NO ' TO ARE-THERE-MORE-RECORDS.
   44       PERFORM A001-PROCESS-AND-READ
                UNTIL ARE-THERE-MORE-RECORDS = 'NO '.
   45       CLOSE PAYROLL-IN-FILE
   46            PAYROLL-OUT-FILE.
   47       STOP RUN.

   48  A001-PROCESS-AND-READ.
            MOVE SPACES TO PAYROLL-OUT-RECORD.
   49       MOVE EMPLOYEE-NUM-IN TO EMPLOYEE-NUM-OUT.
   50       MOVE DEPT-NUM-IN TO DEPT-NUM-OUT.
            MOVE EMPLOYEE-NAME-IN TO EMPLOYEE-NAME-OUT.
   51       MOVE HOURS-IN TO HOURS-OUT.
            ...-OUT-RECORD
                ...CING 1 LINE.
                                         ...MORE-RECORDS.
```

Programming
Concepts

A VIEW OF THE CHAPTER AHEAD

After Reading This Chapter You Will Understand:

- What a program is and why it is necessary.

- The importance of program specifications.

- The use of structure charts, flowcharts, and pseudocode for structured program design.

- The importance of good style and structure when coding a program.

One thing that all computers have in common is that they all require a program to operate. And systems that use computers must then use computer programs. We know that programs may be either purchased, if one exists for the application, or developed, if the application is unique. In this chapter we want to look at how a computer program is developed and at some of the languages used for writing computer programs.

WHAT IS PROGRAMMING?

Or we might also ask: What is a program? A **program** is a series of instructions that define how the computer is to process data. It follows that **programming** is the activity of creating or writing a computer program. But programming is more than simply writing a series of instructions for the computer to follow. Because programs for realistic applications tend to become large and complex, a programmer needs to learn a discipline of creating computer programs.

There are five steps that are followed when creating a computer program. These steps are

- Program specifications.
- Input and output definition.
- Program design.
- Program coding.
- Debugging and testing.

Only the fourth step, program coding, requires the writing of instructions known as program code. The previous three steps are all part of planning a successful program, and the last step ensures that the program was written correctly.

PROGRAM SPECIFICATIONS

Before a program is written, it needs to be defined. Are we writing a payroll program? Accounting? Sales analysis or a mailing list? The specifications define the problem. Not only is the type of program defined, but detailed requirements are identified, such as where the data originates, what process steps are to be applied to the data, and what output is to be produced as a result of running the program.

If we are to have complete and accurate programs, careful definition is required prior to writing the program. Otherwise we are likely to get something other than the results required. Developing program specifications also helps to clarify exactly what we expect the program to achieve.

Figure 11–1 shows a sample program specification for a payroll program. It defines the name of the program, gives a description of it, identifies input and output, and defines the program requirements as a series of steps. Usually the specifications are developed as a team effort with the programmer, systems analyst, and the user all taking part. Once the general specifications are ready, detailed input and output requirements can be developed.

The program specifications define the requirements of the program. Included are input, output, and process needs, which are identified during system design by the user, systems analyst, and the programmer.

Courtesy of Hewlett-Packard Company.

FIGURE 11–1
Program specifications are developed prior to writing the payroll program.

PROGRAM SPECIFICATIONS

PROGRAM NAME: Payroll   PROGRAM ID: PAY
PREPARED BY: Don Cassel   DATE: January 15, 1989

Program Description:
   The payroll program produces a basic pay statement from an input of hours worked and rate of pay.

Input File(s): Keyboard provides hours and rate.

Output File(s): Screen.

Program Requirements:
   1.   Accept as input the hours worked and rate per hour for an employee.
   2.   Calculate gross pay by multiplying hours worked by rate per hour.
   3.   Calculate a basic tax deduction of 15 percent.
   4.   Determine the net pay by subtracting the tax from the gross.
   5.   Display all values on the screen.

INPUT AND OUTPUT

The three main components of a program's activity are input, process, and output. Input to a program is the data that the program reads from a keyboard or other device. The input provided to the program determines what data the program has available for processing. Data that is provided as input can be either numeric, alphanumeric, or alphabetic. Table 11–1 shows some types of input data in each category, with an example of how the data might look.

TABLE 11–1
Three types of data that are commonly used as input to a computer program. Some languages, such as dBASE IV, group alphanumeric and alphabetic together in one category, called character data. A code, such as sex code, might also be defined as a unique field type called logical data.

Type of Data	Example	Value in Field
Numeric	Account no.	34522
	Quantity	25
	Cost	47.29
Alphanumeric	Address	37 Main Street
	Date	6/12/89
	Phone	853-233-0189
Alphabetic	Name	John Wilson
	Description	Compact Disk
	Sex code	F

In addition to this information about the data, some programming languages may require a length that identifies the number of characters or digits in the field. Numeric fields may also require the number of decimal positions in the number to be specified. Many of the specific rules that are required for input definition depend on the language used and can vary widely.

Output defines the results of processing the input data. Your first program usually displays output on the computer's screen to be read directly after it is displayed. Output can also be printed if a permanent hard copy is required. Disk output is frequently used when data needs to be stored for processing at a later time.

Figure 11–2 shows how input is supplied to the program from the keyboard. The program processes this input data and then displays the results on the screen. Output may also have field definitions such as numeric or alphabetic. Specific definitions depend on the programming language and the type of output device being used by the program.

FIGURE 11–2   Input provided from the keyboard is processed by the program. Following processing, the results are displayed as output on the screen.

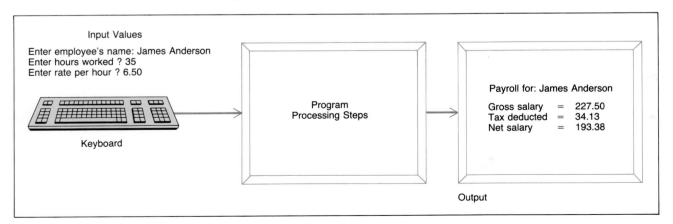

THE TOOLS OF PROGRAM DESIGN

Simple programs, such as one for the payroll problem in the previous section, can often be written directly from the specifications. But programs are frequently more complex than this one. Other factors such as employee pension, government social security, unemployment insurance, overtime pay, and so on need to be considered in a real payroll application. To design programs such as these effectively, tools such as structure charts, flowcharts, and pseudocode are both helpful and necessary.

Structure Charts

A **structure chart** shows the solution to a problem in a hierarchical fashion from the top level to the bottom. At the top of the chart is a general statement about the problem. The next level shows more detail that may be expanded to a third level as required until the solution is completely defined. Each box is a **module** that represents a **task.** A lower-level box is a subtask that further defines the module.

Figure 11–3 shows a general structure chart pattern that may be used to help think about organizing the solution to a problem. As with any general solution, it may need to be adapted to the needs of a specific problem. In this case the problem is defined in terms of input, processing, and output requirements. Since most programs require all three of these components, this is often a useful way to begin.

A structure chart for the payroll problem is shown in Figure 11–4. It follows the input, process, output pattern, but this time specific references are made to the problem. When a structure chart, such as this one, is developed, the programmer should begin by thinking about the general solution to the problem and record this as the top level of the structure chart. Then each module is expanded further as more details to the solution to the problem are considered. In this way only small parts of the solution are designed at one time, keeping complexity to a minimum.

FIGURE 11–3
The fundamental parts of a structure chart.

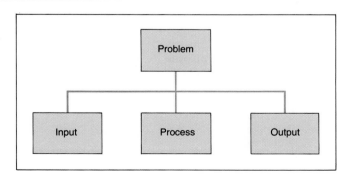

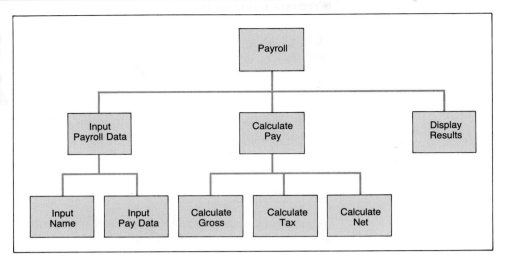

FIGURE 11–4
The structure chart presents a top-down solution to the payroll problem. The top level of the chart is general with more specific details shown as lower levels of the solution are developed.

Pseudocode

Writing **pseudocode** may be thought of as a dry run at writing the program. Pseudocode uses programlike statements without the detailed and sometime more complex syntax required of a programming language. Pseudocode also uses the concept of top-down design used for developing the structure chart. Often, writing pseudocode is the next step in program design after the structure chart has been created.

Pseudocode represents the logic of the program by showing each step taken, decisions that need to be made in the program, and looping or repetition of program code.

Figure 11–5 shows the pseudocode for the payroll problem. The solution at this level includes the possibility of more than one employee, and so the "DOWHILE another employee" entry is included. This entry defines a loop that causes the code to be repeated until there are no more employees to be processed.

FIGURE 11–5
Pseudocode for the payroll program. Each line in the pseudocode represents a line of program code in a simplified form.

```
Program: Payroll

DOWHILE another employee
    INPUT employee's name
    INPUT hours and rate
    Compute gross
    Compute tax at 15% of gross
    Compute net
    PRINT results
ENDDO
```

Program Flowcharts

While pseudocode uses programlike statements to develop program logic, flowcharts use a diagram to develop program logic. Pseudocode is a series of statements written in point form, while flowcharts are a graphic representation of the logic. Although both methods have the same purpose, some programmers have a preference of one over the other.

Program flowcharts use the symbols from Figure 11–6 that can represent all program logic. Symbols are connected by lines and arrows to represent the flow of logic in the program. When creating a flowchart, the flow should normally go from the top to the bottom or to the right in the flowchart. Other directions are permitted, such as when branching left from a decision symbol, but should occur less often. Connectors are used when remote parts of the flowchart need to be connected.

Figure 11–7 shows a flowchart solution for the payroll problem. This flowchart is organized into modules or subroutines that each provide the solution for one part of the problem. Using such an approach is called a structured flowchart and is consistent with the method used earlier for developing the top-down solution with a structure chart.

FIGURE 11–6
Symbols used for creating program flowcharts.

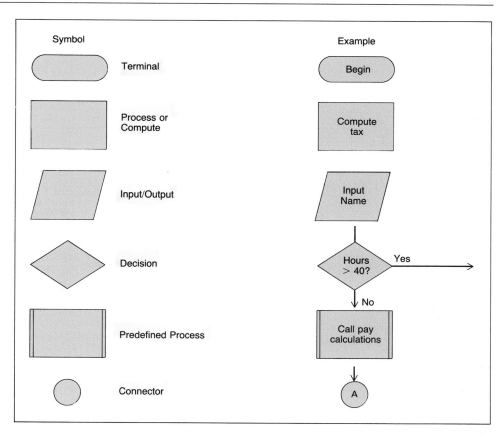

FIGURE 11–7
Flowchart and pseudocode for the payroll problem. The mainline chart provides the calls to access subroutines for reading data, doing the payroll calculations, and printing the results. The mainline also provides a loop so that additional employees may be processed if required.

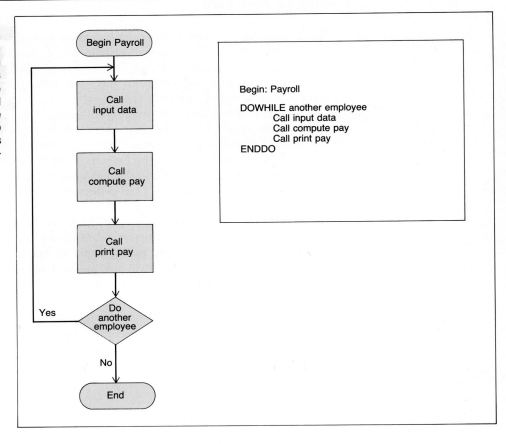

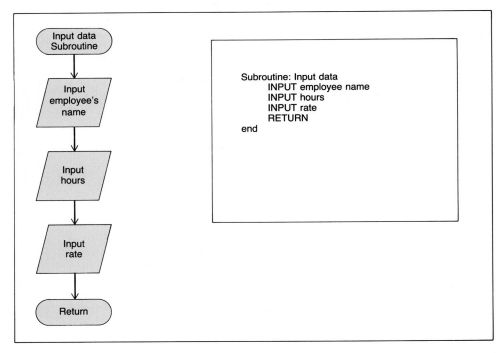

FIGURE 11–7
(Continued)

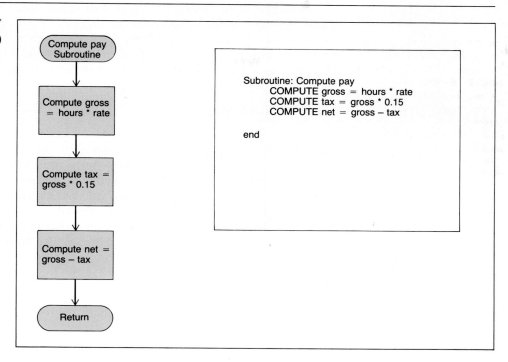

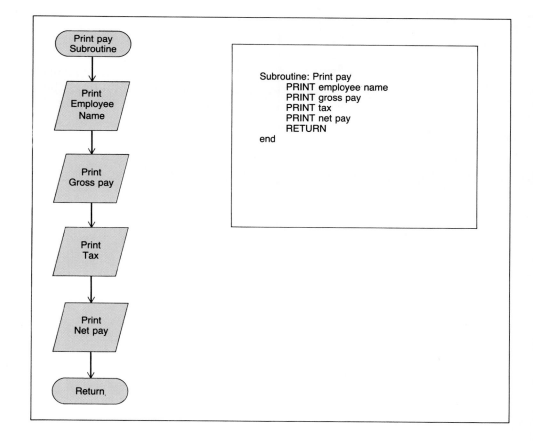

The flowchart begins with a **mainline** section, sometimes called a **driver module.** This module controls the activity of the program and calls other subroutines as they are required. After each subroutine completes its task, it returns control to the driver module, which determines the next activity. Pseudocode is also provided with the flowchart for comparison purposes.

CONTROL STRUCTURES FOR PROGRAMS

A structured program is one that is based on the use of three kinds of program structures called control structures. Early programmers frequently produced programs that were not well organized and used frequent branching or looping. These programs were hard to follow and were sometimes known as "spaghetti code" because of their unorganized structure (or lack of structure). Using the program structures defined here is a method of creating a structured program without unnecessary complexity of logic. The three types of structures are defined as follows:

1. Sequence structure
2. Selection structure
3. Repetition or loop structure

These structures apply not only to programs, but also to pseudocode and flowcharts. They are really quite simple and can be thought of in the following ways.

Sequence Structure

The sequence structure refers to a simple sequence of activities such as reading, printing, calculating, or calling a subroutine. The sequence structure is fundamental to all programming. It does not make decisions or loop but simply

Sequence structure.

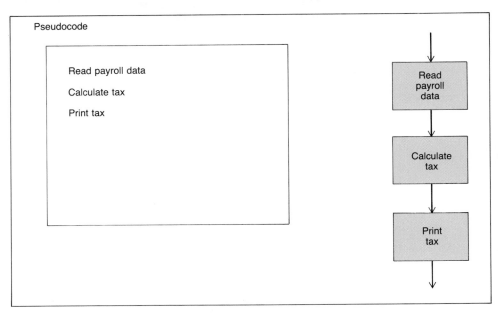

Pseudocode

Read payroll data

Calculate tax

Print tax

Read payroll data

Calculate tax

Print tax

proceeds from one statement to the next. Here is an example of three pseudocode statements that are a sequence structure. To the right of the pseudocode is a flowchart that graphically portrays the same structure.

Selection Structure

The selection structure represents decision making in the flowchart or pseudocode and ultimately in the program. A decision has a condition that is evaluated. If the condition is determined to be true, one action is selected to be done. If the condition is determined to be false, the other action is selected. Notice that only one action or the other is selected; never both.

Selection structure.

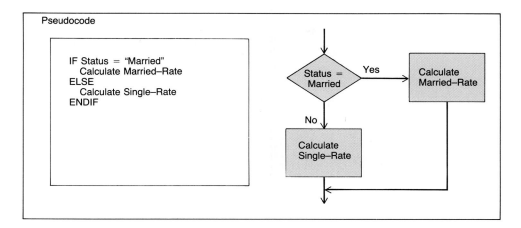

```
Pseudocode

IF Status = "Married"
    Calculate Married–Rate
ELSE
    Calculate Single–Rate
ENDIF
```

Repetition Structure

The repetition or loop structure also contains a decision, but the difference lies in the use of repetition. In this structure the decision determines if the action is to be repeated or if the program is to leave the structure.

Repetition structure.

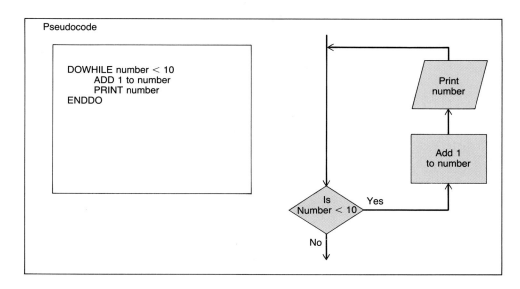

```
Pseudocode

DOWHILE number < 10
    ADD 1 to number
    PRINT number
ENDDO
```

PROGRAM CODING

When the program has been designed using the tools of program design, then the program code is written. Figure 11–8 shows a program written in the BASIC language for the payroll application developed in this section. The program code follows the logic developed in the pseudocode and flowchart but now uses correct BASIC to implement the solution.

Programming requires not only that the program code be written to implement the solution but also that the code is written clearly. The programmer should be able to read the code easily and understand how it works. Clear programming style is necessary so that the program can be tested and debugged with a minimum of confusion. Good style also makes it easier to change the program when the needs of the application change.

The payroll uses good style by including several standards for program coding. These standards are

FIGURE 11–8

A BASIC program using good techniques of style to implement the payroll application.

```
100  REM ******************************************************************
110  REM *            Sample Payroll Program                            *
120  REM * Description:                                                 *
130  REM *   This program reads hours and pay rate data for an employee *
140  REM *   and calculates a gross salary. A 15% tax deduction is      *
150  REM *   computed and the net salary to be paid. After the results  *
160  REM *   are printed the user is allowed to repeat the process.     *
170  REM * Programmer:                                                  *
180  REM *   Don Cassel                                                 *
190  REM ******************************************************************
200  Y$ = "yes"
210  WHILE Y$ = "yes"
215       CLS
220       GOSUB 1000
230       GOSUB 2000
240       GOSUB 3000
250       INPUT "Input another employee (yes/no)";Y$
260  WEND
270  END
1000 REM ******************************************************************
1010 REM *               Input Payroll Data Subroutine                  *
1020 REM ******************************************************************
1030 REM
1040 INPUT "Enter employee's name ",EMP$
1050 INPUT "Enter hours worked ";HOURS
1060 INPUT "Enter rate per hour ";RATE
1070 PRINT
1080 RETURN
2000 REM ******************************************************************
2010 REM *                  Compute Pay Subroutine                      *
2020 REM ******************************************************************
2030 REM
2040 GROSS = HOURS * RATE
2050 TAX = GROSS * .15
2060 NET = GROSS - TAX
2070 RETURN
3000 REM ******************************************************************
3010 REM *                  Print Payroll Subroutine                    *
3020 REM ******************************************************************
3030 REM
3040 PRINT "Payroll for: ";EMP$
3050 PRINT
3060 PRINT "Gross salary = ";GROSS
3070 PRINT "Tax deducted = ";TAX
3080 PRINT "Net salary   = ";NET
3090 PRINT
3100 RETURN
```

1. Begin the program with comments including the name of the program, a description, and the name of the programmer.

2. Begin each subroutine with a remark that identifies the purpose of the subroutine.

3. Use descriptive variable names such as HOURS rather than a single-letter variable. If necessary, use a descriptive abbreviation such as EMP$ for an employee name.

4. When nested code is used, such as in a WHILE loop, indent code within the loop a common number of columns to make the nesting obvious.

5. Use spaces around operators such as +, −, /, *, and = to improve readability.

Figure 11–9 shows a sample screen from the payroll program. The first three lines of the screen display show the input data requested by the program and the values entered. The remaining lines are the results created as output from the program. In this example some of the calculated values have from one to three decimal places depending on the results of the calculations. This is a common characteristic of BASIC and can be modified by more extensive programming.

FIGURE 11–9
A screen display from the payroll program.

```
Enter employee's name James Anderson
Enter hours worked ? 35
Enter rate per hour ? 6.50

Payroll for: James Anderson

Gross salary =   227.5
Tax deducted =   34.125
Net salary   =   193.375

Input another employee (yes/no)?
```

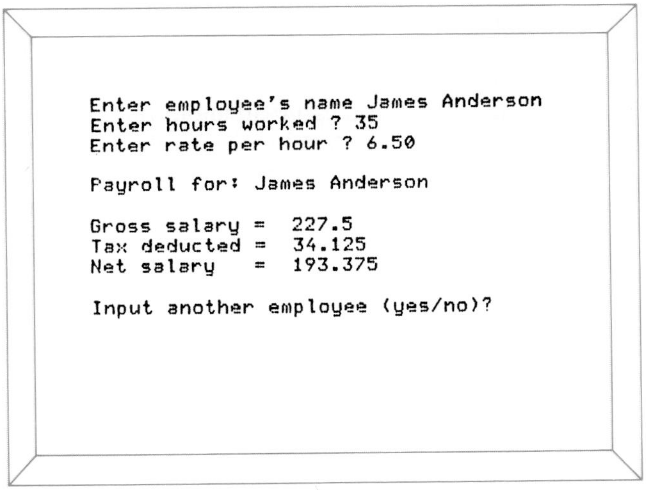

PROGRAMMING LANGUAGES

Coding is the process of writing the computer program in a language such as BASIC. Programmers often write the program on paper before entering it on the computer, although some prefer to type it as the program is developed. In either case constant reference to the design documents is necessary to ensure a correct program.

After the program has been written, it is run on the computer to ensure that it contains no errors. Because the program is written in a language such as BASIC, it must first be interpreted into a computer language that at the lowest level consists of ones and zeros. Several methods of interpretation are used depending on the language or computer.

An **interpreter** is a program that reads each statement in the BASIC program (or other language) and interprets it for the computer. This process is something like a human interpreter who listens to your English and after each sentence you speak interprets it into French for a listener who only understands the French language.

A **compiler** performs a similar function to an interpreter but in a different manner. When a compiler translates the program, it creates an entirely new program that is in the computer language. You might compare this process to a human interpreter who interprets an English language book and creates a French book from it. A compiled program will run much faster than an interpreted one and is desired on systems where lack of speed can be a problem.

When a program is compiled, the original program is called the **source program,** and the compiled version is the **object program.**

A program that is compiled or interpreted may contain errors such as statements that are coded incorrectly. Maybe a comma is missing or a parenthesis is used in the wrong place. In such cases a diagnostic error message is produced, and the programmer must find the error and correct it. The procedure is known as **debugging** the program and is a necessary process for every program.

Finally, program **testing** is done. Data is entered and the results are checked to ensure the program is operating correctly. Good testing procedures will also attempt to use data that is in error to see if the program will reject it rather than attempt to process incorrect data. Testing can be as much of an art (and some science) as programming and is a time consuming but essential task for the producers of business software.

In Appendix A you can read about the differences between four generations of languages and the development of programming from machine language, through symbolic, to high-level languages and now fourth generation. The main difference between the last two generations is that high-level languages

Where did a term such as debugging originate? Allegedly, in 1945 a problem occurred in the Mark I computer, and Grace Hopper, a computer pioneer of the day, was asked to find the problem. Eventually, a moth was found in the relays, and the term "bug" was from then on associated with an error in computer hardware and software.

Courtesy of Naval Surface Warfare Center.

are procedural while fourth generation are frequently nonprocedural. These are the two categories of programming languages used on personal computers today.

Procedural Languages

Languages such as BASIC, COBOL, FORTRAN, and Pascal are called procedural languages because they are coded and written as sequentially ordered statements. Decision making and looping are an essential part of procedure-oriented languages, and the language structure provides statements to accommodate this need.

Procedural languages are in widespread use on both mainframe and personal computers and have developed into dependable and competent languages.

BASIC

The name BASIC means Beginners All-Purpose Symbolic Instruction Code. BASIC was developed at Dartmouth College for use on a mainframe computer in a time-sharing environment. When personal computers came on the scene, BASIC was adopted as the primary programming language. Computers such as the Apple, Commodore 64, and the IBM PC all provided BASIC as a standard language.

BASIC was ideal for the PC because of its interactive nature. Keyboard input and screen output are easy to use and form the basis for many PC applications. BASIC is considered an easy language to learn, but there are many variations of it on different computer systems. Although BASIC is often a first language that a programmer learns, it does have many limitations, which results in the programmer moving to more recently developed and sophisticated languages such as C or Pascal.

COBOL

The name COBOL means COmmon Business-Oriented Language and was developed primarily for business applications. COBOL was developed in 1959 and gained prominence during the 1960s as the leading mainframe computer language. Its foothold in the industry is so strong that the majority of mainframe applications today continue to use COBOL.

COBOL's main strength is its file-handling ability. It was designed to process a variety of file types and can handle sequential, relative, ISAM, or VSAM files equally well. However, it is not particularly well suited to interactive applications using the screen and keyboard. If applications require heavy interaction, other software is used with COBOL to provide the link with the user.

With personal computers exceeding the memory size and capacity of mainframes of only a few years ago, COBOL is now able to run on many PCs. Although the applications are few, some companies are using COBOL programs originally developed for the mainframe on personal computers. Thus the application can be taken to where the user needs it.

Figure 11–10 shows a sample COBOL program that prints a simple expense report. The example demonstrates both a major strength and a major weakness of COBOL. The strength is COBOL's readability. Even someone who sees a COBOL program for the first time can make some sense of it. The weakness is COBOL's wordiness. Even the most elementary program requires many lines of code, whereas a few lines can produce a useful BASIC program.

```
        IDENTIFICATION DIVISION.
        PROGRAM-ID.
            EXP01.
       *REMARKS.
       *     PRINTS DEPARTMENTAL EXPENSE REPORT.

        ENVIRONMENT DIVISION.
        CONFIGURATION SECTION.
        SOURCE-COMPUTER.
            IBM-370-138.
        OBJECT-COMPUTER.
            IBM-370-138.
        SPECIAL-NAMES.
            C01 IS TO-NEW-PAGE.

        INPUT-OUTPUT SECTION.
        FILE-CONTROL.
            SELECT EXP-IN   ASSIGN TO SYS004-UR-2501-S.
            SELECT EXP-RPT ASSIGN TO SYS005-UR-1403-S.

        DATA DIVISION.

        FILE SECTION.
        FD  EXP-IN
            RECORD CONTAINS 80 CHARACTERS
            LABEL RECORDS ARE OMITTED
            DATA RECORD IS IN-REC.
        01  IN-REC.
            05  IN-DEPT     PIC 9(03).
            05  IN-DATE     PIC X(08).
            05  IN-TYPE     PIC X(13).
            05  IN-AMOUNT   PIC 9999V99.
            05  FILLER      PIC X(50).

        FD   EXP-RPT
             RECORD CONTAINS 133 CHARACTERS
             LABEL RECORDS ARE OMITTED
             DATA RECORD IS OUT-REC.
        01   OUT-REC.
             05  FILLER      PIC X(133).

        WORKING-STORAGE SECTION.
        01 WORK-AREA.
            05 EOF-FLAG    PIC 9        VALUE ZERO.
            05 WORK-TOTAL PIC 9(5)V99 VALUE ZERO.

        01   OUT-HEAD-1.
             05 FILLER      PIC X(015) VALUE SPACES.
             05 FILLER      PIC X(118)
                            VALUE  'DEPARTMENTAL EXPENSE REPORT'.
```

FORTRAN

FORTRAN has been a widely used programming language in the engineering, mathematical, and scientific communities for many years. The name FORTRAN is taken from FORmula TRANslation, which implies correctly that the main use of the language is for programming mathematical formulas. Although many other languages are taking its place, it endures as a popular language when the applications are of a mathematical nature. (See Figure 11–11.)

The language was first developed by IBM and released in 1957. As one of the first high-level languages, it made computer power more readily available, and its use became widespread. During the 1960s FORTRAN became available on most computers of the period and is still widely available from PCs to mainframes today.

FIGURE 11–10
(Continued)

```
01   OUT-HEAD-2.
     05 FILLER      PIC X(030)
                    VALUE ' DEPARTMENT        DATE          '.
     05 FILLER      PIC X(103)
                    VALUE 'TYPE OF EXPENSE     AMOUNT'.

01   OUT-DETAIL.
     05 FILLER      PIC X(004) VALUE SPACES.
     05 OUT-DEPT    PIC 9(003).
     05 FILLER      PIC X(010) VALUE SPACES.
     05 OUT-DATE    PIC X(008).
     05 FILLER      PIC X(005) VALUE SPACES.
     05 OUT-TYPE    PIC X(013).
     05 FILLER      PIC X(006) VALUE SPACES.
     05 OUT-AMOUNT PIC 9999.99.

01   OUT-FOOTER.
     05 FILLER      PIC X(049) VALUE SPACES.
     05 OUT-TOTAL  PIC 9(4).99.

PROCEDURE DIVISION.

000-HOUSE-KEEPING.
    OPEN INPUT  EXP-IN.
    OPEN OUTPUT EXP-RPT.
    PERFORM 150-PRINT-HEADINGS.

100-MAINLINE.
    PERFORM 200-READ-ROUTINE.
    PERFORM 300-PROCESS-DATA
        UNTIL EOF-FLAG = 1.
    PERFORM 400-TOTAL.
    CLOSE EXP-IN.
    CLOSE EXP-RPT.
    STOP RUN.

150-PRINT-HEADINGS.
    MOVE OUT-HEAD-1 TO OUT-REC.
    WRITE OUT-REC
        AFTER ADVANCING TO-NEW-PAGE.
    MOVE OUT-HEAD-2 TO OUT-REC.
    WRITE OUT-REC
        AFTER ADVANCING 2 LINES.
    MOVE SPACES TO OUT-REC.
    WRITE OUT-REC
        AFTER ADVANCING 1 LINES.
```

```
200-READ-ROUTINE.
    READ EXP-IN
        AT END MOVE 1 TO EOF-FLAG.

300-PROCESS-DATA.
    ADD  IN-AMOUNT  TO  WORK-TOTAL.
    MOVE IN-DEPT    TO  OUT-DEPT.
    MOVE IN-DATE    TO  OUT-DATE.
    MOVE IN-TYPE    TO  OUT-TYPE.
    MOVE IN-AMOUNT  TO  OUT-AMOUNT.
    MOVE OUT-DETAIL TO  OUT-REC.
    WRITE OUT-REC
        AFTER ADVANCING 1 LINES.
    PERFORM 200-READ-ROUTINE.

400-TOTAL.
    MOVE WORK-TOTAL  TO OUT-TOTAL.
    MOVE OUT-FOOTER  TO OUT-REC.
    WRITE OUT-REC
        AFTER ADVANCING 2 LINES.
```

```
C       SUM OF A SERIES 1 TO 100
        INTEGER COUNT, SUM
        SUM = 0
        DO 20 COUNT = 1, 100
            SUM = SUM + COUNT
   20   CONTINUE
        PRINT 30, 'THE SUM OF 1 TO 100 IS ', SUM
   30   FORMAT (' ', A23, I6)
        STOP
        END
```

Because of its orientation to solving mathematical problems, FORTRAN was not suited to the business community. Programs that create reports or do file processing are not as easily developed in FORTRAN as in other languages such as COBOL. More advanced business applications using indexed files or interactive user operations are best done using a language oriented to these operations, leaving FORTRAN for the engineers and scientists.

Pascal

Pascal is a language that was developed by Nicklaus Wirth, a widely recognized computer scientist. Wirth intended Pascal to be independent of the computer on which it was run so that a program written on one make of computer could run equally well on a different make with no program changes needed. Pascal was one of the first languages to provide for the language structures needed for effective structured programming (Figure 11–12).

Pascal is easy to learn, although perhaps not as easy as BASIC, and is taught as a primary language in many computer science courses. Pascal is also useful for software development and has been used to develop many software packages for business. It is frequently used on personal computers, thanks to the well-known Turbo Pascal that made the language affordable for the micro.

Modula-2

Ten years after Wirth developed Pascal, he set a goal to improve on the language. The result was Modula-2 (Figure 11–13). The new language was

```
program interest(input, output);
    var Balance, Interest, Principal: real;
        Period: integer;
    begin
    {Read initial values}
    read(Principal, Interest, Period);
    {Calculate balance with interest}
    Balance := Principal*(1 + Period*Interest)
    writeln('The new balance is',Balance);
    end.
```

FIGURE 11–13

Modula-2 is a language derived from the Pascal language. Both languages were developed by Nicklaus Wirth.

```
MODULE Sampleprogram;
FROM InOut IMPORT
     Writestring, WriteLn;
BEGIN
     WriteString ('Sample Lines of Modula-2 Output');
     WriteLn;
     WriteLn;
     WriteString ('These are sample lines of printed output');
     WriteString ('from a Modula-2 program.');
     WriteLn;
END Sampleprogram.
```

created to help programmers avoid some kinds of errors that were easily created in Pascal and to simplify advanced programming applications. Many computer science courses are now making the switch from Pascal to Modula-2. Changing to the new language is relatively easy because much of the language structure is identical to Pascal.

C language

The C language was developed by Bell Laboratories in the early 1970s and used on UNIX-based operating systems for software development. C creates object code that is comparable to an assembly language in efficiency while using high-level language features for programming. Structured programs are easily written in C (Figure 11–14) owing to its language structure that promotes top-down coding.

Like Pascal, C is independent of the computer on which the program is written. This feature, as well as its efficiency, have caused it to be adopted by many software developers for the PC. New versions of C let it be used under the MS-DOS and PC-DOS operating systems.

Although C is considered to be a relatively difficult language to master, C language programmers are in great demand.

FIGURE 11–14

A C language program that finds the sum of integers from 1 to a number entered by the user of the program.

```
/*        Sample C language program        */
/*  Finds the sum of integers from 1 to number */
main()
{    int counter = 0; number; sum = 0;
     printf("This program finds the sum of integers from 1 to");
     printf("a number that you enter. Enter the number and ");
     printf("press the return key");
     scanf("%d",&number);
     while (counter < number)
        {
           counter + + ;
           sum = sum + counter;
        }
     printf("The sum of the numbers is %F",sum);
}
```

User-friendly software made computers available to users from many disciplines. No longer is it necessary to be a computer programmer to develop applications for the PC. Using nonprocedural languages, users can develop some of their own applications without the need for writing a computer program.

Courtesy of Hewlett-Packard Company.

Fourth-Generation Languages

What attracted early users to the personal computer was its natural productivity. Instead of submitting requests to a mainframe computer and then waiting days or weeks for a result, users could spend a few hours at a PC and get the information needed for their job. Because of its apparent simplicity, demonstrated by its user-friendly nature, the PC was available to many more users than the mainframe.

Early PC users had to write their own programs in a procedural language, usually in BASIC. But with software such as Lotus 1–2–3 and dBASE IV, fewer programming skills were needed and the user could concentrate on the application rather than on using a procedural language.

More software for the PC is becoming available on a continuing basis that is nonprocedural in its use. These packages, such as PC/FOCUS, provide nonprocedural commands for easy access to data and for data analysis. A number of fourth-generation languages (4GL) were first developed for use on mainframe computers and have now filtered down to personal computers. Frequently, applications developed on the PC can be run on the mainframe, and vice versa.

Users can learn to use 4GL tools very quickly without a lot of prior training, thus reducing the load on programmers for new application development. Fourth-generation languages can both speed up and simplify the process of developing a new application. Coding and testing the system can be done by the user by using easy-to-understand nonprocedural, English-type statements. Prototyping, which is the development of a sample of how the system will function, can be more readily developed with 4GLs.

4GLs offer facilities for doing queries in a data base, generating reports, and updating files. For programmers, 4GLs can be used for automatic code generation, which permits faster program development than writing program codes directly. By using these tools, the professional can reduce the backlog of applications waiting to be developed and improve the time needed for software maintenance.

The mechanism that is fast becoming a standard for communicating between a 4GL and a data base is IBM's Structured Query Language (SQL). SQL is a language used for submitting queries to a data base. Originally developed for mainframe application, SQL is now appearing in PC software products, such as Ashton-Tate's dBASE IV. Users write queries in SQL as part of a 4GL to extract information from their data base.

Using 4GLs in the corporation is leading to a new phenomenon in the way systems are developed and maintained. Formerly, systems design used a linear methodology, as we will discuss in the chapter on systems analysis. The sequence of events was analysis, design, test, and implementation. With 4GLs a more circular systems methodology is beginning to be apparent: analysis, prototyping, user review, and prototype enhancement. Testing is done at various levels of the development instead of near the end. Best of all is the more complete user involvement at all levels of systems development.

CHAPTER SUMMARY	1. A program is a series of instructions that define how the computer is to process data.

1. A program is a series of instructions that define how the computer is to process data.

2. Programming is the activity of creating or writing a computer program.

3. Program specifications define where the data originates, what process steps are to be applied to the data, and what output is to be produced as a result of running the program.

4. Input to a program is the data that the program reads from a keyboard or other device.

5. Output defines the results of processing the input data and may be a screen display or data written on a file.

6. To design programs effectively, tools such as structure charts, flowcharts, and pseudocode are used.

7. A structure chart shows the solution to a problem in a hierarchical fashion from the top level to the bottom, from general to specific. Each box in a structure chart is a module that represents a task.

8. Pseudocode is a dry run at writing a program that uses programlike statements without the detailed and sometimes more complex syntax required of a programming language.

9. Flowcharts use a diagram of connected symbols to represent program logic. A flowchart begins with a mainline section, sometimes called a driver module, and calls subroutines as they are required by the program.

10. A structured program is one that is based on the use of three kinds of program structures: sequence, selection, and repetition.

11. Coding is the process of writing the computer program in a language such as BASIC. The program code follows the logic developed in the pseudocode and flowchart.

12. When programming, not only must the program code be written to implement the solution but the code must be written clearly, using good style, so that it is easy to read and understand.

13. An interpreter is a program that reads each statement in the BASIC program (or other source language) and interprets it for the computer.

14. A compiler translates the program and creates an object program that is in the computer language.

15. Debugging is the process of finding coding errors from diagnostic messages and correcting them in the program.

16. Testing is the process of running the program with test data to discover if it works according to the specifications.

17. Languages such as BASIC, COBOL, Pascal, and C are called procedural languages because they are coded and written as sequentially ordered statements. Decision making and looping are an essential part of procedure-oriented languages.

18. Nonprocedural languages require fewer programming skills and let the user concentrate on the application rather than on using a procedural language.

IMPORTANT TERMS AND CONCEPTS

Computer generations	Interpreter	Pseudocode
BASIC	Mainline	Repetition structure
C language	Modula-2	Selection structure
COBOL	Module	Sequence structure
Compiler	Nonprocedural	Source program
Control structures	Object program	Specifications
Debugging	Output	SQL
Driver module	Pascal	Structure chart
Flowcharts	Procedural languages	Style
FORTRAN	Program	Task
Fourth-generation language	Programming	Testing
Input		

REVIEW QUESTIONS

Fill-in Questions

1. A(n) _____ is a series of instructions that define how the computer is to process data.

2. The _____ chart is a tool to show the solution to a problem in a hierarchical fashion from top to the bottom level.

3. _____ _____ is a dry run at writing the program using program-like statements to represent program logic.

4. The _____ control structure represents decision making in the flowchart or pseudocode.

5. The original program that is compiled is called the _____ program, while the compiled version is the object program.

6. Program _____ ensures that the program is operating correctly.

7. Languages such as BASIC, COBOL, FORTRAN, and Pascal are called _____, because they are coded and written as sequentially ordered statements.

8. The _____ language was developed by Bell Laboratories based on the UNIX operating system.

Matching Questions

Match each term with the description given below.

a. programming   d. interpreter
b. specifications   e. module
c. flowchart   f. debugging

_____ 1. These define the requirements of the program, including the input, process, and output needs.

_____ 2. The process of correcting errors such as a missing comma or a misplaced parenthesis in a program.

_____ 3. A box in a structure chart that represents a specific task in solving the problem.

_____ 4. The act of creating or writing a computer program.

_____ 5. This is a program that reads each statement in the program and acts on it rather than creating a new machine language program.

_____ 6. A diagram used to develop program logic.

Discussion Questions

1. Discuss the terms program and programming.
2. Discuss the reasons for developing program specifications prior to writing a computer program.
3. What type of information about input data is required for writing a successful program?
4. Explain the procedure for developing a structure chart. What is the relationship between the different parts of the structure chart?
5. Discuss how writing pseudocode benefits the program design process?
6. Explain how the use of flowcharts differs from pseudocode when developing program logic.
7. Describe the three different types of control structures that form the basis for structured programming.
8. Discuss the importance of writing clear, readable program code. What are some standards that contribute to good programming style?
9. Explain the difference between an interpreter and a compiler.
10. Choose one procedural language discussed in this chapter, and research some of its characteristics from other sources.

System Analysis and Design

12

A VIEW OF THE CHAPTER AHEAD

After Reading This Chapter You Will Understand:

- The importance of information to the operation of today's business.

- The concept of a business system.

- Each of the components of the information system's life cycle.

I nformation is an integral part of all business systems and understanding it is a vital part of the process of systems analysis and design. Whether we are developing a new system or automating an old one, information is an important key to knowing how the system functions.

THE IMPORTANCE OF INFORMATION

Whether it is a clerical worker who processes orders from customers or a sales manager who directs the marketing staff, information is vital to the operation and productivity of a company. The order clerk may require access to current inventory so that orders taken will be processed quickly to maintain customer satisfaction. Information about the customer's credit status with the company may also be needed to ensure that orders can be sent without requiring advance payment.

This order system provides immediate information to the order clerk when an order is received. Information such as the available inventory of an item and the customer's credit status is quickly available from the system by making a simple query.

Information for the daily operation of the company can be made available from printed reports or by direct inquiry from a computer screen. The benefit of the computer is in its ability to provide timely and accurate information while printed reports can become outdated rather quickly. In either case an information system is needed to collect, process, and distribute this information when it is needed.

TO PURCHASE OR DEVELOP A SYSTEM?

An information system can be either purchased or developed by the company. Because there are many PC-based systems available for accounting, inventory, and order processing applications, many companies purchase this software rather than develop their own. There are three major advantages to purchasing a packaged system:

■ The system can be implemented in a relatively short period of time. By getting the system up and running, the company can receive immediate benefits from its use.

- A packaged system generally costs less to purchase and install compared to the cost of developing a new system.
- A packaged system has usually been in use by other clients and therefore has a track record. Because of this experience, the system is more likely to be trouble-free than a new system which has yet to be proven.

Packaged systems also have a significant disadvantage. They are developed based on the needs of the average company. An accounting package will provide for the needs of the usual business operations but often does not consider special needs that are peculiar to a specific industry. So companies with special requirements must adapt the package to their needs, adapt their operation to the package, or, if these alternatives are not feasible, develop their own system.

If a system is to be developed from the beginning by the company, a complete cycle of systems development is necessary to complete the task. Even packaged systems were originally developed by going through the process of system development.

But this does not mean that buying a packaged system will eliminate the need for systems development. On the contrary. Usually a packaged system is only part of the overall information systems operation of the company. And so it is important that the package fit in with other system requirements so that the entire operation will function as a complete information system.

WHAT IS A SYSTEM?

We have been using the word system rather informally until now, but what is the real meaning of system? A **system** is a set of organized and related procedures used to accomplish a specific task. We are quite familiar with the term system when it is related to natural phenomenon such as the solar system with the sun and its collection of planets, moons, and asteroids. Although the solar system does not have a set of procedures, as a business system might have, it does follow certain laws of physics such as the law of gravity.

A **business system** is a set of procedures that are followed to ensure that the business and the people in it perform the necessary functions to meet the company objectives. For example, an accounting system processes transactions each day against its accounts. On the thirtieth day of the month, a billing cycle is completed, and current bills are sent to the accounts outstanding. If payment is not received within 15 days, a follow-up letter is sent to remind the customer that payment is past due. This is one example of a business

This business system uses both hard copy documents and computer files to function. Invoices, orders, and billing all require paper documents, but the system also uses the computer for necessary functions such as record keeping and automatic billing.

Courtesy of IBM.

system that operates on a cycle that is performed repetitively over a period of time.

A **computer system** is a system that uses a computer as one of its components. Today most business systems use a computer to help automate their procedures and improve productivity and accuracy of the information that is processed. Part of the design of a system frequently requires a computer program in its solution.

The **systems analyst** is the person who analyzes an existing system, determines the needs of the user, and designs a new system to meet those needs. A systems analyst must be familiar with the way the company operates and know how to use or adapt existing procedures or design new ones. The analyst needs to understand how a computer can be used in the solution and be knowledgeable about packaged computer software as well as the development of new software.

INFORMATION SYSTEMS LIFE CYCLE

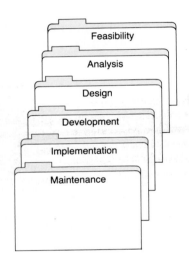

Developing an information system involves a cycle of five phases. These steps are always followed when a system is being developed, and after implementation the cycle repeats itself as changes and new requirements are built into the system. The six phases of the systems life cycle are

1. **Feasibility study.** This stage determines whether the system should be developed and if the necessary resources are available.
2. **System Analysis.** In this phase the existing system is analyzed to develop an understanding of it and to establish system requirements.
3. **System Design.** The new system is designed based on the needs determined during the feasibility and analysis phases.
4. **Program Development.** During this phase, computer software is acquired or programs are written and tested to meet the needs of the system.
5. **Implementation.** Old files are converted to the new system, users are trained in the use of the new system, and it is placed into operation.
6. **Maintenance.** Problems with the system are corrected as experience is gained with its use. New requirements can also be implemented such as the need to address changing tax laws.

These six phases outline the topics that we will discuss in the remainder of the chapter. As we will see, each phase has unique characteristics and form an important part in the process of developing and using a system. As a system is developed each phase of the cycle will contribute to the understanding of the system or provide tools for its development.

FEASIBILITY STUDY

When a new information system is proposed by management, the first stage in the systems process is to do a feasibility study. The **feasibility study** determines if the proposed information system is economically, operationally, and technically possible. **Economic feasibility** is used to determine whether the system can be developed within the cost restrictions defined by management.

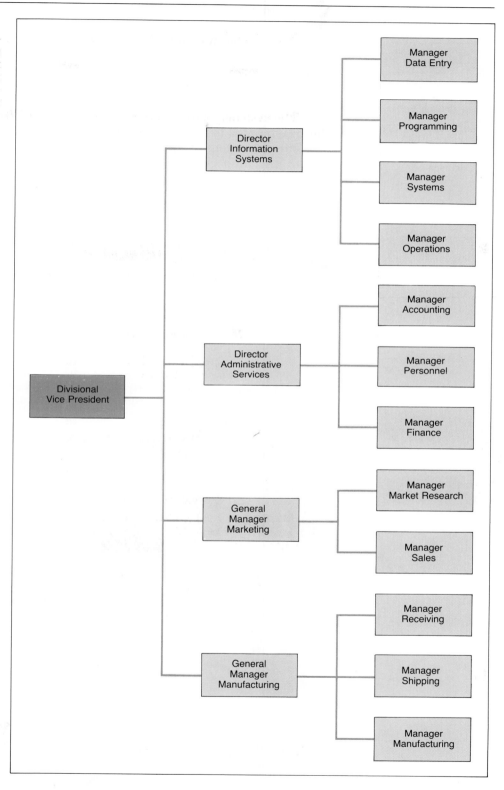

FIGURE 12–1
The organization chart identifies the formal reporting structure of management within a company. This chart shows the lines of responsibility for management under a divisional vice president.

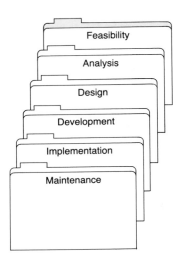

Feasibility

Analysis

Design

Development

Implementation

Maintenance

Operational feasibility is part of the study that determines whether the operation of the system is practical, or even possible. **Technical feasibility** decides if the hardware and software components are available or can be developed if necessary to complete the system. The feasibility study is an essential part of systems analysis because it determines the need, practicality, and economics of designing and implementing a new system.

The systems analyst, who conducts the study, will be a central figure in all stages of system development and implementation. A major responsibility of the analyst is to involve individuals in the company who either understand the current system or will be affected by the new one. To aid in this work the organization chart (Figure 12–1) will prove valuable for identifying the formal reporting structure of management within the company.

System Definition

In the first part of the feasibility study the system must be defined so that it is clear exactly what the system is intended to accomplish. The definition should identify the nature of the problem that is to be resolved by designing a new system. Early in the cycle we must be sure that the new system will indeed resolve the problem before too much time and effort has been expended on a solution that will not really do the job.

The birth of a new system begins at the idea stage, which quickly gives way to the feasibility study. The systems analyst defines the needs of the new system with other experts in the organization and determines whether it is economically feasible.

Courtesy of Hewlett-Packard Company.

The study must also determine the effect of the system on the company and define the limits of its impact. Systems have a tendency to reach out to all areas of an organization, and unless some limits are imposed on the new system, its development may be an unending process. While the overall impact may expect to be far reaching, it is best to limit the scope of the system both organizationally and within a clearly defined time frame.

Economics

A new system will have a cost to implement including the cost of personnel and other resources in the company. Computer costs for the system generally encompass both hardware and software unless existing resources can be used without further upgrading. The total cost of developing the system is then compared to the economic benefits derived from having the system in operation.

Economic benefits are not strictly limited to cost savings associated with increased productivity, reduced work force, or increased sales. These are tangible benefits that are important to the company and can be readily measured. A new system may also provide management with intangible benefits, such as providing information that was not readily available from the old system and improving user or customer satisfaction. Both tangible and intangible benefits need to be evaluated against the cost of developing the new system.

Feasibility Report

The final step in the feasibility study is to prepare a feasibility report that outlines the results of the system definition and the economic benefits. The report defines a proposed solution in general form and suggests a timetable for the design and implementation of the project. At this time only general timing can be considered. More specific times will be formally established early in the design phase of the system.

System objectives will also be specified in the feasibility report. These objectives identify the user's needs and how they can be met by the new system. Getting the report and the system approved will require the support of both management and the user group. By specifying complete objectives, these parties can see how the new system will help to solve some of their problems.

When the proposed system has been approved, the next stage of development is the systems analysis phase, which begins getting into the specific details of the new system.

SYSTEM ANALYSIS

Providing management has given the "go ahead," the next stage in developing a new system is the analysis phase. In analysis, complete details of how the system operates is collected in a form that can be used for supporting the design of the new system. Analysis is the process that gives the systems analyst a complete and thorough understanding of the system that is a necessary prerequisite before proceeding to the design stage. The first step in analysis is the process of data gathering.

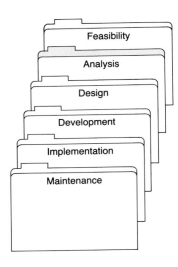

Feasibility

Analysis

Design

Development

Implementation

Maintenance

Data Gathering

Data gathering is the procedure for collecting information about the system. Some information obtained during the feasibility study is available, but this was more general in nature. In the data gathering process, detailed data is accumulated in preparation for in-depth analysis. Some of the following sources may be used in the data gathering process.

- Observing existing procedures
- Interviews
- Questionnaires
- Data collection

Observing existing procedures

One approach to data gathering is for the analyst to spend some time observing how the task is currently being done. One advantage of this approach is that the independent observer is often better at understanding a process than the person doing it. A trained analyst is frequently able to identify important components of an operation that the operator cannot readily verbalize. Usually the analyst will take notes to create a record of the observation period.

Another component of observation is to collect documents, such as procedure manuals, that describe the operation. The procedure manual can be a great aid to the analyst in becoming familiar with any special terminology or technical jargon used in the job. Unfortunately the procedure manual (if one exists) may not reflect the job as it is currently being done but rather how it was originally defined.

Interviews

Because informal changes to procedures are common, the second technique for data gathering is the interview. Through the interview the analyst becomes

Part of the function of systems analysis is data gathering. One method of collecting data about the existing system is by observing the system in action.

Courtesy of IBM.

The interview is one method used for data gathering. In the interview the analyst asks questions about the current system and collects information from the user's viewpoint on how the system operates. Such information becomes an important resource when designing the new system.

Courtesy of Apple Computer, Inc.

familiar with the realities of the day-to-day operation and involves the user in the early stages of systems analysis. The user is also made to feel a part of the new system by being placed in a position of providing input for its design.

Interviews take place with a user representative who is knowledgeable about the system rather than attempting to talk to all potential users that can be very time consuming. An interview can be either structured or unstructured, depending on the objectives to be met by the analyst.

Structured interviews are interviews based on a detailed set of questions that the analyst has developed beforehand. In a structured interview, the questions are asked without deviation, and no informal questioning is done. Structured interviews are useful if adherence to government regulations or laws are required or if consistent responses are sought.

Unstructured interviews are frequently more useful to the analyst than structured ones. In the unstructured interview, the analyst may also begin with a list of questions to give a pattern to the interview. But, as answers are received, informal questions may arise that can be pursued immediately. The benefit of an unstructured interview is that it permits the user to contribute information believed to be important and may open up areas that were not previously considered in the data gathering phase.

Questionnaires

When large groups of users are involved then data gathering can be done effectively by the use of questionnaires. Using a questionnaire can be less costly and less time consuming than interviews; however, they do lack the personal touch that is part of an interview.

Questionnaires should be easy to use and to tabulate the results. Several formats are possible, such as requiring a yes or no response, selecting one of several possible answers by checking a box, or responding with a range of agreement between the values of 1 to 10. There is also the open-ended questionnaire that lets the respondent write in a response. This last approach is not usually a good one because results from it are difficult to tabulate. Which format used by the analyst depends on the type of information to be collected and the kind of results that are expected.

Data collection

Current systems contain a wealth of data that can be useful to the systems analyst. Procedure manuals, mentioned earlier, are one source of data that describe the operation of the system. Other data that may prove useful are forms such as invoices, reports, form letters, and other documentation that is used in the system. If the current system is computerized, then copies of files, data bases, inputs, and outputs will all be essential. These data are useful resources for understanding the current system and will also become an important ingredient of the implementation when converting from the old system to the new one.

Charting the System

When all data about the system has been collected, the next step is to organize it into some coherent pattern. Data gathering tends to produce a lot of unconnected data that needs to take on an organized pattern if a solution to the problem in the form of a new system is to be the end result. To this end a number of charting tools are available to the analyst that not only organize the data but help it to be understood in preparation for the system design phase.

Data flow diagrams

Understanding the operation of a system in large part requires a knowledge of how data moves or flows from one area to another. The **data flow** diagram is a chart used by systems analysts to document the flow of data within the company. The diagram is a model that shows where data originates, how it moves from one location to another, and where it is stored when not being used. In other words the data flow diagram shows on paper how data moves in the real world of the system.

To create a data flow diagram, the analyst first relies on the data gathered from various sources in the company. Then, by using the symbols in Figure 12–2, a diagram can be constructed to show the flow of data. There are four symbols used in data flow diagrams.

FIGURE 12–2
Four symbols used in creating data flow diagrams.

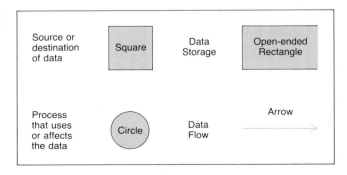

- The square symbol represents either the source of the data or its destination.
- A circle identifies a process where the data is handled in some manner such as validation or order preparation.
- Open-ended rectangles are used to show where data is stored such as in a file. The file can be a physical file or one on a computer system.
- Lines in the data flow diagram show the direction of data flow, where it begins and where it ends.

Figure 12–3 shows a data flow diagram for an order entry system that links inventory, shipping, and accounting. The system flow begins with the customer placing an order, which is represented by the source symbol at the left of the data flow diagram. The order then flows through the system where it is edited and credit is verified if a credit order. Prepaid orders immediately update the accounts file to show that payment has already been received.

The order also goes to the inventory process where the item ordered is picked from inventory, or if there is not sufficient quantity, a backorder is placed. The order then goes to shipping, where a shipping notice and invoice are produced and the item is shipped. A copy of the invoice goes to accounting for follow-up if the bill is not paid.

Another input to the system is the customer payment, which originates at the customer source. When a payment is received it is sent to accounts receivable/payable where the file is updated to show that payment has been made.

It should be made clear that the data flow diagram shown here for processing orders is a general one. In **structured systems analysis** a decomposition method is used to show the progressively finer details of the system. Structured systems

FIGURE 12–3
A data flow diagram for an order entry and processing system. In structured systems analysis, each process in this high-level diagram is decomposed into detailed data flow diagrams to give a complete diagram of each component of the system.

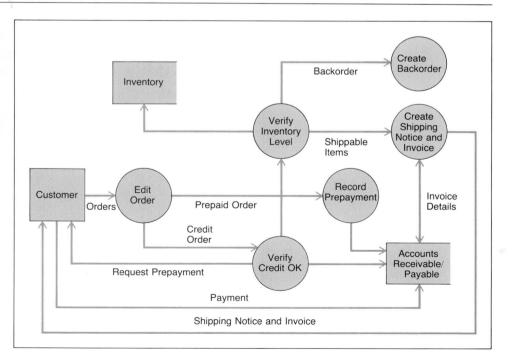

FIGURE 12–4

Symbols used for systems flowcharts approved by American National Standards Institute (ANSI).

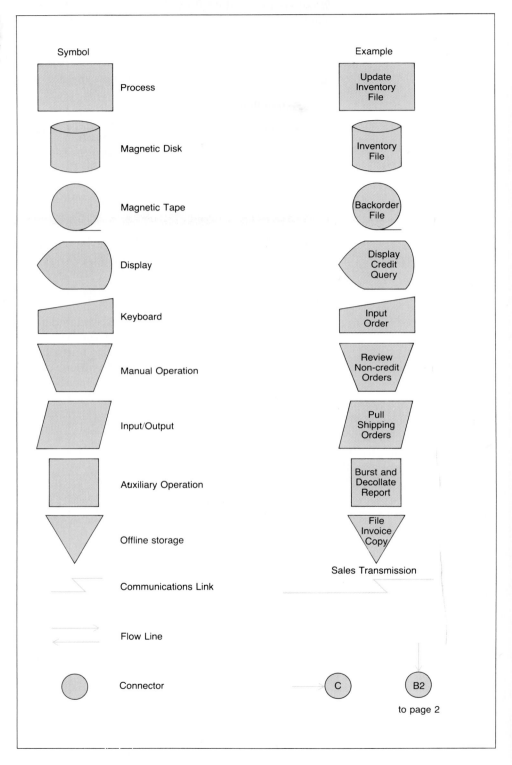

analysis uses a data flow diagram to provide an overview of the system. Then each process, represented by a circle, is decomposed to show the details of a specific operation. In our diagram, the circle representing the editing of the order will become a separate data flow diagram that shows all the steps required for doing the editing. This diagram may also have several processes, flow lines, and data storage as required for the operation.

System flowcharts

Another type of chart used for showing the flow of data in a system is the system flowchart. This chart goes back to the early years of computer system design and is still used by some analysts today, although the data flow diagram is gaining popularity because of its structured approach. Figure 12–4 shows some of the symbols used for system flowcharting. These symbols are based on an American National Standards Institute (ANSI) standard for systems flowcharts and are widely recognized by the computer industry.

A system flowchart is shown in Figure 12–5. In it, a computer program is used to process inventory requests from a keyboard. The display shows the status of inventory items accessed from the disk file by the program. When items are in short supply, a backorder is created and written on the backorder file, which also resides on the disk.

The activity report is a printed report that is first separated into individual pages (burst) and then analyzed for unusual activity against inventory. Such

FIGURE 12–5

A system flowchart shows the flow of data between components of the system.

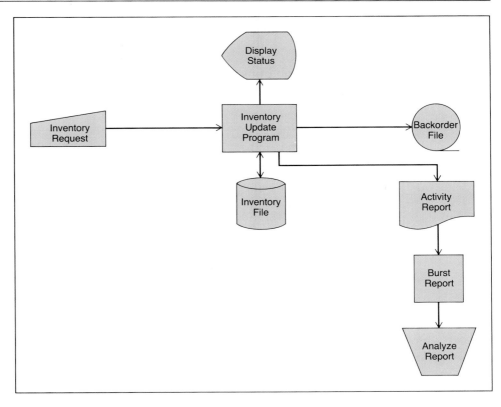

a report can help to identify items that have unexpectedly high sales and may require special attention.

Systems flowcharts have the disadvantage of being nonstructured and thus more difficult to design. Attempts to do decomposition of the system using a system flowchart is more of a problem because of its fundamental unstructured properties. For this reason data flow diagrams are becoming more widely used by analysts who favor the structured approach to systems analysis and design.

Decision tables

A **decision table** is used for expressing a logical solution to a problem in the form of a table. Decision tables are useful where related decisions are to be made and a variety of actions need to be selected. Unlike data flow diagrams or system flowcharts, they do not portray the flow of data but rather express the logic needed for decision making in the system. Decision tables are particularly well suited to developing some types of programming logic.

Figure 12–6 shows both the general format of a decision table and an example of its use for an order system. The decision table consists of four basic components as follows:

- **Condition stub.** This is the decision that is to be made such as "Is the item in stock?"
- **Condition entry.** This entry is expressed as a rule that selects cases where the decision is either true or false or, in some situations, not applicable.
- **Action stub.** The action stub lists the actions to be taken under all conditions.
- **Action entry.** The action entry selects the actions that apply to a specific set of conditions.

The decision table lists all the decisions to be made in the condition stub. The condition entry contains a set of rules. Each rule identifies a combination of conditions using true and false indicators. The action stub lists all actions

---

FIGURE 12–6   A decision table for processing an order. If there are enough items in stock an invoice is prepared for the order quantity and shipped to the customer. If the item is in stock but there is not enough to fill the order, then the stock quantity is placed on the invoice so the customer will receive a partial order. The difference between the order and stock quantity is backordered. Last, if the item is out of stock, the total quantity of the order is backordered.

Heading	Rules				
	1	2	3	4	5
Condition Stub (IF condition)			Condition Entry		
Action Stub (THEN action)			Action Entry		

Order System	Rules				
	1	2	3	4	5
Sufficient Stock Quantity	Y	N	N		
Partial Quantity in Stock		Y	N		
Out of Stock			Y		
Prepare Invoice	X	X			
Enter Order Qty on Invoice	X				
Enter Stock Qty on Invoice		X			
Ship Invoice Qty to Customer	X	X			
Order — Stock on Backorder		X			
Order Quantity on Backorder			X		

while the action entry checks off the actions that are to be followed for a particular rule.

For example, the order system has one rule that is in effect when there is "sufficient quantity in stock" for the order. In that case the actions to be taken are (1) prepare the invoice, (2) enter order quantity on the invoice, and (3) ship invoice quantity to the customer.

SYSTEM DESIGN

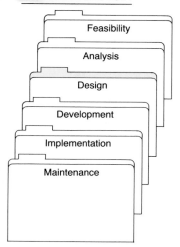

When the analysis stage is complete, the systems analyst has a thorough understanding of the present system and is now ready to begin the design of the new system. By now management has given the go-ahead for the system and detailed design begins in earnest. Many of the tools used for systems analysis may also be used during the design phase. Data flow diagrams, system flow-charts, or decision tables may all be used at different times during the design process. However, one of the first things to be done is to establish a timetable for completing the system.

Project Scheduling

Users and management who will benefit from a new system are the first to ask "When will it be finished?" And, because time is money, management also wants to know how much time will be required to complete the project. A well-known tool used for graphing a project schedule is a Gantt chart mentioned briefly in Chapter 9.

The Gantt chart (Figure 12–7) identifies major areas of work to be done before the system is installed. Each area is represented by a horizontal bar that shows the amount of time required to complete the task. Because some tasks are done concurrently with others, there is an overlap of some bars on the chart. Using a Gantt chart also helps to determine if the project is on

---

FIGURE 12–7   A Gantt chart for scheduling the many phases of system design and implementation. Each bar shows the number of weeks allocated to a task. The beginning and end of a task are shown by its position on the horizontal axis.

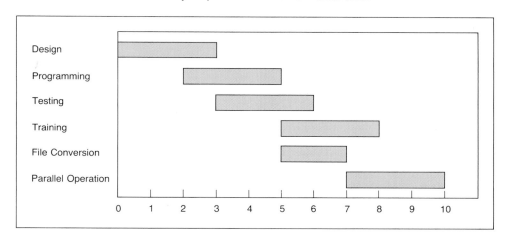

schedule at any point in time by comparing what has been completed to date with the plan represented by the chart.

Output Design

A major part of designing a system involves the outputs that the system is to produce. Outputs can be in the form of reports, screen displays, files, or data bases. Each of these outputs has different features, and many of them may be interdependent. Reports are generated from data present in a data base, while the data base depends on data that has been entered as input through a screen display. Each output may contain similar data but in different forms. Output is also dependent on input of data, which is another component of the design process.

Reports and screen displays have many features in common. They both have headings and labels to identify the data. Data itself is shown with decimal points and possible commas, dollar signs, and minus signs or parentheses for negative numbers. Figure 12–8 shows how a report appears after it has been printed by a computer program. This report is known as a two-up report because there are two columns of data, which has the effect of reducing the

FIGURE 12–8

A report that lists detailed budget figures for an international corporation. Totals for each department, division, and country of the company are printed at the end of the relevant group. Budget or accounting software is designed to produce reports such as this one.

```
                                              BUDGET ANALYSIS
                                                    BY
                                          COUNTRY/DIVISION/DEPARTMENT

COUNTRY  DIVISION  DEPT.  ACCOUNT   BUDGET   ACTUAL DIFFERENCE   COUNTRY  DIVISION  DEPT.  ACCOUNT   BUDGET   ACTUAL DIFFERENCE

   1        1       10     123     10,000   10,000       0          2        1       10     123     10,000   10,000       0
   1        1       10     124     15,000   10,000     5,000        2        1       10     126    120,000  120,000       0
   1        1       10     126    120,000  100,000    20,000        2        1       10     130     45,000   50,000   (5,000)
   1        1       10     130     45,000   40,000     5,000        2        1       10     123      3,000    2,050     950

          DEPARTMENT TOTALS      190,000  160,000    30,000               DEPARTMENT TOTALS      178,000  182,050   (4,050)

   1        1       11     123      3,000    3,500     (500)        2        1       13     126      5,905    1,600    4,305
   1        1       11     126      5,900    6,000     (100)        2        1       13     127    120,000  130,000  (10,000)
   1        1       11     127    120,000  100,000    20,000
                                                                          DEPARTMENT TOTALS      303,905  313,650   (9,745)
          DEPARTMENT TOTALS      128,900  109,500    19,400
                                                                          DIVISION TOTALS        481,905  495,700  (13,795)
   1        1       14     126    115,000  107,550     7,450
   1        1       14     130     45,000   45,500     (500)
   1        1       14     123      3,000    3,500     (500)        2        2       12     126      5,905    6,000     (95)
   1        1       14     126      5,905    6,000      (95)        2        2       12     127    120,000  111,000    9,000
   1        1       14     127    120,000  119,000     1,000        2        2       12     126    120,000  130,000  (10,000)

          DEPARTMENT TOTALS      173,905  174,000      (95)               DEPARTMENT TOTALS      245,905  247,000   (1,095)

          DIVISION TOTALS        492,805  443,500    49,305         2        2       15     130     45,000   50,000   (5,000)
                                                                   2        2       15     123      3,000   30,500  (27,500)
   1        2       11     126      5,905    5,600      305          2        2       15     226      5,905    5,600     305
   1        2       11     127    120,000  130,000  (10,000)
                                                                          DEPARTMENT TOTALS       53,905   86,100  (32,195)
          DEPARTMENT TOTALS      618,710  579,100    39,610
                                                                          DIVISION TOTALS        299,810  333,100  (33,290)
   1        2       12     126    115,000  117,500   (2,500)
   1        2       12     330     45,000   42,000     3,000               COUNTRY TOTALS         781,715  828,800  (47,085)
   1        2       12     126    120,000  110,000    10,000
   1        2       12     130     45,000   50,000   (5,000)
   1        2       12     123      3,000    2,800      200                COMPANY TOTALS       2,067,135 2,019,800   47,335
   1        2       12     226      5,905    5,600      305

          DEPARTMENT TOTALS      173,905  168,400     5,505

          DIVISION TOTALS        792,615  747,500    45,115

          COUNTRY TOTALS       1,285,420 1,191,000    94,420
```

FIGURE 12–9
A screen display format design for a college registration and grade reporting system.

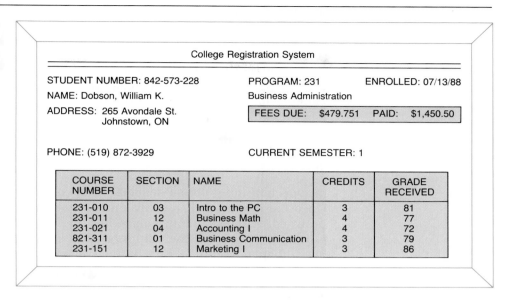

College Registration System

STUDENT NUMBER: 842-573-228 　　　PROGRAM: 231 　　　ENROLLED: 07/13/88

NAME: Dobson, William K. 　　　Business Administration

ADDRESS: 265 Avondale St.
　　　　　　Johnstown, ON

FEES DUE: $479.751 　PAID: $1,450.50

PHONE: (519) 872-3929 　　　CURRENT SEMESTER: 1

COURSE NUMBER	SECTION	NAME	CREDITS	GRADE RECEIVED
231-010	03	Intro to the PC	3	81
231-011	12	Business Math	4	77
231-021	04	Accounting I	4	72
821-311	01	Business Communication	3	79
231-151	12	Marketing I	3	86

length of the report and at the same time places more data within the user's view at one time.

Reports can become complex because of the amount of data contained in them and as a result of the totals and formatting required. Although display screens can be thought of as a report that displays on a screen, there is more to it than titles, numbers, and formatting, as the screen in Figure 12–9 seems to indicate.

In addition to the layout considerations, a screen is often used for input as well as output. This means that the analyst must decide which fields are output values to be displayed and which are input to be entered by the user. And, because screens are part of an interactive terminal, certain inputs, such as a query, will result in an output that will be defined as a screen layout in the design stage.

Screen design frequently requires the use of boldface or highlighting and often uses color to emphasize specific areas of the output. Some displayed data is in the form of graphics or charts. All these needs are identified by the analyst and become part of the output design for the screen display.

Input Design

Data to be entered into a computer must be defined as input. Input design depends on the source of the data and the type of device used for input. Personal computers mostly use the keyboard for data entry, and its input design goes together with the screen definition as discussed in the previous section. Input may also be entered from a modem, and in some cases from a document reader, or even voice input.

When designing the input, control over the type of data entered is often an essential part of the design process. Correct data is imperative to successful system operation and depends on a validation procedure that will accept only correctly entered data. Validation considers detecting some of the following errors made during data entry.

■ Nonnumeric data exists where numeric should be entered. Values such as dollar amounts, account numbers, and quantities should always be numeric.

■ Numeric values should normally be entered as positive values without the need for a sign.

■ Values such as amounts or quantities might need to be tested for being within a given range. Rate paid per hour in a payroll system should not exceed $100.00 or even a value much less than 100. Some items may require a minimum quantity to be ordered.

■ Missing data needs to be detected. When an input requires a name, address, or other data, then the design should provide a test to ensure that it is entered during the input operation.

Much of input design depends on the output requirements of the system. Once the output is thoroughly understood, then the input can be properly designed. Although input comes first in the system's operation, its design follows the design of the output because the output design reflects the user needs that are identified early in the system design process.

File and Data Base Design

Most computer-based systems make use of files or data bases in their operation. Designing these files is part of the input and output design process. However, a file or data base is generally used as both input and output, depending on the operation being done at the time, so one design will serve both purposes.

On personal computers the file design is often inherent in the input design for data entry. This is true for data base packages such as dBASE III Plus, where the input format is often a function of the data base and can serve for both data entry and the data base file itself. However, dBASE does provide for input design that is separate from the data base format for easier data entry (Figure 12–10).

Other software, such as Lotus 1–2–3, uses files but does not require the analyst to design its format. However, spreadsheet layout can be an important part of the design and is part of the design phase.

Prototyping

Prototyping is building a miniature model of the real system to demonstrate its operation. A prototype is a limited working system that has the major attributes of the system under design. In a short period of time the model is built, including display screen formats, data bases, and query capabilities. Using the prototype gives the user a feel for the system and results in immediate feedback if the results are not satisfactory.

A prototype has many limitations, which separates it from the real system. First, it will not have the full range of edit checks normally provided in a complete system. Although users may have access to a data base, they must ensure that the data they enter is valid because these controls are not included in the prototype. There may be a limited amount of data available for access by the prototype and security to the system may be minimal. Reports may be incomplete, and totals and summaries may not be fully accurate but only representative of the real thing.

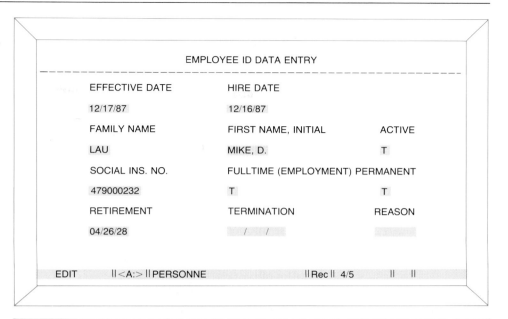

Benefits of Prototyping

By getting immediate user feedback, the systems team can act on revising system requirements before too much investment of time and money has been made. Ordinarily a new system may require months of development before the user is able to use it, which delays useful feedback on potential design problems. A prototype can often be developed in a matter of a few days. Thus immediate feedback from the use of the prototype can actually reduce the amount of time for systems development by reducing the time committed to making revisions to the system.

A prototype can also be used as a tool for selling the user on the benefits of the new system. By using the prototype, the user can see more readily the advantages of the system over previous methods of operation.

Although a prototype is usually built once and then discarded, it can become the foundation for the final system. When a prototype is developed using productivity tools such as fourth-generation languages, it can become a forerunner of the real system. As the prototype is produced, it is massaged based on user feedback and the evolving understanding of the system requirements. Changes are made to the prototype until the complete system emerges from the process.

Tools for Prototyping

Third-generation software technology only occasionally gave rise to prototyping because of the time required to develop a working model. Usually prototypes were developed only for very large and complex systems. Today, with the availability of fourth-generation languages and other productivity tools, a prototype can be built in a few days, which formerly might have taken weeks or months of work.

Besides the use of 4GL, there are application generator software tools that are used for program development. Display screen generators, report generators, natural language query systems, and data base management systems can all be used for developing a prototype and ultimately the final system.

PROGRAM DEVELOPMENT

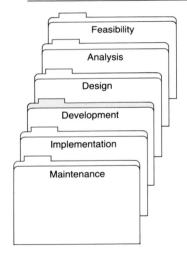

Feasibility

Analysis

Design

Development

Implementation

Maintenance

Designing the system's input and output is only a preliminary step toward creating an operational system. The computer-based components of the system now require detailed development, programming, and testing to create functional application programs. In some cases, existing software is adapted to the needs of the new system. This section considers the specific requirement of developing new computer programs to implement components of the system design. Developing programs will be considered in more detail in the following chapter.

The Steps of Program Development

Most people consider writing a program to be the main occupation of a computer programmer. Although programming may be the most visible and best understood part of developing computer programs, there are really several layers of activity that go into the development of a successful computer program. Briefly, these activities are as follows.

- Developing program specifications.
- Designing input and output.
- Designing the program.
- Writing program code.
- Debugging and testing the program.

Table 12–1 elaborates on these steps, discussing some of the activities that occur at each level of the program development process. It is clear that programming can be as complex a task as systems analysis and design is intricate. The programmer also has tools for the design process, such as structure

	Function	Description
TABLE 12–1 **The Basic Steps** **of Program Development**	Program specifications	The specifications describe the program to be written, identify the files to be used, and outline the processing steps to be performed. This is an essential document needed for the program design stage.
	Input and output design	Designing the inputs and outputs may be part of the systems design phase in some applications. By this time in the development of the new system, inputs and outputs need to be described in detail and the formats finalized. These designs are essential to the program design and coding stage of program development.
	Program design	The program is designed using structure charts, pseudocode, or structured flowcharts. The structure chart shows a program design in a top-down or hierarchical manner as the programmer gets into progressively finer details of the design. Program logic is developed using pseudocode or structured flowcharts.
	Program coding	The program is written based on the information presented in the design documents. Coding is done in a language such as BASIC, COBOL, Pascal, dBASE III Plus, C, and so on, depending on the needs of the system.
	Debugging the program	Debugging is the process of finding and correcting errors that were accidentally coded into the system.
	Testing the program	Testing determines if the program works the way it was intended to work and if it satisfies user requirements. There is a fine line between debugging and testing, and often the two are considered part of the same process.

Not all systems require programs to be written. Often a software package will be adequate. But other applications will require the services of a professional programmer to develop new programs for some components of the system.

Courtesy of Intel Corporation.

charts and pseudocode, just as the systems analyst does, although the specific tools vary somewhat.

Some of the work done by the systems analyst may reduce or eliminate some of the steps taken in program development. For example, the system design process often creates the design for inputs to and outputs from the system. If these designs are done accurately, then the programmer will not need to duplicate this effort. In some systems, developing program specifications is part of the systems analyst's duty and would not be included in the programmer's job description.

IMPLEMENTATION

The final stage of the information system development is the process of implementing the new system. This stage puts the newly designed and programmed system into operation. All the new or revised procedures are implemented at this time, and computer programs that receive or supply information to the system are installed and placed in operation.

Implementation is the time when all the hard work and long hours reach their culmination. Finally, the payback of the investment into developing the

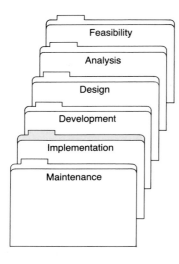

system begins, and the company can now reap its reward. But the new system can also create new or unforeseen problems, and so the process of implementation is as important as any other step in the system.

Training

Users who will be working with the new system need to understand its operation and know what is expected of them. The user needs to understand the use of the system's software and the commands that are available for use. Documents and reports that are part of the system's operation must be understood by the user if the operation of the system is to be successful.

All these components of the system's operation are brought together in the training process of the user. Training can begin before the system is completed and usually continues until the system begins operation. User training may be as simple as a few hours of instruction to many days or weeks of classroom training, depending on the complexity of the system.

Preparation for user training may require the development of documents or manuals to be used in the instruction process. Hands-on experience on the new system is also an important part of training and may use files that have to be especially prepared for the training process. After the training period, the user is ready to begin using the actual system. Training should be scheduled so that it is completed close to the time when the user will begin operation on the new system; otherwise, much of the newly learned material will be forgotten if there is a lengthy delay before the system is actually used.

Conversion

New systems are rarely implemented on their own merit. Rather, the new system is usually intended to replace an old one that no longer does the job effectively. Thus implementation often involves the conversion from an existing system to the new one. There are two aspects to converting to the new system.

- **File conversion.** Existing files and data need to be changed to the format used by the new system. Old files may become part of a relational data base in the new system and will need to be copied to the new format. Formerly manual files may need to be entered on the computer to create magnetic files. File conversion may require both computer programs to be written and data entry to be done to complete the conversion.
- **System conversion.** Users of the old system have been accustomed to operating in a given manner following older procedures that may no longer be valid with the new system. New forms and documents may also be used. System conversion requires the change of procedures, forms, and documents to the new mode. Often, system conversion is integrated with the user training process.

Parallel Operation

When the new system is put into operation, there may be a degree of uncertainty about whether it will do all that was intended. Less optimistic management may even be concerned about whether it will function correctly at all. To put these concerns aside and to prepare for the worst, if it occurs, good system planning demands that the old system should operate in parallel with the new for a short period of time until it is clear that the new system functions correctly.

Because of the cost and time required to operate in parallel, some systems use the old only as a backup in the event of an early failure of the new system. In the unlikely event that the new system "crashes," the user can quickly revert to the old system until the problem has been corrected. When this is done, another conversion will be needed to get the new system back into operation.

MAINTENANCE

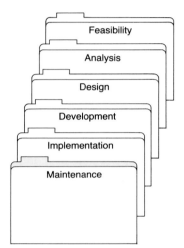

No matter how much time, effort, and planning have gone into the development of a new system, some errors or dissatisfactions with it are likely. No matter how well tested, programs can have undetected bugs that appear only after the system is implemented. These bugs will need to be found and corrected. And the system's operation may look good, even to the user, during the design and implementation stages, but when it goes into operation with a full work load, some weaknesses are likely to appear. These defects need to be corrected to ensure both user satisfaction with the system and effective operation.

Most systems can benefit from ongoing improvements that become part of the maintenance stage. While improvements to the system early in its life may be implemented with little question, later changes are frequently implemented only if they will be cost effective or offer some other benefit for improved system operation. Eventually, this system will age and be less useful as the organization changes, and a new system will need to be designed. Thus the system cycle will repeat itself once more.

CHAPTER SUMMARY

1. For the day-to-day operation of the company, it is necessary to collect, process, and distribute information when and where it is needed. The computer provides the ability to produce timely and accurate information.

2. Information systems may be either developed from the ground up, or an existing system may be purchased and adapted to the company's needs.

3. A system is a set of organized and related procedures used to accomplish a specific task.

4. A business system is a set of procedures that are followed to ensure that the business and the people in it perform the necessary functions to meet the company objectives.

5. A computer system is a system that uses a computer as one of its components.

6. The systems analyst is the person who analyzes an existing system, determines the needs of the user, and designs a new system to meet those needs.

7. The six phases of the systems life cycle are the feasibility study, system analysis, system design, software development, implementation, and maintenance.

8. The feasibility study determines if the proposed information system is both economically and technically possible.

9. The organization chart identifies the formal reporting structure of management within a company.

10. System analysis is the phase that gives the systems analyst a complete and thorough understanding of the system, which is a necessary prerequisite before proceeding to the design stage.

11. Data gathering is a procedure for collecting information about the system. Methods used for data gathering are observing existing procedures, interviews, questionnaires, and data collection.

12. The data flow diagram is a chart used by systems analysts to document the flow of data within the company. In structured system analysis, a decomposition method is used to progressively show the finer details of the system.

13. The system flowchart is another method for showing the flow of data in a system. It uses symbols based on the American National Standards Institute (ANSI) standard for systems flowcharting.

14. A decision table is used for expressing a logical solution to a problem in the form of a table. Unlike data flow diagrams or system flowcharts, they do not portray the flow of data but rather express the logic needed for decision making in the system.

15. Systems design uses many of the same tools used for systems analysis. Data flow diagrams, system flowcharts, or decision tables may all be used at different times during the design process.

16. The Gantt chart identifies major areas of work to be done before the system is installed. Each area is represented by a horizontal bar that shows the amount of time required to complete the task.

17. A major part of designing a system involves the outputs that the system is to produce. Outputs can be in the form of reports, screen displays, files, or data bases.

18. Data to be entered into a computer must be defined as input. Input design depends on the source of the data and the type of device used for input.

19. The computer-based components of the system now require detailed development, programming, and testing to create functional application programs.

20. After the system has been designed and programs developed, the process of implementing the new system follows. Implementation may involve the areas of user training, file conversion, system conversion, and parallel operation of the old and new systems.

21. The systems life cycle is completed when maintenance begins on the system and changes and additions are made to it.

IMPORTANT TERMS AND CONCEPTS

Business system	Interview	Structured systems
Computer system	Organization chart	analysis
Data flow diagram	Packaged system	System
Decision table	Parallel operation	System analysis
Feasibility study	Program	System conversion
File conversion	development	System design
Gantt chart	Project schedule	System flowchart
Implementation	Questionnaire	Systems analyst
	Software	Systems life cycle
	development	

REVIEW QUESTIONS

Fill-in Questions

1. A(n) _____ system is a set of procedures that are followed to ensure that the business and the people in it perform the necessary functions to meet the company objectives.

2. The information systems _____ cycle is a series of steps that are followed when a system is being developed.
3. The _____ chart identifies the formal reporting structure of management with a company.
4. A procedure for collecting information about the system is called _____ _____ .
5. Project scheduling frequently uses a(n) _____ chart to identify and schedule major work areas of the project.
6. Program coding is part of the program _____ step of the system development life cycle.

Matching Questions

Match each term with the description given below.

a. system   d. data flow diagram
b. feasibility study   e. decision table
c. system analysis   f. conversion

_____ 1. This is the stage where a complete and thorough understanding of the system is developed.
_____ 2. This is a chart that expresses a logical solution to a problem in the form of a table.
_____ 3. This is a chart used to document the flow of data within the company.
_____ 4. This process is necessary when an old system is replaced by a newly designed system.
_____ 5. A set of organized and related procedures used to accomplish a specific task.
_____ 6. Determines whether a system should be developed and if the necessary resources are available.

Discussion Questions

1. Discuss the different considerations when a business must decide whether to purchase or develop a new system.
2. Explain the differences between a business system and other natural systems.
3. What are the six major phases of the information systems life cycle?
4. Discuss the purpose of a feasibility study, explaining the various components of the study.
5. What is the function of the system analysis phase?
6. Describe four methods used for data gathering in the system analysis phase.
7. Discuss the use of data flow diagrams and system flowcharts for charting a system. What role does the decision table play in system analysis?
8. Discuss the importance of input and output design in the system design phase.
9. Define and discuss the five steps of program development.
10. Review the parts of system implementation both before and after the system goes into operation.

Management Support Systems

A VIEW OF THE CHAPTER AHEAD

After Reading This Chapter You Will Understand:

- The purpose of management information systems.

- The need for decision support systems and how they are used for business decision making.

- How a spreadsheet can be an effective tool for developing a decision support system.

- The concept of expert systems and how they can be used in a variety of business applications.

S everal categories of systems are used by today's businesses to assist in the daily operation of the company and for far-reaching business decisions. In this chapter we will look at the most common system—the management information system. Next comes the decision support system and lastly a relative newcomer to the scene—the expert system.

MANAGEMENT INFORMATION SYSTEMS

Managers of business operations require information about the operation of the business to assist in the day-to-day transaction of business. Usually this information is supplied through a management information system that collects data and either presents it in the form of reports or makes it available in the form of queries to a data base.

Defining an MIS

While all businesses have methods or procedures for providing information, they may not have a true MIS. A **management information system (MIS)** is a computer information system that is integrated with manual or automated methods of providing information for management decision making. The computer is used for collecting and storing data that is then processed and supplies the data base for management information.

In a fast-food franchise, the computer may collect data on the sales of each item. The data collected may also include the cost of raw materials, salaries, and property. Processing this data can provide information on the profit margin of each product and help management to make decisions on future pricing and promotion of the firm's products. Other far-reaching decisions can be made from the information that may include closing unprofitable stores and opening new ones in areas where business has been exceptional.

MIS and Business Objectives

An MIS, such as the one described for the fast-food chain, needs to function with clearly defined objectives. Clearly, the types of information made available in the MIS are a result of using data collection and computer programs with a specific outcome in mind. A business objective might be to promote a new product. The MIS can produce reports showing how the product is doing, the pattern of sales, and the profits that result from the campaign. As these results are reviewed decisions can be made about the promotion and its results.

Figure 13–1 shows the relationship between the objectives of the corporation, the decisions essential to its implementation, and the information required to carry out the decisions and track its results. None of these components can stand on their own merit. Rather, there is a flow of influence in both directions, because as objectives are defined and decisions made, the information gathered can be used for further decision making and developing new or modified objectives.

Information Reporting

The traditional method for reporting within the MIS is by printed reports. Many systems also provide online information, but reports on paper are still

FIGURE 13–1
Information is used by management to help in making informed decisions. Good decision making contributes to effectiveness in implementing company objectives.

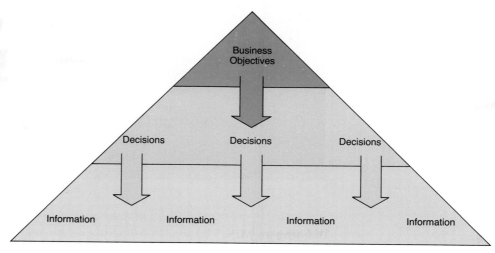

the preferred method because of their ease of use and portability—you can easily take a few pages into the board room. There are generally four types of reports (Figure 13–2) provided by an information system.

1. **Scheduled reports** are provided on a regular basis whether daily, weekly, monthly, or some other interval.

2. **On-demand reports** are provided only upon request. These reports often address a specific need or decision that is not made on a regular basis. With data base query systems, the demand report is becoming an online activity that is done at the keyboard.

3. **Forecasting reports** are used to make future projections. These reports play an important role in the decision-making process and help management to plan strategy for setting company objectives. Often models are used and "what if" questions asked in what is called a decision support system.

4. **Exception reports** are created to identify abnormal situations such as low or out-of-stock inventory or customers who are behind in their payments. This information can be useful for planning corrective action and getting the system back on track.

Data for these reports come from the data base, which is an integral part of the MIS. Data bases for all areas of the company from accounting to engineer-

FIGURE 13–2
Four types of reports used in a management information system. Reports can be hard copy, as shown here, or they may be displayed on the computer's screen. Hard copy reports can get out of date rather quickly while displayed reports make use of current data from the system's data base (DBMS).

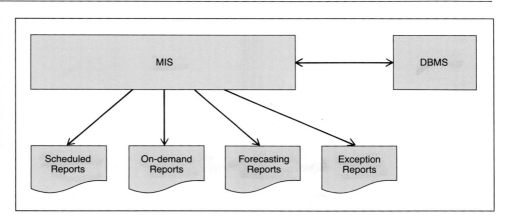

Reading and acting on reports are an essential part of a manager's job.

Courtesy of Gregg Mancuso/Stock Boston.

ing and finance to production may all be needed to generate the necessary information for good decision making by management. Thus a well-designed system is required—one that has been developed with careful and detailed planning with appropriate information links between each component of the system. Rarely does this occur without the techniques of systems design, which was discussed in the previous chapter.

The Organization of MIS

If a well-designed system is important to the functioning of the company, then the organization of MIS is also crucial. In small companies the MIS may be only a few people, such as the president and accountant, while in large organizations, many individuals will be involved in decision making. Information systems in most large corporations come in two parts: MIS as seen in the corporate structure and the information systems department, which services the MIS.

Corporate structure

This is the group of managers who use information from the MIS and define its function. Figure 13–3 shows a typical corporate structure. Each of these positions in the company reports directly to the president and form the corporate structure. The controller is the chief accounting officer who manages the firm's accounts payable and receivable and payroll. This office

FIGURE 13–3
The structure of management in a corporation. While all divisions require the services of information systems, it is also a separate division that reports to the company president or frequently to a vice president.

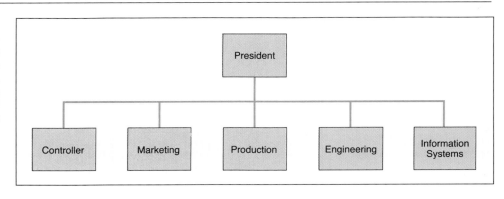

is the source of the financial records that report on the well-being of the company.

Marketing manages the sales force and the promotion of the company's products or services. Production deals with the acquisition of materials and the manufacturing of a product, while engineering develops new or improved products. Each of these parts of the organization depends on MIS for their own operation and effective communication between each area of the company.

Information systems department

In Chapter 1 we saw the need for an information systems department in a large organization. When a large mainframe computer is used in the MIS, a central body of professionals is required to design, implement, and operate the system. In organizations where personal computers are used, a central authority may also be required to ensure that standards are defined and followed. In many companies today, both the mainframe and personal computer are important to the functioning of the MIS.

Figure 13–4 shows an organizational structure of the information systems department. These are the people who design systems, write programs, interact with the users, operate the mainframe computer, and manage the data base. Just as managers require specialized education for their position so do the information systems personnel.

A successful MIS requires the cooperation of the management identified in the organizational structure and the personnel in the information systems department. These two groups make many of the decisions about the information and reports supplied by the system. Operational employees such as accountants, clerks, engineers, salespeople, and others provide the data for the MIS that is used by management for their planning and decision making.

While most companies have a management information system of some form, only some are moving into a new level of system. This new development in business planning by using advanced computer software is called a decision support system, which is our next topic.

FIGURE 13–4

The organizational structure of an MIS department. Large organizations will have more levels than this, while a small company may only have a few positions. The MIS structure was a product of the influence of the large mainframe system on the operation of the company. As personal computers and interactive terminals came into widespread use in the organization, a new position, the information center, arose to provide technical support to these users.

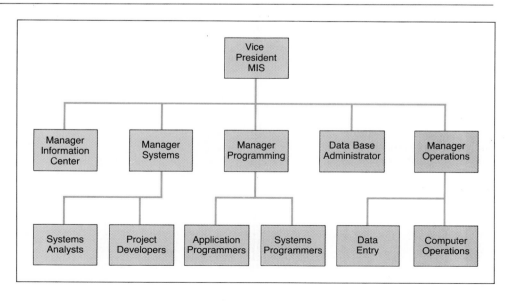

DECISION SUPPORT SYSTEMS

A **decision support system (DSS)** may be thought of as going beyond the MIS to provide information for decisions about the future. Decisions that affect the future of the company such as what products to promote, how to meet the competition, or how to respond to government regulations must be considered. Making such decisions are much more difficult and challenging than are the routine operational decisions made daily by management. These choices often require a different level of information than that provided from the MIS.

Decision support systems should provide more than just the operational data and thus require access to more or different information than an MIS. Historically, this separation between MIS and DSS was valid, but today there is a distinct blending of the two in the practical operation of the business establishment. Although there is a tendency for the systems to overlap, there is a class of software that is presented as decision support software. Some of this software is specialized for DSS, a limited number of programs use expert system techniques, while others simply make use of general-purpose software such as a spreadsheet.

Models

One of the early approaches to decision support systems was the use of a model. A model could mathematically represent a real-life system by using a computer program. When models were first used in business, the manager would supply the data to a computer programmer who would then write a program or modify an existing one to simulate the activity.

Programs used input values called **independent variables** because they could be changed as necessary. These values would be represented by data such as the current sales dollars for a product or the expected growth of sales represented as a percentage. The output data from the model are called **dependent variables** because they depend on the values entered. Dependent data could be the dollar sales projected for next year because it would depend on the current sales and expected growth for the year.

One of the problems with early modeling applications was the time required to get the data back to the manager. By the time the request was submitted for programming, the programming done, and changes made to test the model,

FIGURE 13–5

A spreadsheet is a useful tool for developing models in a decision support system. By entering growth rates for each product, the model projects the sales for the product over a period of five years.

	A	B	C	D	E	F	G	H
1				5 Year Sales Projection				
2								
3	Product	Growth	Current	Year	Year	Year	Year	Year
4		Rate	Year	1	2	3	4	5
5								
6	AH123	8.0%	200,000	216,000	233,280	251,942	272,098	293,866
7	AH145	15.5%	150,000	162,000	174,960	188,957	204,073	220,399
8	AH200	12.0%	100,000	108,000	116,640	125,971	136,049	146,933
9	AK121	15.0%	125,000	135,000	145,800	157,464	170,061	183,666
10	AZ400	5.5%	750,000	810,000	874,800	944,784	1,020,367	1,101,996
11	BG455	18.0%	20,000	21,600	23,328	25,194	27,210	29,387
12	CJ500	30.0%	58,000	62,640	67,651	73,063	78,908	85,221
13								
14								
15								
16								

the results were frequently too late to do much good in the planning process. But with personal computers, this has all changed; now the manager can develop the model in a short time using a software package such as a spreadsheet.

Figure 13–5 shows a spreadsheet that presents a simplified model of a sales projection. With such a model the manager can quickly try different growth rates for each product and observe the results immediately on the screen. Instead of waiting weeks or months for the results, only a few minutes of time is needed for the decision support information to be provided.

"What If" Questions

Spreadsheets are particularly good for asking "what if" questions of the data. In the sales projection spreadsheet the question is asked "what if we can get an 8 percent growth in the sales of product AH123?" to which the answer is that in five years, sales will have reached almost $300,000.

When questions like this one are asked on the PC, the results are returned quickly so that effective management decisions can be made. The personal software used for decision support systems will also permit trying many values in quick succession. Thus the planner manager can quickly suggest a variety of growth scenarios and immediately observe the results.

Using such software is an aid to effective management, but the user must still have management and planning skills that the software cannot replace. It might look good on the computer to suggest that product AZ400 should have a growth rate of 30 percent per year, but the corporate reality might be that it is an aging product with a limited life span. Thus the growth rate of 5.5 percent might be more realistic and obtainable.

Figure 13–6 shows a breakeven analysis where the profit margin is found

FIGURE 13–6

This breakeven analysis spreadsheet is a tool used by financial planners to determine what sales are needed to break even if a given gross margin is used.

Source: Adapted from William R. Osgood and Dennis P. Curtin, "Preparing Your Business Plan with Lotus 1–2–3" (Englewood Cliffs, N.J.: Prentice Hall, 1984).

```
                        Breakeven Analysis

Fixed Expenses ..........................................  $200,000
Gross Margin Percent ....................................       40%
---------------------------------------------------------------------
Breakeven Point:                                          $500,000
=====================================================================
    Net        Fixed      Variable     Total     Profit or    Profit
   Sales      Expenses    Expenses    Expenses    (Loss)      Margin
---------------------------------------------------------------------
        $0    $200,000          $0    $200,000   (200,000)       NA
   $50,000    $200,000     $30,000    $230,000   (180,000)     -360%
  $100,000    $200,000     $60,000    $260,000   (160,000)     -160%
  $150,000    $200,000     $90,000    $290,000   (140,000)      -93%
  $200,000    $200,000    $120,000    $320,000   (120,000)      -60%
  $250,000    $200,000    $150,000    $350,000   (100,000)      -40%
  $300,000    $200,000    $180,000    $380,000    (80,000)      -27%
  $350,000    $200,000    $210,000    $410,000    (60,000)      -17%
  $400,000    $200,000    $240,000    $440,000    (40,000)      -10%
  $450,000    $200,000    $270,000    $470,000    (20,000)       -4%
  $500,000    $200,000    $300,000    $500,000          0        0%
  $550,000    $200,000    $330,000    $530,000     20,000        4%
  $600,000    $200,000    $360,000    $560,000     40,000        7%
  $650,000    $200,000    $390,000    $590,000     60,000        9%
  $700,000    $200,000    $420,000    $620,000     80,000       11%
  $750,000    $200,000    $450,000    $650,000    100,000       13%
```

FIGURE 13–7
Using goal seeking in an investment spreadsheet with a split window so that investment values at the top and current values on the bottom line may be seen together. As the user enters trial values for the annual amount, the goal cell will change in value until the amount needed to reach an investment goal of $1 million after 30 years is displayed.

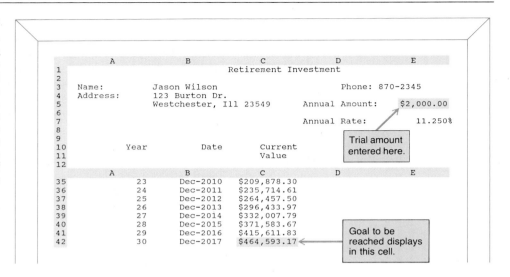

for a gross margin of 40 percent and fixed expenses of $200,000. Different values for expenses and margin can be used to analyze the effect these amounts have on the profit margin for the product.

Goal Seeking

Goal seeking is the opposite of the "what if" question. A "what if" question uses a spreadsheet to ask what happens "if" a specific value is entered on the spreadsheet. This is what happened on the breakeven spreadsheet where the question is asked "What if a profit margin of 40 percent is used?" and the result is shown as a breakeven point.

Instead of asking the question of what happens if a given value is used, the goal seeker asks what it will take to reach a specific value or goal. This goal may be a complex one such as what changes need to be made in tax preparation to reduce the tax payable to a given amount. Changes to entries such as charitable contributions, investments, claim of deductible capital losses, and so on may all be part of the goal-seeking process.

Figure 13–7 shows an example of goal seeking in a financial planning spreadsheet for retirement investment. Assuming that the investor has a goal of reaching $1 million in 30 years, this bottom line in the spreadsheet may be found by trying various annual amounts. Alternatively, the goal-seeking process may take place by establishing a given annual amount but trying different interest rates until the goal of $1 million is reached.

EXPERT SYSTEMS

Introduction

Expert systems are the leading edge of artificial intelligence (AI) tools that have been developed in the computer science labs in recent years. An **expert system** is a computer system that is developed with a series of rules based on the advice of human experts. The program advises or takes action based on the knowledge it has of human behavior in a similar situation.

An expert system is different from other programs that follow a strict set of rules or instructions. Instead, an expert system learns a set of rules and from them infers answers that may not be directly stated by the rules. As an expert system is used, it may pick up new knowledge about the application from the people that are using the system. However, expert systems emphasize the solution to structured problems as opposed to problems that require inventive or creative solutions. Problems that are well defined with clearly defined solutions are a good prospect for an expert system.

A **knowledge-based system** is a system that uses a collection of facts to assist in the making of decisions. Often the terms knowledge based and expert systems are used interchangeably. Expert systems, then, are knowledge-based systems because they have the knowledge of an expert built into them. For example, an expert system on financial planning is developed with the aid of an expert financial planner. The rules that are coded into the program are based on the knowledge that the expert planner has and how they are used for financial planning. For this reason the term knowledge-based system is often used to mean expert system.

Once the expert system has been given all the rules for financial planning, it can simulate the actions of the human financial planner. Instead of going to a professional financial planner, which may be in short supply, you could do your own financial planning by using the program. The program would ask a number of questions about your objectives and financial status. Then based on the rules, it can advise you on handling your finances to meet your goals, much like the expert could do.

Expert System Applications

Many different expert systems have been developed in recent years. Systems in financial planning (Applied Expert Systems), sales (Sales Edge), insurance risk analysis (Syntelligence), locomotive diagnosis (General Electric), and medical diagnosis are a few of the systems already available. Revenue from expert system software was $35 million in 1986. This is expected to grow to $900 million by the year 1991 (Figure 13–8) according to AIM Publications (Natick, Mass.), which publishes the *Artificial Intelligence Markets* newsletter.

Business

Although business is one of the biggest users of computers, it has been slow getting on the road to expert systems. But since the early 1980s, more applications for business have been developed using knowledge-based systems. These applications range from financial planning to credit card charge analysis from direct mail to data base queries. Most systems are currently mainframe based, but, with software becoming available on the personal computer, more expert systems will be developed for a broad range of applications.

One such expert system was developed for American Express,[1] a leader in the credit card business (Figure 13–9). The American Express card is popular with businesspeople not only because of its recognized status but also due to its no preset spending limit.

---

[1] Dwight B. Davis, "Artificial Intelligence Goes to Work," *High Technology*, April 1987, pp. 17–18.

FIGURE 13–8

Expected growth in revenues from expert system applications to 1991.

Source: *High Technology*, April 1987, p. 26.

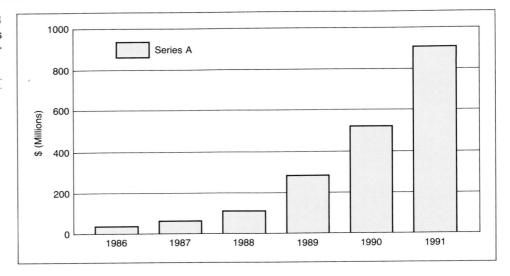

But this policy, contrasted with a bank whose preset limit made analysis easy, created administrative headaches when determining when charges get too high. American Express uses a sophisticated network of authorizers who access up to 13 different databases when making authorization decisions. To help reduce this complexity, an expert system, with about 800 rules, was devised to look for charge and spending patterns of card holders.

When a merchant phones American Express to have a purchase approved, the expert system, developed by Inference in Los Angeles, looks for unusual spending patterns. If such a pattern is detected the authorizer gives the merchant and the customer a wait signal. Then further searches can be done to see if the customer is the true card holder and if the charge is likely to be paid.

Basically, the expert system implements the rules that an authorizer would use but in less time and with greater accuracy. Using such a system for credit card spending approval increases American Express's ability to reduce fraud and unpaid charges. The productivity of the authorizers has also been increased by 20 to 30 percent.

FIGURE 13–9

Using an expert system at American Express helps to detect credit charges that fall outside predicted spending patterns.

Courtesy of Bill Ballenberg.

Another type of expert system developed for business is the Business Strategy Software series of programs published by Human Edge Software. One of these programs, the Sales Edge, is used by budding salespeople who need an edge in meeting with a prospect.

The session on the computer begins with a series of about 100 questions about the user. Questions like "Job disappointments don't bother me for long," and "People usually have hidden motives when they negotiate," are asked. Then a second series of questions are asked about the sales prospect.

When all the questions have been answered, the program generates a series of long and detailed reports on how to close the sales with this person or company. Also included with the software is a manual that is to be used to help interpret the report.

The problem with this type of software is that there are many assumptions made about the person filling in the form and about the way sales negotiations are conducted. Although an inexperienced salesperson might get some useful help from the program, some costly or embarrassing errors could also be made.

The danger with the current status of expert systems in areas that are not well defined is that it can persuade you it has expertise that it doesn't. In areas such as medicine, however, there are diagnostic skills that can be well defined and built into an expert system.

Health-related professions

Expert systems are a branch of artificial intelligence research that began in the mid-1960s. One of the early pioneers was Edward Feigenbaum of Stanford University who began work on computerizing the thought processes of scientists. One of his projects was automating medical diagnosis. This research was done in collaboration with Edward Shortliffe, a physician. The result was a program they called Mycin that was able to diagnose a narrow class of diseases.

Mycin was a landmark system in several ways. It was the first expert system to use the rule-based inference method that is commonplace in today's expert systems. And it was the first such system that could explain how it arrived at a given conclusion. Although it operated on a narrow class of medicine, its diagnosis was almost as good as a physician's in the same discipline.

The program works by interviewing the patient's physician. By displaying questions on the screen to which the physician responds, a profile of the problem is created. First, basic facts such as the patient's name, age, and sex

Expert systems are particularly useful for fields such as medicine where complex decisions are often made. Because there are no fixed equations for diagnosing a patient's disease, expert systems work well at capturing some of the complex process of human reasoning and arriving at a solution.

Courtesy of Pete Saloutos/The Stock Market.

are entered, followed by more detailed questions about the disease. When all the data has been supplied, Mycin produces a ranked list of possible diagnoses.

To make a diagnosis, Mycin has a knowledge base of about 500 rules that describe what medical experts know about diagnosing disease. The rules are expressed as a series of statements in the form of "IF some condition or conditions are true; THEN some conclusion is likely." Each rule has a value from 0 to 1 attached to it to signify its certainty because not all rules are absolute.

Next, Mycin uses an inference engine (a computer program) that can interpret the rules in a meaningful way. Inference is an important component of expert systems that provides the reasoning ability that is used to derive a conclusion from the analysis of many different rules.

Although most doctors do not yet use expert systems for their diagnosis, the development of such systems as Mycin is an important step forward. Many physicians may hesitate to use such a system in their office, and yet this type of application may be a significant development for the Third World and other nations where there are too few physicians for the populations they are attempting to serve.

Financial planning

Financial planning is something that everyone should do but few people are willing to pay for a professional financial planner's services. Expert systems make financial planning a good candidate for computerization. An expert system can learn a set of rules that a financial planner would follow and from these infer a plan that a nonexpert can follow. Some systems, such as PlanPower from Applied Expert Systems, are beginning to be used by accounting and legal firms. Most home systems have not yet used expert system techniques.

A financial planning expert system begins by asking you questions in plain English about a wide range of financial matters. The program then analyzes the input based on rules that have been designed into the system. The system can produce a report, including charts and graphs, in about a quarter of the time required for a human planner.

PlanPower's knowledge base includes some fundamentals such as interest rates and inflation rates. It also knows the tax laws and standard investment strategies that an experienced financial planner would use. After creating the financial plan, the program can also explain why it made the choices it did. This can be an immense aid to the planner so that the reasons for certain investment strategies used by the expert system are known.

Because of the relatively high cost, $45,000 for PlanPower including the computer, software for financial planning is primarily used by professionals. Software for home use is often good software, but is not knowledge based and cannot be expected to draw inferences that the more costly systems can deliver. As further developments occur in this field, we will likely be seeing expert systems that are affordable for the average consumer.

Knowledge Engineering

The practice of building an expert system is called **knowledge engineering.** When an organization seeks to develop an expert system for medical diagnosis or financial planning, there are a number of professionals that must be involved in the process. One of these is the knowledge engineer who is familiar with the construction of expert systems.

A VARIETY OF EXPERT SYSTEMS	Expert System	Application
	AUDITOR	An accounting system used to model the judgment of an auditor when analyzing a firm's allowance for bad debts.
	PRICE	A knowledge-based simulation of management decision making used by business students to understand the maximizing of profit in a firm.
	ZOG	A knowledge-based AI system used by the U.S. Air Force for price analysis and procurement.
	GARI	An expert system that plans a series of processing steps for the machining of mechanical parts.
	ISIS	A knowledge-based system that considers shop constraints when creating job schedules.
	INNOVATOR	An expert system–based framework that uses analogies to draw inferences. One use is by NASA to emulate an inventor/engineer.

A knowledge engineer is a computer scientist or programmer who has specialized in the field of expert or knowledge-based systems. Because this is a young field there are few experts who are educated in this discipline.

In addition to the knowledge engineer, a professional from the task that is being developed into an expert system is needed. If the system is for medicine, then a skilled physician would be used; for financial planning, an expert financial planner. It is important when developing an expert system to use an expert from that field because the system is only as good as the person who supplies it with the knowledge base.

When Is an Expert System Useful?

An expert system may seem to be like an employee that is brilliant on the job, is always on time, and never gets tired or bored. But does this make any job a candidate for an expert system? The answer is a clear no as we will see. There are a few basic requirements for an expert system candidate.

1. The rules or procedures of the system must be clearly definable.
2. The system must normally require a trained expert or professional to function.
3. If there is a shortage of skilled people, then the system is a good candidate.

To be a good prospect for an expert system, an application must first be definable. Medicine is a good case for an expert system because much of diagnosis requires collecting the symptoms and comparing them to a pattern of disease. This is not as simple as it sounds because physicians rely on the accumulation of thousands of past cases and, by applying a few general principles, are able to abstract a diagnosis.

That brings us to a second consideration for a candidate for an expert system. Is the system complex enough to require a trained expert to solve problems? A task that may only require a few days or weeks of training is hardly a candidate for an expert system. But one that takes years of training and more years of experience would justify the time and expense of developing the knowledge base. Thus medicine is one of many fields that presents an excellent opportunity for the development of expert systems.

THE TURING TEST

Suppose you sat down at your computer and it began to converse with you. As you type a statement on the keyboard, it either answered your request or responded more or less intelligently to it. If your computer was linked to other computers on a network, how could you be sure that it was the computer talking to you (actually the software) or just someone else at another computer that you were communicating with?

In 1950 a British mathematician, Alan Turing, proposed a method to determine whether a computer possesses intelligence. This method came to be known as the Turing test and was similar to the scenario just presented. Turing's idea was to have a panel of judges who would pose questions on teletype machines that would be either attached to a computer or to another human on a similar teletype. If the panel could not tell which machine was attached to a computer and which to a human, then the computer could be considered to possess intelligence.

Today computers can do humanlike activities such as play chess, give expert advice, write poetry, or compose music, and in some of these activities, it is difficult to tell the human result from the computer's. Turing, who died in 1954, never lived to see his dream of a computer that could pass for human come true.

A shortage of skilled professionals may also be a strong indicator that an expert system is a potential solution. When there is a shortage, workers with less training can often function well until a complex problem occurs that would normally require a specialist. That is where the expert system can step in. Instead of going to the specialist, who is in short supply and may not be easily available, the expert system provides the same level of support.

Developing an Expert System

Expert systems are developed by knowledge engineers by building a knowledge base while working with an acknowledged expert in the field. Questions are asked of the professional who provides the answers and explanations until a knowledge base is built based on a set of rules. These rules will be used to analyze questions that are presented to the system. When the expert system is used, the solution to a problem is a goal that is found by analyzing the rules that were originally entered during system development.

One such system was developed because there was a shortage of skilled people. When Aldo Cimino at Campbell's Soup Company in Camden, New Jersey, was nearing retirement, he was considered to be irreplaceable.[2] Mr. Cimino was the resident expert on "cookers," and no one had his talent for troubleshooting them. Because Campbell's had more than 90 of these cookers around the world, Cimino's expertise was critical to the continued success of the company.

Working along with Michael Smith of Texas Instruments, Cimino began to transfer his knowledge to an expert system. The system was eventually completed and contained more than 150 rules in the knowledge base. The

---

[2] *Personal Computing*, November, 1985.

An expert system is used at Campbell's Soup to assist in the maintenance of soup cookers. The knowledge of a human expert is built into the computer software which can then be used at plants around the world.

Photos courtesy of Campbell Soup Company.

system went into operation in eight plants in the United States, Canada, and Britain. When a problem arises that the technicians or maintenance managers can't solve, they use the expert system, at least for 95 percent of the problems. It seems that a computer can't entirely replace Aldo Cimino.

Expert system architecture

Expert systems are built with a knowledge base containing rules or facts about a specific application. This knowledge base is attached to a program called an inference engine (Figure 13–10). An **inference engine** applies the rules of the knowledge base to the queries entered by the user and attempts to infer a conclusion.

The inference engine begins its task when the user consults with the expert system. First, there is a **natural language interface** that lets the user consult with the expert system and engage in a question and answer period. The user may also question the expert system on the reasoning for a given conclusion. The inference engine processes this activity by using a process called goal seeking, which is the specific value or answer it is looking for to solve the problem.

FIGURE 13–10
Expert system architecture consists of the knowledge engineer who defines the rules for the knowledge base. The user communicates with the system through a natural language interface. Input is analyzed by the inference engine based on the rules in the knowledge base and data in working memory. Working memory is used to analyze entries and to store the results of new knowledge.

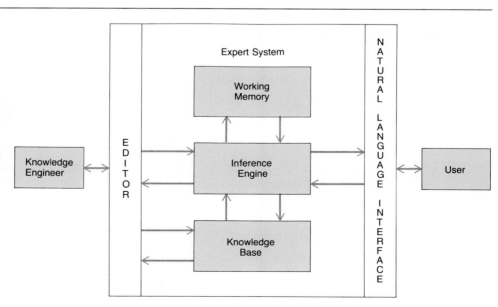

SOFTWARE FOR POWER USERS

Hypercard.

Courtesy of Apple Computer, Inc.

A high resolution graphics display is a product of both hardware and software. Hypercard is an add-on to the Apple Macintosh that provides far greater resolution on a computer that already has excellent graphics capability. This screen shows the detailed graphics capability created by this add-on.

Paradox data base management system.

Courtesy of Symantec.

Paradox is one of the leading data base management systems developed for use on personal computers. In this application, an employee data base query is being made on a local area network. The current screen, as indicated, is read only because another user on the network is currently editing the record.

Memory resident desktop manager.

Courtesy of Borland International.

SideKick Plus is a widely used memory resident desktop manager. When activated, SideKick uses windows that display over other work currently in progress on the screen. Here a calendar and an appointment book have been made active.

Additional SideKick Plus features.

Courtesy of Borland International.

SideKick Plus also provides notepads, file management, a calculator, and a communications window. Here, three notepads have been invoked together, along with a file management window. SideKick provides up to nine separate notepads.

Q & A data base program.

Courtesy of Symantec.

Q & A is another widely used data base program on personal computer systems. In this application a personnel data base (on the right of the screen) is used to provide information that is used to generate form letters (on the left). When the data is combined the resulting form letter is printed.

(Continued)

Lotus Agenda is a relatively new concept in computer software. Agenda is an information and idea manager that can help a manager to organize information and tasks relating to a project. Here, priorities are being assigned to a list of tasks.

Lotus Agenda.

Courtesy of Lotus.

Lotus Agenda organizes the activities relating to a specific project. After the priorities have been assigned by the manager, Agenda reorganizes the tasks according to the priority structure.

Tasks organized by priority.

Courtesy of Lotus.

Rules

A **rule** in an expert system is an IF-THEN relationship of the form

> IF   condition
>
> THEN action

A condition may be an expression such as

> Money to invest > $1000

An action might be

> Purchase Money Market Fund

The complete expression would be written as

> IF   Money to invest > $1000
>
> THEN Purchase Money Market Fund

A sequence of rules may be connected to form a list as shown in Figure 13–11. If the first query is true, then the next is considered and so on. This process continues until a solution for investment is found for the amount that the investor has available. In a complete system more complex rules would be used to consider how the user prefers to invest. Some prefer more security in their investment, while others prefer to take greater risks with a chance of receiving greater returns.

FIGURE 13–11
A rule tree of IF-THEN relationships in an expert system.

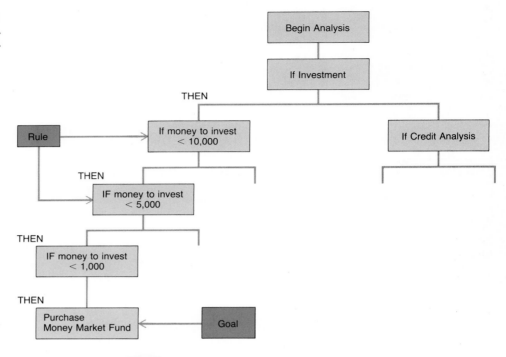

FIGURE 13–11
A rule tree of IF-THEN relationships in an expert system.

Languages for Expert Systems

Programming an inference engine requires specialized computer languages. One such language is LISP (LISt Processing), which was developed by John McCarthy at the Massachusetts Institute of Technology in 1958. LISP is used for programming applications that do list processing, which is a fundamental part of artificial intelligence (AI). Some of today's expert systems also use LISP to formulate the rules in the inference engine and for coding the knowledge base. Some computers have been especially designed to work effectively with LISP.

Another language used for artificial intelligence and expert systems is PRO-LOG (PROgramming LOGic). It was developed by Alan Colmerauer at the University of Marseilles in 1972. PROLOG is a logic-based programming language that has seen widespread use in Japan for the development of artificial intelligence projects. In the 1980s PROLOG is fast replacing LISP as the language of choice for AI applications.

Because developing an expert system from the ground up is a difficult and time-consuming task, many organizations adopt an expert system shell. An **expert shell** provides the supporting software for developing an expert system. Using a shell, the knowledge engineer only needs to concern himself or herself with the application and the user expert. No knowledge of programming is required. The availability of expert shells is an important step forward in the growth and development of expert systems.

*CHAPTER
SUMMARY*

1. A decision support system (DSS) may be thought of as going beyond MIS to provide information for decisions about the future.

2. One of the early approaches to decision support systems was the use of a model.

A model could mathematically represent a real-life system by using a computer program.

3. Programs used input values called independent variables because they could be changed as necessary. The output data from the model are called dependent variables because they depend on the values entered.

4. "What if" questions are asked of the decision support system. The benefit of the personal computer for DSS is that the results are returned quickly so that effective management decisions can be made.

5. Goal seeking is the opposite of the "what if" question. Instead of asking the question "what happens if a given value is used," the goal seeker asks what it will take to reach a specific value or goal.

6. An expert system is a computer system that is developed with a series of rules based on the advice of human experts. The program advises or takes action based on the knowledge it has of human behavior in a similar situation.

7. A knowledge-based system is a system that uses a collection of facts to assist in the making of decisions.

8. Since the early 1980s applications for business have been developed using knowledge-based systems. These applications range from financial planning to credit card charge analysis and from direct mail to data base queries.

9. The practice of building an expert system is called knowledge engineering. A knowledge engineer is a computer scientist or programmer who has specialized in the field of expert or knowledge-based systems.

10. To be a candidate for an expert system, the rules of the system must be clearly definable. The system must normally require a trained expert or professional to function, and a shortage of skilled people is an advantage.

11. An expert system contains a knowledge base that is attached to a program called an inference engine. The inference engine applies the rules of the knowledge base to the queries entered by the user and attempts to infer a conclusion.

12. The system uses a natural language interface that lets the user consult with the expert system and engage in a question and answer period. The inference engine processes this activity by using a process called goal seeking, which is the specific value or answer it is looking for to solve the problem.

13. A rule in an expert system is an IF-THEN relationship.

14. Two widely used programming languages for developing expert systems are LISP and PROLOG. Frequently, they use an expert shell that provides the supporting software for developing an expert system.

IMPORTANT TERMS AND CONCEPTS		
Decision support system (DSS)	Inference engine	Model
Dependent variables	Knowledge base	Natural language interface
Expert shell	Knowledge-based system	PROLOG
Expert system	Knowledge engineering	Rule
Goal seeking	LISP	"What if" question
Independent variables	Management information system (MIS)	

Fill-in Questions

1. The _____ can produce reports showing how a product is doing, the pattern of sales, and the profits resulting from a sales campaign.

2. _____ reports are provided on a regular basis such as daily, weekly, or monthly.

3. _____ _____ systems should provide more than just operational data such as provided by the MIS.

4. A(n) _____ is used to represent mathematically a real-life system by using a computer program.

5. A(n) _____ system is a computer system that is developed with a series of rules based on the advice of human experts.

6. The practice of building an expert system is called _____ engineering.

Matching Questions

Match each term with the description given below.
a. MIS
b. Decision support system
c. exception report
d. expert system
e. goal seeking
f. rule

_____ 1. This document is produced only when abnormal situations occur.

_____ 2. This represents an IF-THEN relationship in an expert system.

_____ 3. This is the opposite of "what if" questions and looks for a specific value.

_____ 4. A manual or automated system for providing management with required information for making business decisions.

_____ 5. A system that is developed with a series of rules based on the advice of human experts.

_____ 6. This system goes beyond MIS to provide information to support decisions about the future.

Discussion Questions

1. What is a management information system? What role does the computer play in an MIS?

2. Describe the four types of reports that are typically used in MIS.

3. Discuss the organization of management in a corporation and the specific structure of the MIS department.

4. Discuss the concept of a decision support system. What role do models play in a DSS?

5. Explain how "what if" questions can be used for decision making in a decision support system.

6. What is the difference between "what if" questions and goal seeking? How is goal seeking used in a DSS?

7. Discuss the meaning of expert system and explain why it is sometimes known as a knowledge-based system.

8. Discuss the purpose of rules in an expert system.

9. Explain the role of knowledge engineering in building an expert system.

10. What are the basic requirements for an expert system candidate?

11. Discuss the importance of an inference engine in an expert system. How is the natural language interface used in this system?

12. Discuss the need for programming languages to develop expert systems.

14

From Fears
to Careers

A VIEW OF THE CHAPTER AHEAD

After Reading This Chapter You Will Understand:

■ The types of fears and fantasies associated with computers.

■ Some methods used to thwart software piracy.

■ The types of computer crime and some of the methods used to
ensure computer security.

■ The various career opportunities available in the computer profession.

The computer has spawned a wide range of uses over its short life span. In this book we have examined many of these but have not considered its social impact. For some, the computer represents an object to be feared. For others, it becomes a tool for crime. But for many people the computer offers an exciting and rewarding career.

FEARS AND FANTASIES

When a machine as powerful and productive as the computer comes onto the human scene, there are likely to be certain fears associated with it as well as fantasies about its potential. To get these two extremes into balance, it's best to remember that the computer is just an electronic device, although a complex one. Because at times it may seem to exhibit some humanlike qualities, such as the ability to do mathematics much better, or at least much faster, than people do, the computer is often considered far more capable than it really is. This perception causes many potential computer users to approach the computer with an excessively high level of anxiety.

William James, a turn-of-the-century psychologist, was to have said that "the best way to get rid of your fears is to face them." While this may seem to be simplistic advice to us today, it does seem to help when encountering computer phobia. Those people who have a fear of using the computer usually find that after the first few sessions at the keyboard their fear has disappeared. There is virtually nothing that a computer user can do to hurt or damage the computer, and so the only real problem is that of making a few mistakes. Fortunately, today's computers are designed to handle our errors and thus as users there is little to fear from initial fumbling as we learn to make use of the computer.

Computer Errors

While users do not need to fear the occasional mistake when using the computer, programmers must be more concerned about their role. These professionals have a greater responsibility because every instruction that a computer follows must be supplied in the form of a program. Programs are written by computer programmers, and the program code requires exacting detail. Because of the level of detail required in a program, it is quite possible for the programmer to introduce errors in the program writing stage. Some of these **program errors** are obvious and are corrected immediately, while others may remain hidden for months or years before they surface, maybe in the form of a telephone bill for $100,000 or a paycheck for $1,000,000.

While these types of programming errors are rare, they do receive the most notice and often seem to suggest that computers are error prone. When an error does occurs on the computer, it is most frequently due to human error as a result of either writing the program or entering data incorrectly.

By contrast, the computer itself has many error-checking circuits built into it so that computer-generated errors are quite rare. These **hardware errors** are totally different from programming errors. Usually they result from component failure but may sometimes be the result of a design problem with the circuitry. Hardware errors are very unusual and are normally self-correcting. In fact, many computers today will operate for several years before a hardware failure occurs.

Computers also depend on the data they are supplied with if the results produced are to be useful to the user. If inadequate or inaccurate data is supplied to the computer, then the information the computer generates will either be in error or at least misleading. Thus the term **garbage in, garbage out (GIGO)** is used, which clearly explains the effect of using incorrect data.

Unemployment

Unemployment is another fear associated with computer use. When computers were first used by business and industry, a significant concern was that the computer would put people out of work. Indeed in some cases this did happen. But with the computer also came many new job opportunities: programmers, systems analysts, computer operators, computer maintenance technicians, manufacturing, and sales were only some of the many new jobs that were created as a result of the computer. So the computer did result in a shift of employment. Significantly, the shift was often from the more menial and unfulfilling jobs to many jobs that represented excitement and challenge while the computer itself took on the drudgery.

Computers and the Solution to Your Problems

"Get a computer in your business and all your problems will be solved." That seemed to be the credo at one time and certainly represents a common fantasy, but the more realistic business person is aware that a computer can only do what is is told. And, unlike a human, it is not very good at making its own judgments. As a result, implementing a new computer will often create some problems of its own, which will take time and effort to correct.

Installing a computer will require training of the users, and some time will be needed to get experience with the system before the computer can be used to its utmost potential. Most companies find that there is a learning curve required of their personnel when a computer is originally installed. At first, the new system may even operate a bit more slowly than the one that it replaced, but as experience with the system is acquired, the full benefits of the change will begin to take effect.

You Need to Be Good at Math or Be a Programmer to Use a Computer

This mistaken belief has led more than one person to abandon their quest for using a computer in their work. Contrary to popular notion, to use a computer successfully does not require a high level of mathematics. The average businessperson who understands the basic concepts of arithmetic needed to function effectively in business can also use a computer successfully.

Most computer users do not have or require programming skills and probably never will. While the computer professional certainly needs to be trained in programming, the business user of the computer needs no programming ability or training to use the computer effectively. However, training in the use of some computer software is usually needed to use the computer successfully. Ordinarily this training is of short duration, lasting only a few days, and does not normally include mathematics or programming. The tutorials that accompany this book provide some basic training in popular hardware and software use.

**SOFTWARE PIRATE
GETS 5 MONTHS**

Randy Trent (not his real name), the owner of R/T Software, has been sentenced to five months in jail for the unauthorized copying and selling of copyrighted software.

Trent was convicted on March 26, 1987, on three counts of fraud involving copied software. His company was in the business of copying commercial software for the questionable purpose of customer evaluation. Presumably customers who evaluated the software and found it suitable would then purchase the legitimate package. But many customers simply continued to use the copied software on their system and never purchased a legitimate copy from the software publisher.

Complainants, including IBM, Ashton-Tate (the dBASE IV company), and Lotus, flew in expert witnesses from California and Texas to Toronto where the trial was held. The software industry watched the trial closely for a precedent to be set to help in their fight against software piracy.

SOFTWARE PIRACY

The accompanying box tells a true story of a person who ran a business selling copied software. This story is an example of software piracy at its most obvious. **Software piracy** is the act of illegally copying software. Selling copied software is clearly illegal as the story tells us, but the act can be illegal even if the copy is not for sale.

Copying a program is not automatically an illegal act. For example, many software packages come with instructions to copy the software onto new disks before using the program. This procedure ensures that if something goes wrong with the disks you are using to run the program, it is always possible to go back to the original. However, the same companies will often state that the program can only be used on one computer at a time, thus prohibiting the user from making copies for all his friends.

But what is to stop the person who purchases a program from running off any number of copies? In many cases there is nothing to stop the person other than their own code of ethics. In the case of corporations, making illegal copies can cost the software publisher millions of dollars. Such was the case when Lotus Corporation sued Rixon Corporation for $10 million for making illegal copies of 1–2–3.

COPY PROTECTION

Software publishers are in the business of making money by selling computer software. To protect their rights, some of these companies have produced software on floppy disks that contain a built-in **copy protection** scheme. By copy protecting a disk, it is not easily reproduced on the purchaser's computer.

Software purchasers, on the other hand, want to protect the software they have paid hundreds of dollars for. One common method for protecting your software is to use a DOS COPY or DISKCOPY command to make a second copy or backup copy of the software. Then the original disk is stored in a safe place, while the copy is used on the computer. Software publishers are concerned that customers will not only make a backup copy but also make free copies for their friends thus causing a loss of business.

Lotus Corporation is probably one of the best known developers of copy-protected software. To use Lotus 1–2–3 Release 1A or 2.0 an original systems disk must be used; a copy will not work. If the program is loaded on a hard disk, the system disk is used with a **key disk** that must be inserted in a floppy disk drive when the program is first loaded. To answer customers' concerns about the lack of protection afforded by making their own backup disk, Lotus supplies an extra backup disk as part of the 1–2–3 package.

Although this approach protected Lotus Corporation from users making illegal copies, it caused the ire of many customers who had good reasons for copying the software. After many years of arguments from both sides, Lotus Corporation is beginning to view this situation differently. In 1988 the firm announced that future releases of 1–2–3 will not use the former copy protection schemes.

Other software companies have provided copy-protected software too, but dropped the protection in answer to user complaints. Ashton-Tate, the supplier of dBASE III Plus, originally copy protected the program but in a second edition dropped the copy protection scheme. Other products such as WordStar and WordPerfect have not copy protected their software.

Licensing

When you buy a piece of software it invariably comes with a **license agreement** (Figure 14–1). Often, simply by opening the package containing the diskettes, you agree to the conditions of the license. These conditions may include not making other copies (sometimes one copy is permitted for backup reasons), using the software on only one machine, and not using it on a network. You may also agree to the return of the package to the publisher upon request, although this is rarely, if ever, requested. Of course, the license also includes a warranty that protects the purchaser if something goes wrong with the original disk. It can usually be returned for replacement.

Site Licensing

Licensing becomes a problem in sites where several computers use the same software. Naturally the purchaser would prefer to buy one package and run it on several computers in the company. This practice is illegal according to the license agreement of most software publishers.

There are two legal approaches for solving this problem. One is to buy as many copies as you have computers that will be running it. The other is to buy a **site license** that permits the use of multiple copies of the same software. Site licenses are frequently less costly than buying multiple copies and are of special importance to companies that have many PCs using the same software.

Network Licensing

A **network license** permits a single copy of a program to be used by several stations served by a network. When networks are used, frequently only one

FIGURE 14–1 A software license agreement.

Microsoft License Agreement

(SINGLE-USER PRODUCTS)

This is a legal agreement between you, the end user, and Microsoft Corporation. BY OPENING THIS SEALED DISK PACKAGE, YOU ARE AGREEING TO BE BOUND BY THE TERMS OF THIS AGREEMENT. IF YOU DO NOT AGREE TO THE TERMS OF THIS AGREEMENT, PROMPTLY RETURN THE UNOPENED DISK PACKAGE AND THE ACCOMPANYING ITEMS (including written materials and binders or other containers) TO THE PLACE YOU OBTAINED THEM FOR A FULL REFUND.

MICROSOFT SOFTWARE LICENSE

1. GRANT OF LICENSE. Microsoft grants to you the right to use one copy of the enclosed Microsoft software program (the "SOFTWARE") on a single terminal connected to a single computer (i.e., with a single CPU). You may not network the SOFTWARE or otherwise use it on more than one computer or computer terminal at the same time.

2. COPYRIGHT. The SOFTWARE is owned by Microsoft or its suppliers and is protected by United States copyright laws and international treaty provisions. Therefore, you must treat the SOFTWARE like any other copyrighted material (e.g., a book or musical recording) except that you may either (a) make one copy of the SOFTWARE solely for backup or archival purposes, or (b) transfer the SOFTWARE to a single hard disk provided you keep the original solely for backup or archival purposes. You may not copy the written materials accompanying the software.

3. OTHER RESTRICTIONS. You may not rent or lease the SOFTWARE, but you may transfer the SOFTWARE and accompanying written materials on a permanent basis provided you retain no copies and the recipient agrees to the terms of this Agreement. You may not reverse engineer, decompile, or disassemble the SOFTWARE.

4. DUAL MEDIA SOFTWARE. If the SOFTWARE package contains both 3½″ and 5¼″ disks, then you may use only the disks appropriate for your single-user computer. You may not use the other disks on another computer or loan, rent, lease, or transfer them to another user except as part of the permanent transfer (as provided above) of all SOFTWARE and written materials.

5. LANGUAGE SOFTWARE. If the SOFTWARE is a Microsoft language product, then you have a royalty-free right to reproduce and distribute executable files created using the SOFTWARE. If the language product is a BASIC or COBOL product, then Microsoft grants to you a royalty-free right to reproduce and distribute the runtime modules of the SOFTWARE provided that you: (a) distribute the runtime modules only in conjunction with and as a part of your software product; (b) do not use Microsoft's name, logo, or trademarks to market your software product; (c) include Microsoft's copyright notice for the SOFTWARE on your product label and as part of the sign-on message for your software product; and (d) agree to indemnify, hold harmless, and defend Microsoft from and against any claims or lawsuits, including attorneys' fees, that arise or result from the use or distribution of your software product. The "runtime modules" are those files in the SOFTWARE that are identified in the accompanying written materials as required during execution of your software program. The runtime modules are limited to runtime files, install files, and ISAM and REBUILD files.

LIMITED WARRANTY

LIMITED WARRANTY. Microsoft warrants that (a) the SOFTWARE will perform substantially in accordance with the accompanying written materials for a period of 90 days from the date of receipt; and (b) any hardware accompanying the SOFTWARE will be free from defects in materials and workmanship under normal use and service for a period of one year from the date of receipt. Any implied warranties on the SOFTWARE and hardware are limited to 90 days and one (1) year, respectively. Some states do not allow limitations on duration of an implied warranty, so the above limitation may not apply to you.

CUSTOMER REMEDIES. Microsoft's entire liability and your exclusive remedy shall be, at Microsoft's option, either (a) return of the price paid or (b) repair or replacement of the SOFTWARE or hardware that does not meet Microsoft's Limited Warranty and which is returned to Microsoft with a copy of your receipt. This Limited Warranty is void if failure of the SOFTWARE or hardware has resulted from accident, abuse, or misapplication. Any replacement SOFTWARE will be warranted for the remainder of the original warranty period or 30 days, whichever is longer.

NO OTHER WARRANTIES. MICROSOFT DISCLAIMS ALL OTHER WARRANTIES, EITHER EXPRESS OR IMPLIED, INCLUDING BUT NOT LIMITED TO IMPLIED WARRANTIES OF MERCHANTABILITY AND FITNESS FOR A PARTICULAR PURPOSE, WITH RESPECT TO THE SOFTWARE, THE ACCOMPANYING WRITTEN MATERIALS, AND ANY ACCOMPANYING HARDWARE. THIS LIMITED WARRANTY GIVES YOU SPECIFIC LEGAL RIGHTS. YOU MAY HAVE OTHERS, WHICH VARY FROM STATE TO STATE.

NO LIABILITY FOR CONSEQUENTIAL DAMAGES. IN NO EVENT SHALL MICROSOFT OR ITS SUPPLIERS BE LIABLE FOR ANY DAMAGES WHATSOEVER (INCLUDING, WITHOUT LIMITATION, DAMAGES FOR LOSS OF BUSINESS PROFITS, BUSINESS INTERRUPTION, LOSS OF BUSINESS INFORMATION, OR OTHER PECUNIARY LOSS) ARISING OUT OF THE USE OF OR INABILITY TO USE THIS MICROSOFT PRODUCT, EVEN IF MICROSOFT HAS BEEN ADVISED OF THE POSSIBILITY OF SUCH DAMAGES. BECAUSE SOME STATES DO NOT ALLOW THE EXCLUSION OR LIMITATION OF LIABILITY FOR CONSEQUENTIAL OR INCIDENTAL DAMAGES, THE ABOVE LIMITATION MAY NOT APPLY TO YOU.

U.S. GOVERNMENT RESTRICTED RIGHTS

The SOFTWARE and documentation are provided with RESTRICTED RIGHTS. Use, duplication, or disclosure by the Government is subject to restrictions as set forth in subdivision (b)(3)(ii) of The Rights in Technical Data and Computer Software clause at 252.227-7013. Contractor/manufacturer is Microsoft Corporation/16011 NE 36th Way/Box 97017/Redmond, WA 98073-9717.

This Agreement is governed by the laws of the State of Washington.

Should you have any questions concerning this Agreement, or if you desire to contact Microsoft for any reason, please write: Microsoft Customer Sales and Service/16011 NE 36th Way/Box 97017/Redmond, WA 98073-9717.

copy of the software is needed on the file server. All other computers on the network can download the software for use on their machine. But using one copy in this situation is not acceptable to the software publisher. Users argue that only one copy of the software is used and that it is protected by the network from illegal pirating of the program. But the software publisher argues that each station on the network is using a copy (in memory) of the program, and thus the company should purchase a network license.

COMPUTER CRIME

A computer vandal broke into the computers of at least 21 different companies and destroyed the files of 1 of these companies. Thieves used a computer to break into the computer of a bank in Vancouver and transferred $2.8 million to a bank in Los Angeles. Employees of a company tapped into the company mainframe to use computer time for personal profit by running jobs for outside clients without their employer's knowledge or approval. An exporting company is buying computers in the United States and selling them illegally to countries in the communist block of Eastern Europe.

All these true stories are examples of computer crime today. Crime, of course, is not unknown in any industry, but computers are unique in the sense that some of these crimes can be perpetrated at a distance. The person who commits the crime does not need to be at the scene but could operate from the comfort of his or her own home or from a remote computer in a school or business. The foregoing examples identify different categories of crimes perpetrated with the use of computers that will now be examined separately.

Unlawful Computer Entry

This category of crime is probably the most widespread misuse of computers. Unlawful entry involves the access to a computer system, usually from a remote computer by modem, for the purpose of accessing programs or data on the system. Gaining access usually means breaking a security system of some sort, stealing a password, or finding a weakness in the software that provides security against unlawful entry.

Most people who perform this crime are not intent on destroying data or files, although some do, but are more curious about looking at information that is not legally theirs to see. Although accessing a computer in this manner to satisfy one's curiosity may not seem to be a harmful act, it is an illegal act and like all computer crimes is a punishable offense. To guard against this activity many systems now require several levels of passwords to access sensitive data. Some systems are designed to record your phone number, which is then checked against a list of approved numbers. If you are on the list, it then phones you back and connects you to the system.

Theft of Currency by Computer

Using a computer to transfer money from one bank to another is routine business today. The crime occurs when a computer user intentionally directs the computer to transfer money from another person's account to their own account.

This is really no different from stealing money directly, but the computer is used as a part of the transaction. More sophisticated thieves have tried to accomplish similar thefts but by deducting only a few cents from many thousands of accounts, hoping that no one would notice. Advanced auditing techniques are being adopted by computer auditors to ensure that even methods such as this do not go undetected.

Theft of Computer Time

Using the company computer to run off your Christmas card list or to calculate your loan payments might be considered a theft of computer time. These are rather trivial incidents, but we are concerned here about the illegal use of computer time for personal gain. An employee who runs mailing lists that are sold to outside companies for personal profit commits a more serious type of computer crime. Companies are within their rights to charge the employee with theft but often simply terminate the employee rather than go to court.

THE AGE OF THE COMPUTER VIRUS

In November 1988 a computer virus spread across the United States affecting the performance of thousands of computers. Included were computers in a nuclear weapons lab, the Pentagon, and several major universities. Very little information was lost, but the virus inconvenienced many thousands of computer users.

A **computer virus** is a program that is hidden in other programs in the system. The virus is written by a programmer who intends to corrupt or interfere with users of computer systems. Usually the virus program is hidden on a network that many computer users access regularly.

After writing the virus program the malicious programmer hides it in a program that other computer users are likely to use. It might be a game or a more serious application or utility program. This program is generally accessed from the network over the telephone lines. Frequently, the virus copies itself to DOS's COMMAND.COM program, which is necessary for the operation of most personal computers.

When a user accesses the program or the system containing the virus, things may seem to be normal for a while. But, after a given time period, or when a certain day occurs (such as Friday the 13th), the virus program is activated. It may simply display a harmless message, but the more sophisticated ones may do damage to files or programs on the user's system. Some have been known to wipe out the entire contents of a hard disk. The virus may also copy itself to other programs, so that if the original program is erased from the disk, the virus will still be present.

Hearing about virus programs often causes users to believe they have caught a virus on their system. It is relatively easy for some errors to occur on a system without a virus being at fault. Erasing a file or even an entire disk can result from simply using the wrong DOS command or using a command incorrectly. Power fluctuations, magnetic media wear, dust, or smoke particles can all cause data errors that have nothing to do with a virus. So be sure that when a problem is encountered, it is not due to one of these factors.

However, there are several practices to follow that can help you to avoid being hit by a hidden virus. First, don't load programs on your system from sources that are not known to be reliable. Frequent use of bulletin boards that are not strictly controlled can open up one's system to the potential of getting hit by the next virus.

Networks are a major source of viruses, so minimizing the use of a variety of networks can reduce the danger. However, for many users, especially those dependent on the use of electronic mail, this solution may not be practical. Using software from reliable sources, such as the major software companies will also minimize the chances of being infected.

Last, there is the use of a vaccine program. A **vaccine program** looks for the presence of a virus in software before it is used on the system. Unfortunately, vaccine programs are not foolproof, and a bright programmer intent on creating a virus can usually bypass the vaccine as well. Ultimately, the best solution to the computer virus is to know the source of your software and accept only proven programs for residence on your system.

How a computer virus spreads.

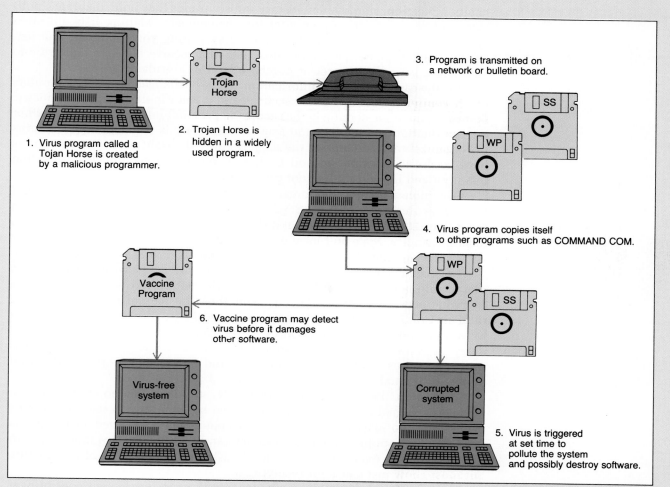

1. Virus program called a Tojan Horse is created by a malicious programmer.

2. Trojan Horse is hidden in a widely used program.

3. Program is transmitted on a network or bulletin board.

4. Virus program copies itself to other programs such as COMMAND COM.

5. Virus is triggered at set time to pollute the system and possibly destroy software.

6. Vaccine program may detect virus before it damages other software.

Theft of Computer Hardware

Whether selling computers to foreign countries is a crime depends on the laws relating to that country. Certainly selling computers to many countries in the free world is not a crime, and many companies do well financially in this marketplace. However, other countries, primarily communist countries, cannot legally purchase computers from the United States. Thus companies that surreptitiously buy computers and ship them via other countries for the purpose of selling to these communist countries are committing a computer crime.

PRIVACY AND SECURITY

Computers are exceptionally efficient machines for storing and disbursing information about all kinds of things. When data is collected about things such as products and sales, most people are indifferent, but when the data contains personal information, many become quite concerned about their privacy and the security of the information. Data about a person's credit rating, spending habits, education, employment history, subscriptions they hold, insurance policies, and so on is all on computer files somewhere. Mailing lists are often bought and sold as a commodity, and so by getting your name on one list, you may soon appear on many other lists and receive offers to subscribe to magazines, get a credit card, or purchase land in Florida.

It is the ease with which information can be exchanged between computers that has raised the concern about security and privacy in the computer industry. **Privacy** is the issue about who has access to personal information and whether the information is complete and accurate. **Security** is the issue that concerns the organization that controls the data. Do only the right people or computers have access to information and is there sufficient protection to ensure that unauthorized individuals cannot get access?

Government is only one organization that stores data on individuals but it is by far the largest. The U.S. government has over 200 million records on more than 100 million people, and data is traded regularly by as many as 15 federal agencies. State and local governments also maintain computer records and exchange data about taxes, welfare recipients, crime, and student loans.

To ensure that individuals have a right to privacy, two major acts were placed into law in 1970. The Freedom of Information Act was passed to give everyone access to data collected about them by federal agencies. Second, the Fair Credit Reporting Act was also passed in 1970 to give persons access to information stored about them by credit agencies. As a result of these acts, everyone can have access to records kept about them. However, getting access to these records is not always automatic and may even require court action by the individual.

The Federal Privacy Act, legislated 1974, stipulates that no secret personal files be permitted and that individuals must be permitted to see the contents of files that do exist and how the data about them contained in the file is used. The law applies to both government and private agencies that deal with the government. Agencies cannot simply ask for a certain type of information but must show just cause for receiving it.

Many critics of the act have shown that there is insufficient control over the exchange of information and that agencies have more freedom of access than the act provides. The lack of a government watchdog to ensure that information is not easily traded has reduced the effectiveness of the Privacy Act.

ETHICS

Crimes such as stealing a computer or the illegal transfer of funds to a personal account are obviously criminal acts. To perform crimes such as these is a calculated attempt to steal or commit fraud, which is clearly subject to prosecution by the legal authorities.

These acts obviously demonstrate a lack of ethics on the part of the person who commits the crime. But what about the person who makes a copy of a spreadsheet or word processing program to avoid the expense of buying the package? Or the student who uses the college computer to gain illegal access to the registrar's records or dials into the company's mainframe from a home computer?

Ethics refers to a moral code and relates to what one perceives as right or wrong. When someone copies a program to avoid the expense of purchase, there are several moral ideals that are being broken. First, the person is obtaining a program that clearly has some value to him or her without paying the price for it. Breaking this moral code is more apparent when we are talking about taking a car or even a book. In the case of a program, the copying may seem to present a different situation from appropriating a car or book.

We can't easily copy a car, and although a book could be copied, the price of the copy is usually more than the original cost of the book so no one bothers to take this approach. Copying the software also denies the software company, the programmer, and the distributor a rightful profit for creating the program and making it available to their clients. It's easy to say that a software company is wealthy and can afford it, but, with a little thought we can see that if every one had this attitude, the software business would be out of business. The wealth of the company cannot justify taking an unethical position on the copying of software.

Another ethics issue is the illegal use of computer systems. Breaking into a computer by using an unauthorized password or by forcing entry through a weakness in the security system is not much different from physically breaking into an organization's office. Although one activity involves a physical act and the other an electronic one, the principle is essentially the same.

Gaining access to unauthorized files also demonstrates a lack of respect for the privacy of the individuals' records that are viewed by the computer hacker. The Privacy Act discussed earlier was passed for the very reason that the files of others should be respected. Hackers also may inadvertently cause damage to the files by not being totally familiar with the system operation and the organization of the files. Although this damage may be unintentional, it nevertheless is real and can result in serious consequences for both the company and the hacker.

To stress the importance of taking a position on the matter of ethics, several organizations that represent computing professionals have adopted a code of ethics that their members must adopt. Organizations such as the Data Processing Management Association (DPMA) and the Association for Computing Machinery (ACM) have a statement of ethics to which their members subscribe.

Ethics is not a concern that is limited to the computer profession. Management in many companies and organizations are concerned in the standards of conduct demonstrated by their people. Dr. Kenneth Blanchard and Dr. Norman Vincent Peale in their book *The Power of Ethical Management* provide an ethics check that goes as follows:

1. Is it legal? Will I be violating either civil law or company policy?
2. Is it balanced? Is it fair to all concerned in the short term as well as the long term? Does it promote win-win relationships?
3. How will it make me feel about myself? Will it make me proud? Would I feel good if my decision was published in the newspaper? Would I feel good if my family knew about it?

These are simple questions that can have a profound influence on the individual's decision-making process when ethics are involved. Ethics is not always a standard that begins with the passing of some law or determined by some authority figure, but it is something that each of us can and should develop as a personal standard of conduct.

COMPUTER CAREERS

In the 1970s, a career in computers was considered one of the most desirable a college student could undertake. Thousands of graduates descended on this employment market and found satisfying and financially rewarding careers as a result. By the late 1980s this career path has undergone many changes and will continue to do so into the twenty-first century.

Ten years ago a computer career was primarily in the mainframe computer area. Programmers, operators, and systems analysts were in the mainstream of employment opportunities. Because of many changes and new developments in the mainframe and its use, and due to the extensive use of personal computers in business, the job market in computers has broadened considerably. But with the expansion, the number of positions has not increased accordingly but are of wider variety, which appeal to a greater range of aptitudes and interests.

We must not overlook the fact that other careers are being impacted by the widespread use of computers. College graduates in a variety of disciplines from business to technology need to be not only computer literate, but to have specific computer skills to find suitable employment in their own discipline. Thus computer courses have sprung up in many educational and training programs that in themselves may not directly lead to a computer career.

Career Opportunities

On the following pages we will look at several categories of jobs that are typical of the computer career (Figure 14–2). Some of these jobs are strictly mainframe, others are related to the personal computer, while some may require knowledge of both areas. The path one takes depends mainly on personal interest and the type of courses chosen at college. Programs are available that stress either career path, and one should choose a direction with personal priorities in mind.

Data entry requires keyboard skills and training in the use of computer hardware and software.

Courtesy of Kingsport Press.

FIGURE 14–2   Computer-related career paths.

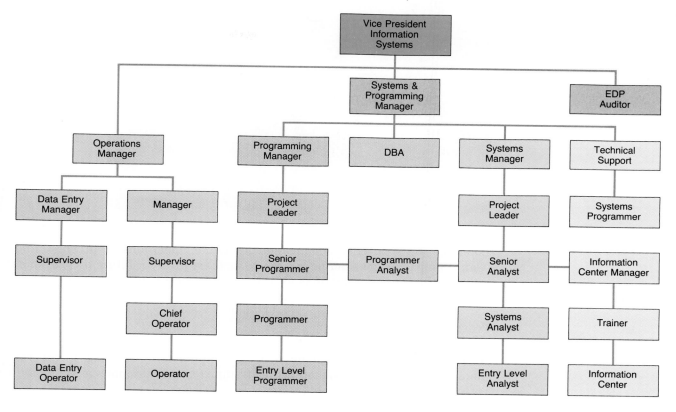

Data Entry Operator

Data entry is the process of entering source data, usually by keyboard, into the compuer. A **data entry operator** is a person who has typing or keying skills and has been trained in the use of the computer. Training is oriented as to application and as to the use of specific software required by the application. Data entry positions are available for all levels of computers from micros to mainframes but are declining in numbers as more automated means of source data entry become available.

Computer Operations

A **computer operator** is someone who runs the computer and is responsible for the monitoring, control, and operation of the computer hardware. This is a mainframe job and often has other supporting positions such as librarians, quality assurance, and management. An operator mounts tapes, disks, feeds paper into the printer, brings up programs, and solves operational problems.

Operators generally begin with a limited amount of responsibility, which is increased as their skill and maturity grows. An operator will frequently

A computer operator runs the mainframe computer, mounts tapes, monitors the operation, and solves operational problems.

Courtesy of Hewlett-Packard Company.

enter the job with college education for either operations or programming. Many companies consider operations to be entry level for future programmers and use the time in operations as a training period to acquaint the employee with the company's computer system.

Programmers

This is a term that covers many areas of computer programming. In general, there are systems and applications programmers, and these jobs relate to both personal and mainframe computers.

Systems Programmer

A **systems programmer** works on systems software such as compilers, operating systems, macros, and other general use software. Usually this is a position for the technically oriented programmer who has had a few years of experience in the applications programming area. An education in computer science or similar discipline is a necessary background for this position.

A computer programmer has the challenging task of designing, coding, testing, debugging, and maintaining computer programs.

Courtesy of Hewlett-Packard Company.

Applications Programmer

The **applications programmer** is one who designs, codes, tests, and debugs applications programs. Program maintenance of existing programs is becoming an important part of the applications programmer's job. Application programs include accounting, payroll, inventory control, education, insurance, and many other applications.

This is the most widely available position in computers today and continues to be one with a strong career potential. Entry-level jobs are available for those who have completed a college program in data processing, information systems, or computer science. As the employee progresses in his or her career, other job levels from junior to senior programmer and programming management are available.

New directions are developing for the applications programmer including fourth-generation languages, data base administration, and expert systems. The personal computer has also opened many new opportunities for the individual with knowledge and skills relating to the PC and its software.

Systems Analyst

The **systems analyst** is the person who designs and implements applications for the computer. Because applications involve people in the organization and their information needs, the analyst needs to be a people-oriented person. Someone who can talk the language of the application and yet communicate in a more technical way with the programmer is required for this position.

Often, the systems job is a promotion from programming and may be considered an alternate career path. Education in information systems is important with a strong business and management component being helpful. Systems analysts spend much of their time with user departments in many areas of the company. As a result they become intimately familiar with the internal operations of the corporation. This background is often an excellent basis for promotion into management.

Business Analyst

The **business analyst** position is similar to the systems analyst with a greater stress on knowledge of the business operation. A business analyst is frequently promoted from a career path in the company that was not information systems related. People from accounting, finance, marketing, and other disciplines who well grounded in the operation of their area of expertise often make good business analysts after receiving some training in analysis and design methodology.

Data Base Adminstrator

A **data base administrator (DBA)** is a position in the information systems department responsible for the design, control, and administration of the company's data bases. In large corporations one or more people may have this

Selling computers combines
business training, marketing
skills, and an interest in computers.

Courtesy of Computerland.

function. In smaller organizations, it may be combined with other functions. The DBA establishes data definitions, defines the data base standards for the company, determines who has access to what information, and maintains the integrity of the data.

Information Center Staff

The **information center** is usually a small department in the company that assist users with day-to-day operational problems. They may assist with problems users have with computer use and even act as an interface between a user and the information systems department. When new software or systems are placed into operation, the information center frequently provides the training for the user departments. This is especially true when personal computers are used and training is needed in the use of PC software. Information center support usually encompasses both PC and mainframe systems.

Marketing

Strictly speaking, this is not a computer job but one in sales. Selling mainframe and minicomputers was a highly lucrative profession in the 1970s and is still one with great potential. Marketing of computers ranges from the large mainframe systems to the relatively small personal computer sold from the local computer store.

First, and foremost, an education in marketing is important to this career path. A business administration program with a minor in marketing is also well accepted as background for entry into computer marketing. Second, to the marketing diploma, is training in computers. Many colleges also offer this as part of the overall program, but the employer will often supplement this with training on the specific products the salesperson is selling. An individual with a strong business program and an interest in the computer field might consider computer marketing as a potential career.

*CHAPTER
SUMMARY*

1. To get the two extremes of fear and fantasy into balance, it's best to remember that the computer is just an electronic device, although a complex one.

2. Program errors are introduced when writing a computer program. Some are obvious and are corrected immediately, while others may remain hidden for months or years before they surface.

3. Hardware errors usually result from component failure but may sometimes be the result of a design problem with the circuitry. Hardware errors are very unusual occurrences and are normally self-correcting.

4. Installing a computer will require training of the users and some time will be needed to get experience with the system before the computer can be used to its utmost potential.

5. Contrary to popular notion, to use a computer successfully does not require a high level of mathematics or programming ability.

6. Software piracy is the act of illegally copying software.

7. To protect their rights some software companies have produced software on floppy disks that contain a built-in copy protection scheme to interfere with the copying of the program.

8. When you buy a piece of software it invariably comes with a license agreement that defines the conditions for making other copies, using the software on only one machine, and not using it on a network.

9. A site license is a license that permits the use of multiple copies of the same software by a corporation or agency.

10. A network license permits a single copy of a program to be used by several stations served by a network.

11. Computer crime is unique from most other crimes in the sense that crime committed by computer can be perpetrated at a distance.

12. A computer virus is a program that is hidden in other programs in the system with the intent of creating malicious activity or damage in the system.

13. Privacy is the issue about who has access to personal information and whether the information is complete and accurate.

14. Security is the issue that concerns the organization that controls the data and who has access to that data.

15. Ethics refers to a moral code and relates to what one perceives as right or wrong.

16. A data entry operator is a person who has typing of keying skills and has been trained in the use of the computer.

17. A computer operator is someone who runs the computer and is responsible for the monitoring, control, and operation of the computer hardware.

18. A systems programmer is one who works on systems software such as compilers, operating systems, macros, and other general-use software.

19. The applications programmer is one who designs, codes, tests, and debugs applications programs such as accounting, payroll, inventory control, education, insurance, and many other applications.

20. The systems analyst is the person who designs and implements applications for the computer. This position requires someone who can talk the language of the application and yet communicate in a more technical way with the programmer.

21. The business analyst position is similar to the systems analyst, with a greater stress on knowledge of the business operation, areas such as accounting, finance, and marketing.

22. A data base administrator is a position in the information systems department responsible for the design, control, and administration of the company's data bases.

IMPORTANT TERMS AND CONCEPTS			
Applications programmer	Hardware errors	Security	
Business analyst	Information center	Site license	
Computer operator	Key disk	Software piracy	
Copy protection	License agreement	Systems analyst	
Data base administrator (DBA)	Network license	Systems programmer	
Data entry operator	Privacy	Unemployment	
Ethics	Program errors	Vaccine program	
GIGO		Virus	

REVIEW QUESTIONS

Fill-in Questions

1. A(n) _____ agreement spells out the rights of the software publisher and the purchaser of the program.

2. A program that is hidden in another program on the computer with malicious intent is called a(n) _____.

3. _____ is the issue about who has access to personal information stored on computer files.

4. A code of _____ is a statement about personal conduct and the difference between right and wrong actions of the individual.

5. The position of computer _____ refers to someone who runs the computer and monitors its operation.

6. An applications _____ develops, codes, and maintains programs for applications such as accounting and payroll.

7. The _____ _____ is a person whose profession is designing and implementing applications for the computer.

8. Staff in the _____ _____ are responsible for the training of computer users and assisting with systems implementation.

Matching Questions

Match each term with the description given below.

a. ethics
b. license agreement
c. privacy
d. software piracy
e. systems analyst
f. virus

_____ 1. Select the professional who designs and implements applications for the computer and business environment.

_____ 2. A moral code that one follows in making decisions on personal actions.

_____ 3. This term refers to the act of copying software illegally especially when the copies are sold to other parties.

_____ 4. A program hidden in a Trojan Horse that duplicates itself into other programs in the system. When activated, it may cause damage to files or programs.

_____ 5. This is a contract supplied with a software package to which the purchaser agrees when the package has been opened.

_____ 6. A concern of many about the degree to which personal data is transferred from one computer file to another.

Discussion Questions

1. Describe some of the fears and fantasies that people have about computers.
2. Discuss the meaning of the term software privacy.
3. What is the purpose of a license agreement? What special forms of licenses are available from software companies?
4. Identify four different types of computer crime that are frequently committed.
5. Explain what a computer virus is and how it works.
6. Define the terms privacy and security.
7. Select four computer-related positions. Define the position and discuss some of the functions of the job.

Origins

A History

of Computing

and Information

Systems

You are probably familiar with the names Apple, Commodore, and Atari and rightly associate them with home computers. But these are a recent event in the history of computers. Computers go as far back as the early 1940s when John W. Mauchly and J. Presper Eckert, Jr., constructed ENIAC at the Moore School of Engineering at the University of Pennsylvania. But the origins of the concepts behind the computer go back much farther in time. In this section we will look at a few of the highlights in the evolution of the computer.

ABACUS

Back around 2000 B.C. a device known to us as the abacus was in widespread use in China and the Far East for arithmetic calculations. By 1200 A.D. the abacus used consisted of a rectangular frame that could be easily held by hand. In the frame were several fixed rods strung with movable beads. The beads were arranged in two groups separated by a fixed bar. The top group consisted of rows of two beads each, while the bottom group had five rows of beads. The beads on the rightmost rod represented the units (1's) position, the second rod the tens (10's) position, and so on. Each bead on the top bar represented a value of five, and the beads on the lower rod had

a unit value. By moving the beads toward the bar, a number was recorded.

In parts of China and other Asian countries, the abacus is still in use today. As primitive as it seems, it is still an effective device for numerical calculations. When adding a column of numbers, a skilled abacus operator can keep pace with the user of an electronic calculator, thus demonstrating its effectiveness. However, doing other arithmetic operations are considerably more difficult on the abacus, and the calculator is clearly the superior device.

BLAISE PASCAL

Blaise Pascal was known as a genius for his work in many disciplines. Born in 1623, he was a French philosopher, scientist,

and mathematician with works on projective geometry, the theory of the behavior of fluids, and a series of letters that influenced church reform. Between 1641 and 1647 he invented the first calculating machine. It used pinwheel gearing and numbered disks, something similar to the wheels used for an odometer in today's cars.

His reason for inventing the calculator showed the dislike Pascal had for routine, menial types of work. It all began in 1638, when his father, who was a lawyer and mathematician, formed a protest against the policy of the government's treasury department. This kind of activity was not taken lightly at that time, and the senior Pascal was required to go into hiding to save his life. But he was soon to be

DATE LINE

3000 BC	1642	1642

Abacus

Courtesy of IBM Archives

Blaise Pascal

Courtesy of IBM Archives

Pascal calculator

Courtesy of IBM Archives

pardoned and given the job of special tax commissioner in Normandy.

It was a difficult job and Blaise Pascal was conscripted into the work by his father. Young Pascal was more interested in abstract mathematics and had little interest or patience for the hard and boring work of calculating tax tables. In the interest of self-survival, he invented the calculator to help in this work. The calculator operated on the decimal principle and could do addition and subtraction.

Pascal gave up the scientific life at the age of 27 to pursue a life of religious contemplation with the Jansenists, a religious order of that time. When he died at the age of 39, civilization lost one of its greatest philosophers and mathematicians.

GEORGE BOOLE

The invention of calculating machines is not the only important development leading to today's computers. Systems of thought and computation also made an important contribution to the development of new techniques.

Such was the work of George Boole (1815–1864), an English logician and mathematician. Boole was one of the developers of the algebra of logic, which expresses and manipulates problems in logic by the use of mathematical symbols.

Boole defined an algebra in which all variables could take on only two states: true and false. By manipulating these variables according to his special algebra, he found that he could describe and investigate many real-world problems. Boole's algebra became the perfect tool to design complex binary logic circuits of the computer, a century after he invented it. Fortunately, we can use computers today without needing a formal understanding of Boole's laws, which are often called Boolean algebra.

CHARLES BABBAGE

Charles Babbage was another genius who conceived of a machine that would go beyond addition and subtraction. Born in 1792 in Devonshire, England, Babbage was a sickly child who

spent much of his time with books and in deep thought (he called it childish reasonings). By the time he went to college, he was astonished to discover that he knew more about calculus than his instructors.

One day he was sitting in the rooms of the Analytical Society daydreaming, as usual, over a book of logarithm tables. When asked by a friend what he was doing, he announced that he had been thinking it might be possible to calculate the logarithms by machinery. That was the idea that spurred him on to the development of the Difference Engine. The first model built could produce the tables mechanically with an accuracy of 20 digits. That model had 96 computing wheels mounted on 24 shafts. It required such precision to build that wide-scale manufacturing proved impossible.

No sooner had Babbage designed the Difference Engine than he had an idea for a new device called the Analytical Engine. Although it was also mechanical, it contained many of

---

1847	1833	1833
George Boole	Charles Babbage	Difference Engine
Courtesy of The Bettmann Archive	Courtesy of The Bettmann Archive	Courtesy of IBM Archives

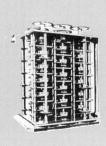

the concepts used in today's computers. It had memory, a control unit, an arithmetic unit, and input and output capabilities. Surprisingly, it also had the ability to be programmed by punched cards. While this new machine represented a significant step forward in Babbage's thinking, the world was not yet ready for this development.

Then he met Ada, the Countess of Lovelace. She was the daughter of Lord Byron and a gifted mathematician, certainly an unusual occupation for a woman in the nineteenth century. Ada took an interest in Babbage's work and was one of the first to appreciate and understand fully the designs of his machines. In 1842 she began to translate Babbage's notes into French, which helped considerably in making his work known around the scientific world.

One hundred and forty-one years later, in 1983, the U.S. Department of Defense adopted a single programming language for all its computer applications. That language is called Ada, named after the world's first programmer, the Countess of Lovelace.

JAMES RITTY AND NCR

In 1878 James Ritty was an American restaurant owner and not a mathematician unlike many of the other people we have discussed. During that year he took an ocean voyage to Europe and was captivated by the operation of a gauge that counted the number of revolutions of the propeller. Being interested in simplifying business operations, he decided that a similar device could be constructed that would record the transactions made each day in his business.

Following Ritty's arrival home he and his brother John constructed a machine with two rows of keys and a large clocklike dial containing two rows of figures showing dollars and cents. This device was the forerunner of the cash register. Sales were recorded by punching holes in a roll of paper with a sharp pin. Ritty's cash register business did poorly and

was eventually sold to Jacob H. Eckert for $1,000.

Eckert added a few more features such as the cash drawer and a bell to indicate a sale. But his register did not do much better, and the business was sold to John H. Patterson. Patterson had a keen business sense, and after calling the company the National Cash Register Company (NCR), sales began to improve. His first factory employed 13 workers who built four or five cash registers a week. Today NCR is one of the largest producers of business machines, data terminals, and computers.

WILLIAM S. BURROUGHS

William Burroughs was born in 1857. His first job was in a bank where the adding and checking of columns of figures were more work and drudgery than he could handle. He soon left the bank and went to St. Louis where he began working in a machine shop.

Soon he became intrigued by the idea that a machine could be built not only to add figures, but

---

DATE LINE

1842	1842	1878

Ada Lovelace

Courtesy of The Bettmann Archive

Mark I computer

Courtesy of IBM Archives

Ritty's cash register

Courtesy of NCR Corporation

also record them in a column on paper with a running total so that by pressing a key, the total could be printed at any time. He sought the help of Thomas Metcalf and with an initial investment of $700 began to build a machine based on his concepts.

The first machine didn't work properly unless Burroughs himself operated it. It seems that you had to pull a lever at just the right time or else the numbers printed were incorrect, and only Burroughs had the right feel for the machine.

In 1886 Burroughs formed the American Arithmometer Company with Metcalf and several other backers. The first machine sold for $475, and gradually the company got off the ground and became a worldwide organization, Burroughs Corporation, well known in the computer field today.

HERMAN HOLLERITH

Herman Hollerith was born in Buffalo in 1860. In 1879 he was hired by the U.S. Census Bureau and by 1880 was deeply into the operation of the census for that year. Five years later, Hollerith and the Bureau were still struggling to compile the results from the 50 million citizens of the country.

Hollerith saw the possibilities inherent in the problem of census recording and began work on a machine that would compile population and other statistics. One day he was watching a conductor punch tickets with a basic description of each passenger and was inspired to use a similar idea in his machine. To develop the idea further he left the Census Bureau for a job at the Massachusetts Institute of Technology, and then moved to the patent office in 1884.

His early work consisted of a machine using a roll of paper, but by the 1890 census he had devised a punched card that was the forerunner of the standard IBM card, which was used for many years by data processors.

Hollerith's method was so successful that the 1890 census was tabulated in less than two months. In 1896 Hollerith formed the Tabulating Machine Company and began selling his equipment to railroads, to audit freight statistics, and insurance companies, for use in classifying risks. By 1911 the company had merged with the International Time Recording Company, the Dayton Scale Company, and Bundy Manufacturing to form the Computing-Tabulating-Recording Company (CTR). In 1924 CTR was renamed International Business Machines (IBM), which is today's largest computer company.

THOMAS WATSON and IBM

Thomas Watson made his start in the business world in 1892 in a butcher shop in Elmira, New York. His job was bookkeeping, which like many of his predecessors he found to be drudgery. He promptly quit and got a job selling pianos, organs, and sewing machines. He found this more challenging and eventually moved to Buffalo where he took a sales job with NCR.

At this time in NCR's history, other companies were being formed by enterprising individuals

---

1886

William Burroughs

Courtesy of UPI/Bettmann Newsphotos

1890

Herman Hollerith

Courtesy of IBM Archives

1890

Punched cards

Courtesy of IBM Archives

to repair used NCR equipment and then resell it, undercutting NCR's profits in the process. John Patterson, NCR's president, picked Thomas Watson, his star salesman, to head up a new organization to fight the competition and let NCR do its own repair. Watson was so good at the job that he soon became the third man from the top in NCR. But this proved his undoing. He couldn't get along with the boss and was soon fired by Patterson. Watson soon joined forces with the Computing-Tabulating-Recording Company, which became IBM. For many years Thomas Watson was the driving force behind the spectacular growth of IBM, to be followed by his son Thomas Watson, Jr.

PRESPER ECKERT, JOHN MAUCHLY, AND ENIAC

ENIAC is an acronym for Electronic Numerical Integrator and Computer. Developed by Mauchly and Eckert at the Moore School of Electrical Engineering at the University of Pennsylvania in the early 1940s, it was the first electronic general-purpose computer and consisted of 18,000 vacuum tubes. The tubes were so unreliable that maintenance men had to run around with spares and replace burned-out tubes while the computer operated. ENIAC could do 300 multiplications per second and was a great improvement over manual methods of calculation.

Eckert and Mauchly founded their own company in 1946 and developed a new computer that was to become known as UNIVAC I. At that time IBM was a fledgling accounting machine company and had not yet moved into the computer business. Beginning in 1951 UNIVAC I was successful in

---

DATE LINE

1937	1914	1941
Howard Aiken	Thomas Watson	John Mauchly (left) and Presper Eckert
Courtesy of IBM Archives	Courtesy of IBM Archives	Courtesy of Sperry Corporation

COMPUTER GENERATIONS

First Generation (1951–1959)

The computers produced during the 1950s were to be known as **first generation** computers. They were built with vacuum-tube circuits and were usually used for scientific or mathematical applications. Programming these computers, by wiring the circuits, was a time-consuming task and required great skill and

replacing some of IBM's punched card equipment at the census bureau and so IBM moved quickly to get into the computer business by releasing the 650 computer in 1954. Later UNIVAC was to merge with Sperry Corporation to become Sperry-Univac. In 1986 Burroughs Corporation and Sperry Corporation merged to form Unisys Corporation.

JOHN VON NEUMANN AND EDVAC

Further computer developments at the Moore School led to the Electronic Discrete Variable Automatic Computer or EDVAC. It was designed with improved techniques over the ENIAC and only required 5,900 vacuum tubes. EDVAC also used the first solid-state devices known in computer design: 12,000 diodes. EDVAC was completed in 1949; it was considerably faster than ENIAC and could add two numbers in 864-millionths of a second.

Mauchly and Eckert worked on the EDVAC, but John von Neumann, from Budapest, Hungary would also become involved. von Neumann came to the Moore School as a consultant in 1944. He often conferred with Mauchly and Eckert on the design of the EDVAC computer and has frequently been named as the inventor of the stored program concept used in virtually all computers today. However, recent data suggests that the stored program concept was discussed prior to von Neumann's appearance at the Moore School and did not originate with him.[1]

[1] Joel Shurkin, *Engines of the Mind—A History of the Computer* (New York: W. W. Norton, 1984).

1946

ENIAC

Courtesy of Sperry Corporation

1946

UNIVAC

Courtesy of Sperry Corporation

1949

John von Neumann next to EDVAC

Courtesy of IBM Archives

expertise. The physical computer was called the **hardware,** and the programs that give it its instructions were the **software.**

Data and programs were entered into the computer using punched cards, which were slow compared to tape and disk that were to follow in later generations. The computer's memory was often a magnetic drum and had slow access time because of the need to wait for the drum to revolve to the address the computer needed. Very few people had the training or skills to use first-generation computers, and so their use was not widespread.

IBM 704.

Courtesy of IBM Archives.

Second Generation (1960–1964)

In 1960 IBM announced a **second generation** of computers using solid-state transistors instead of vacuum tubes. These computers were faster and more compact than the first generation. One of these computers was the IBM 1401, which became popular as a business computer. Other competing companies such as NCR, Sperry UNIVAC, Honeywell, and Burroughs also produced second-generation computers.

Both magnetic tape and disk began to be used as secondary storage for faster and easier storage of data and programs. Today's personal computers have disk drives that are faster and have greater capacity than disks used on second-generation mainframe computers.

A parallel development was the higher-level language, such as FORTRAN and COBOL. Symbolic and assembly languages were still the most popular and were easier to use than machine language. However, they still required a

IBM 1401.

Courtesy of IBM Archives.

high level of training and competence to use. Second-generation computers were the first used largely by business, and applications such as accounting, payroll, and corporate finance were gradually moved to the computer.

Third Generation (1964–1970)

By 1964 a **third generation** of computers was ushered in when IBM announced their System/360 series of computers. These led to the System/370 family in the 1970s followed by the 4300 and 3000 series. These computers were characterized by increased use of miniaturization in their circuitry, and **integrated circuits (ICs)** became the new buzzword. Offering a family of computers provided the customer with upward compatibility. Programs written for one model of computer in the family would run on all other models without the need for change. By adopting such a computer, users could begin with a lower-level, and less costly, computer, and then, as their need for increased computer power grew, a larger, faster computer from the same family could be installed.

High-level languages like BASIC and RPG (Report Program Generator) were developed and adopted for many needs because they improved the programmer's productivity. Third-generation computers are still in use today, and most medium- to large-scale businesses make use of these computers for an extensive range of applications.

All these computers were called **mainframe** systems, intended for centralized use, and required computer professionals for their implementation and operation. The user rarely had direct access to the computer until the late 1970s, when remote terminals began to be used interactively at the user's site. The mainframe computer was located centrally, and data was either transported physically or by electronic means to the computer for processing. Results were then delivered back to the user with resulting delays of days or even weeks.

During the third-generation time period, many smaller computers were developed by companies such as Digital Equipment Corporation (DEC) and Data General. These **minicomputers,** such as the DEC PDP-8 and PDP-11, were

IBM System/360.
Courtesy of IBM Archives.

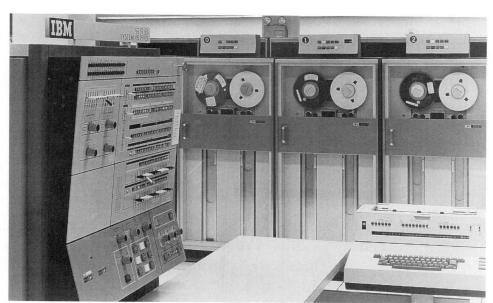

intended for the smaller company that could neither afford the larger mainframe nor had the need for a larger system.

COMPUTER LANGUAGES AND SOFTWARE

Computers are instructed in their operation by a program that is written using a specific programming language such as BASIC or COBOL. Languages for programming the computer have a history that is separate yet parallel to the development of the hardware. Early computers, like the Mark I, were wired to perform specific operations. If new operations were required, the computer would be rewired to the new specifications.

The next computer, UNIVAC I, could store its program in a memory device; thus UNIVAC used the first **stored program** and was the forerunner of today's computers, which load their programs from a magnetic disk. Changing UNIVAC's program was as easy as reading the new requirements (the program) into the store or memory, and the computer was then ready to solve a new problem.

Four computer generations are outlined here showing the characteristic features of each generation.

First-Generation Computers

The first computer generation had a memory, usually a magnetic drum or magnetic core in which the program was stored. The program consisted of binary numbers in the form of 0's and 1's, which represented the instructions. These programs were written in machine language. The symbolic instructions were only for the programmer to read, not the computer. The programs were difficult to write, and even more difficult to read. If they contained bugs (errors), which was inevitable, it was extremely difficult to find and correct the error.

Machine Language

Symbolic Language		Machine Language	Description
A	A1,B3	011101011010	Add
M	Z2,Z3	110100101011	Move
B	START	10101001	Branch

Second-Generation Computers

As faster computers with greater capacity became available, the demand for computer languages that were easier to use and to debug also grew. This demand resulted in true symbolic languages being developed where the programmer wrote the program code in the symbolic language and the computer translated it into machine code. Thus the programmer did not need to understand the machine's language but just the symbolic language. Although this language was certainly easier, it was still no simple task to create a sophisticated program.

Languages such as FORTRAN and COBOL came on the scene at this time but did not come into widespread use until third-generation computers were available.

Symbolic Languages

Assembly Language	Description
A AMT, TOTAL	Add instruction
MVC NAME,PRINTA	Move instruction
B AGAIN	Branch

FORTRAN—1954

```
      READ(5,110) XLEN,WID
      AREA=XLEN*WID
      WRITE(6,220) AREA
      STOP
  110 FORMAT(2F5.1)
  220 FORMAT(1X,I5)
      END
```

Third-Generation Computers

As computer languages became easier to use, they also required more of the computer's resources. So the next major development in languages had to wait for the increased power and lower cost of the third generation of computers. Although languages such as FORTRAN and COBOL had been around since second generation, most computers lacked the power to use them efficiently. Now faster computers with more memory opened new doors for computer applications in engineering, the sciences, business, and education. Other languages, including PL/1, RPG, and Pascal, were only the leading edge of many new programming languages introduced with third-generation computers.

High-Level Languages

COBOL—1959

```
PROCEDURE DIVISION.
TOTAL-ROUTINE.
        ADD AMOUNT TO TOTAL.
        MOVE NAME TO PRINT-AREA.
        WRITE PRINT-LINE
            AFTER ADVANCING 1 LINE.
```

BASIC—1964

```
100 T1 = T1 + A
110 PRINT A, T1, N$
120 GO TO 100
```

Computers and Fourth Generation

While the distinction between the first three generations of computers and their technology was clear, the fourth generation did not have as clear a definition. Certainly, the personal computer was an important component of computer development. Perhaps the PC was the single new development that affected the most people.

But other developments in large-scale and supercomputers also had an impact on software development. The evolution of fourth-generation languages such as Intellect and Focus was a significant step forward in the growth of user-oriented languages. On the personal computer the term **user friendly** described the type of software that was coming to be expected by the user.

User-Friendly Languages

Mainframe Language
iNTELLECT

PRINT THE COMPANY NAME, 1989 SALES,
1989 INCOME, SORTED BY COMPANY NAME.

PC Language
dBASE III Plus

SORT ON COMPANY—NAME TO NAME
DISPLAY ALL COMPANY—NAME, SALES—89
INCOME—89

THE FIRST PERSONAL COMPUTERS

In 1972 INTEL Corporation announced a new integrated chip called the 8000 series microprocessor. These small integrated circuits (ICs) could do everything a large computer could do, provided they were connected to a power supply, keyboard, and display screen. One of these makeshift microcomputers was advertised in *Popular Electronics* magazine in 1975 and sold either as a kit (for $395) or completely assembled ($695). Few people saw the vision at that time and few of these computers were sold.

The Birth of Apple and the IBM PC

Soon after the INTEL computer was announced, two friends, Steve Jobs and Stephen Wozniak, decided to build their own microcomputer as a result of enthusiasm developed by their membership in the Homebrew Computer Club in the San Francisco Bay area. They built a small computer and demonstrated it to their friends at the club. Encouraged by the positive response, they decided to form a company and sold Jobs' Volkswagen and Wozniak's calculator and borrowed $5,000 from a friend to get started. The first microcomputer, called the Apple I, cost $666.66. The term "personal computer" was to come into popular use a few years later.

An integrated circuit chip contains thousands of circuits engraved in less than a square inch (6.54 cm^2). ICs made possible the personal computer by offering computer power in a small space with very low power requirements.

Courtesy of Commodore Systems.

The Apple II was the first runaway best-seller in the microcomputer market. Although other computers were previously available, including an Apple I, Steven Jobs' and Stephen Wozniak's Apple II opened the door to the micro market, and many other manufacturers soon flooded it with their own offerings.

Steven Jobs courtesy of Rick Browne/ Photoreporters; Stephen Wozniak and Apple II courtesy of Apple Computer, Inc.

The name personal computer became synonymous with the IBM PC following its announcement in 1981. Although not truly a new computer, the name IBM lent it credibility not previously found with other computers. In the few years following its release, thousands of software packages followed to make the PC a truly worthwhile addition to any small or large business. Spreadsheets, word processing, and data base programs became the primary software packages that were used on these computers. In 1987 IBM announced its new line of computers, the Personal System/2. The PS/2 offers greater computing power and storage capacity than the PC, which was discontinued to make room for this newly developed computer.

Courtesy of IBM.

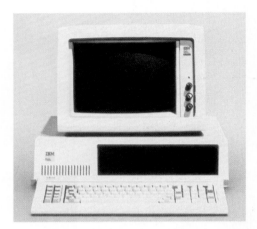 

In 1977 they improved the microcomputer and produced the Apple II, which became a runaway best seller. From 1977 to 1981 sales rocketed to over $300 million, and Apple became the fastest-growing company in America. Again two dreamers made computer history, but this time it was a personal computer that could be used by virtually anyone. Parallel developments came from Commodore and Radio Shack. The personal computer came to be understood as a computer that could be used by one person.

Not to be kept out of the picture, IBM developed the IBM Personal Computer (PC), which was released in 1981 and quickly became the standard for personal computing. Until IBM produced the PC, the microcomputer was not taken very seriously by computer professionals or by business. But once the leader of the computer industry took the plunge, the computer became a serious business tool and there has been no looking back.

Parallel developments in software made these computers easy to use. They required a minimum of training, whether used for business or personal applications from spreadsheets to financial planning or accounting to computer graphics.

B

Number Systems

All computers use numbers for their operation, and certainly we depend on the computer to provide information in the form of numbers after processing is complete. While we are accustomed to using decimal numbers, and that is how the computer normally displays or prints them, internally things are different.

In RAM, a computer represents data in the form of bits, which are based on the binary number system. **Binary numbers** consist of the digits 0 and 1, unlike decimal numbers, which consist of digits 0 to 9. Binary is a base 2 number system because it uses only two digits, whereas decimal is base 10. Most people use base 10 numbering, which was developed in Egypt as far back as 3400 B.C., but there have been times and places when other systems were in use. The Papuan language tribes of the Torres Strait of Australia and parts of New Guinea use a base 2 number system. Some tribes in the Terra del Fuego used base 3 and 4 number systems, and a South American language called Saraveca used a base 5 system.

Table B–1 compares decimal numbers with equivalent values in binary, octal, and hexadecimal. Because hexadecimal numbers must count up to 15, the letters A to F are used to represent digit values 10 to 15. Base 8 (octal) and base 16 (hexadecimal) have been widely used in computers over the years. Today binary and hexadecimal are the most common way of interpreting numbers in computer memory.

TABLE B–1
Comparison of Different Number Systems.

Decimal	Binary	Octal	Hexadecimal
0	0	0	0
1	1	1	1
2	10	2	2
3	11	3	3
4	100	4	4
5	101	5	5
6	110	6	6
7	111	7	7
8	1000	10	8
9	1001	11	9
10	1010	12	A
11	1011	13	B
12	1100	14	C
13	1101	15	D
14	1110	16	E
15	1111	17	F
16	10000	20	10

DECIMAL NUMBERS

0 1 2 3 4 5 6 7 8 9

Decimal or base 10 numbers are those most commonly used in today's world for counting. Each of the ten digits in the number system has a specific value, but when two or more digits are used in the number, then the value of the digit depends on its position in the number. We call this the place value.

For example, the number 545 may be understood as follows.

5	4	5
↑	↑	↑
5 Hundreds	4 Tens	5 Units
5 × 100 +	4 × 10 +	5 × 1

The 5 in the 1's position represents the digit value of 5. The 4 in the 10's position represents the value 4 times 10 or 40, while the 5 in the 100's position is 5 times 100, or 500. Although its digit value is still 5 its positional value is different from the 5 in the 1's position.

Counting to 16 in Decimal
1
2
3
4
5
6
7
8
9
10
11
12
13
14
15
16

Powers of 10

$$10^0 = 1$$
$$10^1 = 10$$
$$10^2 = 100$$
$$10^3 = 1,000$$
$$10^4 = 10,000$$

All this may seem elementary and is intuitive to most of us. But the principle becomes important when we want to understand other number systems that we don't use every day.

The number 545 has a position notation that is used to represent all decimal numbers. The position notation is given as follows:

$$5 \times 10^2 + 4 \times 10^1 + 5 \times 10^0$$

The 10's used in this expression are called the base. The values 0, 1, and 2 are the exponents or powers of 10. If we multiply these values and add each result, we get the following:

$$5 \times 100 + 4 \times 10 + 5 \times 1 =$$
$$500 + 40 + 5 = 545$$

The sum of this expression gives 545, which is the original number.

Numbers used by computers are often referred to by their high-order or low-order digit. In a number such as 7034, the digit 7 is the high order, sometimes called the most significant digit, and 4 is the low order, or least significant digit.

```
    7    0     3    4
    ↑               ↑
High-Order Digit   Low-Order Digit
(most significant)  (least significant)
```

BINARY NUMBERS

0   1

Early in the development of computer technology it was discovered that binary numbers were better suited to computer usage because of the two state nature of electronic devices. Two states mean that only two values, on-off, true-false, or 0 and 1, may be represented.

Counting to 16 in Binary
0
1
10
11
100
101
110
111
1000
1001
1010
1011
1100
1101
1110
1111
10000

Powers of 2

$2^0 = 1$
$2^1 = 2$
$2^2 = 4$
$2^3 = 8$
$2^4 = 16$

A binary number such as 1101 may be understood by applying the rules of positional notation as used in the decimal number system. Instead of using the base of 10 we use a base 2, which gives the following expression for the number 1101.

$$1 \times 2^3 + 1 \times 2^2 + 0 + 2^1 + 1 \times 2^0$$

Simplifying the expression by first applying the powers of 2 and then calculating the values gives the following result.

$$1 \times 8 + 1 \times 4 + 0 + 2 + 1 \times 1 =$$
$$8 + 4 + 0 + 1 = 13$$

In effect, by calculating the expression using the positional notation, we have converted the binary number to decimal, which is easier to understand.

Another method for converting a binary number to its decimal equivalent is to sum the positional values. The following chart simplifies this method for finding the decimal value of 1101011.

64	32	16	8	4	2	1	Positional values
1	1	0	1	0	1	1	Binary number

To convert to decimal, simply add the positional values as follows.

$$64 + 32 + 8 + 2 + 1 = 107$$

HEXADECIMAL NUMBERS

0   1   2   3   4   5   6   7   8   9   A   B   C   D   E   F

Although computers are designed based on the binary principle, we sometimes find it easier to work with other representations. One, of course, is decimal, but programmers often use hexadecimal because of the way memory and addressing is organized. Writing program code in an assembly language often requires the use of hexadecimal.

Counting to 16 in Hexa-decimal
1
2
3
4
5
6
7
8
9
A
B
C
D
E
F
10

Powers of 16	
$16^0 =$	1
$16^1 =$	16
$16^2 =$	256
$16^3 =$	4,096
$16^4 =$	65,536

Hexadecimal is base 16 meaning that each digit position has a positional value of 16. With 16 digits, it is necessary to use letters A to F to represent the digits 10 through 15 (see insert).

To understand how hexadecimal works, let's take the number 1A5. To change this number to decimal, write it using the positional notation method used for both decimal and binary, but this time use the exponent 16 as follows.

$$1 \times 16^2 + 10 \times 16^1 + 5 \times 16^0$$

Notice that the letter A in the hexadecimal number is entered as 10 in the positional notation. Expanding this expression gives the following result:

$$1 \times 256 + 10 \times 16 + 5 \times 1 =$$
$$256 \; + \; 160 \; + \; 5 \; = 421$$

The number 421 is decimal equivalent to the hexadecimal number 1A5.

CONVERTING BETWEEN BINARY AND HEXADECIMAL

Converting between binary and hexadecimal is an easy process because four binary digits are equal to one hexadecimal digit. The reverse is also true. One hexadecimal digit converts to four binary digits. For example, the binary number 1011 can be converted as follows.

```
8  4  2  1     Positional value
1  0  1  1     Binary digits
         B     Hexadecimal value
```

We arrive at the hexadecimal value of B because the binary number 1011 is equivalent to 8 + 2 + 1, which is 11 in decimal. And 11 in decimal is expressed as B in hexadecimal.

A second example converts the hexadecimal number 1A5 to binary. Each hexadecimal digit converts to a group of four binary digits.

```
   1      A      5      Hexadecimal digits
0001   1010   0101      Binary digits
8421   8421   8421      Positional values
```

The binary equivalent of 1A5 is 000110100101, or if we delete the leading zeros, the number is 110100101. By using the groups of four binary digits for each hexadecimal digit the conversion is easily done.

CONVERTING DECIMAL TO OTHER BASES

Decimal numbers may be converted to binary or hexadecimal and other bases by the method of successive division. This is done by dividing the decimal number by the base of the number system to which you want to convert. To convert to binary, divide by 2. To convert to hexadecimal, divide by 16. Next record the remainder of this step. The quotient is then divided again and the remainder recorded. This process is repeated until a quotient of zero is reached.

For example, to convert the decimal value 13 to binary 1101, the following steps are taken.

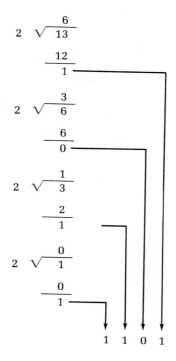

To convert decimal 2620 to hexadecimal A3C the following steps are taken. Remainders between 10 and 15 are substituted with the letters A to F.

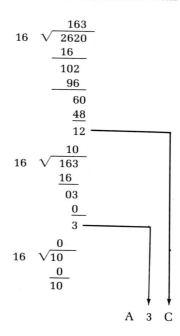

Glossary

absolute addressing Address formulas in a spreadsheet that do not adjust row and column references as the formula is copied or moved.

access arm The arm on which the disk's read/write head is mounted.

access time The time taken to access a record from disk. It includes the time to position the read/write head to the track or sector and to rotate the disk to the required record.

accounts payable A system or program that keeps track of the debts owed to a company by its suppliers.

accounts receivable A system or program that keeps track of the dollar amount that the company has credited the customer.

acoustic coupler A modem that attaches to a telephone by placing the handset onto rubber cups in the coupler.

address bus The path that carries memory addresses to all devices connected to the data bus.

ALU See *Arithmetic and logic unit.*

American Standard Code for Information Interchange (ASCII) A 7-bit coding system used for representing characters in the computer.

append The process of adding a record to the end of a file or data base.

applications software Software that is designed to perform a specific function such as accounting or inventory control.

arithmetic and logic unit The part of the processor that performs arithmetic and decision making in the computer.

ASCII See *American Standard Code for Information Interchange.*

assembler A translation program that converts assembly language programs into machine language.

assembly language A second-generation language that uses symbolic program code.

asynchronous transmission A mode of data transmission that uses start and stop bits to identify the beginning and ending of the data.

autoanswer Automatic answering by a modem of a call from another modem.

autodial Automatic calling from a modem of another modem.

automatic recalculation A process where formula values are computed after a change has been made to a spreadsheet.

backup A procedure for maintaining copies of crucial files on tape or disk in the event of a loss or failure of the primary file.

BASIC A high-level programming language standard on most personal computers.

Basic Input Output System (BIOS) A program stored in ROM that assists in the process of starting up the computer and doing basic input/output operations.

batch A method where data is collected over a period of time and processed as a group.

batch file A disk file containing a series of DOS commands.

binary A two-state number system based on the values zero and one.

BIOS See *Basic Input Output System.*

bit The smallest element or value represented in the computer. Derived from binary digit.

bit mapping A method of displaying information on a screen by controlling individual pixels.

bit rate The rate at which data is transmitted on a communications line. Transmission speed is measured in bits per second.

block A group of text ranging from one or more characters or words to sentences, lines, or paragraphs that may be moved, copied, or deleted in a word processor.

boilerplate Commonly used text such as phrases or paragraphs.

booting The process of starting up the computer and loading the operating system.

bus An electronic circuit that sends data and messages between the various components of the computer system.

business system A set of procedures designed for the purpose of collecting and analyzing business information.

byte The basic unit of data in the computer. A byte is used to represent a character, digit, or symbol and is usually composed of 8 bits.

C language A high-level programming language developed by Bell Laboratories with assembly language efficiency.

CAD See *Computer-aided design.*

CAM See *Computer-aided manufacturing.*

CD-ROM A form of compact disk that contains computer-readable data. Storage capacity typically exceeds 1 billion bytes.

cell An element of a spreadsheet at the intersection of a row and column that contains a value, label, or formula.

central processing unit (CPU) An electronic device made of one or more silicon chips consisting of memory, ALU, and control unit sections operating under the direction of the program.

COBOL A high-level computer language used mainly for developing business applications on mainframe computers.

coding The process of writing a computer program.

cold start The process of booting the computer by turning on the power.

command driven Programs that require the user to type each command. PC-DOS is one of the most common command-driven programs.

communication medium A line that links computers together for the purpose of data communication.

compiler A program that translates a source language program and creates a machine language program called an object program.

computer-aided design (CAD) Using a computer graphics system to assist in the design of a product.

computer-aided manufacturing (CAM) Using a computer system to assist in the manufacturing of a product.

computer system An electronic device that consists of several components that provide the capability of executing a stored program for input, output, and processing.

concurrent processing A software system that permits the user to switch between several tasks without leaving the current task.

control structures The basic types of patterns used for controlling logic flow in a program. The three basic structures are sequence, selection, and iteration.

control unit Decodes each program instruction and directs the activity of the CPU.

copy protection A hardware or software method that prohibits the user from making unauthorized copies of the software.

CP/M Control Program for Microcomputers is an operating system developed by Digital Research Corporation for 8-bit microcomputers. CP/M-86 is the 16-bit version.

CPU See *Central processing unit.*

CRT See *Display screen.*

cursor The flashing symbol on the display screen that shows where the next entry will be made.

daisy wheel An impact printer that creates a solid character by impacting the paper with the character contained on a spoked wheel. Use for letter-quality printing.

data A collection of facts or raw material that are gathered and used for input to the computer.

data base An integrated collection of data stored on a direct access device; a collection of files containing data relating to a given application with query and update capabilities.

data base administrator (DBA) A position in a company with the responsibility for designing, implementing, and maintaining the data bases in a mainframe environment.

data base management system (DBMS) A software system for maintaining and accessing data on the computer for one or more related applications.

data bus The path through which data or instructions flow between the components of the computer.

data dictionary A definition of the contents of a data base, including file, record, and field definitions.

data entry The process of entering data into the computer for storage or processing.

data flow diagram A chart used by sys-tem analysts to document the flow of data within a system.

data rate The speed in bytes per second at which data is transferred to and from an input/output device.

DBMS See *Data base management system.*

debugging The process of finding and correcting syntax and logic errors in a computer program.

Decision Support System (DSS) A system that provides management with information for making decisions that affect the future operation of the company.

decision table A table for representing the logical solution to a problem by showing decisions and related actions.

desktop managers A memory-resident software package that provides services such as a calendar, calculator, clock, and phone dialing.

desktop publishing Software used to integrate text, with a variety of fonts, and graphics, including clip art, to produce a WYSIWYG document.

device driver Software that is used to interface an input or output device with a program. Drivers are frequently used to interface printers in word processing programs.

directory A list of the names of files contained on a disk. The list may also include the size, date, and time each file was created.

diskette See *Floppy disk.*

disk operating system (DDS) An operating system program that aids in the handling of disk and other input and output operations. See also *Microsoft disk operating system.*

display screen An output device composed of a cathode ray tube (CRT) that displays computer output.

DOS See *Disk operating system.*

dot matrix A type of impact printer that forms a character with a pattern of dots by pressing a set of wires against an ink ribbon to make the character on the page.

downloading The process of receiving data at the PC from a mainframe computer.

EBCDIC See *Extended Binary Coded Decimal Interchange Code.*

electronic mail (E—mail) A computer network that provides for the trans-mission of mail electronically between subscribers to the service.

Electronic Private Branch Exchange A private communication network that operates electronically.

EPBX. See *Electronic Private Branch Exchange.*

expansion board A circuit board that is plugged into an expansion slot to provide the computer with additional capabilities such as color graphics or the use of a mouse.

expansion slot Provides a space for expansion boards for adding extra features such as a mouse or modem to the computer.

expert shell The supporting software used for developing an expert system.

expert system A computer-based system that is developed with a series of rules derived from human experts.

Extended Binary Coded Decimal Interchange Code (EBCDIC) An 8-bit coding system for data representation used primarily in mainframe computer systems.

feasibility study A study that determines whether a system should be developed and if the necessary resources are available.

field An item of data such as a quantity or name. A component of a record.

file A collection of records relating to a specific application.

file locking A software control that prohibits a user from accessing a data base when it is currently in use by another user.

file server A central computer on a network that provides data storage and software for other computers on the network.

fixed disk An external storage device of large capacity consisting of a fixed magnetic platter that is rotated under a read/write head. Also called a hard disk.

floppy disk A removable mylar disk that stores data magnetically. Common sizes are 5¼ inches and 3½ inches.

flowchart A chart used to develop the logic of a computer program. See also *System flowchart.*

fourth-generation languages A computer language for applications development that is essentially nonprocedural.

function key driven Software that primarily uses function keys to receive user commands.

function keys A set of 10 or 12 keys, labeled F1 to F10 or F12 on the keyboard, that are assigned specific operations for the software in use.

Gantt chart A chart used for scheduling the different phases of system design and implementation.

garbage in—garbage out (GIGO) An expression that suggests the output from a computer can only be as good as the input data provided.

general-purpose computers A computer system that may be used for a variety of applications.

goal seeking A technique used in models and spreadsheets for determining the necessary actions required to reach a specific goal.

graphics Software that assists in the preparation, editing, and presentation of graphic data.

hard disk See *Fixed disk.*

hierarchical directory See *Subdirectory.*

IC See *Integrated Circuit.*

Icon A graphic image displayed on the screen to identify an action that may be selected by the user of the program.

impact printers A type of printer that forms a character by impacting an ink ribbon against the paper. Includes dot matrix, daisy wheel, and chain printers.

indexed sequential access method (ISAM) A file access method that uses an index to provide access to any record in the file. The file may also be accessed sequentially.

inference engine A component of an expert system that applies the rules of the knowledge base to queries entered by the user.

information Data that has been processed and organized into a useful form.

information system (IS) A system that collects and organizes data into a useful form.

ink jet A printer that forms characters by firing a jet of ink at the paper to form the character.

input Data supplied to the computer for processing or storage.

input device A peripheral device such as a keyboard, disk, or mouse that provides input data to the computer.

install program A program that is used to install software to customize it to the configuration of the computer on which it is used and to set defaults to user preferences.

integrated circuit (IC). Silicon chip that contains a number of transistors. ICs are the foundation for microprocessor technology.

integrated software Software that provides a variety of applications usually including word processing, spreadsheet, data base, graphics, and communications.

interface A port or device used to attach an input or output device to the computer.

interpreter A program that reads each statement in a BASIC or other source language program and translates it for computer execution.

ISAM. See *Indexed sequential access method.*

job control language (JCL) Commands for use on mainframe operating systems.

kernel The core program in the UNIX operating system that is a common component of all implementations of the system.

keyboard template A plastic overlay for function keys that identifies the use of each key for a specific software package.

knowledge-based system A system that uses a collection of facts about an application to assist in the decision-making process. See also *Expert system.*

knowledge engineer A person with computer science or engineering background who has specialized in the field of expert or knowledge-based systems.

knowledge engineering The process of building a knowledge-based expert system.

LAN See *Local area network.*

laser printer A nonimpact printer that uses laser technology to print computer output a page at a time.

license agreement A legal contract with a software publisher giving the user the rights to install and use the software on a computer or network.

life cycle See *Systems life cycle.*

light pen A pen that detects light to make choices from the menu on the display screen.

local area network (LAN) A network that links computers together for purposes of data and program sharing. Computers on a LAN are generally in close proximity to each other.

machine language A low-level language written in binary for direct computer execution.

macro A method of storing frequently used keystrokes or commands for use by a program.

mainframe computer A large-scale computer system capable of supporting many users with a variety of peripheral devices.

management information system (MIS) A computer information system that is integrated with manual or automated methods of providing information for management decision making.

megabyte A measure of millions of bytes of storage.

megahertz (MHz) The number of cycles per second at which the clock operates to control the speed of the computer.

memory A device that stores the program and the data being processed by the computer.

memory resident A program that resides in memory (RAM) while other programs are active.

menu A list of options presented by a program from which the user makes a selection.

menu oriented A software package that uses menus as the primary user interface.

microcomputer A small-scale computer based on the microprocessor chip. See also *Personal computer.*

microprocessor The integrated circuit or chip that contains the processor, arithmetic and logic unit, and control unit.

microsoft disk operating system (MS-DOS) A disk operating system developed by Microsoft for use on microcomputers. A version is also known as PC-DOS.

minicomputer A medium-scale computer system that usually supports multiple users.

MIS. See *Management information system.*

model A mathematical representation of a real-life system.

modem An electronic device that converts a computer's digital signal to analog or the reverse for the purpose of data communication.

monitor   See *Display screen.*

monospace   A method of printing where each character occupies the same amount of space on the line.

mouse   An input device that attaches to the serial port and moves the cursor or icon on the screen by rolling the mouse on a flat surface.

MS-DOS   See *Microsoft disk operating system.*

multiprocessing   A system that uses more than one processor to run several programs simultaneously.

multiprogramming   A system with the ability to run more than one program concurrently.

multitasking   An operating system that may do two or more tasks at the same time.

multiuser   A system that permits many users to access the same data base and share software resources on a central computer.

natural language interface   A software interface that lets the user respond with English language queries.

near letter quality (NLQ)   A mode of operation for a dot matrix printer where printing quality approximates that of a letter-quality printer.

network   A communication system that provides for data transfer between the computers on the network.

network topology   The type of physical organization of communication lines and devices used in a network. Three basic topologies are star, ring, and bus.

nonimpact printer   A group of printers that forms a character without the need to impact the paper with a physical object. Includes laser and ink jet printers.

nonprocedural language   A problem-oriented language that defines the task to be done rather than how to accomplish the task.

object program   A machine language program produced as a result of compiling a source program.

online   A method where data is entered into the computer and processed as it is received.

operating system   See *Disk operating system.*

Operating System/2 (OS/2)   The disk operating system for IBM's Personal System/2 line of computers.

organization chart   A chart that identifies the formal reporting structure of management in an organization.

OS/2   See *Operating System/2.*

output   The information created as a result of computer processing.

output device   A peripheral device, such as a display screen, disk, or printer, that records or shows output data from the computer.

packet switching   A method of data communication that sends data in groups of characteristics called packets.

page composition software   Software that is used in desktop publishing to compose the contents of a page by integrating text and graphics.

parallel interface   An interface that transmits or receives one byte at a time. Printers generally use a parallel interface.

path   A PC-DOS/MS-DOS expression that defines the subdirectory to be used in a disk operation.

PBX   See *Private Branch Exchange.*

PC-DOS   A version of MS-DOS used on the IBM personal computer.

personal computer (PC)   A desktop microcomputer for personal use.

pixel   The smallest dot or point of light that can be displayed on the display screen.

plotters   An output device that creates graphics or charts by drawing the image using a collection of colored pens.

pop-up menu   A menu that appears somewhere in the middle of the screen.

port   A plug or socket provided to attach input and output devices to the computer.

presentation graphics   Software used to prepare material such as bar or line graphs, pie charts, or other information suitable for presentation as overhead transparencies, slides, or other forms of figures.

printer   An output device for producing printed output.

Private Branch Exchange (PBX)   A communication system for private use within an organization.

procedural language   Languages such as BASIC, COBOL, Pascal, and C that are

coded and written as sequentially ordered statements that include decision making and looping. Procedural languages define how to accomplish a task as contrasted to nonprocedural languages.

processor   See *Central processing unit.*

productivity software   General-purpose software such as spreadsheets, word processing, data base, and graphics, that are suitable for a variety of applications.

program   A set of instructions written in a language for computer use.

program development   The process of designing, writing, debugging, testing, and implementing a computer program.

programmer   A person who is trained in the design, coding, debugging, and testing of computer programs.

programming   The process of writing a computer program.

programming language   A language designed specifically for the purpose of writing computer programs.

prompt   A question or statement from a program to which the user types a response. Can also be a symbol such as the DOS prompt (>) or the dot prompt in dBASE.

proportional spacing   A method of printing where each character occupies a different width based on its size.

pseudocode   Programlike statements that are written as an aid to structured program logic development.

pull-down menus   A menu that comes down from the top of the screen.

query   A process for making an inquiry and receiving a response from a data base.

RAM disk   A part of RAM that is set aside to store data or programs from a disk file for faster access.

random access memory (RAM)   Volatile memory where a program resides during execution by the computer.

read-only memory (ROM)   A memory chip that stores information permanently in the computer.

record   All the data pertaining to a single transaction.

relational   A data structure where the relations in the data are presented in logically related tables.

relative addressing   A cell address in a spreadsheet such as D12 that automatically adjusts the row or column reference if the formula containing the address is moved or copied.

relative file   A file access method that permits access to the record by its record number that corresponds to its position in the file.

resolution   The number of pixels that can be displayed on the display screen that determines the clarity of characters or graphics on the screen.

RGB   A color display screen that receives three different signals for the red, green, and blue colors.

rule   An IF—THEN relationship in an expert system.

secondary storage   A storage device such as disk or tape that stores data external to the computer.

sequential file   A file that stores its records in order from the first to the last records. Records must also be accessed this order.

serial interface   An interface that transmits or receives only one bit at a time. A modem generally uses a serial interface.

shell   In general a shell is a program that passes control to other modules in a system and receives control when the module is finished. The part of UNIX that communicates with the user.

single tasking   An operating system that performs only one task at a time.

software   A program that provides the instructions for the computer's operation.

sort   The procedure of rearranging records or data into a predefined sequence.

source program   The original program written in a high-level language prior to compiling or interpreting.

special-purpose computer   A computer that is designed for a specific application such as in a digital watch or microwave oven.

spreadsheet   A program that permits the entry of data and formulas in rows and columns on the screen.

stored program   See *Program.*

structure chart   A chart that is used to develop the solution to a problem in a hierarchical fashion.

structured system analysis   A decomposition method that analyzes the system from the general to the more detailed level of the system.

subdirectory   A directory on fixed disk that has several branches each of which contains files or programs.

supercomputer   A large-scale, high-speed computer system used for scientific or other complex computing activities.

synchronous transmission   A method of data transmission that synchronizes the data with a clock to establish the timing of sending and receiving data bits.

system   A set of organized and related procedures used to accomplish a given task.

system analysis   The process of analyzing a system to develop an understanding of it and to establish system requirements.

system analyst   A person who analyzes the needs of a system and designs and implements a new system to meet those needs.

system design   The process of designing the procedures and components of a new system.

system flowchart   A chart used to represent the flow of data in a system.

system life cycle   The five stages of development of an information system. These stages are feasibility study, system analysis, system design, program development, and implementation.

system software   General-purpose programs, such as DOS, that are used to make the computer and other software function effectively.

terminal   An I/O device with a screen and keyboard that attaches to the computer.

testing   Running a program with test data to ensure that it produces the correct results.

UNIX   A multiuser multitasking operating system developed by Bell Laboratories.

uploading   The process of sending data from a PC to a mainframe computer.

user   A person who makes use of the computer hardware and software.

utility   An operating system program that is used to perform disk maintenance or other frequently encountered activities.

video display terminal (VDT)   See *Terminal.*

virtual storage   A memory technique that uses both primary and secondary stage. Programs and data in primary storage are swapped to disk when they become inactive and are swapped back to memory when they are again needed.

virtual storage access method (VSAM)   A disk access method used primarily on mainframe computers that uses an index system to both maintain and provide access to records either directly or sequentially.

voice recognition   A computer input device that converts the human voice into equivalent digital code.

warm start   Booting the computer by using a keystroke combination and without turning off the power.

what if question   A question asked by entering a value on the spreadsheet and observing the effect it has on other cells in the model.

Winchester disk   See *Fixed disk.*

window   A window is used in a spreadsheet or other software so the user can see two or more parts of the same file or data from two or more files.

windowing software   Software that provides the user with the ability to display several interrelated items of information in separate areas on the screen.

word   A measure of storage consisting of a number of bits or characters.

word processing   A program that aids in the typing, editing, and formatting of text ranging from short memos to long manuscripts.

worksheet   See *Spreadsheet.*

WORM   An optical disk storage device that can be written once but read many times. Useful for backup applications.

WYSIWYG   An acronym for "what you see is what you get."

Index